THINKING ABOUT NOTHING

TO

THE MEMORY OF MY FATHER

THOMAS P. CONLON (1892–1981)

LIBERTY, LAWS AND PEACE ARE THE GREATEST GIFTS

(These words frame Anselmus van Hulle's portrait of our subject.)

Thinking about Nothing

Otto von Guericke

and the

Magdeburg Experiments

on

The Vacuum

by

Thomas E. Conlon

The Saint Austin Press
2011

ISBN 978-1-4478-3916-3

The author and publisher are grateful to:

University of Chicago Press for permission to quote from P. Duhem, Medieval Cosmology (tr. Ariew) ©1985 by the University of Chicago.

Cambridge University Press for permission to quote from C. S. Lewis, The Discarded Image ©Cambridge University Press 1964

Hugh Lawson-Tancred for permission to quote from Aristotle, The Metaphysics ©Hugh Lawson-Tancred 1998

Published by the Saint Austin Press

2011

Contents

PREFACE

As an undergraduate in the summer of 1971, I betook myself to work as a Gastarbeiter on a Baustelle in Mainz. I had learnt some German from a teach-yourself book and had thought it best to suspend judgment on the pronunciation of the language until I actually arrived in the Bundesrepublik. My preparation proved to be a perfectly adequate preparation for the tasks I had to undertake and many of my colleagues, mostly from Turkey, Italy and Spain, were managing without even the benefit of a teach-yourself book. For a period, my boss was a man of about fifty who had fought on the Eastern front, been a prisoner of war in Siberia and had been ransomed by the Adenauer government in the early 1950s. It was the first time I had met, on ordinary human terms, someone who had lived at the sharp end of history. It was a formative and salutary experience for a young person. Before returning to Belfast, I made a trip to Berlin and took the opportunity of crossing into East Berlin. At a distance of forty years my recollections have condensed themselves into a montage of images — the Berlin Wall seen through the central arch of the Brandenburger Tor, Checkpoint Charlie, the car with the concrete-filled door panels that had been used by escapees to the West, the one-way currency exchange from D-marks to Ostmarks on entering the East, the contrast between the frenetically commercialised Kurfürstendam and the stark, hoarding-free, grand buildings of Stalinallee and Karl-Marx-allee. Buildings where Hegel, Weierstrass, Planck and Einstein had taught were now occupied by the Staatspolizei. This first experience of Germany left me both with an admiration for the traditional German virtues of thoroughness and industry and with a sharpened, more personal, awareness of the equivocal history of a great nation.

Thirty-five years after my first visit, my wife and I toured the cities of the old DDR whose names still have a resonance throughout Europe — Berlin, Dresden, Potsdam, Wittenberg, Magdeburg, Jena and Brandenburg. Magdeburg was still in the process of reconstructing itself physically after the destruction of the war years and the subsequent period of neglect under Communism. Psychologically too, it appeared to be putting down roots to a more worthy past from which to draw nourishment for a better future. Otto von Guericke looms large in Magdeburg's past as a figure with whom it can unabashedly identify and in whom it can justly take pride.

Like my old boss, he too was a man who had been at the sharp end of history. He had survived the previous annihilation of the city in 1631, escaping the flames, with his wife and children, as a destitute refugee. From this, the lowest point of his life, he had gone on to play a leading role in the city's rebuilding. While pursuing a busy political and diplomatic career, he had carved out a niche for himself in the scientific pantheon of the seventeenth century. By way of a souvenir of our visit, I bought a copy of the facsimile of the *Experimenta Nova*, originally published in 1672, and reproduced in 2002 for the 400th anniversary of von Guericke's birth.

This was the beginning of my interest in von Guericke. Men of intense piety, intellectual passion, political and administrative acumen, equally at home with Scripture, the Church Fathers, the philosophers and poets of classical antiquity as well as the leading writers and thinkers of their day are no longer familiar figures. On the other hand, they are not imaginatively and psychologically alien to us in the way that the men of classical antiquity, or great figures from non-European cultures are. Von Guericke is one of us, a man with whose mind, character and preoccupations we can confidently empathise. To misquote Ranke, we feel we can know him *wie er eigentlich war*.

Personal interest, however intense, would not, on its own, have been sufficient to write this book. Two other factors have been indispensable. The first has been the astonishing growth in the dissemination of information enabled through the internet. With a mouse-click, I was able to obtain biographies of von Guericke from otherwise unknown German antiquarian booksellers. In an even more gratifying development, Googlebooks have made freely available a vast amount of seventeenth century source material including the *Mechanica Hydraulico-pneumatica* and the *Technica Curiosa* of Fr. Kaspar Schott, the priest whose writings first brought von Guericke to international attention. Additionally, many of the individuals, some prominent on the international stage and some just of local fame, with whom von Guericke had dealings are now featured in the German language Wikipedia. These two factors have made it possible to track down virtually all of von Guericke's allusions and references.

These new possibilities may have provided the means to write this book, but motivation has been sustained, in more traditional fashion, by the help and encouragement of my friends and family. I am grateful to Dr. John Mayberry of the University of Bristol for many insights about Aristotle and his continuing influence on mathematics. Mr. Terence Cole and my sons Joseph and Thomas have read and commented helpfully on sections of the text. Mr. Kenneth Asch has been untiring in his reading and commenting upon the entire manuscript. The expertise of Miss Nancy Hoyos in the use of image editing programs has shown me that pictures as well as words can be translated. Herr Duschanek of the Otto von Guericke Gesellschaft provided, at various points in the project, useful guidance to the German studies of von Guericke's life. I would like to thank Mrs. Louiza Savvides for making me see clearly that in addition to advancing the agenda of one's employer, one's colleagues, one's students and one's family it is a good thing to set some time aside unapologetically to pursue one's personal interests. Without a decision to do so, this book would not have been started. Finally, I would like to thank my wife Theresa for her many years of support and companionship before this book was begun and for her patience during the writing of it. Her careful proof-reading of the last but one draft of the text has ensured that the traditional sole responsibility of authors for errors and omissions weighs less heavily.

T.E. Conlon
Reading, U.K., June 2011

Part I

Otto von Guericke

a

Short Biography

Portrait of Otto von Guericke

(Anselmus van Hulle)

Liberty, Laws and Peace are the greatest gifts.

Introduction

The biographical sketch is largely based on three German biographies:

(a) Friedrich Wilhelm Hoffmann. *Otto von Guericke, Bürgermeister der Stadt Magdeburg: ein Lebensbild aus der deutschen Geschichte des siebzehnten Jahrhunderts.* (Verlag Emil Baensch 1874)

(b) Hans Schimank. *Otto von Guericke, Bürgermeister von Magdeburg.* (Magdeburger Kultur und Wirtschaftsleben Nr. 6 1936)

(c) Ditmar Schneider. *Otto von Guericke: Ein Leben für die Alte Stadt Magdeburg.* (Verlag B. G. Teubner 1997)

Other important sources for both the biographical section and my translation from the original Latin of von Guericke's writings on the vacuum have been:

(a) The facsimile of von Guericke's magnum opus — *Ottonis de Guericke Experimenta Nova (ut vocantur) Magdeburgica de Vacuo Spatio.* (Verlag Janos Stekovics 2002)

(b) Fr. Kaspar Schott. *Mechanica Hydraulico-pneumatica.* (1657) (Googlebooks)

(c) Fr. Kaspar Schott. *Technica Curiosa.* (1663) (Googlebooks)

(d) Friedrich Dannemann. German translation of Book III of the *Experimenta Nova.* (Ostwald's Klassiker der Exakten Wissenschaften, Band 59. Verlag Harri Deutsch 2002)

(e) Hans Schimank. German translation of the entire *Experimenta Nova.* (Verlag des Vereins Deutscher Ingenieure 1968)

(f) Alfons Kauffeldt. *Otto von Guericke Philosophisches über den leeren Raum.* (Akademie-Verlag Berlin 1968)

I have chosen to abide by Hoffmann's use of Julian calendar dates, which von Guericke himself used in dating all his writings. Gregorian calendar dates are obtained by adding ten days to the corresponding Julian dates.

Glossary

Many German terms, particularly terms denoting titles, have no accurate English equivalents. Bürgermeister, for instance, is only loosely translatable as "Mayor". Accordingly, in the text, the correct German terms are used and their meanings are given below.

Ausschuss. An advisory committee. The Magdeburg constitution provided for two independent advisory committees comprising in all fifty members. In a Magdeburg context, the term Ausschuss refers to one of these two committees.

Bürgermeister. The nearest translation is "mayor". The administration of Magdeburg was presided over by four Bürgermeister, elected for life. During any given year two were active and two were passive and in the following year the roles were reversed. The two active Bürgermeister each served a six month term as president of the Rat. (Ratsvorsitzender).

Domherr. Cathedral canon or prebendary.

Dompropst. Cathedral provost. This and the position of Domherr, formerly clerical roles, were held by laymen in the secularised archdiocese of Magdeburg.

Freiherr. A title equivalent to the English "Baron".

Fürst. Prince. One of the rulers of the hundreds of territories making up the Holy Roman Empire.

Geheimrat. Privy Councillor. An advisor in confidential matters to a Fürst or to the Kaiser at the Imperial Court at Vienna.

Graf / Grafin. A title equivalent to the English "Earl/Countess".

Herzog / Herzogin. A title equivalent to the English "Duke/Duchess".

Hofburg. The official residence of the Kaiser in Vienna.

Hofkriegsrat. The Court Council of War of the Habsburg Monarchy. It was founded in 1556 as a body of men of military experience who could take charge of the army both in war and in peacetime.

4

Hofrat. Court counsellor. An advisor to a Fürst. The term is also used to denote the body of counsellors.

Kaiser. Emperor. The Holy Roman Empire was inaugurated with the coronation of Charlemagne in 800 A.D. and survived until its dissolution by Napoleon in 1806.

Kämmerer. Chamberlain. A senior civic official of Magdeburg. The constitution provided for four elected Kämmerer, in addition to the four elected Bürgermeister.

Kirchenordnung. An instruction from the civic authorities regulating the affairs of the Lutheran Church.

Kreisdirektor. Each of the ten Circles had a Director responsible to Vienna for the affairs of the Circle.

Kreistag. An assembly of one of the ten Circles of the Holy Roman Empire. Magdeburg was in the Lower Saxony Circle.

Kurfürst. Prince Elector of the Holy Roman Emperor. Eight of the Fürsten had the right to vote for the election of a new Kaiser.

Landstadt. A town falling under the authority of the Reichsstand.

Magistrat. The municipal authority of a German town or city.

Mediatstadt. A town under intermediate authority, particularly one that had lost or been refused Reichsunmittelbarkeit – autonomy within the Holy Roman Empire.

Möllnvogt. Chief Attorney. A legal official of the archdiocese of Magdeburg. The "Mölln" refers to his official residence in an old mill house.

Nachlass. A body of unpublished writings by a deceased author.

Rat. Town or City Council. In Magdeburg this consisted of the four Bürgermeister, the four Kämmerer and sixteen other members.

Rathaus. Town Hall. The building in a German town where the Rat held its meetings.

Ratscollegium. As well as the four Bürgermeister and four Kämmerer the constitution provided for sixteen Ratmännern. This collective entity formed the Ratscollegium.

Ratmann. A member of the Ratscollegium other than the Bürgermeister or the Kämmerer.

Referent. Consultant. Official adviser.

Reichsdeputation. An executive committee, chosen by the Kaiser from among the representatives of the Reichsstände, with a brief to deal with some area of Imperial business.

Reichsgeheimrat. Imperial Privy Counsellor. The title signifies that the holder was a confidential adviser to the Kaiser.

Reichshofrat. The Reichshofrat (also known as the Aulic Council) was, alongside the Reichskammergericht, one of the two highest courts in the Holy Roman Empire. It had particular responsibility for matters to do with Imperial feudal rights and Imperial privileges.

Reichsgrafenstand. The collective noun for those with the status of "Graf".

Reichskammergericht. The Imperial Chamber Court. This was, alongside the Reichshofrat, one of the two highest judicial institutions of the Holy Roman Empire. Virtually all legal proceedings in the Holy Roman Empire could be brought to the *Reichskammergericht.* Only the rulers possessing the "de non appellando" Imperial privilege were exempted from its jurisdiction.

(Reichs)Stand. A state of the Holy Roman Empire, whose representatives were entitled to vote on the deliberations of the Reichstag.

Reichstag. A gathering of the representatives of the territories of the Holy Roman Empire to take decisions affecting the whole Empire.

Resident. Consul. The representative of the government in a region. The older meaning of the word "Resident" survives in English in the Irish legal title "Resident Magistrate".

Early Life and Family

Otto von Guericke was a remarkable and interesting human being. As a young man from a prosperous background, he was well educated and widely travelled. An effective architect and engineer, impatient of mere talkers, he was a solid family man and one of strong but eirenic religious conviction. His entire life was characterised by a deep attachment to his native Magdeburg. In May 1631, like Aeneas from Troy, destitute and accompanied by his wife and sons, he fled the flames which consumed it. Unlike Aeneas however, he returned two years later to become a leading figure in the rebuilding of the city which he later served for many years as Kämmerer, diplomat, and Bürgermeister.[1] Behind the local politician and small businessman, behind the family man and the man of religion there stood the scientist and truth seeker. Working entirely as a self-funded amateur, he gained a permanent place in scientific history through three major original achievements — the invention of the vacuum pump, the first demonstration of electrostatic repulsion, and the pioneering of the concept of absolute space. The latter proved to be a key part of the Newtonian synthesis and remained indispensable to scientific progress until the latter half of the nineteenth century. Inter alia he also independently invented the barometer, associated low pressure with stormy weather, weighed air, investigated sound and combustion in the vacuum and estimated the height of the atmosphere. His single most famous experiment, simply known as Magdeburg's Hemispheres, speaks to his talent for scientific showmanship and remains to this day a popular item of elementary physics curricula.

He was a scion of a family with a long tradition of public service to Magdeburg stretching back to the fourteenth century. His father,

---

[1] Magdeburg was a city of the Hanseatic League. According to the 1630 reform, its administration should consist of an executive body - the Rat - consisting of four Bürgermeister, four Kämmerer and sixteen Rathmännern, collectively comprising the Magistrat. These twenty-four were elected for life. During any one year half were active and half were passive and at the end of the year the roles were reversed. The passive members were nevertheless obliged to attend the meetings of the whole group. Each of the two active Bürgermeister held the chairmanship for six months of their year of activity. Additionally there was an advisory group — the "Ausschuss" — of fifty members which was summoned for important issues. This was divided into two sections which held independent separate meetings. Before the reform, the Rat was elected by the city's guilds. (Hoffmann p. 49)

Hans, had been a widely travelled diplomat in the service of the king of Poland. His grandfather and grand uncles had served in the office of Bürgermeister, the highest civic office of the city. In January 1602, Hans, then a widower of forty-seven, married the twenty-one year old Anna von Zweidorff from Braunschweig. Otto, their only child, was born on November 20th 1602.

His parents enjoyed nineteen years of married life together and Otto grew up a gifted and much-loved child for whose education no expense was excessive or trouble too much. In addition to attending an excellent school, he was taught privately by the ablest tutors that his devoted parents could hire. In 1617, well prepared at the age of fifteen for university, he studied at Leipzig where he took introductory courses in the sciences. The clouds of the Thirty Years War, which were to inflict destitution upon him, utter destruction on his native city, and suffering and misery on the whole of Germany, were already gathering. As the war spread from Bohemia to neighbouring Saxony his father, concerned for his safety, recalled him from Leipzig early in 1620 and sent him instead to the Academia Julia at Helmstedt. Here too, events curtailed his studies. His father, rendered unable to speak by a stroke in June 1620, died on September 4th whereupon his distraught widow summoned her son to the parental home. Not till the summer of 1621 did his grieving mother give her permission for him to resume his academic pursuits. This time he went to Jena where for two years he dedicated himself to the study of jurisprudence. His university education was completed by a spell at Leyden where his studies proved decisive for the future. In addition to the study of English, French and Dutch they included attendance at lectures on physics, applied mathematics and fortification engineering. Before settling down to what was expected to be a conventionally successful and well rewarded career of public service, assured for him both by his talents and his family connections, the final polish to his education was supplied by a nine month long trip to France and England.

After three years of widowhood his mother married again in May 1623. Her new husband was a distinguished lawyer, Christoph Schulze, soon to become Möllnvogt of the archdiocese of Magdeburg. His stepfather was to be of crucial assistance in the restoration of von Guericke's fortunes in the years of the rebuilding of the city after its destruction in 1631. This marriage was without issue and Anna was widowed again in 1642. Von Guericke and his mother maintained throughout their lives the close relationship one might expect between a mother and a gifted only son. After the death of her second husband she moved from the official residence of the Möllnvogt back to the home she had shared with her first husband, Hans. Here, after von Guericke's own bereavement in 1645, she presided over his household and the care and education of her sole surviving grandchild. Natural and inevitable though her death in September 1666, one day short of her eighty-sixth birthday, may have been, it was felt keenly by her son. Her coffin, richly ornamented and covered in the family coat of arms, was borne among a throng of mourners to the churchyard of Ulrichskirche where she was laid to rest on October 14th by the side of her first husband.

Shortly after his return to Magdeburg in 1626, von Guericke joined the Ratscollegium of the city. Apart from a short interruption at the time of the destruction of the city, he belonged to this body until his old age. A second important development for such an eligible bachelor was his marriage, a major event reflecting the social status of his family, on September 18th to Margarethe Alemann.[2] Of their three children, a daughter, Anna Catharina, born in 1627, died within two months of her birth; a son, Hans Otto, born on October 28th 1628, survived his father; and a second son, Jacob Christoph, born in 1630, died, a casualty of the siege, at just over a year old. Margarethe herself, suffering greatly from kidney stones, died in September 1645 during a particularly frenetic period of von Guericke's diplomatic journeying on behalf of the city. After seven years as a widower, he married Dorothea Lentke, the daughter of a Bürgermeister colleague, Stephan Lentke, in May 1652. This marriage was childless and Dorothea survived her husband, dying in Hamburg in March 1687.

The young Hans Otto received, under the watchful eyes of his parents, grandmother and step-grandfather, the same kind of affectionate and careful upbringing as his father had enjoyed. He was well educated both in the sciences and in languages. At the age of eighteen he accompanied his father to the Peace of Westphalia negotiations which brought to an end the Thirty Years War. Subsequently, in 1649, he

---

[2] The genealogy of this family is on the Internet — accessible by searching "Genealogie der Familie von Alemann" They were also a family with a long record of public service to Magdeburg with recorded roots going back to the thirteenth century.

again accompanied his father to Nuremburg and to Vienna where he embarked upon a period of academic study of jurisprudence. Following the successful completion of his studies in the autumn of 1651, he expressed a wish to follow, like his grandfather, a diplomatic career and to take up a position as an attaché at Constantinople. His father and grandmother were appalled at this prospect and only managed to dissuade him by proposing to him the alternative of a trip to Italy. With seven friends he embarked on the trip in September 1651, finally returning to Magdeburg in June 1652 after more than three years away from home. In the course of this sojourn he conveyed his father's greetings to the celebrated Jesuit scholar, Fr. Athanasius Kircher,[3] a man whose views on the vacuum von Guericke would later be at pains to rebut. Later, Hans Otto was his father's companion on diplomatic missions to the Imperial Court at Prague and to the Reichstag at Regensburg in 1654. Ambitious for a diplomatic career on a wider stage, he became a Hofrat in the service of the Fürst of Anhalt-Cöthen and undertook missions on behalf of Anhalt-Cöthen as well as of Magdeburg. On one such mission he met his future wife, Catharina Dorothea von Bunsow, whom he married in 1655. The following year she bore him a daughter, Juliane, who died at the age of nine months. Four years later, on March 24th 1660, Catharina herself succumbed to consumption and was laid to rest alongside her daughter in the Johanniskirche. On February 11th 1662, encouraged by his father and grandmother, Hans Otto married again. His new bride, Hedwig von Ulchen (1631–1687), was from a well-connected family in Hamburg and bore him five children,[4] three of whom survived infancy — Leberecht (1662–1737), Dorothea (1669–1706) and Friedrich Wilhelm (1672–1717). In 1662 Hans Otto left the service of the Fürst of Anhalt-Cöthen and the following year entered that of the Elector of Brandenburg, Friedrich Wilhelm,[5] as his Resident to the Lower Saxony Circle. In March 1659 Hans

---

[3] Letter to Fr. Schott of 22nd July 1656. *Technica Curiosa* p. 29.

[4] Hoffmann (p. 165) claims two sons and four daughters. The "Genealogie der Familie von Alemann" records the five named above.

[5] Friedrich Wilhelm (1620–1688), the Great Elector, acceded to the title on the death of his father Georg Wilhelm in 1640. His long reign saw the development of Brandenburg into an efficient, religiously tolerant, militarily powerful, scientifically progressive, politically absolutist state and paved the way for his son Friedrich to declare himself the first King of Prussia. By the treaty of Westphalia the archdiocese of Magdeburg was to revert to Brandenburg on the death of August of Saxony. This gave Friedrich Wilhelm a strong interest in opposing Magdeburg's

Otto had become a Canon of Magdeburg's Nicholaikirche but resigned the position following his departure for Hamburg where, as a requirement of his new employment, he took up residence in 1663. He remained there until his death in January 1704. His son, Leberecht, returned to Magdeburg and resumed the family tradition of public service to the city where he is laid to rest in the family vault in the Johanniskirche. The home of Hans Otto in Hamburg provided a refuge from the plague for his elderly parents from January 1681 until Otto's death in May 1686.

---

aspirations to autonomy within the Empire. His other importance to this biography arises from his personal interest in von Guericke's experiments dating from the late 1650s. While he himself espoused Calvinism, his general outlook was one of religious tolerance. Von Guericke dedicated the *Experimenta Nova* to him.

Johann Georg, Elector of Saxony (1585–1656)

(Anselmus van Hulle)

Friedrich Wilhelm, the Great Elector (1620–1688)

(Anselmus van Hulle)

13

Gustavus Adolphus, King of Sweden (1594–1632)

14

The Siege and Destruction of Magdeburg (1626–1632)

During the five years following his return to Magdeburg von Guericke closely witnessed, without being able decisively to influence, the play of external pressures and internal responses that culminated in the siege of 1631.

Magdeburg, where Luther himself had been a schoolboy, was an overwhelmingly Lutheran city. The archdiocese of Magdeburg had been under secular control since 1545 and since 1598 its affairs were administered by Christian Wilhelm,[6] the son of the Elector of Brandenburg. Initially he maintained the title of Archbishop but, subsequent to his marriage in 1614, replaced it by that of Administrator. The Magdeburg Rat did not however concede that his position, derived from ecclesiastic office, accorded him any authority over the city.

As Wallenstein[7] marched northwards through Germany, Christian Wilhelm, associating himself and the city with the Danish intervention on behalf of the Protestant cause, took command of a body of Saxon troops. Following defeat by the then irresistible Wallenstein at the battle of Dessauer Bridge in 1626, he became a fugitive, fleeing ultimately to Sweden. In 1628 he was deposed from his position as Administrator by the cathedral chapter in favour of the thirteen year old August,[8] younger son of Johann Georg,[9] the Elector of Saxony. At

---

[6] Christian Wilhelm (1587–1665) was the son of Joachim Friedrich, Elector of Brandenburg. After his return to Magdeburg in 1630, he played a leading role in inciting resistance to the besieging armies. In the course of the siege, he was wounded and captured. Perhaps opportunistically, he converted to Catholicism in 1632, a step which secured his release from imprisonment. At the Peace of Prague in 1635 he was allocated an annual income of 12,000 thalers. Further emoluments accrued to him at Westphalia and in 1651 he purchased the Herrschaft Neuschloss in Bohemia. He married three times and died in the Kloster Zinna in January 1665. Schimank (p. 10) describes him as "an arrogant and vain prince without any gift of leadership"

[7] Albrecht von Wallenstein (1583–1634). A convert to Catholicism in 1606, he was a successful generalissimo of the Imperial Armies during the early part of the Thirty Years war. He was dismissed by Ferdinand in 1630, but recalled in 1632. He was murdered in 1634, at the probable instigation of Ferdinand, because he was justly suspected of seeking to negotiate a separate peace with Ferdinand's then enemies.

[8] Augustus of Saxony (1614–1680) was the sixth child of John Georg and his second wife Magdalene Sybille.

[9] Johann Georg (1585–1656) was Elector of Saxony from 1611 to his death. Imbued neither with religious fervour nor military zeal, he pursued a policy of pragmatically seeking peaceful accommodation with the more aggressive powers with which he was surrounded. Consequently he appears to cut a rather pusillanimous figure in comparison with his more driven and ambitious contemporaries. He was a reluctant ally of Gustavus from 1631 to 1635 and a tepid supporter of the Kaiser after the Peace of Prague.

the same time the Kaiser claimed the administratorship for his son, the Archduke Leopold Wilhelm. Magdeburg resisted the claim of Leopold and, in consequence of this defiance of the Kaiser's authority, was subjected to a twenty-eight week blockade by Wallenstein in 1629. In the course of this siege von Guericke suffered considerable losses of income from land he owned outside the city walls.

August finally took up the position of Administrator in 1638 in the much transformed circumstances following the Peace of Prague in 1635. Through many vicissitudes he remained in post until his death in 1680. He and his diplomatic agents proved indefatigable opponents of Magdeburg's aspirations to become an Imperial Free City like Augsburg or Cologne. Much of von Guericke's subsequent diplomatic activity consisted in seeking to counter their policy of maintaining the status of Magdeburg as an "episcopal town"[10] thus falling under the authority of the Administrator of the archbishopric rather than being directly subject to the Kaiser.

By 1630 Wallenstein's continued military success, culminating in the occupation of the Baltic ports early in that year, had, on the one hand, led to a justified suspicion that personal ambition rather than the Catholic or Imperial cause was his driving motivation, and on the other, had fired the King of Sweden, Gustavus Adolphus,[11] with a resolve to ensure the maritime security of Sweden by establishing a beachhead in northern Germany. In consequence of the former, Wallenstein was dismissed from his position and retired to his estates in Friedland, leaving the army he had raised and the responsibilities of quartering and paying its troops in the hands of the Imperial general, Johann Tserclaes, Graf von Tilly.[12] In consequence of the latter, Gustavus Adolphus, following a period of diplomatic activity aimed at securing allies among the Protestant north Germans, landed in Usedom on the Pomeranian coast on June 25th 1630. The military triumphs wrought by his genius as

---

[10] v. C.V. Wedgwood. The Thirty Years War. p. 245. (Jonathan Cape)

[11] Gustavus Adolphus (1592–1632) was king of Sweden from 1611. His reign saw Sweden emerge as a European great power, principally owing to the efficiency of his administration and his genius as a military commander. He died at the battle of Lützen in 1632.

[12] Johann Tserclaes, Graf von Tilly (1559–1632) was born in Brabant and educated by the Jesuits at Cologne. He was a successful commander of the troops of the Catholic League during the earlier part of the Thirty Years War, but was defeated by Gustavus Adolphus at Breitenfeld in 1631. He died at Ingolstadt of wounds sustained at the Battle of Rain on the river Lech in April 1632.

a commander were accompanied by a rapid expansion in the scope of his ambition — from the initial aim of securing a beachhead, to the championship, at a price, of the Protestant cause in Germany, to the conquest of all of Germany and the permanent establishment of a Swedish empire in mainland Europe. These ambitions were checked only by his ignominious death at the battle of Lützen in 1632.[13]

Perhaps because of the Edict of Restitution of 1629 which would have restored to the Catholic Church property expropriated since the Peace of Augsburg, perhaps because of the purchase on the popular Protestant mind of a belief that Gustavus Adolphus was the realisation of a prophesy of Paracelsus[14] foretelling the advent of a "Lion from the North", or perhaps just because of sheer naïveté, Magdeburg proved susceptible to manipulation by Swedish diplomacy. In contrast to the canny wariness of Swedish intentions shown by the Electors of Saxony and Brandenburg and the leaders of other cities, Magdeburg openly declared its support for the Swedish king on August 1st 1630, the first and the only territory to do so without some degree of coercion. On hearing of Magdeburg's readiness to ally itself with the Swedish cause, Gustavus memorably declared "This is the brand that will fire rebellion throughout Germany".

Within the city, von Guericke, judging by his own subsequent account,[15] was distrustful of the trend of developments. He had already suffered the destruction of his property outside the city walls by the blockading troops in 1629. Now, in January 1630, delegates of the Hanseatic League arrived in Magdeburg to oversee the reform and democratisation of the government of the city. The new constitution, by which the members of the Rat were elected for life[16] directly by the citizens, rather than by the city's guilds, did not especially commend

---

[13] Wounded and fallen from his horse he was shot as he lay face down in the mud. His body was stripped of valuables and was discovered later among a pile of corpses. On its return to Sweden his widow, Maria Eleanor of Brandenburg, refused to have it buried and kept it in an open coffin visiting it and communing with it daily until constrained to cease by an armed guard. His funeral finally took place in Stockholm in the summer of 1634.

[14] Theophrastus Bombastus Paracelsus (1493–1541) was a radical Swiss physician and medical reformer. He inspired much opposition to his proposed reforms and spent much of his life as a vagrant intellectual.

[15] His recollections of the siege form part of his handwritten Nachlass. They were translated by his biographer Friedrich W. Hoffmann and published in 1860 under the title *Geschichte der Belagerung, Eroberung und Zerstörung Magdeburgs*.

[16] The Hanseatic cities agreed a new constitution in 1630.

itself to him. As a member by birth of the old "ruling élite", a dislike of populism came naturally to him. The motto, "Liberty, Laws and Peace are the greatest gifts", with which he later associated himself in a portrait by van Hulle, sum up his lifelong political outlook. However, his co-option to the new Rat as one of five outgoing members to be reinstated and his appointment to an office with responsibility for the defence and fortification of the city speak to the respect his person and talents already commanded.

On July 27th 1630 Christian Wilhelm, who had come back to Germany with the landing party of Gustavus Adolphus, returned secretly to Magdeburg as a Swedish agent. The mood of the city had changed from the time of his deposition two years previously. Possibly because of a new optimism among Protestants inspired by the arrival on German soil of Gustavus and because the recent democratic reforms had allowed the translation of this mood into action, he was able to exert immediate influence on the affairs of the city. He successfully advocated the alliance with Gustavus Adolphus and by the end of the year Magdeburg was quartering a Swedish garrison of some 2,400 men under the command of Dietrich von Falkenberg.[17] He gave the Rat Gustavus' written promise to protect Magdeburg from the Imperial troops and he himself took command of the fortification and defence of the city, placing himself at the head of a pro-Swedish party within the city. Since the end of November an army of Imperial troops under Gottfried Heinrich, Graf zu Pappenheim[18] had been encamped outside the city. In March 1631 von Tilly himself arrived with extensive reinforcements. The city was surrounded and the siege began in earnest.

Magdeburg's 7,000 defenders faced the 30 000 strong besieging army as a house divided against itself. The divisions ultimately rested on the ambivalence of their religious and political aspiration. Their Lutheran religious leanings prompted them to solidarity with the Swedish invaders, while their political ambitions for autonomy within the Empire

---

[17] Dietrich von Falkenberg (1580–1631) was the son of the Drost zu Blankenau. After a period in the service of the Landgraf of Hesse, he entered the service of Gustavus Adolphus in 1615. He rose to the rank of Hofmarschall and in the autumn of 1630 Gustavus appointed him military commander in Magdeburg where, disguised as a sailor, he arrived on October 19th 1630.

[18] Gottfried Heinrich Graf zu Pappenheim (1594–1632) converted to Catholicism in 1614 and devoted the remainder of his life to the Catholic cause. On the outbreak of the Thirty Years War he abandoned a diplomatic career for a military one and was a dashing and courageous commander until his death at Lützen in 1632.

were best served by reaching an accommodation with the Kaiser, Ferdinand II. On the ground, these divisions reflected themselves in the existence of two parties in dispute as to the right course of action to follow. In the early weeks of the siege, Christian Wilhelm and von Falkenberg sought to take the initiative with an aggressive defence, loosing off cannon balls against the enemy in a strategy as ineffective as it was wasteful of the scarce resource of gunpowder. As the outer defence works fell one by one to the besiegers, von Falkenberg ordered, on April 21st and 23rd, the evacuation and razing of the suburbs of Neustadt, to the north, and Sudenburg, to the south, in order to deny them to the Imperial enemy. By the beginning of May the stocks of powder were dangerously low and the state of the city's defences parlous. Its only hope was to hold out until Gustavus' promised relief arrived.

For what then followed, von Guericke's own account of the siege, albeit partisan, is an important source. Although the account was written some forty-five years later it describes events to which he was an eye witness. On May 8th von Tilly had an envoy bring a message to the Rat urging them to surrender and not wantonly to plunge themselves into the ruinous disaster that would inevitably follow if the city were taken by storm. The Rat was reluctant to take full responsibility for such a momentous decision. It embarked instead on a consultation, in eighteen separate districts, of those entitled to vote. Pending the outcome, von Tilly's envoy was detained. The consultation took place on the following day. Some districts, fearful of the devastation that a plundering army might wreak, voted for surrender negotiations and some voted that they would abide by the decision of the Rat whatever it might be. The Swedish party, still maintaining the arrival of Gustavus to be imminent, urged that no negotiations be entered into and that it would be better to hold out to the last man than fall into the hands of such an enemy.

On that same day, May 9th, von Guericke conducted a personal inspection of the city's defences. He was alarmed to see the besiegers raising scaffolding against the ramparts at Neustadt and, aware that ammunition was running out, concluded that an attack, which they had no realistic hope of repelling, was imminent. That afternoon he reported his findings to the assembled Rat who instructed him to make von Falkenberg aware of what he had established. Von Falkenberg promised to repel the enemy advance to the walls with a counterattack that same night. In the event this did not happen. It has been supposed that von Falkenberg received subsequent but, as it turned out, false intelligence that the Imperial troops were retreating from their positions of their own accord and might even be abandoning the siege.

At 4 a.m. the following day, Tuesday May 10th, a general meeting of the civic authorities resolved unanimously to open surrender negotiations with von Tilly. A party of four, including von Guericke, was dispatched to the leaders of the Swedish party — Christian Wilhelm, von Falkenberg and the Swedish ambassador Stahlmann — closeted in a separate room of the same building to finalise surrender terms for the city. The intention was that von Tilly's envoy of May 8th should return accompanied by a delegation from the city empowered to negotiate surrender. The meeting did not go well. Von Falkenberg embarked on a long monologue, recalling Gustavus' promise of relief, dismissing the fears of his interlocutors as exaggerated and cowardly, and assuring them that Gustavus' arrival was imminent. Every extra hour was now worth a ton of gold; the city should hold out and no truck was to be had with the enemy. After more than an hour of this, the meeting was interrupted by a message that the Imperial troops were on the move and drawing near to the city. To the bearer of this news, von Falkenberg replied that he hoped that the Imperial troops would be so bold as to try and storm the city for they would meet with a reception not to their taste, and calmly resumed his discourse. The next interruption to the meeting was the sounding of the alarm that the enemy was within the walls.

With this, von Guericke left the meeting and discovered that Croatian soldiers had entered through a poorly protected gate at Fisherman's Bank (Fischerufer) and had already begun pillaging and plundering. Rushing back to the Rat to communicate this development, he found that von Falkenberg's own scouts were reporting that the city wall at Neustadt had also been stormed and troops were entering here too. Von Falkenberg, in the terrible realisation that what he had mocked as impossible just a few minutes previously had now come to pass, jumped to horse and led a brave but doomed assault on an overwhelmingly superior enemy. Shot from his mount, he was borne to a nearby house where he perished in the fire that shortly afterwards consumed it. The council sought a meeting place of greater safety in the Marktplatz to organise further resistance. This too proved a hopeless undertaking and it became each man's duty to look to his own as best he could.

Von Guericke has left us a vivid pen portrait of the terror and carnage inflicted on the civilian population by Pappenheim's Croatian troops. He writes:[19]

"'It's all ours, it's all ours.' they whooped in triumph and soon the streets and houses were scenes of beatings, murder, arson and pillage. As long as a householder had still something to part with, he was able to protect himself and his family until others arrived who also demanded something. Finally, when everything had been surrendered and there was nothing more to surrender, aggression began in earnest. The enemy started their harassment and beatings. They threatened people with shooting, bayoneting or hanging so that they had to dig out and hand over everything even if it was buried under the ground or made secure by a thousand locksmiths. In the midst of their fury and to the grisly sounds of murderous shrieking, many thousands of innocent men, women and children were pitilessly cut down or met gruesome deaths in countless other ways. There are not words enough to describe, or tears enough to bewail, their fate. The agony endured for just over two hours. Then, unexpectedly, the flames, fanned by the strong wind, took hold."

From about 10 a.m. fire raged through the city. It remains unclear and disputed whether it was initiated by the Swedes as an extension of the scorched earth policy already followed in the suburbs of Neustadt and Sudenburg, whether by von Tilly as a deliberate punitive measure, whether by the Imperial troops out of control and running amok, or whether simply by the accident of strong north east winds fanning local fires into a general conflagration. The city was reduced to smoking ruins and some 25,000 of its inhabitants perished either of suffocation in the fires or at the hands of the Imperial troops. Its destruction shocked Europe. Von Tilly and his Imperial troops bore the opprobrium for its fate and, at least in the short term, the tragedy for the city and its inhabitants became a propaganda triumph for the Protestant cause.

Von Guericke fled to his waiting wife Margarethe, young son Hans Otto, and infant, Jacob Christoph. They witnessed helplessly the out-of-hand butchery of their servants and saved their own lives only by surrendering all their money and possessions to the looting soldiery. Von Guericke led his family together with the nurse of his infant son Jacob Christoph, who had been wounded by a soldier and was being carried in her arms, to the house of his uncle, Johann Alemann, where

---

[19] Schimank p. 16 cites von Guericke's original German.

21

other friends and relatives were gathered. Alemann had had previous contact with officers in the Imperial army and, owing to his influence, von Guericke, his wife, his two children and the nurse were taken as prisoners to a camp at Fermersleben, where they were treated with relative mildness. Here, some weeks later, Jacob Christoph died of the injuries he had sustained.

In later years von Guericke would recall that for fixing the watch of an Imperial officer he received payment of a ducat[20] which enabled him to support himself and his family.[21] Nevertheless they had to remain in prison until a ransom of three hundred thalers had been paid. His release was secured by financial assistance from Ludwig, Fürst of Anhalt-Cöthen,[22] and he was able to make his way to his mother's relatives in Braunschweig where, still destitute, he sought employment to support his family. Through the recommendation of Graf Wilhelm of Saxony-Weimar, he obtained a position as a quartermaster and engineer in the service of the now triumphant Gustavus Adolphus and, in this capacity, spent some months working on fortifications at Erfurt. This remained his occupation until his return to Magdeburg to take a leading role in its reconstruction.

---

[20] The ducat was a gold coin dating from medieval Venice. It became a standard currency throughout Europe after its sanction by the Kaiser Maximilian II in 1566. It remained a legal currency until 1866.

[21] The source for this incident is an earlier historian of Magdeburg, Heinrich Ratmann, author of *Geschichte der Stadt Magdeburg* (1816)

[22] Ludwig Fürst von Anhalt-Cöthen (1579–1650) became, having travelled widely as a young man, ruler of Anhalt-Cöthen in 1606. He was a humane ruler whose main interest was in agricultural reform. Gustavus Adolphus transferred control of Magdeburg and Halberstadt to him but after Gustavus' death, he, at the bidding of Oxenstierna, relinquished this position.

FERDINANDVS III. ROMANORVM
IMPERATOR. SEMPER
AVGVSTVS.

Ferdinand III Holy Roman Emperor (1608–1657)

(Anselmus van Hulle)

The Rebuilding of Magdeburg (1632–1642)

When Pappenheim vacated the ruins of Magdeburg in January 1632 the town came under Swedish control. The Swedish commander, Field Marshal Baner,[23] issued a proclamation summoning the former residents of Magdeburg back to the city. Von Guericke and his family returned from Erfurt in February 1632 where they were again able to take possession of their property. Von Guericke's stepfather, Möllnvogt Christoph Schulze,[24] was appointed Commissar by Ludwig of Anhalt-Cöthen to whom Gustavus had entrusted responsibility for the administration both of the city and of the archdiocese. Schulze was made responsible for the rebuilding of the city and on February 12th 1632 issued an instruction that a street plan be drafted for approval by Gustavus before further ad hoc work proceeded. The drawing up of the plan was entrusted to von Guericke who submitted his proposals on April 10th. It comes as no surprise that von Guericke produced a far-reaching, logical and ambitious plan. Schimank writes of it:[25]

"The plan that von Guericke drew up was magnificent and far seeing. It was the sort of plan that only an engineer who had deep roots in the city would conceive. It showed his awareness of the city's proud past and it dreamt of a no less glorious future. The hard exigencies and pressure of the time did not permit the bringing to fruition of such a bold conception. .... Only after a century and a half did Magdeburg, which of all German cities had suffered the most, regain the population and economic status that it had before the destruction."

Subsequently he successfully applied for a remunerated position as an engineer. His first responsibilities in this capacity were the rebuilding of the bridges over the Elbe and the restoration of the city's

---

[23] Fieldmarshal Johann Baner (1596–1641) served under Gustavus in Poland and Russia from 1626 to 1629. He accompanied Gustavus to Germany in 1630. After the latter's death and the Swedish defeat at Nördlingen he became the commander of the Swedish troops in Germany. He re-established Swedish military prestige with victories at Wittstock (1636) and Chemnitz (1639). As a leader he was erratic and disorganised, driving his troops to mutiny. He died on May 10th 1641 and was succeeded by Torstenson.

[24] Like von Guericke, Schulze was a captive after the siege of Magdeburg and had to buy his freedom. When, under Swedish control, Ludwig of Anhalt-Cöthen became responsible for the affairs of Magdeburg, he appointed Schulze as overseer of the city's reconstruction. In 1635, following the peace of Prague, he was able to leave the service of Ludwig and work directly for the city of Magdeburg as a jurist. In this capacity he assembled a collection of documents bearing on the historic privileges of the city and its relationship to the archdiocese. These provided the legal basis for von Guericke's long diplomatic advocacy of Magdeburg's ancient rights.

[25] Schimank p. 19.

defences which Pappenheim, as part of a wider policy of leaving behind nothing of value to the enemy, had blown up on his retreat from the city.

In the course of 1632, in addition to von Guericke, many of the former Ratmännern returned and, while remaining subject to the authority of the Swedish military commanders, began to resume their administrative functions in the city. For the next few years von Guericke appears to have been fully occupied with the rebuilding of his own and the city's fortunes. Meanwhile, events on a wider stage were determining the future of the city and of von Guericke personally. Gustavus Adolphus had died. His despoiled and naked corpse was discovered under a pile of bodies at the battle of Lützen in November 1632. His demise drained the élan from any possible Swedish project for the conquest of Germany and the installation of Gustavus as Kaiser. Johann Georg, the Elector of Saxony, ever an uneasy and unwilling ally of the Swedes, began to negotiate peace with Ferdinand and, along with other Protestant electors, concluded the Treaty of Prague in May 1635.

The treaty defused religion as a continuing casus belli among Germans. The Edict of Restitution of 1629, requiring restitution of Church property expropriated since 1555, was all but revoked by dint of exempting secularisations before 1627 and the "cujus regio, illius religio" (the religion of a territory is the religion of its ruler) principle was reaffirmed. Added inducements of territorial concessions, including the granting of the archbishopric of Magdeburg to Saxony, proved sufficient to obtain the signatures of most of the Protestant princes to the treaty. As a result of this last provision, John Georg's son, August, was finally able in 1638 to take up, uncontested, the office of Administrator to which he had been elected a decade earlier. Although the Thirty Years War continued for a further thirteen years, it became, after the Treaty of Prague, a war on German soil rather than a war between Germans. The real protagonists were, on the one hand, France, under the tutelage of the icy Richelieu and his protégé Mazarin, in an alliance of convenience with Sweden, and, on the other, the Spanish and Austrian branches of the House of Habsburg. To von Guericke, as to the great majority of his compatriots, whose natural loyalties broadened from family, to native city, to the wider German speaking world as represented by "The Holy Roman Empire of the German People", the experience of the war was one of invaders quartering armies on German soil and bringing misery, disease and economic ruin in their wake.

Following the Treaty of Prague in 1635, the Elector Johann Georg of Saxony renounced his Swedish alliance and thereafter Saxony became an ally of the Kaiser. The city was again besieged, this time, by Saxon troops alongside the Imperial Fieldmarshal von Hatzfeldt.[26] The Swedish garrison capitulated without bloodshed and, on July 15th 1636, withdrew with military honour. Magdeburg passed into Saxon control and accepted a garrison of 1,500 Saxon and Imperial soldiers and their dependents. For the next decade Magdeburg was to endure greater vexation and harassment from German troops than it had suffered during the occupation by the Swedish foreigners.

Without any visible straining of consciences, loyalties were transferred from the Swedes and their agent Ludwig of Anhalt-Cöthen, to the Electorate of Saxony. Christoph Schulze, von Guericke's step father, resigned his Swedish commission to become a lawyer in the service of the Magdeburg civil authorities. Von Guericke himself became an officer in the service of Saxony and remained working as an engineer.

The picture that emerges, from his own correspondence as well as the public record, of von Guericke's activity in the years 1632 to 1640 is, on the one hand, that of a disinterested servant of the interests of Magdeburg, and on the other, that of an energetic businessman and local politician engaged in restoring the position and prosperity of his family. In 1637 we find him engaged in an activity which greatly exercised him right to the end of his life — arguing about his tax liabilities. In a letter to the Rat of March 14th he writes[27] that, as the Rat well knew, he had left the service of Sweden and, as an engineer in the service of Saxony, he had thus far been exempt from municipal taxation. However, Kämmerer Hermann Körver had, only the previous week,

---

[26] Melchior von Hatzfeldt (1593–1658) belonged to an ancient and still extant family from Hesse. His elder brother became Prince Bishop of Würzburg and Bamberg and he too was initially intended for a clerical career. He was educated by the Jesuits at Fulda and took orders as far as the diaconate. In 1620 he enlisted as an officer and rapidly rose through the ranks under Wallenstein and subsequently, after the latter's assassination, under Gallas. Towards the end of the Thirty Years War he retired from the Imperial service but later, in 1657, assisted the Poles against the Swedes. He was unmarried. His body is buried in Praussnitz and his heart in Laudenbach.
[27] Hoffmann p. 28.

imposed a tax of one thaler on the cost of milling a bushel of rye. As it was unlikely that Körver was acting on his own authority, he had no option but to ask the Rat to treat him like other officers in respect of civic exemptions and to cease their exactions from him. He didn't desire to do anything prejudicial to the interests of the city, but just wanted that to which he was entitled. An official of the Rat evenly replied that on the milling of grain for his personal or household consumption no tax would be levied but he was obliged to pay tax on grain used in his recently resumed brewing business and consequently the exaction stood.

The city, still very much in the process of rebuilding, laboured under the burden of quartering and feeding an occupying garrison. Foodstuff prices rose to unprecedented levels in 1636 and 1637 and a plague induced by malnutrition swept the city. The deterioration of the currency further exacerbated the state of economic misery. An application to the new Saxon commander, August Adolph von Transdorff,[28] for some easing of the economic burden was harshly met by an increase in the very exactions of money and provisions whose mitigation had been sought.

The Rat now considered that its best hope of obtaining some relief from the severity of von Transdorff lay in sending an emissary to the court of the Elector at Dresden to make the city's case directly. Von Guericke, being both an engineer in the service of Saxony and a man of deep loyalty to his native city, was the ideal choice. Many years later, recalling this period in a memorandum of 1677,[29] von Guericke noted:[30]

"There was no-one, both because of the hostility and threats of the Saxon commander and military, and also of the dangers of travel owing to the activity of hostile Swedish troops in the electorate of Saxony, who wanted to travel to Dresden to seek help from Johann Georg, the Elector."

---

[28] August Adolph Freiherr von Transdorff was a captain (Hauptmann) in the Imperial army, later becoming a commander (Obrist) in the service of Saxony. He was gravely wounded at Breitenfeld in 1631. In 1636 he was commandant at Leipzig as the city withstood a year long siege by troops under Baner. For his role in the 1637 defence of Leipzig he was honoured by the Kaiser in 1644. From 1640 to 1646 he was commandant at Magdeburg. He was also involved in the unsuccessful defence of Leipzig against Torstenson's troops in 1642.

[29] On February 6th 1677, in connection with a financial dispute with the city, von Guericke sent a memorandum, comprising 26 folio pages, to the Rat setting out his record of service to Magdeburg.

[30] Hoffmann p. 44.

His transition from the occupations of civil engineer, town planner and local entrepreneur to a diplomatic career began with his willingness to undertake this particular journey to Dresden. It was to be the first of many subsequent burdensome and hazardous missions undertaken over nearly a quarter century on behalf of Magdeburg.

The Years of Diplomatic Success (1642–1648)

Now in his late thirties, his personal fortunes somewhat restored, von Guericke seems imbued both with a sense of his own capacity to give leadership and that leadership was expected from him. By 1641 he had commanded the trust of his fellow citizens sufficiently to have become a Kämmerer. In September of the following year he undertook, as an envoy of Magdeburg, the dangerous journey to Dresden to bring the city's grievances to the personal attention of the Elector Johann Georg. This, his first diplomatic mission, was a success and the requested concessions[31] were granted. The return journey was, if anything, even more hazardous. Swedish troops, since 1635 Saxony's enemy rather than ally, had invaded the Electorate. Returning by boat to Magdeburg, von Guericke witnessed the sacking of the villages of Muritz and Mühlberg, where he had stopped for the night. At the latter place he thought it prudent to abandon his boat and continue on foot.

Despite the Elector's apparent sympathy for their predicament, von Transdorff's harsh and arbitrary treatment of Magdeburg's citizens continued unabated. During the harvest period, the soldiers, their wives, children and servants simply ran out into the fields taking what they wanted and leaving the people to cope as they might. Von Guericke recalls how the people of Magdeburg suffered.[32]

"They were like the children of Israel in bondage to the Pharaoh. From the highest to the humblest, all lived in fear that, on a pretext plucked out of thin air, their house would be taken over by the military, that they might be subject to beatings, and even that they would be sent as criminals in irons to the Elector. All letters were opened in the hope of finding a word here or there which could be held against the writer so as to provide an opportunity of dragging him before a court and imposing a more or less severe penalty."

In 1643 the Rat resolved on another mission to Dresden to seek mitigation of their distress by making their plight known directly to John Georg. Von Guericke agreed to make the journey provided that he was accompanied by colleagues so that he alone would not be the sole object of von Transdorff's resentment. In May 1643 he set out again for Dresden, this time in the company of his colleagues Johann

---

[31] The concessions were to do with stopping the commercial activities of the military which were undermining the ability of the citizens to make their living. (v. Hoffmann p. 44)
[32] Hoffmann p. 43.

Alemann and Gottfried Rosenstock.[33] Johann Georg received the delegation warmly but little concrete amelioration of their situation ensued. The principal positive development was the change in the Rat's policy away from merely seeking remedies for specific grievances towards the greater goal of being free of the Saxon garrison entirely.

Having established his credentials as a diplomat, von Guericke was now entrusted with the realisation of the much-cherished hope of the city fathers to be rid of occupying garrisons, whether Swedish, Saxon or Imperial. They longed to be relieved of the burden of supporting them and to be allowed to administer their own affairs. This involved a series of complicated negotiations with Johann Georg's court at Dresden, with the Kaiser Ferdinand's in Vienna and with the Swedish military authorities commanded by Fieldmarshal Torstenson.[34] To this end, in August 1645, von Guericke embarked on his third perilous journey to Dresden. In December of that year we find him battling snow and ice to reach Halle, the seat of the Administrator August, who himself coveted the right to station a garrison in the city. From Halle, he travelled to Leipzig to negotiate with Torstenson, who was also considering the city as possible quarters for a Swedish garrison, and then returned to Magdeburg to report to the Rat. On January 9th 1646 the diplomats were on the move again — von Guericke to Leipzig and Eilenburg and his colleague Steinacker to Dresden. Their energetic diplomacy, supplemented by the activities of the city's representatives in Vienna, was finally rewarded. On April 14th 1646 the Imperial cavalry along with von Transdorff's infantry withdrew and were replaced by a 250 strong garrison provided by the city itself. On the following Sunday Thanksgiving services were held to mark the city's deliverance from sixteen years of oppressive occupation.

---

[33] Gottfried Rosenstock (d. 1677) was a Bürgermeister colleague of von Guericke from 1662 to 1677. He was born in Belzig, married into the Alemann family and took an active part in the rebuilding of Magdeburg.

[34] Lennart Torstenson (1603–1651) was a commander under Gustavus Adolphus and Baner in the earlier part of the Thirty Years War. Illness compelled him to return to Sweden but on the death of Baner he was recalled to Germany as generalissimo of the Swedish forces and was promoted to fieldmarshal. He inflicted severe defeats on the Imperial army at the second battle of Breitenfeld (1642) and at Jüterbog in 1644. Crippled with gout and unable even to sign an order, his request for a recall to Sweden was acceded to in 1646 and Carl Gustav Wrangel was appointed his successor. Torstenson passed the remainder of his life in high administrative positions in Sweden.

Writing in 1936, perhaps with the Treaty of Versailles in mind, Schimank notes that the city's liberation had been dearly bought and made subject to humiliating conditions, against which the Rat immediately began to protest. He writes:[35]

"Clearly the city had paid dearly for its delivery from alien occupation and had to consent to an agreement that severely constrained its rights. Never in history has the validity of an imposed agreement, where a population has felt its most natural rights abused and its honor besmirched, been maintained. Scarcely had the occupying troops withdrawn, before the Rat began to register its protest before lawyers and witnesses against the conditions imposed on it. It declared that the city would pay the traditional dues as soon as its grievances against the former Archdiocese and in particular against the cathedral chapter were addressed, but, in any case, they would not meet these obligations in the demeaning manner that was expected. They would not countenance any foregoing of the privilege, expensively purchased from two Kaisers, of extending the fortification works. As regards the right to station a garrison, which had been in former times clearly and indisputably conceded to them, they did not intend to enter negotiations."

The course of events over the next twenty years would show that these fine words, gratuitously courting the enmity of the powerful Electors of Saxony and Brandenburg, were mere bluster. In the meantime however, perhaps as an expression of the understandable pride of a city enjoying new liberty, the Magistrat, which had fallen below the norms specified in the 1630 reform, was augmented by the appointment of six new Ratsmännern. Von Guericke himself, hitherto a Kämmerer, was elevated to a vacant Bürgermeister position which he assumed on September 5th 1646. Of this advancement Hoffmann notes:[36]

"On his elevation to the highest civic office, he justified the great expectations, which his talents, his experience and his zeal for the welfare of the city allowed one to cherish. For more than thirty years he remained untiringly active, fighting Magdeburg's cause on his diplomatic missions and furthering its interests with inexhaustible energy but, nevertheless, with only modest success."

Diplomatic forays continued. Von Guericke's first mission as a Bürgermeister elect was in May 1646 to Leipzig where Torstenson, sick and about to return to Sweden, assured him that Stockholm had no objections to the city's becoming a Free City with its own garrison. As a mark of his esteem and gratitude, von Guericke presented Torstenson

---

[35] Schimank p. 23.
[36] Hoffmann p. 49.

with an expensive pen and a brass celestial globe powered by an internal clockwork mechanism. This gift is of interest because it gives us a rare glimpse of a private life of engineering and craftsmanship behind the busy public persona. His own account suggests that he had constructed the globe himself. In correspondence with the Rat in September 1646 he writes[37] that it would have been worth more than a hundred thalers, but it had made a more favourable impression than a thousand ducats. He could have asked for payment for it but had, in the interests of the city, refrained from doing so. An allusion to a conversation with Torstenson provides the earliest explicit reference to von Guericke's scientific interests. He writes:[38]

"When, because of his illness, the fieldmarshal (Torstenson) stayed in Magdeburg, I discussed with him, in addition to fortification engineering, other valuable scientific and mathematical topics."

On the larger stage, the long agony of the Thirty Years War was moving to a close. The Peace of Westphalia, negotiated among no fewer than 109 delegations over about five years and finally resulting in the treaties of Osnabrück and Münster of May and October 1648, brought to an end wars of a specifically Christian confessional character in Europe. The Peace settled the religious character of the regions of Europe by reaffirming the Augsburg formula *"Cujus regio, eius religio"* — a doctrine that could be understood to justify alike the revocation of the Edict of Nantes and the anti-Catholic penal laws in England. The period of the Counter Reformation, where the religious affiliation of whole territories might be subject to sudden change, drew to an end.

The political settlements of the Peace were in large measure the work of Mazarin. In implementing the policy of his mentor and predecessor Richelieu, he enhanced the power and prestige of an absolutist Bourbon monarchy in France at the expense of the authority of the Habsburgs of Spain and Austria. The Empire was fragmented beyond repair and the authority of its Kaiser fatally undermined by the granting of independence from the Empire to Switzerland, the Netherlands, Savoy and several other Italian states. The reduction of the Empire to an impotent patchwork of territories was further assured by ceding to some 400 German rulers, in the name of the liberties of the German

---

[37] Hoffmann p. 49.
[38] Schimank p. 38. "anderen raren mathematischen Wissenschaften".

princes, an authority equal to that of the Kaiser. The stage was set for a century and a half of French ascendancy in Europe, curbed initially by the Duke of Marlborough at Blenheim and subsequently by the Duke of Wellington at Waterloo. The emergence of a unified state in Germany, which might otherwise have taken place under the Kaiser, was postponed until the era of Bismarck. When it did take place, it did so according to a very different dynamic — that set in motion when the Elector of Brandenburg became King of Prussia in 1701.

Magdeburg's concerns, in comparison with the events unfolding on the European stage, were parochial but nonetheless passionately felt. The city feared that the assurances given it by the Kaiser and the Queen of Sweden in respect of its former rights and privileges might be lost sight of amidst the welter of far reaching settlement negotiations. Magdeburg's aim was to secure a formal reaffirmation by the Treaty signatories of promises already made to it. Among the chief objectives of the city's emissaries were the following:

1 - That the privileges granted to it by Kaiser Otto I[39] in 940 AD be renewed.

2 - That the status of Magdeburg as an Imperial Free City be confirmed and the payment of all dues to the Administrator be abolished.[40]

3 - That the right to extend the city by a quarter of a German mile[41] be recognised and that the city be accorded complete jurisdiction over this new territory.

4 - That the rebuilding of the demolished suburbs of Sudenburg and Neustadt be prohibited.[42]

5 - That the independence of the city from the diocese of Magdeburg be formally implemented by the transfer of various sovereign powers and responsibilities to the city.

---

[39] Otto I, Holy Roman Emperor (912–973), is buried in the Cathedral of Magdeburg. Von Guericke certainly believed that a document setting out such privileges existed and provided the legal foundation of Magdeburg's rights. It seems likely, however, that there never was any such document and Magdeburg's privileges were based simply on tradition and custom.

[40] This was imposed as a punishment by Pope John XXII in 1325 as a penalty for the murder of the Archbishop Burchard III. (Hoffmann p. 55)

[41] A German mile is approximately 7,600 kilometres.

[42] The concern of the city fathers was that if these suburbs were rebuilt people would choose to live in them and escape the contributions to the fortification and garrisoning of the city exacted from the residents proper within the city walls.

Fearful that the agent of the Administrator August, Dr. Johann Krull, would be poisoning influential minds against the city, the Rat considered that it was vitally important to send the best possible representative to the talks. Von Guericke did not want to be burdened with the responsibility of missions to Osnabrück and Münster. He felt used and exploited. His earlier diplomatic missions, in addition to being onerous and hazardous, had also severely impacted his ability to earn a living from his brewing and farming interests. The city fathers wanted his talents and experience as an ambassador but, like their legendary colleagues of Hamelin, were determined to pay no more than the barest minimum. Von Guericke's correspondence with the city authorities at this period, as it was frequently throughout his life, is much taken up with personal financial matters.

In the event, he was prevailed upon to accept this commission and in October 1647 set out in his own wagon drawn by four of his own horses. His eighteen year old son, Hans Otto, and a young servant accompanied him. On a personal level he had a miserable time. The horses sickened with the effort of pulling a wagon along roads turned into quagmires by the autumn downpours. After eight days of travel they finally arrived in Osnabrück on October 28th. All three shared a single first floor room with cracks in the floorboards and ceiling so that they could see the ground below and the attic above. Osnabrück was teeming with diplomats and their entourages from all over Europe and it would have been surprising had local landlords and shopkeepers not taken the opportunity to profiteer. Von Guericke was shocked to be charged two thalers a week for accommodation, eight for substandard meals and three for stabling the horses. He complained that his servant boys and girls in Magdeburg kept a better table. From the initial 270 thalers given to him for the entire trip, he had already spent 130 by the time he wrote to the Rat on November 11th asking for at least fifteen ducats to be sent with the next courier. The need for money and weariness at the hardships he had to endure remained a recurring theme of his correspondence. His mission dragged on into the summer of the next year. We find him writing in May 1647:[43]

"However distasteful it is to me to be writing about money, there is no alternative. I need to have one hundred thalers as soon as possible. .... I have no doubt that there are quite a

---

[43] Hoffman p. 58.

few people who are cursing me and think that it's all very well for me sitting here and living off their money. But they would think differently if they saw what a grim and soul-destroying business it is to be endlessly hanging about here hoping and waiting to see whether, how and what, settlement of our issues will finally be reached. Just when I have brought something to a satisfactory state, along he[44] comes and turns everything upside down and I have my work cut out to get our wagon back on its wheels. ...... A thousand and one times, I have wished that I didn't have to be here, though someone else would have had to be. ...... Upon my soul and more than you could believe, I miss my home so much; but there's nothing for it, I have to stick it out here."

His attendance at the peace negotiations proved protracted. His return to Magdeburg, delayed by the smallpox to which his son and servant had succumbed, was finally underway on August 13th and he arrived back in his native city on August 24th 1648.

Despite the many trials and inconveniences, his experience had not been an unrelieved tale of woe. We catch sight of the impression he could make on influential people. He was then a widower of forty-five with an experience of life of a depth and richness that must have seemed unrivalled. He was a man of wide education and profound intellect, who had survived tragedy, destitution and bereavement to rebuild a life of some prestige, worthy of his family name, and to be a leader of his city. The Swedish plenipotentiaries, Johann Oxenstierna,[45] son of the Swedish chancellor, and Johann Salvius,[46] were major figures at the conference. On May 6th von Guericke came to pay his respects to the wife of Salvius, a lady who exercised considerable influence on her husband. She received him alone in the informal setting of her living

---

[44] "he" was the representative of the administrator August, Dr Johann Krull, an indefatigable opponent of the aspirations of Magdeburg. As well as inheriting a strong animus against the city from his father-in-law, Möllnvogt Berthold Struve, he also had his own quarrels with the city. Both Struve and Krull fell foul of city regulations on the conduct of businesses. Von Guericke, normally judicious and calm in the expression of his opinions, could not contain his dislike of the behaviour of both.

[45] Johann Oxenstierna (1611–1657) was the son of Gustavus' Chancellor Axel Oxenstierna. He served in the Thirty Years War from 1632 and was entrusted by his father with various diplomatic missions. As a diplomat his role was restricted to representing his father's precisely expressed positions with little latitude for personal initiatives. From 1650–1652 he was governor general of Swedish Pomerania and was elevated to Marshal of the Realm by Charles X in 1652.

[46] Johann Salvius (1590–1652) was a Swedish lawyer and diplomat from a humble background. He gained the confidence of Gustavus Adolphus through a construction project at Gothenburg. He began his diplomatic career in 1622, becoming a secretary of state in 1624. He and Oxenstierna ensured that the provisions of Westphalia were favourable to Sweden. He was appointed to the Privy Council and became a Baron in 1651 and is still considered one of Sweden's foremost diplomats.

room. Like Dido to Aeneas, she listened raptly to his long account of the fate that had befallen Magdeburg in 1631 and was moved to tears. She promised to intercede with her husband and proved as good as her word. The very next evening von Guericke found himself dining with Oxenstierna, the senior of the Swedish representatives. Though the latter was unconvinced about the authenticity of the Ottonian Privileges,[47] both he and Salvius were induced to support Magdeburg's political aspirations.

On behalf of the city, von Guericke needed to make influential friendships wherever they could be found. On the Imperial side he successfully cultivated the Kaiser's senior emissary, Maximilian Graf von Trautmannsdorf[48] and persuaded him to favour Magdeburg's claims. The hostile briefings of Dr Krull, which had changed the hitherto supportive attitude of the Elector of Brandenburg, were successfully countered. To the great joy of the city fathers, von Guericke's untiring diplomatic efforts appeared to have been brought to a triumphant conclusion when, in October 1648, Article 8 of the Treaty of Münster declared:[49]

"The city of Magdeburg, by virtue of its humbly submitted request to His Majesty the Kaiser, shall have its ancient freedom and the Privileges promulgated by Otto I on June 7ᵗʰ 940 renewed, notwithstanding that the document has been lost through the ravages of time. In addition, the privilege conferred by Kaiser Ferdinand II of fortifying the city and extending it by a quarter of a mile, is also duly and lawfully reaffirmed. Also hereby confirmed is the unrestricted and unthreatened exercise of its rights and privileges both spiritual and tem-

---

[47] The privileges supposedly granted to Magdeburg by Otto I in 940.

[48] Maximilian Graf von Trautmannsdorf (1584 –1650) was the son of an official at the Imperial Court. As a young man he converted to Catholicism and served in the Imperial army from 1593 to 1606 in campaigns against the Turks. His diplomatic career began under Rudolph II. He became Reichshofrat in 1612 and, following successful negotiations on behalf of the Kaiser with Spain and Bavaria, was elevated to the Reichsgrafenstand in 1623. In the following years he conducted negotiations with Bavaria, was the Kaiser's chief counsellor at the Reichstag at Regensburg in 1630 and played a part both in the recall of Wallenstein and in his assassination in 1634. He influenced the Kaiser's abandonment of the Edict of Restitution which facilitated the reconciliation with the Elector Johann Georg of Saxony achieved by the Treaty of Prague in 1635. He was the principal Imperial representative at Westphalia and strove to obtain a settlement favourable to the Habsburg interest. When political developments conspired to favour the opponents of the Habsburgs, he, ostensibly on health grounds, withdrew from the conference and was succeeded by the inflexible Isaac Volmar. He died in Vienna in 1650 and is buried in Trautmannsdorf.

[49] Hoffmann p. 75.

poral. A special provision is also hereby made that the suburbs, which damage the interests of the city, may not be rebuilt."

The inclusion of this article was due to the direct influence of the Swedish delegates, Salvius and Oxenstierna, and the Imperial delegate Maximilian von Trautmannsdorf. However, goodwill in high but far-removed circles was not a guarantee of an uncontested implementation of the treaty's provisions in the local context. Arguments began immediately. The residents of the disputed suburbs, Neustadt and Sudenburg, appealed against the prohibition on rebuilding and applied to the Administrator to be reclassified as archdiocesan provincial towns (erzbischöfliche Landstädte). The landowners of the affected properties also protested against the proposed quarter mile extension of the city and the construction of new fortifications that it would entail. Despite the protests, the city authorities proceeded on their own initiative with preliminary surveying work in Neustadt. This precipitate action provided the Administrator with a welcome opportunity for another round of diplomacy aimed at reversing the loss to his authority sustained by the provisions of the Treaty of Münster. He reported the Rat to the court at Vienna. The Kreisdirektor of the Lower Saxony Circle[50] issued a warning to the city to discontinue surveying in Neustadt. Johann Georg, naturally taking the part of his son, the Administrator, also issued, in February 1649, an Imperial decree restraining further work pending the decision of a new Commission to review the matter. This decree was communicated to the Magdeburg Rat in March 1649 and was followed by another issued in May but not communicated to the Rat until July.

Aware that they were at the centre of a storm of protest, von Guericke's colleagues on the Rat resolved on another mission to defuse the situation and found themselves calling, yet again, on his services. This next round of diplomacy was focused in three locations — Osna-

---

[50] The Holy Roman Empire was first divided into six "Circles" by Kaiser Maximilian I in 1500. To the original six — Franconia, Bavaria, Swabia, Upper Rhine, Westphalia and Lower Saxony — were added, twelve years later, Austria, Upper Saxony, Lower Rhine and Burgundy. The Circles were administrative units with each having specific financial and personnel obligations to the central government of the Empire. Neighbouring Circles were grouped into three larger units called "corresponding Circles", one of which was Upper and Lower Saxony. (Thomas Salmon. *The Present State of all Nations* Vol. 2. p. 134 (1745). The Lower Saxony Circle (Niedersächsischer Reichskreis) comprised some 28 territories notably Magdeburg, Hamburg, Lübeck, Bremen and Halberstadt.

brück, where delegations were still negotiating final details of the Peace of Westphalia, Nuremburg, where a convention had been summoned to monitor the execution of the provisions of the Treaty, and the Imperial Court at Vienna. In March 1649 we find von Guericke and his son, after a period of respite of only seven months, again on the road to Osnabrück.

In order to persuade him to accept this new commission, the Rat finally acceded to the request, first made in June 1646, that he be immune from general civic taxes and impositions levied on the citizenry, in particular, the obligation to quarter soldiers in their homes as part of the war effort. In support of his request he had cited his arduous continuing service to the city and his inability, while absent on diplomatic missions, to supplement his income from his brewing and farming business. To his chagrin the city fathers had declined his request. They had acknowledged the scope of his services and had promised him a gratuity of one hundred ducats when money should become available. Nevertheless they had refused him his wish on the grounds that such a request was unprecedented and the consequences of acceding to it unforeseeable. Now in 1649, wishing him to undertake yet more missions, and in recognition of his apparent success at Osnabrück and Münster, the Rat and both sections of the Ausschuss granted the long-sought immunity to him, his son and their spouses.

To see in von Guericke's extensive and often tetchy correspondence about money a wily Bürgermeister manouevring to do well for himself would be to take an ungenerous and perverse view of his character. Beyond the normal good reasons why a man in his forties would value financial security, there must also have been a longing on the part of a man no longer young for the time and financial resources to pursue his scientific interests. In considering his conduct one must bear in mind that he was destitute at thirty; when he gave the superbly crafted celestial globe to Torstenson he was forty-four; when he appeared at Regensburg with a thought out position on one of the great philosophical questions of the day and able to support it with experiments, he was fifty-two; when he completed his *Experimenta Nova* he was sixty-one. From his early manhood to late middle age, the Horsemen of the Apocalypse — pestilence, war, famine and death — stalked Germany with Magdeburg's suffering being particularly intense. From the tenor of his writings and the sheer adversity of circumstance that he overcame to accomplish his scientific work, it is plain that his science was not a salon hobby but an abiding passion of his entire adult life. A more just reading of his situation during these years is to see a man seeking the time and the means to requite the deep, truth-seeking impulses of his nature.

The negotiations to rid Magdeburg of an occupying Saxon garrison and his apparent securing of autonomy for the city at Westphalia were the high points of von Guericke's diplomatic career. The record of the next seventeen years of diplomatic activity is one of frustration and failure culminating in the final abandonment of the city's political aspirations and the reluctant acceptance in 1666 of yet another military garrison — this time of the troops of Brandenburg.

Diplomatic Frustration and Drudgery

Arriving in Osnabrück on March 14th and taking up residence in his old lodgings, von Guericke set about his new diplomatic assignment. The Administrator had already been active and, deliberately excluding the original drafters — Oxenstierna, Salvius and von Trautmannsdorf — had organised a conference to clarify the Treaty's contentious Article 8. Restrictive and more liberal interpretations[51] of the exact meaning of Article 8 were respectively advanced by the Administrator and by von Guericke. The latter's position was supported by the representatives of the other Imperial cities but the advocacy of the former, aided by the intervention of both his father Johann Georg and the young Elector of Brandenburg, prevailed. One of the provisions of Westphalia was that, after the death of the current Administrator, the archdiocese of Magdeburg would pass to the electorate of Brandenburg in compensation for territory in Pomerania ceded to Sweden. This finally occurred after August's death in 1680, when the secularised archdiocese became the Duchy of Magdeburg.

Following this setback at Osnabrück, von Guericke and his son returned to Magdeburg while other delegates made their way to Nuremberg to continue negotiation on implementing the Treaty and on the arrangements for demobilising troops. The Rat, fearing the erosion of their influence in the negotiations, resolved to send a representative to Nuremburg and to the Imperial Court at Vienna. Once again there was only one man for the task. The only man for the task once again wrote, on June 12th 1649, a long letter rehearsing his great reluctance to embark on a new mission. He summed up his ragged weariness with travel and diplomacy, appositely citing Ecclesiastes 2:22–23.[52]

"For what does a man gain for all the toil and strain that he has undergone under the sun, since his days are full of sorrow, his work is full of stress and his nights afford him no peace?"

---

[51] In dispute, for instance, was whether the ¼-mile extension conceded at Westphalia was to be in addition to the 77 roods (Ruthen) previously granted to the city by the Kaiser or whether the latter was to be included in the former. Also at issue was the nature of the city's title to the extra land — was it to be freehold (Eigentumsrecht) or merely a right of "oversight" (der Stadt nur ein Obereigentum aber kein Nutzeigentum zuzugestehen sei). Hoffmann p. 78.
[52] Hoffmann p. 81.

By widening the scope of the immunity they had earlier granted him so that it now, as well as his immediate family, covered all his descendants, they persuaded him. On July 17th, accompanied by his son, he set out for Nuremburg. With him, in addition to letters of accreditation to the Kaiser and to the Swedish supreme commander, Field Marshal Carl Gustaf Wrangel,[53] were letters of petition to the Imperial Court written by Jacob Stajus,[54] a colleague on the Rat. The wider aim of his mission was, as before, to secure the implementation of the (suppposed) Ottonian privileges by the awarding of Imperial Free City status to Magdeburg.

Between Bamberg and Nuremburg an unexpected call was made on his diplomatic skills. His wagon was surrounded by a band of drunken and armed peasants emerging from a fair. Von Guericke's initial fears — quite natural in view of the danger of encountering bands of demobbed, footloose, and unpaid soldiers seeking to somehow survive — that a full scale robbery was afoot happily proved unfounded and they were able to continue unmolested, arriving in Nuremburg on July 24th.

His reports back to the Rat from Nuremburg dwell on the difficulties of obtaining appointments with key people and on the severely inflated prices. The latter he attributed to the doubling of duties on commodities as Nuremburg struggled to pay its share of the five million thalers agreed at Westphalia as the total sum required to meet the financial obligations of the Swedish army and to ensure their orderly demobilisation. Magdeburg's contribution in this regard was also a concern of von Guericke when he finally obtained an appointment with Carl Gustaf on August 9th. Their negotiations centred on Magdeburg's share of the reparations to be paid to Sweden but led ultimately to no

---

[53] Carl Gustaf Wrangel (1613–1676) fought as young captain in the Thirty Years War from 1633, rising rapidly to the rank of colonel in 1636 and major general in 1638 while still serving in Germany. In 1644, now as a naval commander, he defeated the Danes at Fehmarn. In 1646 he returned as the successor of Torstenson, to Germany where alongside the French general, Turenne, he fought in Bavaria and Württemburg. After the Peace of Westphalia he became Governor General of Swedish Pomerania. Subsequently in 1655 he campaigned alongside Friedrich Wilhelm of Brandenburg in the Second Northern War, invading Jutland and capturing Kronborg. In 1658 he became supreme judge in the province of Uppland and chancellor of the University of Greifswald two years later. He is buried in the Wrangel family crypt at Skokloster.

[54] Jacob Stajus was the author of a document "Proiect Priveligii" dealing with the Ottonian privileges. (v. Footnote 255 to Dissertation of Heinrich Guido, Impuls und Transfer 2006)

significant concessions. Von Guericke's other important meeting was with Reichsgeheimrat Isaac Volmar.[55] He advised him that, when he went to Vienna, he should separate the issues of the Ottonian privileges and the request for Free City status, warning him that the Elector of Brandenburg would be a determined opponent of the latter. His sense that the interests ranged against Magdeburg were now too strong and too influential to be resisted can only have been reinforced when a private letter of the Administrator to Carl Gustaf was divulged to him. In it the Administrator asks the Swedish commander to give no hearing to the Magdeburg deputies and their outrageous demands. When von Guericke had done all he could in Nuremburg, he set out, towards the end of August, for Vienna.

To avoid the plague, then rampant and a particular hazard on an overland journey, he chose to travel first to Regensburg and from there to continue the journey by boat along the Danube. In addition to his son he took with him a young man from Regensburg, a relative of a prosperous Nuremburg friend[56] recommended to him for the sake of his good contacts in Vienna. The little party disembarked on September 5th and took up residence in a two-room rented apartment.

He was to spend the next year and a half in Vienna. He had a frustrating and rather wretched time and his letters give vent to his continuing unhappiness and desire to be back in Magdeburg. He was no longer a young man. Coming up to fifty, he was, by the standards of time, on the threshold of old age. His health was no longer robust. He was experiencing both severe headaches and toothache and complained to the Rat that often when he was supposed to be working or thinking about something he simply couldn't and had to lay aside his pen. Touchingly, he asked them to keep the news about his health problems secret from his mother so that she would not be upset. He was finding the local food disagreeable and he had given up the spacious comforts of his home for the privation of a tiny shared apartment. Perhaps these tribulations might have been endured with greater equanimity had he been able to make substantial progress with the main business of his diplomatic mission. This was, as ever, to detach Magdeburg from any

---

[55] Isaac Volmar was an Imperial diplomat who had been chancellor of Alsace before it was ceded to France. He succeeded von Trautmannsdorff as the principal Imperial negotiator at the Peace of Westphalia.
[56] Hoffmann p. 91.

obligations to the former archbishopric, to free it from subordination to the Electors of Brandenburg and Saxony and to have it declared, based on the (supposed) Ottonian Privilege of almost 700 years previously, an Imperial Free City. Here too he was beset by delays, broken promises, uncertain lines of authority and the inability of a still financially straitened city adequately to bribe the decision makers. Above all, his efforts were stymied by the formidable opposition of the Electors of Brandenburg and Saxony and the latter's son, August the Administrator.

With just a little historical hindsight, it is clear that one of the potentially great scientists of the day was having his life wasted on a hopelessly quixotic enterprise. No amount of Imperial pretension or court ceremonial could change the reality that the power of the Kaiser over German affairs had been permanently broken at Westphalia. The desire of some four hundred German princes to enhance their own status aligned itself, to French eyes very opportunely, with a calculation that the centralised and united France created by Richelieu would always have the upper hand over a fragmented Germany. Accordingly, Mazarin energetically promoted the claims of the former with an eye to ensuring the latter.

A frustration that goes unrecorded in his correspondence but which must have weighed heavily on him was the state of his scientific interests. Given that a busy man of fifty, even today, doesn't suddenly start thinking seriously about science, one assumes that von Guericke had by this time worked out his positions on the fundamental questions and had developed at least some experiments to lend support to his ideas. The vacuum pump, for which he is most celebrated, has been dated to 1647, but that too must have been the culmination of work going back to earlier years.[57] Instruments attributed to his devising go back to 1632,[58] when he had just returned to the devastated city. He

---

[57] In the *Preface to the Reader* of the *Experimentum Novum Magdeburgum* Fr. Schott writes: "Its author is the noble and most excellent Master Otto Gericke, Patrician and Bürgermeister of Magdeburg and its ambassador to the general Peace Treaty at Münster and Osnabrück. A few years previously (paucos ante annos) he thought up a device whose intent and purpose you will understand from his words reproduced below."

[58] Von Guericke's great grandson, who died c. 1790, records in his *History of the Duchy of Magdeburg* that he possessed an astrolabe and a spirit level on which were engraved "fait par Otto de Guericke, engineer at Magdeburg 1632". Hoffmann (p. 166) points out that, as von Guericke

was still a lone, self-funded[59] scientist and not part of the extensive network of English, French and Italian scientists that communicated with each other through such figures as Fr. Mersenne[60] at Paris. His scientific work, in which neither the city fathers nor even his immediate family seem to have taken any interest, needed consolidation and communication to a wider audience. Of his scientific isolation Schimank writes:[61]

"Here stood a man entirely on his own. There was no Medici family to put resources at his disposal. Scientifically he was in a less favourable situation than the members of the Florentine Academia del Cimento[62] who could advise each other. He had to think out for himself every little artifact and design every piece of auxiliary apparatus so that it could be made by a Magdeburg based business. Perhaps it is this that is at the root of the preference, that all his experiments show, for a certain unsophisticated directness. When someone in Florence carried out experiments on the pressure of the air, he could rely on the availability of the highest technical expertise. Here in Magdeburg the equipment for scientific research was the solid and durable work of a local forge. While this, on the one hand, made it harder to perform experiments it also, on the other, gave them an overwhelming direct impact."

If consolidation of his ideas into a body of work was ever to be achieved, or recognition of his accomplishments ever to come to him, time was fast running out

Von Guericke, however, finding himself in Vienna on September 6th 1649, set about the tasks he had been given with his customary energy and determination. His most immediate goal was to obtain an audience with the Kaiser. When he learned that the Kaiser was in Ebersdorf,[63] he proceeded thither on September 10th. Unfortunately the Kai-

---

only became entitled to the prefix "von" in 1666, though the inscription may well be true, it can hardly have been done in 1632.

[59] His great-grandson Biedersee estimates that von Guericke spent the enormous sum of 20 000 thalers on his experiments and machines. (Hoffmann p. 202.) This may go some way to explain the motif of worry about money that is a recurrent theme of his correspondence.

[60] Marin Mersenne (1588–1648) was a French theologian, philosopher and mathematician. He was educated by the Jesuits at La Flèche and ordained as a Minim Friar in 1613. He was a strong defender of Descartes, a fellow past pupil of La Flèche, against clerical criticism and maintained an extensive and international scientific correspondence. He was the first to draw the attention of Pascal to the work of Torricelli in Italy. The Mersenne primes are named after him.

[61] Schimank p. 40.

[62] The Academia del Cimento (the Academy of Experiment) was a scientific society founded in Florence in 1657 by students of Galileo, Torricelli and Viviani. It was financially supported by Prince Leopoldo and Grand Duke Ferdinand II de Medici.

[63] Ebersdorf was the location of the Imperial hunting lodge near Vienna.

ser was hunting when he arrived, so he went back to Vienna. The Kaiser returned to the Imperial residence late that evening and von Guericke presented himself at the Hofburg the following morning, September 11th. He submitted his letters of accreditation to Johann Maximilian Graf von Lamberg,[64] whom he knew well from his time in Osnabrück, and an appointment was made for an audience at 4 p.m. Von Guericke duly appeared at the appointed time only to be told that it was the day for the Mail and the officials were too busy, but that, if he could come back tomorrow at the same time, he would be definitely admitted. He finally secured his first audience with the Kaiser on September 12th 1649.

The Kaiser was still in mourning for the death of the Kaiserin, Maria Leopoldine,[65] who had died in childbirth on August 7th. He received von Guericke standing at the end of the room under a mourning canopy and wearing a long cloak that fell to the ground about him. The latter condoled with him, as court protocol required, on the death of the Kaiserin and then turned to the perennial themes of Magdeburg diplomacy. He thanked the Kaiser on behalf of the Rat for his support for the city of Magdeburg in the change of its relationship to the archbishopric and for his reaffirmation of the Ottonian Privileges. He came then to his central purpose and presented his request that, to avoid future disputes, the city of Magdeburg be proclaimed an Imperial Free City and enrolled as such in the Imperial Register. Secondly he reminded the Kaiser that in the Treaty of Prague, negotiated by his father Ferdinand II, the extension of the city by a quarter of a German mile and the associated jurisdiction and building rights had been conceded. Finally he besought the Kaiser to issue a decree to the dissenting Fürsten confirming Magdeburg's new position. The Kaiser procrastinated. He graciously assured von Guericke that he had Magdeburg's petition very much in mind, but that he would have to consider the matter further

---

[64] Johann Maximilian Graf von Lamberg (1608–1682) had a long and distinguished career in the Imperial military and diplomatic service. He was a Kämmerer of Ferdinand II from 1634, a member of the Reichshofrat from 1637, an Imperial representative at Westphalia, a signatory of the treaty, and in 1657 was nominated to the Reichsgeheimrat. He is buried in the Augustinian Hofkirche in Vienna. His youngest son, Johann Philipp von Lamberg, (1651–1712) was a cardinal and Prince-Bishop of Passau.
[65] Archduchess Maria Leopoldine of Austria (1632–1649), was the daughter of Leopold V, Archduke of Austria, and Claudia de Medici. In 1648 she married her first cousin, the Kaiser, following the death of his first wife, Archduchess Maria Anna, in 1646.

before giving a response to the Rat. He accepted a written deposition of Magdeburg's claims from von Guericke and, offering him his hand, brought the audience to an end.

Von Guericke was to remain in Vienna for almost another year and a half — until February 1651 — without being able significantly to advance or clarify the situation of Magdeburg from where it stood at the time of this audience. He was to have a second audience with the Kaiser in June 1650. Both before and after these meetings, he set about cultivating various influential personages of the court, the Imperial and Swedish delegates and the representatives of the German principalities and Free Cities. This was not just a matter of force of personality, persuasive charm or eloquent argument. It also involved the giving of, what were coyly called, "presents". A financially straitened city needed to budget carefully the price of a man's good offices. Von Guericke reported to the Magdeburg Rat, that unless Ferdinand Sigismund Kurtz, Graf von Senftenau,[66] the Reichsvizekanzler, received at least 500 thalers, Graf Oettingen[67] 200, Kammerpräsident Justus von Gebhardt 200, and Reichshofrat Wilhelm Bidembach[68] 200, nothing could be expected from them. The reply from the Rat noted that they had decided to remit 2,000 thalers to him. This was to include 500 for Graf Kurtz and otherwise von Guericke was to use his judgment, taking into account the rank and influence of the possible recipients, as to the appropriate number and value of presents to be given. They added that they would have liked to send him more, but he himself was well aware of the financial difficulties and terrible state of the city. His judgment in the delicate matter of present giving was not always sure. The cities of the Hanseatic League had written in support of Magdeburg's claims and the letter had been given to von Guericke for delivery. He had given it to the Reichsvizekanzler, Graf Kurtz, to pass on to

---

[66] Ferdinand Sigismund Kurtz Graf von Senftenau (1592–1659). He came to the Imperial Court in 1625 as Kammerherr, was named Reichshofrat in 1626 and became a member of the Geheimrat in 1640. He was ennobled to the Reichgrafenstand c. 1636 and became Reichsvizekanzler in 1637.

[67] Joachim Ernst Graf zu Oettingen-Oettingen (1612–1658) was president of the Reichhofsrat during this period. (Hoffman p. 140)

[68] Wilhelm Bidembach von Treuenfels (c.1588–1655) had a career as a law professor at Tubingen and as a court official. He was named a Reichshofrat in 1648, only the second Lutheran to hold such a position. He was ennobled by Ferdinand III in 1654. He was the Referent for the affairs of Magdeburg at the Imperial Court.

[68] Hoffmann p. 129.

the Kaiser. This he had promised to do. Thinking it prudent not to rely solely on his word, von Guericke had presented to his wife, Grafin von Senftenau, seven large containers of Neckarwein, a goblet, and an expensive ring in a case made of silver inlaid with gold. The present was accompanied by an elaborate written address. One can easily imagine his chagrin when the very next day the ring and the goblet were returned with a note from the Graf that these were excessive, but that he would keep the wine and would like to invite von Guericke to come and help him drink it. Reporting this misadventure in his correspondence with Magdeburg, von Guericke ruefully notes that either his present had been of insufficient value or that the Graf had been in receipt of more substantial inducements from the Elector of Brandenburg, and, in any case, that he (the Graf) had no longer anything to fear from von Trautmannsdorf.[69]

His second audience with the Kaiser and his courtiers took place on June 16th 1650. A week later he sent a report of it to the Rat. He had begun by reminding the Kaiser of the purpose of his previous audience some nine months earlier. He had recalled that Otto I had established Magdeburg as an Imperial Free City and that, as a mark of its gratitude, a magnificent statue had been placed in the market place with the inscription:

"In the year of Christ 973 the Senate and people of Magdeburg place this statue in memory of the holy, august and invincible Kaiser Otto I, guarantor of our freedom and father to our city."

Though in the course of time they had given up something of their freedom to the over-reaching spiritual power of the archbishops, this had happened as a concession to their spiritual authority rather than their temporal. Now that there were to be no more archbishops, the archbishopric had no claim to jurisdiction over the city and accordingly at Westphalia the city had been completely freed from both the jurisdiction of the Elector of Brandenburg and of the archbishopric and been confirmed in the "pristine Liberty" (pristina libertas) with which Otto I had originally endowed it. Magdeburg now most humbly, in the light of the endorsement already given by the Reichshofrat, besought the Kaiser to be the most gracious Kaiser and Lord of their city, and to spare it

---

[69] This is an allusion to the fact that Graf Maximilian von Trautmannsdorf, a firm supporter of Magdeburg's case, had died earlier in 1650.

from all further disputes. Brandenburg had already received more than it had lost in Pomerania[70] and, if jurisdiction over the city were to be ceded to Brandenburg, the Elector would become master of the Rhine, the Weser, the Elbe, the Oder and the Vistula, a development which should give pause for thought. Were the Kaiser now to take the city into his jurisdiction, he would receive its obedience and loyalty, even to the shedding of its citizens' blood, and, with a statue similar to the Kaiser Otto's, his fame and glory would be preserved in Magdeburg from age to age and from generation to generation. The better to dispose the Kaiser to look kindly on the city, he presented his last petition on his knees — that the Kaiser would have mercy on an impoverished city rebuilding itself from heaps of rubble and that he would listen graciously to the humble request of the city which, next to God, reposed its trust and hope for its welfare in the Kaiser's favour.

After what was no doubt a tour de force of presentation the Kaiser replied. He spoke so softly and quickly that von Guericke could only partially follow him. His demeanour was friendly but his words, as before, non-committal. He wanted to do the right thing by Magdeburg and would give the matter careful consideration. Von Guericke noted that it was unfortunate that important supporters of Magdeburg — Graf von Trautmannsdorf and Graf von Schlick[71] — were no longer present and that no one could know the outcome of the issue.

At the end of this letter von Guericke renewed a request he had made earlier to be relieved of his position. A certain bitterness had entered his relationship with the city fathers. It is all too easy to imagine that gossip had been circulating in Magdeburg that von Guericke was enjoying the high life at public expense while the rest of the citizenry were eking out a day-to-day and hand-to-mouth existence. Colleagues on the Rat, perhaps jealous of his prestige or perhaps expressing a more

---

[70] This alludes to the provision of the Treaty of Westphalia that Brandenburg was to be compensated with the lands of the archbishopric of Magdeburg for the territorial losses in Pomerania it incurred to the Swedes. This was to take effect on the death of the Administrator August which occurred in 1680 after which the archbishopric and the city became the Duchy of Magdeburg.

[71] Heinrich von Schlick (1580–1650) had a distinguished military career in the Imperial service and is considered one of the most capable commanders in the Imperial ranks. He originally became an officer in the service of Spain in 1604 before returning to the Imperial service. He saw service throughout the Thirty Years War and at the time of his death was a fieldmarshal, Geheimrat and Kämmerer as well as being president of the Hofkriegsrat. He had also received the Spanish honour of the Golden Fleece.

measured disapproval of his acting as plenipotentiary rather than a delegate, were reproachful.[72] He writes:[73]

"I can no longer abide such a wretched existence but want to give myself a life of tranquillity and leave all the praise, fame and glory that you seem to think is my only motive for being here, lock stock and barrel, to someone else. All that I will have from this protracted business dragging on from one year to the next, I will have gained through worry, trouble, exertion, discomfort and the shortening of my life. Better to be rid of it as soon as soon as possible and entrust everything to God."

In early September Magdeburg's case finally came before the Reichsgeheimrat. When von Guericke's supporting documents and the favourable opinion of the Reichshofrat had been read, discussion began in the presence of the Kaiser. After more than a year of waiting for a clear decision, the outcome of the discussion was as crushing as it was unexpected. The meeting's only resolution was that all the documents supporting Magdeburg's case should be copied to their opponents to give them the opportunity of entering their objections. They were given a period of three months in which to do this.

Reporting this setback to his Magdeburg colleagues von Guericke identified the architect of their misfortune as the Elector of Brandenburg, who had recently protested against any confirmation by the Kaiser of the privileges granted by Otto I. Diplomatically and politically he was frustrated. There was no clear way forward and, moreover, he was depressed. He reflected on the possibility of illness with no one to look after him, of dying without a priest and of an unceremonious burial far from home. He warned the Rat of the need for circumspection and for the avoidance of statements or measures that would only make matters worse and give openings to the city's enemies. He deprecated the city's unwisdom in writing to the Kaiser in these terms:[74]

"In the situation where His Majesty does not help the city, or the Administrator cease his interfering in its rights, steps will have to be taken to offer resistance."

Finally he renewed his request for a recall and the sending of another representative.

In early October 1650, the city fathers approved his return to Magdeburg and proposed that Nuremburg's agent, Heinrich Stayger,

---

[72] Hoffmann p. 116.
[73] Hoffmann p. 105.
[74] Hoffmann p. 115.

should also assume responsibility for the affairs of Magdeburg. At this critical juncture for the affairs of the city, von Guericke now felt, notwithstanding his own earlier recommendation of such a course, that the downgrading of the city's representation to a mere agent would send the wrong signal and would be construed as indicating the city's abandonment of its case. He supposed the Imperial officials would think:[75]

"if the Magdeburgers don't rate their future welfare any higher, why should we much care about it?"

He urged the Rat to send someone of appropriate standing as the official representative of the city. The Rat replied that it could spare no one and asked him, as he already was in Vienna and in command of all the details of the situation, to remain in post pending the outcome of the postponed deliberations. Once again von Guericke acceded to the wishes of his colleagues and promised to postpone his departure to February 1651, by which time, as it then seemed, the outstanding issues would definitely, one way or another, be resolved. As the weeks dragged on the relationship of the city to the archbishopric continued to deteriorate and the former continued to seek some protection from the Kaiser against the incursions of the latter on its rights. At the end of the agreed three month period a further two months extension, at the request of the representative of the Elector of Brandenburg, was granted. To von Guericke a scenario of never ending delays was becoming a depressing reality and, this time, with a clear conscience that he had done all he could, he confirmed his departure for the end of February.

On February 20th he had a final audience at court to make his farewell. The Kaiser was again polite, apparently interested, anxious to know how things stood with Magdeburg and, ineffectually as ever, concerned about the delays. Von Guericke informed him that Heinrich Stayger would replace him as Magdeburg's representative and took his leave. The long-awaited day of departure, February 27th, finally dawned and, leaving his son behind to continue his studies in Vienna, he began the journey home. His arrival in Magdeburg was delayed by a throat infection and flu which confined him to bed in Leipzig from where, on March 15th, he wrote to the Rat the final letter of his long period of absence.

---

[75] Hoffman p. 117.

Despite the tensions that had from time to time surfaced, his colleagues on the Rat and in both section of the Ausschuss gave him a warm reception. They credited his industry and perseverance and acknowledged that any blame for the continued absence of a resolution, satisfactory or otherwise, of Magdeburg's claims could not be laid at his door. Moreover, they remained hopeful that the machinations of the Administrator and his allies had merely delayed, rather than prevented, a final judgment in favour of Magdeburg.

Hoffmann leaves it largely to surmise how von Guericke spent the next period of almost a year and a half before embarking on a final round of diplomacy. In his personal life, the period is marked by two happy occasions. On May 13th 1652 the fifty year old widower married the much younger Dorothea Lentke, the daughter of his Bürgermeister colleague Stephan Lentke.[76] The marriage was childless and the couple continued to live with Otto's mother, Anna von Zweidorff, till her death in 1666. A month later, on June 14th, Hans Otto returned safely home after an absence, given over to study and travel, of nearly four years. It can hardly be doubted, even if it is not documented, that a period of personal happiness and relative tranquillity in the affairs of the city, afforded him the opportunity energetically to pursue his scientific interests. If the period at Vienna had been particularly unhappy and frustrating for him, redress was to be made by the next decade of his life which was to witness the consolidation of his scientific achievements and his emergence as an eminent and internationally recognised investigator of nature.

By the summer of 1652 there was still no definite settlement of Magdeburg's case by the Imperial authorities and the city fathers decided upon another attempt. Once again they turned to von Guericke, with his indispensable knowledge and experience of the issues. On this occasion they also assigned to him a colleague, a lawyer, Dr. Bertram Selle. Their written instructions were to liaise with Stayger, the city's agent at the Imperial court, to determine the present status of the city's claims and to consult with various high officials with whom von Guericke was already acquainted as to whether Magdeburg could obtain a

---

[76] Stephan Lentke (1599–1684) was Bürgermeister from 1641 to 1684. The other two Bürgermeister at this time were David Brauns (1637–1660) and Georg Kühlewein (1638–1656). Stephan had seven children of which Dorothea (born c. 1630) was the second youngest. She survived Otto by less than a year, dying in Hamburg in March 1687.

decision before the opening of the forthcoming Reichstag at Regensburg.

The two colleagues, accompanied by von Guericke's son, set out
for Prague to where the Kaiser had transferred his court. As with the
previous diplomatic journeys, prayers for their safety and the success of
their mission were read out in the churches before their departure. On
arrival in Prague on August 23rd, they contacted Stayger. He advised
them that their journey had probably been futile because the Kaiser,
wishing to have his son Ferdinand elected King of the Romans,[77] needed the votes of the Electors of Saxony and Brandenburg and would
not, at least at this juncture, wish to take any steps that might offend
them. Nevertheless von Guericke and Selle embarked on yet another
round of the diplomatic circuit. They renewed influential acquaintance-
ships such as those with Reichvizekanzler Graf Kurtz, Kammerpräsident von Gebhardt and Reichshofrat Bidembach, who had a particular
responsibility for the affairs of Magdeburg. Nor was the cultivation of
important new contacts, such as the Swedish representative Matthias
Biörenklou,[78] neglected. They were granted an audience with the Kaiser
on September 13th. The meeting was brief but seemingly very positive
and the following day von Guericke wrote to the Rat to the effect that
the aim of their mission had now all but been accomplished.

However by a week later bitter disappointment had ousted the
earlier optimism. In his letter of September 21st he writes:[79]

*"Since our last letter we have left no stone unturned to reach our goal, but contrary to what
we had hoped we have, to date, not succeeded. It seems that people here will go to any lengths
to detain us with honeyed words until the start of the Reichstag at Regensburg".*

His letter will evoke a pang of sympathetic recognition from anyone
who has dealt with practitioners of the useful art of letting people down
gently, of those who can sugar with suave assurances the disappointment of cherished hopes. He relates how on the 15th he went to
Bidembach, a man with whom he was on good terms and whom he

---

[77] The title confirmed his right of succession as Holy Roman Emperor. Ferdinand IV was
elected in May 1653 and crowned at Regensburg on June 18th 1653. He predeceased his father,
dying on July 9th 1654.
[78] Matthias Biörenklou (1607–1671) was a Swedish diplomat and scholar. He is the author of
some thirty-five works in various languages, mostly on political topics. His portrait by Anselm
van Hulle, who also painted von Guericke, is still well-known.
[79] Hoffmann p. 129.

regarded as a firm supporter, to urge him to act decisively on the city's behalf to obtain a final settlement of their concerns. Bidembach replied that, of course, if the decision were just up to him the matter would long ago have been settled. But there then followed a rather elaborate explanation of the complications and difficulties that now rendered further assistance impossible. The truth of their situation — that no decision would be forthcoming before the Reichstag — was becoming irresistibly evident. They sought the advice of their colleagues as to what their conduct should now be. The Rat's instructions to them was to seek a further audience with the Kaiser at which, as well as taking their leave, they were to ask for some right of address for Magdeburg at the forthcoming Reichstag. In effect the Rat had accepted that nothing would be achieved at Prague but wanted the right to plead the city's case before the delegates at Regensburg. This further audience seems not to have taken place. However on October 15th they were officially informed in writing by the Imperial Chancellery that no resolution of Magdeburg's claims would take place at Prague, but that the Kaiser would, on his arrival at Regensburg, bring the matter to a conclusion. On receipt of this communication von Guericke and Selle made their way back to Magdeburg. Owing to tensions between Sweden and Brandenburg over the Swedish withdrawal from Pomerania, the Reichstag was postponed from an initially projected starting date of October 31st 1652 to March 10th 1653.

Back in Magdeburg, von Guericke was now one of the serving Bürgermeister. During the short period between the return from Prague and his departure for Regensburg, we can catch a glimpse of him as he involved himself with the management of the internal affairs of the city. Magdeburg's churches had suffered greatly in the fire of 1631 and, having been to a greater or lesser extent rendered unusable, various provisional arrangements for worship had been made. These had been subject to a Kirchenordnung[80] of 1639. A decade letter, the main churches in Magdeburg — the Johanniskirche, the Ulrichskircke, the Jacobskirche and the Heiligegeistkirche — had all been restored to use and the situation called for a new Kirchenordnung. Von Guericke was particularly active in the drawing up of the new regulations, which, duly

---

[80] In reformed German churches Kirchenordnungen, deriving from the secular authority, replaced the canon law, papal and episcopal jurisdiction that had regulated the life of the churches while they remained Catholic.

signed by the civic and ecclesiastical authorities, came into effect in December 1652.

Another and longer term civic interest of the Bürgermeister was education and the state of the schools. Before 1631 their income had come from endowments and regular obligatory contributions levied from a range of sources. The documents detailing these arrangements had been lost in the fires of 1631. Fortunately however, an old school official, who had been responsible for collecting school income, testified on oath to the Rat his recollections of the sources. Based on this, von Guericke, on assuming, in 1655, the responsibility for the provision of education, set about re-establishing the revenue of the schools. When his request to the guilds and other liable parties to renew their contributions proved fruitless, he took advice from lawyers at the University of Jena and began legal proceedings. This proved effective. The guild of garment cutters, initially persuaded by the discovery of an old register of their own that the schools' claims had merit, had their convictions strengthened by two legal judgments against them. These induced them to agree, in 1663, to clear arrears with a payment of one hundred thalers and subsequently to maintain an annual contribution of forty guilders.[81] The guild of bakers and the guild of brewers, both finding themselves in a similar legal position, appealed initially to the Reichskammergericht in Vienna. Subsequently however, realising that the likelihood of a favourable judgment was low, they also settled, agreeing in 1676 to pay 280 thalers to clear the arrears and thereafter to contribute thirty guilders annually. With these precedents in mind the other parties, against whom claims were outstanding, settled without further protest and von Guericke was, in the end, able to secure an annual income of 200 thalers for the school system.

The Magdeburg Rat was unanimous in its desire to be represented at Regensburg. They were equally unanimous in deciding that their representative should be von Guericke, with his unparalleled experience and contacts, supported, as at Prague, by the legal expertise of Dr. Bertram Selle. Once again equipping themselves with the necessary letters of accreditation, and a detailed brief of their remit, the pair set out from the city, arriving in Regensburg on February 15th 1653. The Kaiser,

---

[81] The guilder, also known as the florin, was a silver coin rather than, as its name suggests, a gold one.

along with a number of Electors, Fürsten, Grafen and other notable personages, had previously arrived and were diverting themselves in pre-lenten carnival merry-making.

On arrival the two colleagues began the round of diplomatic visits. Bidembach received them warmly and advised them to submit a position paper to the Kaiser, but not before the Reichstag was in session. The Swedish delegates, Bohlen and Biörenklou, were under firm instructions from Queen Christina to assist Magdeburg to obtain what had been promised to it at Westphalia. Their reception by various other delegates was equally favourable and they seemed, as they often did, set fair for a successful resolution of their city's issues.

However the opposition was no less active. The Administrator, ever seeking to ward off the threat to his power and revenue represented by Magdeburg's ambitions, had sent his representatives, Domherr von Hagen and Dr. Krull, whom the Kaiser received on March 10th. Another opponent was Herzog Franz von Lohringen[82] who, in addition to being bishop of Verdun, was Dompropst at Magdeburg and who, at his audience on March 15th, complained to the Kaiser that the city's proposed expansion would infringe his rights. The most telling opponent of all, the Elector of Brandenburg, whose long term interest was that the city should be included in his inheritance of the archbishopric, and on whose vote the Kaiser was relying, was also active.

In May the Kaiser's son was duly elected Ferdinand IV[83], King of the Romans, and, on June 8th, crowned with ceremony and celebration. The following day von Guericke and Selle were received in audience. They congratulated the Kaiser on the elevation of his son and on the birth of a daughter, Eleanor Maria of Austria, on May 31st. To their renewed request for the fulfillment of the promises of Westphalia, the Kaiser responded that the matter would be entrusted to the Reichshofrat. A particular apprehension for the city was the situation with regard to its ever more menacing creditors. In 1650 von Guericke had negotiated a three year moratorium which would shortly expire. A further rescheduling of their debts was an urgent necessity and the two delegates had been instructed to seek a comprehensive guarantee of a

---

[82] Francois de Lorraine (1599–1672) was bishop of Verdun from 1623 to 1661. The diocese was annexed to France in 1552 and this arrangement was confirmed at Westphalia.
[83] It was to be a short-lived reign. The new king died of smallpox within 3 weeks of his coronation.

period of further protection by the Kaiser. Their request for measures to ease Magdeburg's hard pressed financial situation was referred to the Kammerpräsident, von Gebhardt.

Despite the near insolvency of the city, money for sweeteners was still forthcoming. In the very same exchange of correspondence about the need for a further period of debt remission, we find von Guericke noting that Bidembach, the strongest advocate of the city's case, was something of a bibliophile. He, von Guericke, had seen a large, illuminated, four volume atlas in a local bookshop with a list price of one hundred thalers, but obtainable by him for ninety thalers. Such a book would make a most suitable present for Bidembach, inclining him even more strongly to favour the city's interests. The Rat approved the purchase and the "present" was received with the greatest of pleasure by the influential Hofrat.

The formal opening of the Reichstag took place on June 30th 1653. On July 3rd a request for public prayer for its success was made in the churches of Magdeburg.[84]

"Of your charity, fervently pray and beseech almighty God that, in His omnipotence, he will govern the hearts of our high rulers now gathered at Regensburg for the Reichstag, that He may inspire in them a spirit of charity and good counsel and that He may so direct their efforts that, redounding to Thy divine honour, they may be fruitful in bringing enduring peace and prosperity to our beloved city.
May your charity also encompass in prayer the two members of our administration who have been sent on behalf of our city to the said Reichstag."

Soon after the opening a decision was taken in the Reichsgeheimrat that Magdeburg's issues were to be put before the entire assembly at the Reichstag. This was uncongenial to von Guericke and Selle who tried in vain to have it rescinded. Graf Oettingen, the Reichshofrat president, explained to von Guericke the political reality that the role of Friedrich Wilhelm in the affairs of Magdeburg was becoming decisive. The Kaiser did not wish to take on himself the responsibility for a decision which might not have the approval of the Elector of Brandenburg. Such a decision would not bring the desired peace and stability to Magdeburg but would, in all probability, be contested by the Elector either by appeal to the Stände or perhaps even by a resort to arms against Magdeburg. The Rat was advised of this development on July 18th.

---

[84] Hoffmann p. 137.

They accepted the situation with more equanimity and optimism than their representatives. In its view the assembly, at worst, might establish a commission to look further into the authenticity of the Ottonian privilege, but it surely wouldn't set aside the terms of Westphalia, strict adherence to which it itself had insisted on, nor would it wish to defy the Kaiser's edict on the Treaty's implementation. They counselled against von Guericke's plan to submit a memorandum to the Kaiser to counteract those of the Administrator's representatives and then to circulate this memorandum to the Stände, many of whom were ill informed of the issues. The Rat favoured a less confrontational strategy. The memorandum to the Kaiser should not take the form of a rebuttal. The relevant documents were, in any case, to be circulated to the Stände and they should seek to exert influence solely by a more low-key, networking-with-individuals approach.

Not until the following April did the Magdeburg question come to a vote at the Reichstag. As his correspondence from September to February has been lost, the record of von Guericke's activities during this period is defective. It is however known that his wife Dorothea fell ill in the autumn of 1653. When news of this reached him in mid-October he immediately set out to be at her side, arriving in Magdeburg on October 27th. On the 29th he delivered a report to his colleagues on his and Selle's activities at Regensburg. By Christmas, at the latest, he was back in Regensburg, circulating a document in support of Magdeburg's case to the Stände. With momentous consequences for his future he brought back with him to Regensburg the apparatus needed to demonstrate his experiments on the vacuum.[85]

The remainder of the time was occupied, as ever, with diplomacy and the attempt to counter their opponents' steady undermining of Magdeburg's position. A new source of distress to the city was the campaign of economic sanctions launched against it by the Administrator. This entailed the blocking of trade and the impounding of agricultural revenue due to the citizens. The justification of this was that the city owed a large sum of money in tax arrears but the real purpose was to force the city to submit to the overlordship of the Administrator. As best they could, von Guericke and Selle fought Magdeburg's cause with the limited weapons at a diplomat's disposal. In addition to the issuing

---

[85] Schneider p. 99.

of timely memoranda, they sought new friends for Magdeburg. Among those whose good offices they successfully solicited was the influential archbishop Elector of Mainz, Johann Philipp von Schönborn, who, a short time later, was to play an important role in bringing von Guericke's science to a wider audience. On March 17th they visited the Swedish delegates and, to their disappointment, found that the support the city could count on when they had been dealing with Salvius and Oxenstierna, was no longer forthcoming. Bohlen was coldly indifferent and Biörenklou made excuses to not see them at all. Nevertheless, Queen Christina, soon to abdicate and convert to Catholicism, remained a supporter and, on instructions from her, the Swedish delegates sent a supportive memo to the Kaiser on April 24th.

On the afternoon of their being snubbed by the Swedish delegates, they were received again by the Kaiser, who was, as before, friendly, interested in the progress of their case, but impotent in furthering it.

At the beginning of May, Magdeburg's affairs finally came for consideration by the entire assembly. On May 2nd von Guericke and Selle reported what had transpired. Votes were cast in three "Colleges".[86] The Electors voted against Magdeburg. The Fürsten felt they had not been adequately briefed and refused to vote. The Free Cities voted in favour. The conclusion of the Reichstag was imminent and the Kaiser and the delegates were now preoccupied with preparations for departure. Nevertheless von Guericke succeeded in having the matter considered again and voted on by the Fürsten on Sunday May 6th, the last possible opportunity. The final votes were a meagre reward for the years of unremitting dedication to the cause. The two senior Colleges — the Electors and the Fürsten — voted that the Kaiser could only confirm the Ottonian Privilege if the original document or a credible copy were produced. The extension of the city boundaries was to be regulated by a commission to be set up by the Herzog of Braunschweig and the city would have no claim on private property within the proposed extension.

---

[86] From 1489, the Reichstag was divided into three Colleges — those of the Electors, the Fürsten and the Free Cities. The voting system was territorially rather than individually based, so that, for instance, the Elector of Brandenburg had eight votes in the College of Fürsten in addition to one in the College of Electors. Votes appertaining to a single state could also be shared among multiple individuals.

On the following day, May 7th 1654, the Reichstag was formally closed and the Kaiser departed that same afternoon. At some point[87] just prior to this, the episode occurred that was to propel von Guericke, from being a talented and hardworking diplomat and municipal official for a fairly insignificant city, into a figure of permanent historical interest.

---

[87] Some Internet sources date the episode to May 8th. On this day von Guericke wrote to Magdeburg that the Reichstag had already closed and the Kaiser had departed on the afternoon of the previous day. (Hoffmann p. 149).

Christina, Queen of Sweden (1626 1689)

(Anselmus van Hulle)

Robert Boyle (1627–1691)

Johann Philipp von Schönborn,
Archbishop of Mainz (1605–1673)

The Scientist Emerges

In the *Preface to the Reader* of the *Experimenta Nova*, written some ten years later, von Guericke recalls how casually and accidentally the events of the most decisive day in his life came to pass.

"Later, at the Imperial Assembly held at Regensburg in 1654, where I had been sent on municipal business, some enthusiasts for scientific matters heard something about these experiments and pressed me to give a demonstration. This I tried to do to the best of my ability. Then it transpired that, at the end of the Assembly, just as the final proceedings were underway, these experiments of mine came to the notice of his Imperial Majesty himself as well to that of some Electors and Fürsten, who were already preparing their departure. They wished to see them before they left and I could hardly decline to gratify the wishes of such people. The person most of all taken by them was the Most Eminent Lord Elector, Johann Philipp, Archbishop of Mainz and Bishop of Würzburg. So much so that he was most insistent on having a similar apparatus constructed for himself. Since in the difficult circumstances of the time there were no craftsmen to do this, he prevailed upon me to sell him the apparatus that I had brought with me to Regensburg and he then had it taken to Würzburg."

His natural aptitude for scientific showmanship could not have wished for a better stage on which to display itself. One can hardly doubt that to his distinguished audience he staged a persuasive demonstration of the reality of a phenomenon whose very existence many doubted. It is, however, a much-repeated myth that his demonstration at Regensburg included two teams of twelve horses harnessed to hemispheres and unable to separate them against atmospheric pressure.[88] In a letter to Fr. Schott written two years later and also in Book III Chap-

---

[88] The *Experimenta Nova* describes in Book III Chapters 26 & 27 the experiments carried out at Regensburg. The evidence of the *Technica Curiosa* would date the first demonstration with horses to 1657. On p. 39 Fr. Schott writes: "The author first mentioned to me these hemispheres in a letter of July 22nd 1656, saying that they could not be pulled apart by six strong men. .... He mentions the hemispheres again in a letter of August 4th 1657; here are his words. 'Regarding new experiments, nothing of any note has happened to write to you about. I am busy with various tasks; these and other problems have prevented me from making progress with them. I'll just however mention that that business with the two exactly-fitting dishes or hemispheres has now been carried through. I wrote to your reverence that six men would hardly be able to pull them apart. Shortly afterwards I actually tried it out (which was a costly undertaking) and found that twelve horses could hardly separate them. Indeed if all the air were to be extracted perhaps not even sixteen could do it. As soon as the air is introduced through the opening of the tap, the hemispheres come apart of their own accord.' " In a letter to Fr. Schott of November 16th 1661 von Guericke writes "This summer I have done some new things ..... " and goes on to describe experiments with hemispheres where in one case sixteen horses could scarcely separate them and, in another, twenty-four horses were required. (*Technica Curiosa* p. 37)

ters 26 and 27 of the *Experimenta Nova* von Guericke indicates the experiments he actually performed. Schimank summarises:[89]

"He weighed the very archetype of lightness, the air, and, as if God had revealed to him a share in the secrets of Creation, he caused clouds and wind to form in glass vessels and through this same air, which we don't feel on our necks and shoulders though it washes all around us, he shattered toughened glass into splinters."

Von Guericke and Selle remained in Regensburg for a further three weeks, busying themselves with farewell visits and waiting for copies of the Reichstag's resolutions to be made, before returning to Magdeburg. On June 13th their arrival home was warmly greeted despite the relative failure of their mission. The Rat's chronic optimism had not deserted it. They had indeed the support of the Free Cities and they chose to believe that the Kaiser would not confirm the resolutions of the Electors and the Fürsten, but would be amenable to an appeal from the Kreistag at Braunschweig. Hoffman finds their naiveté hard to credit.[90]

"How possibly could von Guericke, a man of some acuteness and penetration, and how could his colleagues on the Rat, surrender themselves to the illusion that their implacable opponent, the Administrator August, would make no use of the weapons he now had at his disposal or would let slip through his hands this favourable opportunity to reduce the city, which had refused to pay its dues to the archbishopric, to the status of a Landstadt? How little they knew their opponent and his adviser Dr. Krull, now elevated to the rank of vice-chancellor."

On June 19th, at the request of the Administrator, the Kaiser formally commissioned the Elector of Cologne, Maximilian Heinrich,[91] and Herzog August of Braunschweig-Lüneburg,[92] the Lower Saxony Kreisdirektor, to implement the resolutions of the Reichstag.

It was now the turn of Magdeburg to prevaricate and procrastinate in the hope of evading the implementation of measures it disliked.

---

[89] Schimank p. 37. The letter to Fr. Schott of June 18th 1656 is translated later in this text.
[90] Hoffmann p. 153.
[91] Maximilian Heinrich of Bavaria (1621–1688) was the fourth child of Albert VI of Leuchtenberg. He became Archbishop of Cologne and Duke of Westphalia in 1650. He was also Prince-Bishop of Liege, Hildesheim and Münster.
[92] August II (1579–1666) Herzog zu Braunschweig and Fürst von Braunschweig-Wolfenbüttel was the seventh child of Herzog Heinrich von Dannenberg. Having, against the odds, succeeded to power he ruled from 1635 to 1666. He was one of the most cultivated rulers of his time and founder of the Herzog August Library in Wolfenbüttel. A statue of him was erected in the market square in Wolfenbüttel in 1904.

Developments were slow. At the end of 1655 the Kaiser's commissioners demanded that Magdeburg should send representatives to a meeting in Helmstedt. This was met by a flurry of delaying tactics from the Rat. Objections were lodged with the commissioners themselves and the Kaiser was petitioned for a delay. When the Swedish ambassador intervened on behalf of Magdeburg, the Kaiser issued a statement on February 3rd 1656 affirming that it was not his intention to impose burdens on the city against the spirit of the Westphalia Treaty, but merely to assist in its implementation. He demanded that the Commissioners produce a detailed report to him and while this was in preparation no further measures against the city were to be taken.

Unsurprisingly, this development did not find favour with the Administrator. In July 1656 we find him at the Reichsdeputation at Frankfurt, blaming the city for the civil unrest following a penalty imposed on it by the commissioners. In October of that year he was pressing the Kaiser to impose sanctions on the city. In January 1657 continuing to act with characteristic indecisiveness, the Kaiser sent both aggrieved parties — those from Magdeburg as well as those from the Administrator — to his Commissioners, who then set a new date, March 3rd, for a meeting at Helmstedt to attempt to reconcile the two parties. The Magdeburg Rat did not send a representative to this meeting but sought, using behind-the-scenes contacts, to hinder progress on putting the Regensburg resolutions into effect. The Kaiser's death on March 23rd plunged the Empire into an uncertain interregnum. The succession of his son Leopold to the Imperial throne was not automatic. It was only secured, more than a year later, by counteracting the intrigues of Mazarin in favour of a successor more congenial to him than a Habsburg. With a new urgency the Commissioners rescheduled the Helmstedt meeting for May 20th. This time the Rat did send a delegation led by von Guericke which included a legal expert and friend from Lübeck, Dr. David Gloccinus. Dr. Krull and Dr. Jacob Unruh attended on behalf of the Administrator. The Commissioners were also represented. The sessions opened on May 23rd and closed on the 29th. The Magdeburg delegates returned home to deliver, on June 1st 1657, a report to the Rat on yet another inconclusive meeting.

While, so to speak, von Guericke's diplomatic day job was beset with delay and frustration — a circumstance not destined for amelioration — the seeds of interest his demonstrations at Regensburg had sown were bearing fruit. Archbishop Johann Philipp had indeed taken von Guericke's hemispheres to his Jesuit[93] college at Würzburg where it stimulated immediate interest. Von Guericke himself relates the sequel.[94]

"The most Reverend Fathers of the Society of Jesus, who were teaching at the Public Academy of Würzburg, often tried out my experiments in the presence of the aforesaid Elector. They wrote them up and communicated them to scholars at Rome, seeking, at the same time, their opinion of them. One of their number, Rev. Fr. Kaspar Schott, Professor of Mathematics at the Academy, began to correspond with me about these experiments and to seek clarification on various details. This is how it came about that he added an account of these New Experiments as an appendix to his book on the mechanical and hydropneumatic arts, (published in 1657), calling them "Magdeburgica", and making them widely available in printed form."

Fr. Schott had obviously been working on his book *Mechanica Hydraulico-pneumatica* for some time. He had received permission to publish from the Order's General[95] at Rome, in January 1655 and from the Provincial[96] of the Upper-Rhine Province, in January 1656. To defray the costs of publication he had obtained independent funding from the estate of the bookseller Johann Gottfried Schönwetter. His projected work consisted of two parts. The first was to deal with the theory of his subject and the second was to describe a range of practical devices including some which, he claimed, offered the promise of perpetual motion using the power of water.

Fr. Schott and a colleague, the professor of Theology, Fr. Melchior Cornaeus, became absorbed in the significance of the new experimental possibilities revealed by von Guericke's work. At this point, judging by the dates on which he had obtained permissions from his

---

[93] The Jesuits, founded by Ignatius Loyola (1491–1556) in 1539, were, by the early 17th century, a truly remarkable body of intelligent, disciplined, energetic and dedicated men. If indeed the agenda of the Counter Reformation was to plunge Europe into a superstitious, pre-scientific darkness, a view for which the Galileo incident seems commonly to be taken as conclusive proof, then someone in Rome had neglected to brief the supposed shock troops of the new order. Apart from producing their own outstanding scholars like Kircher, Clavius, Zuchius, Viviani and Riccioli they established more than 500 schools across Europe contributing to the education of many of the major scientific figures of the period such as Descartes, Torricelli and Mersenne.

[94] *Experimenta Nova. Preface to the Reader*

[95] Goswinus Nickel (1584–1664) was Superior General of the Jesuit Order from 1652 until his death.

[96] Nithardus Biberus

superiors, Fr. Schott's work was complete. Possibly acting in response to a suggestion of Fr. Kircher, his old mathematics teacher, he decided to add an appendix describing the work of von Guericke. The appendix is, in reality, a separate short book with its own frontispiece and warm dedication to Fr. Kircher. It is entitled *An Account of New Experiments from Magdeburg in which some seek to establish the vacuum and some to disprove it.* The last of its nine sections, written by Fr. Cornaeus, is cast in the form, familiar to his Jesuit training and the academic life of the time, of a disputation between opposing views. The earlier sections describe the experiments and record the opinions which Fr. Schott had solicited from various authorities and particularly from von Guericke himself. On p. 451–452 he writes:

"These and many other considerations are adduced on both sides of this question. Fr. Melchior Cornaeus, professor of Theology at our own university of Würzburg, has learnedly and at some length argued these matters in a discussion of his own dedicated to this topic (see Section 9 below). On several occasions he and I observed and carefully scrutinised the experiments in question. When I first saw them, I sent an account of them to Fr. Kircher at Rome and to some other friends and scholars, asking their opinion of them. All of them sided with the Aristotelians against the Vacuists.[97] Among the replies I received was this from Fr. Kircher."

Fr. Kircher's reply from Rome in February 1656 is alluded to by von Guericke in the *Experimenta Nova.* (Book III, Chapter 36) The tone of the letter makes it clear that, then as now, an eminent and prestigious scholar does not expect to learn anything he doesn't already know from an amateur working in isolation. Evident also, however, is the real conceptual bafflement of someone wedded to the idea, supported by thinkers from Aristotle to Descartes, that all of cosmic space is occupied by a continuous plenum of substance. The idea that a rent could be made in this to expose some underlying nothingness seemed a hardly credible fantasy. Fr. Kircher writes:[98]

"Reverend Father in Christ,
I have seen the account of the experiments sent to my assistant priest and have read through it carefully. I am astonished by what is going on in the minds of such people that emboldens them to assert that a vacuum has been produced when the very experiments themselves

---

[97] The Latin is "Vacuista". The very existence of such a word conveys well the status of the idea at the time.
[98] *Mechanica Hydraulico-pneumatica.* p. 452.

demonstrate abundantly that there isn't a vacuum. The experiments, while they certainly exhibit the presence of great forces, are very far from showing that a vacuum exists and, on the contrary, there can be no better demonstration that a vacuum doesn't exist. For if a vacuum is produced by this experiment, what, I ask, is the source of the need for such great exertion? It is certainly not the air, for that has all been extracted. Therefore it must be the nothingness that is left behind after the extraction of the air. Can anyone conceive that nothingness can offer a resistance? Has anyone ever heard of such a thing in philosophy? The philosophical explanation would be that the small amount of air left behind in the opening, creates the resistance because of the supreme impulse it has to fill the vacuum. But as everybody knows, were the continuity of substance to be once ruptured (which, in my opinion, cannot be achieved by any human undertaking) so little air would have neither the potency to fill the space, nor indeed the impulse. The resistance seen and nature's impulse to oppose are better attributed to the rarefaction of air than to anything else. I have seen this kind of thing a hundred times in similar machines. I am in accord with the considerations you bring up and they clearly demonstrate the truth about the non-existence of a vacuum.

I regret that I do not have enough time for a thoroughgoing refutation from first principles of the claims made on behalf of this whole contraption. Therefore I shall leave the discussion of this issue to your reverence and to Father Cornaeus. Your reverence might be able to do this most opportunely in the Hydraulica where it treats of the vacuum.

By the way, my associate, Fr. Valentine Stanfel, sends you his regards. He is also particularly expert in hydrostatics and had decided to publish similar material to that which you are now in the process of doing. As you have anticipated him, he has abandoned his plan. In the meantime he will not be short of other topics to engage him among the great range of disputed issues. Your reverence should not neglect to correspond with him; for that would be beneficial to you both.

Farewell and keep me in your love,

> *Rome, 26th February, 1656.*
> *your reverence's servant,*
> *Athanasius.*

Fr. Schott first wrote to von Guericke himself on June 4th because he was having technical difficulties with an experiment. Von Guericke answered promptly and Fr. Schott records his reply.[99]

Most reverend Lord and Friend,
I am replying to the letter written on June 4th at Würzburg and received on June 14th. My experiments are particularly directed to showing that air is nothing other than a fume or evaporation coming from the Earth, which it surrounds with a fixed and definite weight. It penetrates everything that is not already filled with some other substance, is carried with the

---

[99] *Mechanica Hydraulico-pneumatica.* p. 454-455.

Earth as it executes both its daily and annual motions and, along with the Earth, constitutes, as it were, a single body. To show this I have set up various experiments but none of them makes the point as well as the one your reverence observed in the presence of the most eminent Elector of Mainz. There you had a pump with two openings. Through one of them the air is introduced and through the other it is expelled. Notwithstanding that I have improved everything a lot since then, the use and point of those experiments is very briefly the following.

1. They make it clear, how great is the weight of the air surrounding us and to what height it drives the water in an evacuated tube.

2. If something else that is not spherical is firmly attached to an evacuated sphere, so that the air from the former is violently drawn into the latter, then it is subject to compression, just like the non-spherical glass containers are, and fragments, with a great bang, into a thousand pieces.

3. We can weigh the air confined in a glass vessel. The weight is given by how much lighter the glass is once it has been evacuated. For example, a Receiver, of the sort that medical people use to distil water, is about three or four loht[100] lighter after the extraction of the air as you and the eminent Elector of Mainz will have seen.

4. From the same experiment we infer the true cause of winds and clouds. For when a wind is created inside a closed glass vessel by shaking it, a cloud appears very shortly thereafter.

Since the time when I produced the exhibition for the said eminent Elector, I have a much better and clearer grasp of all these matters and of many other topics as well.

By the way, some aficionados of curiosities have written to me about these experiments and have extracted various replies from me. I think that those replies, especially the ones I have communicated not long ago to a certain outstanding philosopher, would be a beneficial addition to what your reverence is in the process of publishing. I am keen to oblige your reverence and would be happy to send you some further material in this context.

Commending us both to the divine protection,

I remain your reverend lordship's most humble servant and friend,

Otto Gericke,[101]
Magdeburg June 18th 1656.

Fr. Schott writes attractively and with personal modesty in the persona of an honest broker among various eminent and opinionated authorities. This extract from his *Preface to the Reader*[102] conveys his tone.

---

[100] A small coin that von Guericke uses as a weight — see Book III Chapter 21.

[101] The spelling "Guericke" and the prefix "von" were not adopted until after his ennoblement in 1666.

[102] *Mechanica Hydraulico-pneumatica.* p. 444.

"Now I am bringing to public attention another device which is more effective and very much more ingenious than anything previous. Its inventor is the celebrated and excellent Master Otto Gericke, patrician and Bürgermeister of Magdeburg and the city's delegate to the comprehensive peace treaties at Münster and Osnabrück. A few years ago he thought up this device with an intention and purpose which you will gather from his own words which are reproduced below. At the recent Reichstag in Regensburg he offered it to the most eminent Elector Johann Philipp, Archbishop of Mainz and Bishop of Würzburg, who keeps it in his palace, where, on a number of occasions, I have looked at it, examined it carefully and written a description of it which I have sent to scholars at Rome and elsewhere to obtain their opinion of it. There wasn't a single one who didn't praise the inventor's skill. There are some who, using this kind of device, try in all sorts of ways to produce a vacuum. (Thus far the vacuum has been a chimera as the indestructible plenitude[103] of nature stands in the way of trying, or even of hoping, to produce one.) There are others who insist that there is no more effective way of eliminating the possibility of a vacuum than by these same experiments. They are adamant that Nature, though it may be exposed to enormous force by the operation of the pump that our gifted Elector possesses, transcends all human schemes and exertions.

I have described the actual device in words and pictures below and have set out the arguments of the disputants on both sides. Provided only that my reader come to the subject with an open mind, I invite him to be the judge."

In ordinary circumstances there would be nothing remarkable about the respectful mutual courtesy between two scientifically-minded individuals. However, in the aftermath of the Thirty Years War with its poisonous confluence of religious, dynastic and nationalistic conflicts, their correspondence is something of a tribute to men from different sides of a major divide. Some years later von Guericke was also to develop a warm relationship with his political, and indeed religious, opponent, the Calvinist Elector Friedrich Wilhelm. That relationship was, however, arguably conducted more with an eye to obtaining advantage from a powerful patron than from a depth of shared interest.

On May 2nd 1657, Fr. Schott signed the dedication of the *Magdeburg Appendix* to Fr. Kircher, and von Guericke's work now became available to the wider international community of scholars. In particular, it attracted the notice of the Anglo-Irish nobleman Robert Boyle,[104] then at Oxford. In 1660 he published in English *New Experiments Physi-*

---

[103] This is a technical term associated with the view that nature was a plenum.
[104] Robert Boyle (1627–1691) was born in Waterford, Ireland, the 7th son of the Earl of Cork. He acquired his passion for science during a visit to Italy when he studied works of Galileo. He moved to Oxford in 1654 where he was an active member of the "Invisible College", the precursor of the Royal Society.

co-Mechanical, touching the Spring of Air and its Effects which was almost immediately made accessible to an international readership by being translated into Latin. Boyle acknowledges some indebtedness to Fr. Schott's account of von Guericke's work. He writes:[105]

"And I should immediately proceed to the mention of my Experiments, but that I like too well that worthy saying of the Naturalist Pliny, 'Benignum est & plenum ingenui pudoris, fateri per quos profeceris'[106], not to conform to it, by acquainting your Lordship, in the first place, with the Hint I had of the Engine I am to entertain you of. You may be pleas'd to remember, that a while before our separation in England, I told you of a book that I had heard of, but not perus'd, publish'd by the industrious Jesuit Schottus, wherein 'twas said he related how that ingenious Gentleman, Otto Gericke, Consul of Magdeburg, had lately practised in Germany a way of emptying Glass Vessels, by sucking out the Air at the mouth of the Vessel, plung'd under water: And you may also perhaps remember, that I express'd myself much delighted with this Experiment, since thereby the great force of the external Air (either rushing in at the open'd Orifice of the empty'd Vessel, or violently forcing up the Water into it) was rendered more obvious and conspicuous, than in any Experiment that I had formerly seen. And though it may appear by some of those Writings I sometimes shew'd your Lordship, that I had been solicitous to try things upon the same ground; yet in regard this Gentleman was before-hand with me in producing such considerable effects, by means of the exsuction of Air, I think my self oblig'd to acknowledge the Assistance, and Encouragement the Report of his performances hath afforded me."

Meanwhile, Magdeburg's concerns remained as pressing as ever. Following the inconclusive Helmstedt meeting, the Rat, hoping to make progress by addressing its problems separately, had appealed to the Commissioners on the single issue of the extension of the city boundaries. They had been inclined to favour the request but had consulted the Administrator who, unsurprisingly, opposed it in a letter of November 9th 1657.

The next twist in Magdeburg's declining fortunes was to be significant for von Guericke's future. In January 1658 Friedrich Wilhelm renewed a demand that the city pay dues that it had previously refused. Magdeburg sent emissaries to the Commissioners and the Elector of Saxony, acting with Imperial authority during the interregnum that followed Ferdinand's death, to seek postponement of any payment. Von Guericke himself was sent to Berlin on March 5th to petition the Elec-

---

[105] Preface to *New Experiments Physico-Mechanical Touching the Spring of Air.*
[106] It is a virtue and a manifestation of a fitting modesty to acknowledge anyone through whom one has made progress.

tor to withdraw his demand. The Elector had not been present at Regensburg for von Guericke's demonstration of his experiments and this meeting appears to have been the first encounter between the two men. Politically, it was a failure. Friedrich Wilhelm did not agree to any remission of his demands and affirmed that he would send two advisers to collect the money from the city at the end of month. Their personal relationship was however to flourish. Friedrich Wilhelm took a lively interest in von Guericke's experiments, held him in high regard and within a few years had both employed Hans Otto as his Resident in Hamburg and co-opted von Guericke himself to the Brandenburg Hofrat.

The next fruitless developments were the meetings organised by the Administrator — in Magdeburg itself in May and in Quedlinburg on June 5th — to discuss their longstanding dispute. On behalf of Magdeburg, von Guericke and some associates attended the latter, as did Dr. Krull and Hofrat Barby for the Administrator. Before returning to Magdeburg von Guericke attempted to repeat an experiment described by Pascal[107] and to compare the air pressure at the foot and at the summit of a mountain — in this case, Brocksburg. As he recounts in Book III Chapter 30 of *Experimenta Nova*, the first part of the experiment was successfully conducted. Unfortunately during the ascent to the summit, the servant carrying the glass tube fell, breaking the tube and ruining the experiment. He was soon back in Magdeburg reporting to the Rat that no diplomatic progress had been made. This was to be the last such meeting.

On July 8th 1658 Leopold, then eighteen, was elected to succeed his father Ferdinand as Kaiser Leopold I. The election was not a mere formality. To counter the claims of Louis XIV, advocated by Mazarin, it was necessary to disburse 150 000 thalers to secure the vote of the Elector Friedrich Wilhelm.[108] A key influence was the Elector of Mainz, Archbishop Johann Philipp. Exhibiting a nascent wider German patriotism, recognising Imperial authority as a principle of unity among Germans, crediting Leopold with the advantages of being neither French nor Swedish, and satisfying himself that there was no prospect of a Habsburg instigated merger with Spain, he gave him his support.

---

[107] v. *Nouvelles Experiences touchant le vide*. Pascal 1647. The experiment was performed by Pascal's brother-in-law, Florin Perrier, in September 1648.
[108] Charles W. Ingrao. *The Habsburg Monarchy 1618–1815* 2nd Edition p. 56.

Magdeburg's Rat felt itself obliged to send a delegation to congratulate the new Kaiser on his accession and to take advantage of the occasion to present a petition for the confirmation of the city's privileges. Von Guericke, again reluctant but again bowing to his colleagues wishes, set out, accompanied by a colleague Dr. Peter Iden, for Vienna in July 1659.

Even by the modest standards set by his previous eighteen years in diplomacy, this mission was exceptionally frustrating and futile. The reality was that the great ones of the Empire had wearied of Magdeburg's diplomats. They did not obtain an audience with Leopold and their assiduous currying of favour with the influential began, as their persistence exhausted their hosts' reserves of politeness, to be rebuffed as often as it was indulged. Hoffman records their experience with one of the most important power brokers, the President of the Reichshofrat, Graf von Oettingen. Initially the Graf could not receive them at his home. Undeterred they showed up at 5 a.m. on July 28th to wait for him at the Reichshofrat building. A few days later they were calling on him again. On August 13th they called on the Graf's son. On the fifteenth they found the Graf himself in a local court house and commended Magdeburg's issues to his attention. On the 22nd they visited him at home, giving him a second copy of their memorandum as the first copy seemed to have been ignored. On the 28th they were attending upon him once more. Hoffman[109] notes that on the September 13th, when they sought him out again,

"because their visits had by this time become burdensome to him, and because he didn't want to become involved with their concerns, he did not show them a friendly face".

In the midst of all this frenetic diplomatic activity von Guericke suffered an illness which rendered him feverish and fatigued. From mid-September to mid October the reports to Magdeburg were signed only by Iden, but shortly thereafter von Guericke recovered sufficiently to become again a co-signatory. Increasingly conscious of the futility of their remaining longer in Vienna and having indirectly learned that Graf von Oettingen had stated that consideration of Magdeburg's affairs should be postponed to the next Reichstag, they petitioned the Rat for their recall and departed Vienna on January 29th 1660.

---

[109] Hoffmann p. 162.

The reader will be as relieved to learn as the writer is to record, that this was von Guericke's last foray in diplomacy. Almost twenty years of activity in this sphere was, notwithstanding the seeming triumph at Westphalia, turning to dust. The lasting legacy of those years was his scientific discoveries and inventions to whose consolidation he increasingly turned his attention.

From one of his correspondents, Philip Ernest Vegelin of Cherbourg, Fr. Schott learnt about Robert Boyle and about a recently founded English scientific society which was shortly to become the Royal Society. Fr. Schott writes:[110]

"Not long ago the most noble and excellent Master Philip Ernest Vegelin of Cherbourg wrote to me about an illustrious Englishman, Master Robert Boyle, brother of the Earl of Cork, saying that he had recently made a series of observations and experiments about air ...... and that in the near future similar and even greater developments are expected by him and by other members of the recently founded most noble Society dedicated to just one aim — that of uncovering more and more the secrets of nature by every kind of skillful investigation. I was desperately keen, and tried in all sorts of ways, to obtain some information about these experiments so that I might include them in my Technica Curiosa, which I was then contemplating. Then the same most noble and excellent Master Vegelin ...... sent me the book itself that had been recently produced in England and published at Oxford. With great eagerness I read through the whole book comprising no fewer than eighteen sections, hardly pausing for breath. I was so impressed by it that I thought that, in addition to the English version, it should be published again in a German edition so as to come as quickly as possible to the notice of many more people."

Fr. Schott made good his intention. The first book of the *Technica Curiosa* concerns itself with Von Guericke's work at Magdeburg and the second, entitled *Mirabilia Anglicana,* is dedicated to Boyle's work. While preparing the *Technica Curiosa* Fr. Schott maintained contact with von Guericke and told him something of what Boyle had accomplished. Fr. Schott records the correspondence from von Guericke. From the dates and contents of the letters, and given Fr. Schott's enthusiasm for communicating his subject, one can plausibly infer that the priest had received a copy of the Latin edition of Boyle's book at the very end of 1661 or early 1662. He writes:[111]

---

[110] *Technica Curiosa Proemium* Book II.
[111] *Technica Curiosa* Book I p. 53.

"After I had received the preceding letter and thoroughly absorbed its contents, I requested elucidation on a number of points which arose in this and other contexts. I also mentioned the new English experiments by Master Boyle which, after reading my account of the Magdeburg experiments, he has compiled for publication. To this letter the most noble author sent the following reply, as learned as it is intelligent.

Most reverend, most religious, most venerable Sir, and my very dear friend,

When I returned from the wedding of my son Otto Gericke, Hofrat of the Fürst of Anhalt, at Hamburg, I found that your letter of February 17th had arrived at my home. I understand from it that you have received my last letter of December 30th 1661, in which, at the request of your reverence I gave a detailed account of some experiments I carried out last summer. As well as attracting your reverence's considerable admiration, my letter has raised some fresh difficulties that need clarification. .... Finally, you mention the fact that the distinguished Master Robert Boyle, brother of the Earl of Cork in England, (sic) has, having seen your reverence's account in the Mechanica of our Magdeburg experiments, brought out a book New Experiments about Air. I have not yet seen this book but, in any case, as regards his apparatus and how it performs, your reverence leads me to believe that I have done it all much better and more thoroughly. ....

(Von Guericke goes on to make three specific technical criticisms.)

For these reasons I cannot persuade myself that he has discovered any more experimental phenomena, using apparatus of that kind, than I have now described in my book Concerning my own Experiments. I shall see to it, however, that a copy of the book is sent to me from Holland.

Apart from that, it just remains to commend your reverence to Christ's protection.

Your reverence's willing servant,
Otto Gericke,
Magdeburg, February 28th, 1662.

The book to which von Guericke refers was incorporated as Book III into the *Experimenta Nova* which comprised in all seven books. This substantial work was, according to its own *Preface to the Reader*, completed on March 14th 1663. However because of illness, the pressure of other concerns and difficulties with his Dutch publisher, Johannes Janssonius, the book did not appear until 1672.

Von Guericke's next letter, sent on April 15th, does not mention Boyle and is dedicated to responding to specific queries. By this time

Fr. Schott must have been in possession of at least a draft of *Concerning my own Experiments,* as von Guericke's letter refers him to various chapters for further clarification of some points. At the end of the letter there is the first reference to the emergence of Friedrich Wilhelm, who had been decisive in frustrating von Guericke's diplomatic career, as an admirer and patron of his scientific work. He writes:[112]

"I note that your reverence is considering sending me what he writes about these and other less important experiments for prior review. I shall carefully and safely return everything and there will be no need to make a copy first. If any other queries should come to mind, just ask me and feel free to write to me. I shall be happy to reply to the best of my modest ability. I would be very grateful if your reverence would send me a copy of his Physica Curiosa,[113] for which I shall gladly pay. To my great joy I have gathered that his most eminent highness, the Elector of Mainz, has also been very taken with my experiments. The most serene Elector of Brandenburg is also a great admirer and patron of the mathematical sciences. Commending your reverence to the particular providence and protection of the Almighty, I am and remain your reverence's ever humble

Otto Gericke,
Magdeburg April 15th 1662.

By the time he wrote again he was in possession of Boyle's book and in a position to comment on it. Fr. Schott writes:[114]

"In this letter this most gracious man replies to some questions, which I had put to him after his last letter. The questions I put will be obvious from the context in his reply.
Most reverend, most religious, most worthy Sir, and my very dear friend,
I received your reverence's very welcome letter of April 9th. I hope he has received my last letter of the fifteenth in which I hope I satisfied your reverence's desires. However, if there are still any problems, I can explain them at greater length.
As for Master Robert Boyle's Experimenta Nova Physica-Mechanica, I replied to you as soon as your reverence had sent me an outline of his apparatus and before I owned or had read a copy of his tract. I wrote to you that the air pump of his apparatus was not at all suitable for producing a vacuum, both because the pump was not immersed in water and because the operation of the pump was too slow. I now find that he himself admits as much in various places. For example, on page 65:

---

[112] *Technica Curiosa* p. 59.
[113] This was another book by Fr. Schott published in 1662. It is concerned with biological and physiological topics.
[114] *Technica Curiosa* p. 74.

'Indeed, despite taking the greatest care in the matter, external air was getting in so quickly, that after various experiments had been tried in vain, I gave up attempting them in that particular glass and decided to make a completely fresh attempt in a large Receiver.'
Likewise at the end of page 70 and on page 74, he writes:
'Seeing that even such a little amount of air, which had insinuated itself (and we were not able by any method to exclude absolutely all the air) was sufficient etc.'
Similarly towards the end of the preface i.e. the letter to his nephew,[115] he says that he knows full well from his experiments

> *'that it is such a hard task and more difficult than one might think, to stop air entering through little invisible holes or some tiny crack in a vessel, when the air immediately around it is compressed, so that despite our efforts and enthusiasm, we never manage to completely evacuate the Receiver or to keep it almost evacuated for some period, so that it didn't to some degree leak.'*

From these and other remarks he makes it is clear that the air is indeed for the most part being extracted, but that nevertheless a lot is leaking unnoticed around the sides of the piston head. In my apparatus, an outline of which I sent, not long ago, to your reverence in my last set of notes, this hardly happens at all. Quite often I have kept glass containers, copper spheres and other similar vessels in an evacuated state for three months and even longer. I have kept the copper hemispheres, which have already been mentioned, in an evacuated state for three or four weeks, but this was only possible if they had been glued together at their edges with wax.
I now turn to the seven separate questions that your reverence has formulated.

(The rest of the letter then deals with the seven points raised by Fr. Schott.)
Meanwhile commending us both to the Almighty's paternal protection and favour, I remain, your reverence's faithful and humble servant,

Otto Gericke,
May 10th 1662.

In March 1663 von Guericke brought his *Experimenta Nova* to completion. He had been working on it for at least the previous few years. In a letter to Fr. Schott of November 16th 1661 he relates his progress. He writes:[116]

"As far as my treatise, which is in hand, is concerned, I work on writing it during whatever spare time my other occupations allow. It is divided into eight books. The first is entitled 'About the Cosmos and its organisation according to the more commonly received opinion

---

[115] Boyle's book was cast in the form of a letter to his nephew Charles, Viscount of Dungarvan.
[116] *Technica Curiosa* p. 36.

among philosophers'; the second is 'Concerning my own Experiments'; the third, 'About What is and What is Not' (this particularly demonstrates that space is infinite and immeasurable); the fourth, 'Concerning the potencies operating in the Cosmos[117] and other Associated Topics'; the fifth, 'Concerning the Earth of Land and Sea and its associate Moon'; the sixth, 'Concerning the world of the Planets and their true Organisation'; the seventh, 'Concerning the fixed Stars', and the eighth, 'Concerning what is at the limits of the Cosmos'. However, the task is proceeding very slowly both because of the burden of other affairs and because I am without any assistance. I am also having considerable difficulty writing in Latin, since no fewer than 38 years have gone by since I finished studying in universities and during which opportunities for writing only infrequently presented themselves."

Besides the *Experimenta Nova* von Guericke composed two other unpublished works which formed part of his Nachlass. The first, the manuscript of which is preserved in Magdeburg's city library, was entitled *Civitatis Magdeburgensis pristina libertas* (The Ancient Liberty of the City of Magdeburg). The writing of it was not for him an academic pursuit but an attempt to give historical justification to Magdeburg's incessantly pursued aim of becoming an Imperial Free City by establishing the authenticity of the Ottonian Privilege. This was already disputed by his contemporaries and the settled opinion of subsequent historians is that the Ottonian Privilege, supposedly issued by Otto I in 937 AD, was in fact a later composition. There has never been a suggestion that von Guericke was party to any deliberate deception on the issue but it has been allowed that his civic patriotism perhaps coloured his judgments.

The second unpublished work was a three-part history of Magdeburg. The first part consisted of a heavily annotated copy of a previous historical work by Johann Pomarius, first published in 1587. This was available to Heinrich Rathmann zu Pechau,[118] the author of a history of Magdeburg written between 1800 and 1816 but by the time Hoffman was writing, c. 1860, had disappeared. The second part, covering the period 1585–1630, was already missing at the start of the nine-

---

[117] The Latin is "de virtutibus mundanis". The concept "virtutes mundanae", a precursor of the later idea of "forces of nature" is important in von Guericke's thinking. In Book IV Chapter 1 he formulates the concept in these terms. "All of creation, especially the bodies of the Cosmos, consist of their substance, their way of being (sua vita) and their innate potencies (virtutibus). These potencies are neither substance nor accident, but something which flows out of bodies of the Cosmos (effluentia Corporum Mundanorum) and which is innate in them".

[118] Heinrich Rathmann: *Geschichte der Stadt Magdeburg* (1816).

teenth century. The third part is an account of the siege and destruction of Magdeburg in 1630. Hoffman, working from von Guericke's hand-written document, published it in 1860 under the title *Geschichte der Belagerung, Eroberung und Zerstörung Magdeburg's* (History of the Siege, Conquest and Destruction of Magdeburg). This document remains in print and is an important eyewitness account, albeit written decades after the events it describes, of the horror that descended on the city in May 1631.

On the political side of his life, the years after 1663 saw the final developments of his career. At the beginning of 1666 he was ennobled by Kaiser Leopold. Hoffmann blandly declares that this was an honour awarded solely in recognition of his distinguished services and not one von Guericke or his friends had solicited.[119] The petition to Kaiser Leopold unearthed by Schimank from the Vienna archives shows that a little prompting had been necessary to remind the Imperial authorities of his worthiness to receive recognition.[120] In any case, it was an honour he was very happy to accept. From then on he signed himself "Otto v. Guericke" rather than plain "Otto Gericke". On April 7th he requested that he be referred to by the title "Edel" in official documents. In the event, the Rat went one better and passed a resolution that he be referred to as "Edel, Vest und Hochweiser" (the noble, learned and accomplished).

A development of more moment was that the Elector Friedrich Wilhelm, who already since 1650 had been exacting dues from the archbishopric of Magdeburg, moved to exert his control over the city itself. Von Guericke was the acting Bürgermeister, responsible for the negotiations which took place in May 1666. The background to Friedrich Wilhelm's forceful intervention in the affairs of Magdeburg was

---

[119] Hoffmann p. 166.

[120] Schimank (p. 33) is sceptical of the Hoffmann version for which von Guericke himself is the source and believes it more probable that von Guericke had lobbied for the honour during his second visit to Vienna. He certainly requested the right to use the prefix "von" and the change of spelling from "Gericke" to "Guericke". In a petition to Leopold of January 31st 1665, reproduced in Schimank p. 69, von Guericke, adducing the consideration that he was now well known because of his experiments, writes: "Because of this I have been moved, for the good of posterity, to bring up another matter. The fact that there are many people, here and elsewhere, who share my name (Gericke) though they are not related to me, often leads to mistaken identity. Also, as foreigners pronounce the initial 'Ge' as 'sch', my name is often misunderstood. Both these would be rectified by the title "von" and the insertion of a 'u' between the 'G' and the 'e' so that I write my name as 'von Guericke'."

that an army of the Elector's troops had been raised to subdue the Bishop of Münster, who had taken up arms against Dutch allies of Brandenburg. Having compelled the bishop to accept terms, Friedrich Wilhelm's army marched through the archbishopric of Magdeburg, finally arriving at Wanzleben, a short distance from Magdeburg. Taking possession of the strategically important city presented itself as an attractive and feasible option. The commander of the troops, Fieldmarshal von Sparr,[121] was instructed to meet continued resistance to the Elector's demands for the payment of dues and for the quartering of a garrison by initiating a siege of the city.

Negotiations proper began with the arrival on May 21st of an envoy from Halle to the Magdeburg Rat at the head of which sat von Guericke. The envoy brought letters from the Elector, the Administrator, and from certain Brandenburg counsellors inviting Magdeburg to send representatives to discussions at Wanzleben on May 23rd. A reply was dispatched the following day and on the 23rd a five-strong delegation, with von Guericke's colleague Bürgermeister Rosenstock at their head, proceeded to Wanzleben. Its instructions were to refuse any payment of dues and decline any request to quarter a garrison. When these two demands were duly made to them, the delegates responded that they needed to present them first to the Rat at Magdeburg. They were given until the following Friday, May 25th, to accomplish this and it was made clear to them that a failure to comply would lead to military action.

On the 24th the Rat summoned both Ausschüsse requesting that they deliberate and advise. As at the time of the siege of 1631, the representatives of the people felt that the decision before them was so critical to their city's destiny that the people themselves should be consulted. That same day an exercise in popular democracy was quickly organised. The outcome was that all nine districts were in favour of paying the dues but not of quartering troops. Only one district was prepared to countenance the latter and then only as a worst case scenar-

---

[121] Otto Christoph Freiherr von Sparr (c.1600–1668) was an officer in the Imperial army during the Thirty Years War. After the Peace of Westphalia he briefly led a campaign on behalf of the Elector of Cologne, but in December 1649 entered the service of Friedrich Wilhelm. He was a successful Chief of Staff and Commander in campaigns against Poland and Sweden. He was promoted to fieldmarshal in 1657. The following year, in recognition of his command of troops from Brandenburg fighting against the Ottoman Empire in Hungary, he also became an Imperial fieldmarshal. The subjugation of Magdeburg was his last military mission.

io. Accompanied by a representative from each district, the original five delegates returned to Wanzleben to communicate their decision.

The refusal of a garrison was not well received by the Brandenburg negotiators but they knew how to apply pressure using a classic mixture of cajolery and menace. Friedrich Wilhelm had no designs on the privileges of the city; his only aim would be to enhance its prosperity and well-being; the garrison would in no way oppress the citizenry but would just enable them to defend themselves better against any threat; the delegates would be well-advised to remember that the generous terms and concessions that might be available in the event of a voluntary submission would no longer be in prospect if it came to a settlement by force; they should also bear in mind that, prominent citizens though they might well be, the city and its inhabitants were not their personal property to do with as they liked; they were at Wanzleben to be in the service of their community and theirs alone would be the responsibility for what might be unleashed on Magdeburg as a consequence of their recalcitrance. After several hours of this the delegates requested a further moratorium till May 27th and returned to Magdeburg to report.

At Magdeburg the full representative assembly of the Rat and the Ausschüsse heard and debated at length the report. Their conclusion was that the city neither had enough armaments, nor its citizens sufficient stomach for a fight, to offer effective resistance to the Elector's demands. Again referring the issue to the people, they recommended capitulation to assemblies of the people in the nine districts. The citizenry, intimidated and fearful, accepted that the Rat's options were limited to negotiating the best terms it could get.

On Sunday 27th, the city's delegates proceeded to nearby Klosterberg to where, in the interests of facilitating negotiations, the representatives of the Elector and the Administrator had moved. A final round of discussions lasted until midnight and on the following day an agreement, which became known as the Klosterberg Treaty, was signed. By its terms Magdeburg would quarter a garrison of Brandenburg troops, pay a monthly sum of 1,200 thalers for their upkeep and, additionally, disburse the dues, so long demanded and so long refused, to the Administrator and to the Elector. On behalf of the city the first signature was that of Otto von Guericke.

It was a sad, but perhaps inevitable, moment for both Magdeburg and von Guericke. Hoffmann evokes a note of wistful melancholy at the signing away of long cherished aspirations.[122]

"It ought to register with the reader how painful this step was to the city. The aspiration to autonomy within the Empire, with which the city had so long flattered itself, and which it had thought to have realised at the Peace of Westphalia, had been shattered at one blow and Magdeburg, proud of its freedom, reduced to the status of a mere Mediatstadt. It was little comfort in its loss that, at the same time, the same fate befell other German cities."

It ought to have been a particularly poignant and traumatic moment for von Guericke himself. His signature on the Klosterberg Treaty was acknowledging the futility of some twenty years of his own life doggedly devoted to securing what he was now abandoning forever. There is however no evidence that he was at all distraught. A man who had in 1631 seen at first hand the destruction made inevitable by a hotheaded want of realism among the city's defenders was not likely to be in the vanguard of a reckless charge to the barricades against superior odds. Every consideration of prudence and humanity would have counselled the surrender his signature now endorsed. However, beyond an intelligent willingness to adapt to the inevitable, a major and, to some, a mysterious, change[123] had come over his outlook. The ardent local patriot had become Friedrich Wilhelm's man. The probable reasons are humanly understandable. The Elector esteemed him personally, valued his scientific activity and, since 1663, had employed his son, Hans Otto, in the service of Brandenburg. In this same year von Guericke felt sufficiently confident of his relationship with Friedrich to feel able to ask him to reconfirm the Letter of Immunity from civic impositions which he had first received in June 1649. Given that at the beginning of the year he had already solicited and received assurances on that score from the Kaiser, the request to the Elector was, so to speak, covering all the bases. His correspondence with Fr. Schott and contact with the Jesuits of Würzburg had ceased in 1664 and Fr. Schott himself died in May 1666. The Elector was now his uncontested champion and when the *Experimenta Nova* finally appeared it was prefaced by a fulsome dedication to his new patron. The portrait of a handsome, middle-aged von Guericke, painted around 1649 by Anselm van Hulle, appears immedi-

---

[122] Hoffmann p. 172.

[123] Hoffmann (p. 172) comments on how baffling this transformation at first appeared.

ately after the dedication. The gold chain von Guericke is wearing was a gift from the Elector,[124] who had nominated him to the Brandenburg Rat in 1666. Below the portrait, the title "Counsellor to the most Serene and Potent Elector of Brandenburg" stands before that of "Consul of the City of Magdeburg", a precedence which speaks of his loyalty to his new master and the new dispensation.

---

[124] Erich Regener: *Otto von Guericke, der Erfinder der Luftpumpe und seine Beziehungen zum Grossen Kurfursten.* (1908)

The Experimenta Nova

The magnum opus von Guericke finally produced does not greatly differ from what he had projected in his letter to Fr. Schott of November 16th 1661. The draft Books VII & VIII were merged into a single Book VII and the draft Book III was dropped in favour of a new
and more comprehensive book, *On Empty Space,* which was inserted as
Book II.

Book IV records a side of von Guericke's scientific thinking
which he did not share with Fr. Schott and which remained unpublished until the appearance of the *Experimenta Nova* in 1672. This
centred on the concept of a "virtus mundana" — perhaps best, if
somewhat anachronistically, translated as "force of nature". Gravity, as
manifested by bodies falling to the Earth, was too familiar a phenomenon to provoke new thought and, in any case, had been "explained" by
the Aristotelian doctrine of bodies seeking their natural place. Phenomena associated with magnetism and static electricity, produced by rubbing amber, had been studied by William Gilbert[125] and an account
published in his *On the Magnet and Magnetic Bodies, and on the Great Magnet
the Earth* appeared in 1600. This was an important stimulus to radical
thinking about what came to be subsequently called "action at a distance" — invisible forces of attraction and repulsion unmediated by
any intervening substance. Kepler, for example, proposed the idea that
the force governing the orbits of the planets was magnetic. Von Guericke sought to integrate these new phenomena into a conceptual
framework of "virtutes mundanae", which he thought of as being intrinsic properties of certain materials, manifesting themselves as an
incorporeal outflow (effluentia) towards other bodies. In a letter to the
young Leibniz,[126] written shortly after the publication of the *Experimenta
Nova,* he describes the experiment which demonstrated, for the first
time, the phenomenon of electrostatic repulsion.

*"There are different minerals that, poured together with sulphur into a ball about the size of
two fists, allow a visual demonstration of what I have named "forces of nature" (virtutes
mundanae). Tycho Brahe writes that he would very much like to support Copernicus, if only*

---

[125] William Gilbert (1544–1603)

[126] Gottfried Wilhelm von Leibniz (1646–1716) was one of the giants of the generation after
von Guericke. They corresponded in the years 1671–1672. The quoted passage is cited in
Schimank p. 44.

the Earth were not such a heavy body. My experiments show the contrary is true — the Earth is not as heavy as the lightest feather. Likewise Galileo in his treatise thinks that one cannot grasp the reason why the moon follows the Earth and always presents the same face towards it. I show with the same spherical ball that this happens through particular forces of nature. For example, when the ball is first rubbed somewhat by hand and then a light feather is held close to it, the ball firstly attracts the feather to itself, but then soon repels it as far as the range of its force (orbis virtutis) allows. Then, wherever the ball goes the feather goes too, hovering in the air, so that one can bring it to any desired point even up to someone's nose. .... It always presents the same side to the spherical ball, so that, by means of this ball, once can turn it in the air, as one pleases. Likewise many other remarkable things can be demonstrated using this ball."

The *Experimenta Nova* took a further nine years before it was finally published. In March 1670 he signed the *Preface to the Reader* but not until November 1671, the dedication to his patron and political overlord, the Elector Friedrich Wilhelm. The character of the *Experimenta Nova* is more that of an intellectual "apologia pro vita sua" than a report on latest research findings. He was now past sixty. His reputation as an experimenter had been growing since 1654 and since 1657 had been spreading internationally. Already in 1661 he had noted that important people were coming to see his experiments.[127] In October 1663 the Duke of Chevreuse and another high French official, Balthasar von Monconys,[128] included Magdeburg in a grand tour specifically to meet him. On November 21st he was demonstrating his experiments to Friedrich Wilhelm in Cölln an der Spree.[129] The *Experimenta Nova* was not written to enhance his already growing fame but to communicate to the world the fruits of his study, reflection and experimentation, pursued amidst all his other preoccupations, on the great questions of cosmology and ultimate reality.

The book demonstrates that, in addition to being a successful engineer, local politician and indefatigable diplomat, he was formidably erudite. He alludes to some hundred and fifty sources ranging from the philosophers of antiquity and the prophets of the Old Testament to near contemporaries like Galileo, Kepler, Pascal and Fr. Kircher. He

---

[127] Letter of Nov 1661. *Technica Curiosa* p. 36.

[128] A description of their trip was published in 1666 by the firm "Horace Boissot and Georges Remus" and entitled "Journal des Voyages de M. de Monconsys, Conseiller du Roi en ses Conseils d'Etat et Privé et Lieutenant Criminel au Siège Présidial de Lyon."

[129] The demonstration took place in the library of the Elector and a note of it made in the diary of Otto von Schwerin, a tutor to the Elector's sons. (Schneider p. 113)

was through-and-through a religious man in two senses. First in the cultural sense of being so soaked in Scripture as to be able effortlessly to reach for an apposite scriptural quotation to convey or illustrate his meaning. Secondly, in the intellectual sense that he unquestioningly anticipated harmony between the words of Scripture, intelligently read, and the conclusions he would draw from his scientific investigations. This spirit permeates his writing from the inspiring quotation from St. Basil with which the *Preface to the Reader* opens:

"The contemplation of nature, according to the Blessed Basil, is the antechamber of heavenly pleasure, the undying joy of the intellect and the gateway to serenity. It is the summit of human joy, the meeting place of the spirit of the exalted and that of the down-to-earth. In such contemplation, the soul, heedless of itself and roused, as it were, from a profound torpor enters upon a region of light and seems to take on the character, not so much of a man raised to heaven, but of a divinity come to earth."

to the very last words of Book VII:

"Further knowledge is reserved for the happier eternal life after our resurrection. As the apostle[130] says, 'In this mortal life our knowledge is only partial; after this life has passed to its completion, then all that is in any degree useless shall be removed. Now with dimmed vision we see riddles; then we shall see face to face'. Till then may Authority, Honour and Glory be to God the Father, Son and Holy Spirit, the triune God, creator and preserver of all things, now and forever."

Scriptural allusions pepper the entire work. The literalism of his religious belief is strikingly illustrated by the discussion in Book II Chapter 11 of the location and volume of heaven, taking due account of the total number of bodies it might be necessary to accommodate. His religion was untainted by rancorous sectarianism. Three generations removed from the passions incited by the Reformation in Germany, von Guericke had grown up in an atmosphere of mutual tolerance and cordiality between Lutherans and Catholics. A contemporary document, emanating from Wittenberg, sets out, perhaps through the rose tinted glasses of nostalgia, a perception of a world that had given way to a harsher dispensation.[131]

"For as long as the papists and we, Lutherans, lived together, there was no question of factions or parties. Nobody sought to deprive anyone of what they had justly acquired. We

---

[130] Paul: Corinthians 1:13.
[131] Cited by Kurt Pfister in *Kurfürst Maximilian von Bayern und sein Jahrhundert.* p. 101. Munich (1948).

lived side by side in an easy relationship. We intermarried. The fathers brought up their sons, the mothers their daughters, each in their own religion. Between us Christians there were neither persecutions nor bloody struggles.

In Bohemia, by contrast, Calvin demonstrates that he wants to annihilate both the Luther-ans and the papists. There he is going about a "reformation" which is more a "deformation" or, worse still, a "destruction". He despoils the churches of the images of the saints and insults or burns the relics. If such violence marks his first triumphs, what will be in store for us the day that Calvin has the upper hand in our country?"

As befits a Lutheran first brought to prominence by the Arch-bishop of Mainz, first published by a Jesuit of Würzburg and later pat-ronised by the Calvinist Friedrich Wilhelm, von Guericke's writings are free from confessional animosity. His few lapses from urbane courtesy are provoked by individuals such as Dr. Hauptmann[132] whose particular blend of philosophical pretention, obscure verbiage and ignorance of the simplest experimental facts irritated him beyond measure.

While he clearly enjoyed the theatrical exhibition of his experi-ments to his amazed fellow citizens, his work on the vacuum was not just for spectacle but was firmly embedded in a wider passion for cos-mology. He presents a survey of the main options of the day — the Ptolemaic, Tychonic and Copernican systems — and declares himself firmly in favour of the last of these. A notable omission from his survey is the absence of any mention of Kepler's theory of elliptical orbits which had been included in the final volume of the *Epitome of Copernican Astronomy* (1621). Throughout the *Experimenta Nova* von Guericke shows himself conversant with Galileo's work and alludes to him fre-quently and favourably. But the "Galileo affair", which loomed so large in later centuries, so far fails to excite his indignation that it does not even rate a mention. It may well be that a man who had spent the prime of his adult life amidst the horrors of the Thirty Years War and who exercised political authority as a professional, did not recognise the confinement of an elderly professor to his villa for gratuitously cheek-ing the powerful of the day as the iconic outrage it later transpired to be.[133]

---

[132] Augustus Hauptmann (1607-1674) German doctor and chemist. He was a speculative theo-rist on the nature of venereal and other diseases. See *Experimenta Nova* Book III.

[133] Cf. the case of Lawrence Summers who was forced to resign the presidency of Harvard for inopportunely observing that it may be in the nature of things that the vast majority of profes-sionals mathematicians are male.

Nevertheless, the tension between Scripture and the new astron
omy was as real, and probably as painful to him, as the discovery of
uncomfortable facts about racial or gender differences would be to a
modern investigator committed to ethically inspired, a priori views. It is
best to let him speak for himself on the Pontifical Decree of 1616 de-
nouncing the Copernican system. In Book VI Chapter 16 he writes:

*"Almost all the modern astronomers (including also the most famous astronomer of our time
Fr. Johannes Ricciolus of the Society of Jesus, Professor of Theology and Astronomy in the
Academy at Bologna, who brought out his remarkable work "A New Almagest comprising
Ancient and Modern Astronomy" are now backing away from the Ptolemaic system, which
we have treated in Book I Chapter 4, on account of its blatant errors. Furthermore those
who follow the peripatetic school, or the Pontifical Decree of 1616 published by a Congrega-
tion of cardinals (in which they decree that Copernicus' Pythagorean doctrine of the immobil-
ity of the sun in the centre of the cosmos and the motion of the Earth around it, being contrary to sacred Scripture, is to be interdicted and abominated) are compelled to recognise only
Earth-centric systems. Thus, they are left only with the Tychonic system and whether or not
this is true or false they hang on to it and defend it. The question arises whether by this
procedure Astronomy can truly be pursued or the disposition and relationships of the heavenly bodies be determined.*

*Let us first consider the case of the Peripatetics. Their general practice is to infer probable
truth from what Aristotle has prescribed, so that they feel entitled to argue from his sayings.
Moreover, according to them, it is wicked that a non-peripatetic should prefer to go by the
evidence of the senses. It is exactly because they cling to and trust his authority that they are
completely unmoved by what sound reason and experiments might dictate. There is an important distinction between knowing and believing. To believe is to give assent to a proposition based on the authority of the speaker. To know is recognise the truth of a statement for
a reason. The inescapable inference is that a System which is understood through reason is
truly to be preferred to another to which assent is given because of the authority of the speaker. 'Why do you order me to believe, if I am able to know?' says Augustine. But the Copernican system can be validated through reason, but not the Tychonic (as we have already
proved in many places and also in the sequel). Therefore the Copernican system is true and
to be preferred to the Tychonic.*

*Secondly, it is right that the reverence due to sacred Scripture should be maintained intact
and undiminished and, accordingly, we shall write nothing that might bring Holy Writ into
disrepute. To those who would interpret some or other passage in support of their position
and use it to deprecate the Copernican system and to defend the Tychonic one, we would pose
the following questions. Should the reverence due to Scripture be extended beyond the purposes of Scripture — that of teaching the way to eternal salvation — to resolve philosophical,
mathematical and astronomical issues, including even the most fundamental questions?
Among the first of these is the position of the sun and the Earth in the cosmos. Is it through*

Scripture that the outstanding questions which arise in these subjects are to be dissected and resolved? Or, is it not rather the case that Scripture, leaving all those issues to one side, (which, in any case, are questions of scholarly rather than popular, dispute, for ordinary people can't see what the problems are) speaks of the rising, setting and motion of the sun as well as of the fixity of the Earth in the language of common speech and according to the understanding and views of ordinary people?"

The good sense and eirenic tone of this hardly need recommending, then or now.

The appearance of a comet in early December 1664 which remained visible until the end of January 1665 was a major event for European astronomers. Stanislaus Lubienietski[134] published in 1668 a lavishly illustrated volume, *Theatrum Cometicum*,[135] which provided accounts of over four hundred historical sightings of comets. Much of the book is however dedicated to recording the observations and reaction of scholars to the comet of 1664–1665. Among the eminent whose opinions he solicited were Christian Huyghens, Kaspar Schott, Johannes Hevelius,[136] Athanasius Kircher and von Guericke. (Understandably omitted from the book was the scholar destined to be the greatest of them all, Isaac Newton, then just turning nineteen, who recorded his observations on December 24th, 27th 28th, 29th and 30th and throughout much of January.[137]) Lubienietski's correspondence with von Guericke was conducted from an initial letter of March 4th 1665 to his farewell of April 19th 1666. Von Guericke republished the letters as an appendix to Book V — *On the Earth and the Moon*.

He wanted the book to be published in Holland. In the *Preface to the Reader* he alludes to delays caused by illness and the pressure of other affairs. Detailed negotiations on its publication seem to have only started in 1667. In April of this year a book and map trader, Johann Blaeu, with whom he had previous dealings, wrote to him from Amsterdam that the publishing trade was currently languishing because of

---

[134] Stanislaus Lubienetski (1623–1675) was a Polish historian and astronomer. While resident in Hamburg he was a friend of von Guericke's son. He was a celebrated Socinian minister and, persecuted by Lutherans, died of poison in 1675.

[135] The Theatrum Cometicum is available online at the National Digital Library of Poland. Lubienietski was also the author of a *History of the Polish Reformation*.

[136] Johannes Hevelius (1611–1687) was a councillor and mayor of Danzig, as well as being an astronomer. He was the last significant figure to make observations without the use of a telescope.

[137] Newton. MS. Add. 3996 f 115v.

the war with England but that as soon as there was a recovery, he would attempt to find a publisher. Progress was slow. Two years later, on April 16th 1669, Blaeu was writing again to him to say that he had read the proofs and could see that the book would have a substantial market. However his own presses were booked up for more than two years ahead and von Guericke should apply to another publisher.

Through the agency of a friend, Johann von Gersdorff,[138] von Guericke opened negotiations with another potential publisher, Johann Jansson van Waesberge, also from Amsterdam. In one of these letters he indicates — seemingly as a ploy to extract better financial terms from the publisher — that he was still actively engaged in experimental work, that the *Technica Curiosa* did not contain even a tenth of his experiments and that the final revision would not be complete before the end of 1669. Von Guericke was a canny negotiator and pressed for, in addition to seventy-five free copies of the first edition, fifty free copies of each subsequent edition. However, the publisher would agree, in the latter case, only to twelve. As it transpired, there was to be no second edition until 1962 when the work was reprinted in commemorative form. Friedrich Wilhelm graciously accepted the dedication of the book. Von Guericke himself, using his contacts at Vienna, obtained the Caesarian privilege from the Kaiser, Leopold. The contract with the publisher was signed on March 21st 1670. In the spring of 1671 the publication of the book was announced at trade fairs at Leipzig and Frankfurt. This came to the attention of Leibniz who, on April 23rd, wrote urging him to hasten publication and alluding to the interest he thought the book would arouse in England and France.[139] In a letter of September 1671, von Guericke requested the publisher to print at the end of the text "Completed on March 14th 1663". In making this request, von Guericke, notwithstanding the inclusion of correspondence

---

[138] Johann von Gersdorff was the composer of the droll ditty dedicated to von Guericke which appears after the *Preface to the Reader*.

[139] In a reply to Leibniz of June 6th 1671 (Schimank p. 49) von Guericke summed up the purpose of his book. He wrote: "So far as the main part of the work is concerned, it is principally about the right understanding and perception of the universal vessel or container of all things, which I, to use one word, call space but not understood in its usual three dimensional sense, but as that in which every body and every substance either has its being and subsistence or could so have. Space yields to nothing and is not displaced according to the volume of the body it receives; it is permanent and immobile, everywhere in everything and through everything, whether corporeal or incorporeal and to which nothing brings being whether it is occupied or empty."

from 1665 and his earlier claim that he was continuing to carry out experiments in the late 1660s, asserted, presumably with an eye to his priority, that the substance of the work had been completed before that date. Copies of the book were finally available in early 1672.

When the *Experimenta Nova* was finally published he presented copies to a number of influential acquaintances including Friedrich Wilhelm and the Administrator August. He also had his son send a copy to Queen Christina of Sweden, a former supporter of Magdeburg's cause. As a young adult she had converted to Catholicism, abdicated her throne in 1654 and was now resident in Rome. In her youth a pupil of Descartes, the Queen was a well-educated, highly intelligent, headstrong and somewhat eccentric individual, the value of whose opinion should not be discounted. She replied to Hans Otto courteously and graciously in French.[140]

M. de Guericke,

I have received your father's book which you have sent me. I thank you with all my heart for it and can tell you that I have read it from cover to cover with great care and pleasure. Others are better capable than I of judging its worth and expressing their esteem but my ignorance does not inhibit me from saying that I consider this work to be one of the most worthy and admirable of our century. The experiments, beautiful as they are, have been repeated by others at Paris, London, Florence and even here at Rome. But the deductions and new ideas, or rather conjectures, which he infers from them, are, as it seems to me, specific to him — at least I have read nothing similar — unless British astronomy, which I have not yet had the leisure to consider, has produced something comparable. Be that as it may, it seems to me that no-one else but your father has given us an idea of the universe so worthy of its adorable Author. I leave it to the mathematicians and astronomers to argue his system with him; for myself, I assent willingly to most of his conjectures, in so far, of course, as is permissible to me by the authority of the Church of Rome. Meanwhile I thank you both for your gift and for the pleasure which the reading of such a beautiful book has given me.

May God prosper your affairs,
Rome, this 9th of July 1672,
Christina Alexandra.

Appearing eighteen years after the first public demonstration of his experiments at Regensburg, the *Experimenta Nova* did not have the impact that earlier publication might have secured for it. By allowing

---

[140] Hoffmann p. 229.

Fr. Schott to publish on his behalf he had stolen his own thunder. Schimank notes:[141]

"One might think that a work of such scope and range must have had a strong influence on his contemporaries. I suspect that this was by no means the case. In the majority of instances his book was something to show off rather than to study. Very few had any idea of its riches. Only on this supposition is it understandable why von Guericke's electrostatic investigations were not further pursued and why they were only recalled to mind when the phenomena, which Guericke had already described in Book IV, were newly discovered by others.[142] The reason for this anomaly is to be sought in the tardiness of the book's publication."

It is possible that Schimank has overlooked the influence of its central philosophical idea in one important quarter. Judging by his letter to Leibniz cited above, von Guericke valued, at least as highly as his experimental work, his attaining of a theologically based "right understanding and perception of the universal vessel or container of all things which I, to use one word, call space." Von Guericke's theological view of the nature of absolute space, of which he presents himself as the originator and pioneer, is virtually identical with that expressed by Newton in the scholium to the Principia.[143] This is the view that for two centuries triumphed over the seemingly more sophisticated relationist views of Descartes and Leibniz. This concept of absolute space is a key building block of the Newtonian synthesis and it is legitimate to wonder if Newton owes any of this aspect of his thinking to von Guericke. There are two relevant facts.

The first is that in November 1672 a two page review of the *Experimenta Nova*, written by Henry Oldenburg,[144] appeared in the Philosophical Transactions of the Royal Society. The review is generally dis-

---

[141] Schimank p. 59.

[142] Schimank may be incorrect as to the independence of later investigations from von Guericke's work. Boyle repeated von Guericke's electrostatic experiments for the Royal Society in November 1672 and February 1673 (Schneider p. 127) and Francis Hawksbee, (1666–1713), also a Fellow of the Royal Society, greatly extended von Guericke's electrostatic investigations in the last decade of the 17th century.

[143] In the General Scholium to the Principia Newton writes: "He (the true God) is eternal and infinite, omnipotent and omniscient; that is, His duration reaches from eternity to eternity; His presence from infinity to infinity. ….. He is not duration or space but He endures and is present. He endures forever and is everywhere present; and by existing always and everywhere, He constitutes duration and space."

[144] Henry Oldenburg (1619–1677) was a German theologian and natural philosopher who became secretary to the Royal Society shortly after its creation in 1660. He was founding editor of the Philosophical Transactions of the Royal Society which began publication in 1665.

missive[145] and makes it clear how completely, at least to English eyes, von Guericke's experimental work had been eclipsed by Boyle's. However it does include a fair-minded and neutral presentation of von Guericke's views on Space. Oldenburg writes:[146]

*"As to the space that is between those his (*sic*) Mundan bodies (the Planets,) he conceives it to be not any thing Material or Corporeal but a Meer Space, void of all body, which Space he defines to be as 'twere the Universal Vessel containing all Bodies, declaring herein his dissent from Descartes in whose opinion Space or Extension cannot be without an extended substance: whereas he (our Author) makes Space indifferent to the being or not being filled with Bodies.*

Treating of this Space, which he calls Void and esteems so in its own nature, he maketh it Immense and Infinite: and discussing that so much agitated Question, whether there be a vacuum, he concludes it in the Affirmative, asserting that not only all those parts of Space, to which the Effluvia or Expirations of his World do not reach, are void of all body, but also, that so much of Water, Air or any other thing as is exhausted out of Vessels, no other body succeeding in its room, so much there is of Vacuity there."

Oldenburg was on good terms with Newton and, at his instigation, Newton had been elected a Fellow of the Royal Society in January 1672 for his work on optics. Furthermore it was Oldenburg's custom, as Secretary, to be assiduous in keeping the Fellows informed of developments.

The second fact is that the earliest assertion of the concept of absolute space by Newton appears in the *De Gravitatione*. This critique of Descartes' *Principles of Philosophy* remained unpublished until 1962 and the date of its composition has not been established with any greater precision than "probably before 1685".[147] In language so reminiscent of von Guericke as to seem like a paraphrase of his views on the uncreated nature of Space, Newton writes:[148]

---

[145] E.g. "It will easily appear to sagacious and impartial Readers, to which of these two Gentlemen, Mr. Boyle and Mons. De Guericke, the Curious are most obliged, there having been at first but six Experiments made by the latter of them and published by Schottus in Arte Hydraulico-pneumatica about A. 1656." Nevertheless, Boyle again learning something from von Guericke, demonstrated the electrostatic experiments of Book IV before the Royal Society in November 1672 and February 1673. (Schneider p. 127.)

[146] Philosophical Transactions of the Royal Society. 1672: 7 5103–5106

[147] This dating is given in Janiak: *Newton Philosophical Writings* p. 12. (2004). Writing in 1981, Edward Grant in *Much Ado About Nothing – Theories of space and vacuum from the Middle Ages to the Scientific Revoutiion* (C.U.P.) p. 233 dates it to "probably completed between 1664 and 1668".

[148] Newton: *Philosophical Writings*. Edited Janiak. C.U.P. p. 25–26.

"Space is an affection of being just as being. No being exists or can exist that is not related to space in some way. God is everywhere; created minds are somewhere, and body is in the space that it occupies and whatever is neither everywhere nor anywhere does not exist. …. Lastly, space is eternal in duration and immutable in nature because it is the emanative effect of an eternal and immutable being. If ever space had not existed God at that time would have been nowhere and hence He either created Space later (where He was not present Himself) or else, which is no less repugnant to reason, He created His own ubiquity."

The arrival in Magdeburg of a young law graduate of Jena and Leipzig, Wilhelm Homberg, who in 1674 began practising as an advocate in the city, presented von Guericke with a last opportunity to communicate his scientific enthusiasm and to disseminate his views. Homberg, then 22, was inspired by his contact with von Guericke to abandon the law and devote his life to natural science. After studying medicine at Wittenberg, he finally settled in Paris where, in 1691, he was elected to the Academy of Sciences. Subsequently he became a teacher of physics and chemistry and the private physician of the Duke of Orleans. He made permanent contributions to the then infant subject of chemistry and died in 1715.

The Last Years

After the Treaty of Klosterberg, von Guericke remained a Bürgermeister for a further ten years. The inevitable infirmities of age began to afflict the hitherto energetic and active man as he entered his eighth decade. In his 74th year and aware of his failing powers he desired to lay aside the burdens of office and to pass his remaining years in tranquillity. On February 12th 1676 he was due once again to take over as serving Bürgermeister from Dr. Stiehler.[149] On January 27th he expressed his feeling to the Rat.[150]

"You are aware of my advanced age and that I am in my 74ᵗʰ year. This has left me not just physically weak but my memory has also been badly affected so that I am very slow to grasp the subject of discussions, the content of reports or the burden of grievances. These afflictions, not to mention the other frailties of old age, would be much exacerbated by taking on the leading executive role in the city's administration. It is better to give up of one's own accord than to take on responsibilities that one cannot properly discharge."

As so often before, his colleagues sought to dissuade him from resigning and to serve one more six-month term. On February 11th they were still insisting that he come to the Rathaus and embark on the new term of office. On February 12th von Guericke wrote to them once more. He reminded them:[151]

"One must bear in mind that for everything decline is inevitable and that no one can guarantee that at an age of seventy or more he will remain in full possession of his strength and faculties and be capable of discharging executive office. .... Accordingly I request the Rat not to impose on me beyond my capacity. Otherwise I stand ready and willing to render our city any possible service."

On this occasion the Rat complied with his request and Gottfried Rosenstock, who more than three decades previously had accompanied him to Dresden, took over as Bürgermeister. Six months later, at the expiry of Rosenstock's term, the issue of von Guericke's wishing to be excused the burden of office arose again. His colleagues had robust views about an appropriate age for retirement and were far from being exemplars of patient deference to the great man in their midst. Rosenstock proposed that, in view of von Guericke's pretended feeble-

---

[149] Dr. Ernst Stiehler served as Bürgermeister from 1670 to 1689.
[150] Hoffmann p. 176.
[151] Hoffmann p. 178.

ness, he (Rosenstock), Dr. Stiehler and von Guericke's father-in law Lentke should administer the city's affairs on a rotating month-by-month basis and that Lentke should serve first. Lentke's prompt rejoinder was that he, too, could plead the same excuses as von Guericke and expressed the opinion that von Guericke should be summoned to serve another term.[152] Stiehler concurred arguing that either von Guericke should serve as Bürgermeister or he should resign completely from the Rat. The upshot of these and further deliberations was the dispatch of a messenger to summon von Guericke to the Rathaus. On the grounds of having had a sleepless night, von Guericke declined their request.

Dissatisfied with this response, the Rat dispatched three of its members to attempt to persuade him to continue as Bürgermeister. When this, too, proved fruitless, the Rat finally decided on September 2nd by a majority vote to accept the inevitable and to spare him further solicitation on the matter. Though he had resigned as Bürgermeister, von Guericke remained a member of the Rat for a further two years. In the redistribution of civic responsibilities, which took place in February 1678, he was assigned a role overseeing the Rat pharmacy, presumably a post that made only modest demands on his energies. Not until September 1678 do the minutes of the Rat record him as emeritus, in view of age and incapacity.

His remaining years saw him fight one final battle. The issue was the personal and family immunity from all taxation and civic impositions, which had been granted in 1649 and confirmed in 1666 by the Kaiser and the Elector of Brandenburg. Von Guericke's immunity had become a source of resentment to his colleagues on the Rat and even to the wider population of Magdeburg. In the light of the hard-pressed

---

[152] The relationship between Guericke and his father-in-law appears to have become strained. In his will of 1684, Lentke declared: "Concerning my third daughter Dorothea, wife of Bürgermeister Otto von Guericke, who since her marriage has suffered great misfortune; God knows through whose neglect of her it has come to pass that she has lost the use of her right reason and remains without issue and without any hope of issue. However she will be entitled to an equal share with my other children. It is my earnest wish as her father that the said Dorothea will not receive anything at all to dispose of at her own discretion but only as my eldest son Stephanus, along with my son-in-law Herr Ambtmann Petersen and Bürgermeister Friedrich Andreas Eggeling as executors of this will see fit. My aforementioned daughter is not to have the power to transfer even the smallest sum to her husband Bürgermeister Otto von Guericke or to the son of his first marriage or to the latter's children through her will or in any other way." (Schneider p. 139)

circumstances of the city in a time of war against France their reactions to his position of privilege were perhaps not unnatural. In 1676 legal opinion was sought from the University of Jena regarding the continuing validity and scope of the immunity. On February 8th 1677 the response from Jena, running to some fourteen folio sides, was laid before the Rat.

The thrust of the legal advice was overwhelmingly that von Guericke's claim for complete immunity was without merit. The lawyers rested their conclusions on five main arguments. Firstly, the very concept of immunity was an inequitable one. A well-to-do man's refusal to shoulder a fair share of the obligations of citizenship simply increased the burdens on other, mostly poorer, citizens. Secondly, the immunity had not been freely awarded but that von Guericke had, in effect, extorted it from the Rat in 1649 under duress and hence it had no continuing validity. Thirdly, it had been awarded in recognition of von Guericke's diplomatic accomplishments but these achievements had proved to be illusory and could no longer be considered as a valid justification of a perpetual immunity for him and his heirs. Fourthly, the immunity had been intended to compensate him for the inability to earn a living owing to long absences on the city's business, but now that he was, in fact, overseeing his brewing and garden-produce businesses, the conditions under which the immunity had been granted no longer applied. Fifthly, subsequent to the granting of the immunity, von Guericke had purchased pieces of land which had hitherto been subject to taxation and which he now claimed to be covered by the immunity. Such a removal of sources of revenue was unacceptable to the city treasury.

Von Guericke replied to this legal battering within a few days. On February 10th, the Rat received from him a letter accompanied by a memorandum of twenty-six folio pages. It was the writing of an old man dwelling too much on the past, given somewhat to self-pity and lacking in generosity to the next generation. He denied any duress had been exercised when the immunity was first granted and claimed that his brewing and garden interests were insubstantial and their produce only for private consumption. However, he was mostly concerned to reproach the younger generation with having forgotten his services to

Magdeburg and devoted the bulk of the long memorandum to reminding them of what he had done for Magdeburg. He complained:[153]

"I have done all I can for the city. As you, the Rat and the Ausschuss, have frequently attested, I have, to the neglect of my personal affairs, spared myself no exertion or trouble. In regard to the loss of my salary from the Elector of Saxony[154] and to the foregoing of income due on my late father's properties at Alstedt and NiederRöblingen arising from my services to the city, I have borne greater losses than any recompense provided by the immunity."

From about this time the city exacted various amounts from him. This it could easily do by making deductions from payments of salary and pension due to him. Later, in 1680, as a prophylactic measure against the spread of the plague, he was required to quarter soldiers of the garrison. These infringements of the family's immunity, as they understood it, generated a steady stream of not especially edifying or interesting missives from both father and son, addressed to the Rat and to Friedrich Wilhelm, which continued, on the part of the former, to within a few weeks of his death.

In the summer of 1680 an outbreak of plague, which had been affecting Dresden and Leipzig, reached Magdeburg. To preempt possible infection von Guericke and his wife Dorothea left their home in January 1681 to join the family of his son in Hamburg. He was not to see Magdeburg again.

On April 17th 1686 he wrote a final letter to Friedrich Wilhelm complaining about the continuing exactions of the Magdeburg Rat. This prompted a letter of severe admonition to the Rat from the Elector dated May 7th. By this time von Guericke was on his deathbed.

The days leading to his death were recalled by the deliverer of his panegyric.[155]

"Weakening further with each passing day, he had, some days previously, on May 1st, been reconciled with God and had eagerly received the holy Eucharist as his viaticum. Finally he became so weak and feeble that he held to his bed and, amidst the prayers of his family and household, rendered up his soul on Tuesday May 11th at three in the afternoon. Thus he exchanged this troubled transitory existence for eternal happiness after a span of 83 years 5 months and 21 days. It was also the day on which, fifty-five years earlier, he had been compelled to leave his beloved native city and to see it go up in flames."

---

[153] Hoffmann p. 183.
[154] Von Guericke was officially in the service of the Elector of Saxony in the years 1636, after the Peace of Prague, to 1646 when the troops of Saxony withdrew.
[155] Hoffmann p. 236.

Hoffmann comments:[156]

"A gentle and not unwelcome death — von Guericke died of old age without suffering from any real illness — brought to an end in Hamburg on Tuesday May 11th a life that up to its last years had been so active. He passed away in the arms of his spouse, surrounded by his son and his grandchildren. His physical condition prevented the fulfillment of his wish to see once more his native city. Apart from his loss of memory, he remained in possession of his mental faculties. As profound as it was justified, was the grief of his family and of all who had ever been close to him or who had been acquainted with his virtues and excellences and his services to his city and to science."

On May 21st 1686 his body was carried in solemn procession to the Nicolaikirche in Hamburg. It was intended that interment at this church should constitute only a temporary laying to rest and that his remains would subsequently be taken by barge to Magdeburg for final burial in the crypt of Ulrichskirche where his parents had been interred.

What then actually transpired has only been clarified in recent years. It is the opinion of Hoffmann,[157] writing in 1874, that this transfer never occurred, owing to a state of civil unrest in Hamburg. Schimank, writing in 1936, notes:[158]

"The body was supposed to be later transferred to Magdeburg and buried in the ancestral crypt. The reports as to whether this actually happened contradict each other. None of them seem sufficiently authenticated to inspire confidence. We do not know where Otto von Guericke, one of Germany's finest men, was finally laid to rest."

The work of a more recent biographer, Ditmar Schneider, underwrites the currently accepted account of events following his death. He writes:[159]

"On May 22nd 1686 this son of Magdeburg set out on his last journey. …..The barge of the shipper Christoff Block, who must have received from Hans Otto several authorisations for the transport of a corpse, passed the customs station at Dömitz on June 15th. The shipper notified the station of the transport of the corpse of Otto von Guericke to Magdeburg and referred to an authorization document. ……. On July 2nd all the bells of Magdeburg tolled while the funeral procession made its way from the Grossen Münzstrasse to the Ulrichskirche to interment in the family crypt of Alemann-Guericke in the Johanniskirche."

---

[156] Hoffmann p. 196.
[157] Hoffmann p. 237.
[158] Schimank p. 61.
[159] Schneider p. 144.

Five days after his death von Guericke's house in Magdeburg was struck by lightning causing considerable damage to the property and to the experimental apparatus which had been stored there. Following the decease of her husband, Dorothea left the home of her stepson for her own residence in Hamburg in which she died ten months later in March 1687. Von Guericke's death did not bring to an immediate end the financial wrangling between his family and Magdeburg. His son took up the cudgels on behalf of his deceased father and the affair dragged on with claim and counter claim for another year and a half. A final settlement was reached in January 1688.

For some two centuries Magdeburg was careless of the memory of her greatest son. In 1759 his library was put up for sale by the von Guericke family. The city had first refusal but, pleading financial constraints, declined to purchase any of the books. Not till 1879, with the establishment of the Otto von Guericke School, was his memory honoured in the name of a Magdeburg institution. In 1890 the Alemann-Guericke crypt in the Johanniskirche was converted to a boiler room. No records were kept of the place of reburial of the bodies displaced to accommodate the new use of the space. Hence, today we do not know the final resting place of his bones. In 1862 Friedrich Dies, von Guericke's first biographer, called for the erection of a fitting memorial to this second Otto, who had earned the city's gratitude. After many delays a bronze statue was finally erected in 1907.

In the *History of Ideas* section a perspective is given on von Guericke's ideas in their wider historical context. Here only a brief summary is appropriate.

Thomas Kuhn coined the phrase "paradigm shift" to describe those moments in scientific history when the way forward seemed blocked and the path ahead only reopened by a radical reconceptualisation at a fundamental level. Von Guericke's claim on our enduring interest stems from the role he played in the first great paradigm shift of modern science. His combination of careful, ingenious experiments together with profound reflection proved the classic recipe for decisive scientific progress. Moreover, his achievements were accomplished in the face of the difficult circumstances of his life and against the authority not just of Aristotle but also of Descartes, the greatest thinker among his contemporaries.

He is primarily remembered today for his experimental work on the vacuum and on electrostatics. These should not be the sole source of his reputation. Against Descartes and the Aristotelian inheritance, he, through his idea of "incorporeal potencies", was a pioneer both of a scientifically respectable idea of "action at a distance" and of a theologically based idea of absolute space, anticipating Newton's "sensorium Dei" by a generation. This idea served the progress of science well for the following century until it was supplanted by a Kantian view of space as an inescapable feature of our perception. Kant's humanist views conformed more to the metaphysical and religious temper of the day but did not lead to any striking scientific progress. The decisive advance from both the seventeenth century theological, and the later Kantian, positions came in the nineteenth and twentieth centuries when mathematical developments allowed a new freedom and scope to the scientific imagination. Following the discovery at the beginning of the nineteenth century of the wave nature of light, controversy about the vacuum returned to the centre of the scientific stage. For a second time, the resolution was accompanied by a dramatic paradigm shift — that of Special Relativity — which again affronted the sensibilities of many and defied the cherished certainties of centuries. Though the circumstances of the second vacuum controversy are remote from the first, there are many similarities between the two paradigm shifts. Not the least of which is the enduring greatness of the principal architects of each — Einstein and Minkowski of the second, Torricelli, Pascal and von Guericke of the first.

Part II

This Part comprises a translation of the Dedication and Preface to the Reader of the Experimenta Nova and of Books II and III, in which von Guericke describes his reflections and experiments concerning the vacuum. The appendices contain translations of chapters from other books which are relevant to the topics discussed in Books II and III.

Otto von Guericke's

Experiments

(the so called "Magdeburg Novelties")
concerning

Empty Space

first published by Rev. Fr. Kaspar Schott of the
Society of Jesus and Mathematics Professor at the
Academy of Würzburg

but now, by the originator himself,

more fully presented and extended by various
other experiments

and including discussions of certain other topics —

the weight of the air around the earth, the natural forces, the
planetary system, the fixed stars and the immeasurable space subsisting
between, as well as beyond, these bodies.

Amsterdam
The House of Johannes Janssonius at Waesberg 1672.
(with the Imperial Privilege of his Majesty, the Kaiser)

Serenissimo & Potentissimo Principi ac Domino,

DOMINO

Friderico Wilhelmo

Marchioni Brandenburgensi,

S. Rom. Imperii Archicamerario & Principi Electori,

Supremo Borussorum Domino,

Magdeburgi, Juliaci, Cliviae, Montium, Stetini, Pomeranorum
Cassubiorum, Vamdalorum & in Silesia, Crosnae
Carnoviaeque Duci; &c.

Burggravio Norimbergensi,
Principi Halberstadiensi, Mindensi & Caminensi,

Comiti Marchiae ac Ravensbergii,

Domino in Ravenstein Lauenburgt & Butaiu &c.

Principi Augusto

Prosperitatem Perennem.

Most Serene and Potent Prince and my most clement Lord!

It has pleased the great and good triune God to manifest His majesty, wisdom and authority in the kings and high princes, whom He has placed over so many peoples on this Earth and whom He has given us to revere. Likewise it has pleased Him so to endow their natures that in the most serious matters, as if guided by an innate instinct, they display a god-like power expressed in friendly, wise and prescient discourse. Affairs, which to other mortals appear perplexing or inaccessible, seem to them simple and transparent. They count as well-spent the hours dealing with the concerns reserved for them alone and for their glory. Every epoch, recent as well as re-mote, gives ample witness of their splendid accomplish-ments. It is definite that certain ancient kings, giving free rein to their intrepid spirits, turned their minds to the highest of concerns and made the heavens themselves the object of their reflection. Their zeal and enterprise brought it about that the heavenly bodies, suspended above us as if on a high ceiling, became not just objects of sight but also of thought, and that the trajectories of bodies of stupendous mass, size distance, motion and orbits were studied.

Our times, too, show no slackening in the exertions of the greatest of princes as they underwrite initiatives directed to the acquisition of new knowledge. Such may arise from the princes themselves, or from the scientific investigations of those wise men with whom they surround themselves, or from the researches into unsuspected phenomena undertaken by those professional[160] scholars, to whom their authority and resources give sustenance, motivation, impulse and energy. Nor today do these great lords of the earth lack, nor up until the Last Day will they ever lack, the material for further pursuit of this study. No one will lightly deny that in the scrutiny of nature, there remains much to do both for us and for those who shall come after us. I call to witness the philosopher and rhetorician Seneca, who writes on this topic in his thirty-third letter.

"The men who have made discoveries before us are not our masters but our guides. The truth is open to all and is by no means exhausted. Much has been left for those coming after us."

Mindful of the truth of these words, I could not but enquire into the teaching about Space, the receptacle of all the aforesaid heavenly bodies, particularly as I had observed that this has not been satisfactorily transmitted to us, neither from the ancient nor from the more recent philosophers.

Through the good fortune of the age, it has been granted to us to make advances in the understanding of Space as in all other areas of knowledge. We have been favoured by being able to pursue our investigations more deeply so that the testimony of so many experiments leaves no room for scepticism and I am therefore not deterred by fear of publication. By the favour of the Almighty, all else needful has been given to me; a guide and sponsor is however still required,[161] under whose auspices it would be fitting to emerge from my home

---

[160] The Latin phrase is "successu exituque ex asse respondente". I have taken this as an allusion to the Great Elector's custom of paying scholars to undertake particular projects.
[161] This phrase "dux tamen et author nobis opus est" comes from a letter of Cicero (Ad Fam. 2:6:1.Cicero to C. Curio). The echo may be deliberate, or a semi-conscious allusion, but unlikely to be just a coincidence.

into the public gaze and into whose protection, as sacred vessels into a temple of honour, it would be appropriate to commend and dedicate this work on omnipotent nature. But such a one is to be found! For you, most Serene and Potent Prince Elector, by divine favour, are our sovereign lord and most humane father. Your protection is holy and sacred to us. We bow to your judgments and your slightest wishes compel our compliance. It was my duty to submit this storehouse of discoveries about nature, sprung from the soil of your territory, to you my lord and protector and, indeed, your excellence, manifested in your many great achievements, lays claim to this token of my loyalty. As your feats have been extensively memorialised by other pens, I make here only cursory mention of them. It is enough for me to record, now and for all time, that in addition to all your other deeds, you are a man of singular and gracious humanity. I say this both because of the favour my zeal for the investigation of nature has always found with your Serene Highness and because you, the most gracious and kind of men, have, of your bountiful liberality, honoured my work.

Most Serene and Potent Elector, I pray and beseech you, that you would take this endeavour of mine, such as it is and so deeply unworthy of the greatness of your majesty as it is, under the shelter of the prestige of your name, your sacred patronage and your protection. I pray that it might receive the light of your favour as if from the radiance of the sun. Of your graciousness, may it be permitted a share, which its own merits would not gain for it, in the renown of association with the shining rays of your excellence and power, famed throughout the whole world.

Most serene and powerful prince, most beneficent Elector, may God keep and watch over you. May He preserve, protect and defend your august House so that, playing its part in the Empire, it may rule its subjects wisely and receive increase of its authority: may He grant that it be forever safe, ever flourish and that it endure to eternity.

I remain your Serene Highness' most humble and devoted servant and subject,

Otto von Guericke.

OTTO von GUERICKE

Counsellor to the Elector of Brandenburg
Bürgermeister of the city of Magdeburg

Preface to the Reader

"The contemplation of nature, according to the Blessed Basil,[162] *is the antechamber of heavenly pleasure, the undying joy of the intellect and the gateway to serenity. It is the summit of human joy, the meeting place of the spirit of the exalted and that of the down-to-earth. In such contemplation, the soul, heedless of itself, and roused, as it were, from a profound torpor, enters upon a region of light and seems to take on the character, not so much of a man raised to heaven, as of a divinity come to earth."*

True indeed is that well-known couplet:

"If the hearts of men were to know the essence of things,
Power and authority would seem but a trifle."

Moreover, in regard to the knowledge of nature, rhetoric, elegance of expression and facility at disputation count for nothing. Galileo writes:[163]

"For in this regard, a thousand Demosthenes or a thousand Aristotles are laid low, just by a single man of moderate talent who has a better grasp of the truth. Therefore disabuse yourselves of the hope that there will be found men, more learned and well-read in the authorities than I am, who, flying in the face of nature itself, can make true what is false."

Thus, whatever is demonstrated by experiment or is discernible by the senses should take precedence over all theorising, however probable or plausible: for many things which, when tried in practice, have no validity, can seem true in argument or speculation.

In the Art of Magnetism, p. 570 Kircher writes:[164]

---

[162] St. Basil the Great (330–379). I have been unable to find the source of this quotation. St. Basil however speculated interestingly on many natural phenomena. For instance on the rainbow he writes: "When a ray of light, piercing the haze of clouds, comes to one of the clouds, then there occurs some distortion and the light returns to itself. Being multi-coloured, the ray gets unnoticeably coloured with different shades, in the unseen for us manner concealing the mutual influence of the unequal coloured parts. The reflections of all the coloured rays, seen together, are white." (Vol 3 p. 55. Collected Works St.Petersburg 1911)

[163] *Dialogue Concerning the two Chief World Systems.* Galileo Galilei (1564–1642) published in Florence 1632. The quotation is said by Salvati to Simplicio, the straw man advocate of Aristotelian opinions, on "The First Day". (v. p. 54 of the Stillmann Drake translation (University of California Press 1967)) Prior to this extract Salviati says "If what we are discussing were a point of law or of the humanities, in which neither true nor false exists, one might trust in subtlety of mind and readiness of tongue and in the greater experience of the writers, and expect him who excelled in those things to make his reasoning most plausible, and one might judge it to be the best. But in natural sciences, whose conclusions are true and necessary and have nothing to do with human will, one must take care not to place oneself in defence of error."

111

"Thus it is clear that all philosophy, unless grounded in experiment, is empty, fallacious and useless. What monstrosities are begotten by thinkers, otherwise men of very great and keen intellect, when they do not heed experiment. Experiment alone is the arbiter of disputed questions, the reconciler of difficulties and the one teacher of the truth. It holds a torch to the darkness and when issues have been resolved, it teaches us how to attribute true causes to phenomena."

Thus it is that philosophers who rely solely on their theories and arguments and who discount experiments, can infer nothing solid about how Nature is constituted. For the conceptions of men, if not based on experiment, are apt to stray as far from the truth as the sun is from the earth.

Very recently Gilbert Clerke has also recognised this. In the preface to his book *On the Fullness of the World*, he writes:[165]

"Natural philosophy formerly consisted almost entirely of uncertain and extremely dubious arguments which, decked out in elongated verbiage, were designed to deceive real philosophers and their other readers rather than to instruct them."

From this state of affairs, it came about that a man, just by controversially sounding off, might gain renown and an unjustified reputation for scholarship and would be listened to as if he were a philosopher of the first rank. Such a man would be looked up to as being of the highest intellect, when, in fact, he hardly made sense even to himself — especially when, in the grip of his delusions, he would deliver himself of whatever nonsense had just entered his mind.

But by the grace of the gods, certain scientifically-minded talents have at last shed light on the proper approach and pioneered a new method of doing philosophy that takes counsel from both reason and experiment. From their efforts two great hopes have been conceived. The first is that philosophers will seek the truth in its fullness and not just some ghostly shadow of it and the second, that dissension in the natural sciences will be laid aside and a close bond be established between investigations of nature and the science of mathematics. This will not even be the work of one generation, much less that of a single man. We should, however, not lose hope that, from a steady reliance of suc-

---

[164] Athanasius Kircher S.J. (1602–1680) was a German Jesuit polymath with wide ranging intellectual interests. The Art of Magnetism (*Magnes sive de arte magnetica*) was initially published in 1641. It followed an earlier work on Magnetism published in 1631, the Ars Magnesia.
[165] Gilbert Clerke (1626–1697) was an English mathematician and theologian. *De Plenitudine Mundi*, in which Descartes' work was reviewed, was published in 1660.

cessive investigators on this new method, the passing of time will reveal new secrets of nature and illuminate the darkness of error. We should not lose heart that Truth, like a bride entering on a marriage of the highest promise, shall appear among us in so far as our lowliness can bear her radiance and the wedding bells will indeed ring out.

Nevertheless, I have to say that it grieves me today that I still feel there is a need for disputes with their arguing and counter-arguing because the leaders of the new philosophy themselves do not agree on what, if anything, fills the Cosmos. They stumble on the very threshold of the new science.

For some time now philosophers have been in keen dispute among themselves about the vacuum. Does it, or doesn't it exist? If it does, what is its nature? In fact, once someone is in the grip of an idée fixe on this topic, he defends his opinion with an aggressive tenacity as if he were a soldier holding a position against an attacking enemy. The effect on me has been to inspire a burning determination to get to the truth of this so hugely contentious issue. My determination would not abate, much less subside completely, until I had found the spare time to carry out some experiments related to this issue.

I have, in fact, carried out such experiments and my efforts have not been misguided in so far as I have discovered various ways of experimentally exhibiting the very vacuum, whose existence has been so universally denied. Later, at the Imperial Assembly held at Regensburg in 1654, which I attended on municipal business, some enthusiasts for scientific matters heard something about these experiments and pressed me to give a demonstration. This I tried to do to the best of my ability. Then it transpired that, at the end of the Assembly, just as the final proceedings were underway, these experiments of mine came to the notice of his Imperial Majesty himself, as well to that of some Electors and Princes who were already preparing their departure. They wanted to see them before they left and I could hardly decline to gratify the wishes of such people. The person most of all taken by them, was the Most Eminent Lord Elector, Johann Philipp,[166] Archbishop of Mainz

---

[166] Johann Philipp von Schönborn (1605–1673) was a remarkable German churchman and politician. Having managed to protect the Archbishopric of Mainz, against the representations of the Swedes, from secularisation at Westphalia, his tenure as Archbishop (1647–1673) saw a period of rebuilding and consolidation following the depredation of the Thirty Years War and of seeking to resist the influence of the French and Swedes alike. Apart from his patronage of

and Bishop of Würzburg. So much so, that he insisted on having a similar apparatus constructed for himself. But since, in the difficult circumstances of the time, there were no craftsmen available to do this, he prevailed upon me to sell him the apparatus that I had brought with me to Regensburg and he then had it taken to Würzburg.

The Most Reverend Fathers of the Society of Jesus, who were teaching at the Public Academy of Würzburg, often tried out my experiments in the presence of the aforesaid Elector. They wrote them up and communicated them to scholars at Rome, asking them for their opinion. In particular, one of their number, Rev. Fr. Kaspar Schott,[167] Professor of Mathematics at the Academy, began to correspond with me about these experiments and to seek clarification on various details. This is how it came about that he added an account of these New Experiments as an appendix to his book on the mechanical & hydro-pneumatic arts, (published in 1657), calling them *Magdeburgica*, and making them widely available in printed form.

Indeed, after these experiments had been brought to public attention many others, in addition to the ones that I had earlier performed, were added. These were all published, again by the estimable Fr. Schott, in Book I of his *Technica Curiosa* which is entitled *The Marvels of Magdeburg*[168] (1664). Thus it transpired that, along with *Old Experiments of*

---

scholarship, his prelacy was also notable for the introduction of the reforms of the Council of Trent and for the outlawing, at the urging of the Jesuit Friedrich von Spee, of witch-hunting.

[167] Kaspar Schott S.J. (1608–1666) was a German physicist and mathematician. He was a student of Kircher and a professor at the Jesuit College in Würzburg. The allusion is to Fr. Schott's *Mechanica Hydraulico-Pneumatica*. He writes (p. 444) *"Aliud hic Machinamentum, priore ut operosius, ita longe ingeniosius, in medium produco. Auctor eius est Praenobilis & Amplissimus Dominus Otto Gericke, Patricius & Reipublicae Magdeburgensis Consul, eiusdemque ad universales Pacis Tractatus Monasterij & Osnabrugi Legatus. Excogitavit is paucos ante annos Machinam eo animo & fine, quem ex ipsiusmet verbis infra afferendis intelliges; obtulitq. Ratisponae in nuperis Comitiis Imperialibus [1654] Eminentissimo Principi Johanni Philippo, Archiepiscopo Moguntino, & Herbipolensi Episcopo, qui eam in Arce sua Herbipolensi asservat, ubi non semel, eodem Eminentissimo Principe praesente, artificium totum vidi, examinavi, scriptis mandavi"* (I am bringing here to public attention another apparatus, more effective and much cleverer than its predecessor. Its author is the noble and distinguished Master Otto Gericke, Bürgermeister of Magdeburg and its delegate to the comprehensive Peace Treaties of Münster and Osnabrück. A few years ago he thought up this machine. You can divine his purpose and intention in doing so from his words reproduced below. At the recent Reichstag at Regensburg (1654) he offered it to the most Eminent Lord John Philipp, Archbishop of Mainz and Bishop of Würzburg, who keeps it in his palace at Würzburg where on a number of occasions, in the presence of His Eminence, I have looked at it carefully and taken notes on it.)

[168] The title of Book 1 of the *Technica Curiosa* is *Mirabilia Magdeburgica sive Experimenta pneumatica Magdeburgi exhibita*. Von Guericke is alluding to the fact that the first section of the *Mirabilia*

Magdeburg, New Experiments of Magdeburg also appeared. There were also many others who wrote on these same topics. Indeed, almost all to whose notice they came, were moved to singular wonderment at those instruments and the effects they demonstrated. Fr. Schott gives testimony of this in the Pro-oemium to the *Technica Curiosa* (p. 3) when he writes:

"I do not hesitate openly to acknowledge or unabashedly to proclaim that I have never seen, heard, read of, or imagined anything more marvellous of that kind. Nor do I think the sun has ever before shone on even its like, not to speak of anything more wonderful. This is also the judgment of the most prominent and learned men to whom I have communicated these matters."

Fr. Schott is not alone. All the many treatises that, from various sources, have appeared on these matters have likewise been fulsome in their acknowledgments.

It was never my intention or desire to publish anything on this subject. What finally changed my mind was the utter discord about the vacuum, some supporting that concept and some assailing it, so that one's astonishment at so many differences of view and at the often bizarre ideas that people conceive, knows no bounds. In undertaking to produce an integrated treatise on the spatial vacuum, my intention was to diminish the influence of the plethora of perverse views, while, at the same time, meeting the desires of those who urgently wanted an account of these experiments and of the useful applications that might flow from a deeper knowledge of natural science. I brought the treatise to completion on March 14th 1663. In it, I did not want to correct or refute those diverse and mutually inconsistent opinions. To follow such a course would be unduly verbose as well as being tedious for my readers. (In Book III Chapters 35 & 36, I do however briefly consider at least the common objections explicitly put forward by the aforementioned Reverend Fathers & Professors in the Appendix to *De Arte Mechanico & Hydropneumatico* as well as those of some others.) Also, the publicising of antiquated or poorly thought out fancies of this kind could distract such of my readers as are not wedded to preconceived notions from deepening their experience and knowledge. They will

---

Magdeburgica is entitled *Experimenta Magdeburgica Antiqua* and the second section *Experimenta Magdeburgica Nova*. Both the *Mechanica Hydraulico-pneumatica* and the *Technica Curiosa* are dedicated to Archbishop Johann Philipp von Schönborn.

have freed themselves from misguided influences, will recognise properly carried out experiments and will consider issues with fair-minded truthfulness. When the facts speak for themselves words are unnecessary. There is no point in arguing with or quarrelling with someone who denies the witness of definite and palpable experiment. Let him hold whatever opinion he wishes and, like the moles, let him pursue the darkness. Mathematics isn't aggressive but its unhurried pursuit of the most inoffensive truths triumphs. The conclusions of other philosophical disciplines can be argued about because they lack the evident certainty which Mathematics has the power to give. Thus it is that the human spirit, after long wanderings through the whole range of studies, at last finds rest in the solitary certainty of Mathematics.

As regards the style of this exposition, eloquence and elegance of expression have not been my aim. Accordingly, if there are solecisms I would wish that they be overlooked. For we seek facts not words. Ultimately words are subordinate to facts, not facts to words. It has not been possible adequately to describe everything in words and, in the interests of brevity, much has either had to be omitted or rendered informally. As the old proverb has it:

"One should talk with the many, but disclose one's own mind to the few."

This work has been finished, as has been said, for more than these past seven years. However, partly because of illness and partly because of the relentless pressure of other concerns, I have been prevented from issuing it. In fact it would have continued to languish unpublished had not certain important figures, being convinced, like Lucian,[169] of the utter futility of knowledge extracted only from books and lacking experimental support, dragged me away from further procrastination and urged me to resist no longer the production of this work for the common benefit. I did not want further to postpone meeting their requests. However it is impossible to please everybody; so it is plausible to suppose that there will be no shortage of critics. As the proverb has it:

"Let no one delude himself that he will be spared envy and enmity whenever he thinks to treat of serious matters."

---

[169] Lucian of Samosate (c.125–c.180) Syrian-Greek satirist. His works have been translated into English by the brothers H.W. and G. F. Fowler.

As Seneca[170] says:

"Indeed, no mortal man is untouched by ignorance; we take this contagion from mortality itself. For when a man errs, humanity errs and wrongly to denounce something as an error on the part of an individual man is to injure mortality itself."

One should not reckon that anyone would be so fortunate as to produce a work free from all error. Indeed even as we point out the errors of another we ourselves often commit one. Therefore, where our assertions are not supported by experiment, we expect criticism from the wise and the good and if we should be put to rights on any point, we will accept their correction.

It is a central aim for us that the content of this book remain within the confines of the mathematical sciences and that it should not venture into other fields. It does not, for instance, concern itself with matters of faith but relies solely on mathematical argument and what is made manifest through experiment. However if anything that might cause offence has, perhaps in a moment of thoughtlessness or careless-ness, unintentionally found its way into this book, we hereby desire to retract it. We concede to anybody the right of disagreement and are ready ourselves to follow whatever more conforms to the truth. It only remains to say that, in our opinion, there will be no lack of subtle and observant minds, who, stimulated by this work, will in the future invest effort in deeper and perhaps more fruitful investigations. Farewell, kind reader, and may you look with favour on our endeavour.

Given at Magdeburg, March 14th 1670.

---

[170] Seneca (4BC–65AD) was a Roman Stoic philosopher and letter writer and tutor to the Emperor Nero.

Dedicated

to the most noble and accomplished

Master Otto von Guericke

On the publication of

Experimenta Nova Magdeburgica

To explore in thought the winding ways of nature
Is work for a wise and intelligent man.
But it was a worthier effort, reserved for a rarer talent,
To follow their twists and turns with his marvellous skill.
Venerable greybeard, all Germany has known you as a ruler,
Excellent alike in governance and in probing nature.
Anyone knowing you here in Magdeburg or reading your works
Will have become a witness to this which cannot be denied.
Indulge a jest. A book that proves the vacuum
Is indeed far from vacuous.

I have penned this short poem as mark of my great and
undying gratitude to the most generous of patrons. With warm-
est good wishes for a long life,

Johann von Gersdorff,
Nobleman of Lausitzer

LIBER SECUNDUS

DE

VACUO SPATIO

Book II
Concerning Empty Space

Chapter I – Why the author was led to investigate the Vacuum

No one will deny that in nature, the marks of Almighty God are to be most impressively perceived in the gigantic mechanisms of the Cosmos. Indeed, from Book I (v. Chapter 20 et seq.) we may particularly note the following.

The Earth is to be reckoned as nothing compared with the Sphere of Saturn

Firstly, the remoteness of the heavenly bodies — that of the sun of course, but also of the Moon and of the rest of the Planets — is incomprehensible. It is generally accepted that some of these bodies are of such enormous magnitude that their sizes are not just greater than our Earth, but are many times greater, by factors of ten, a hundred or even more. Is there a mortal man that can imagine or properly grasp the size of the Earth, which is of diameter 1720 (and thus of radius 860 and circumference 5400) German miles?[171] When, however, this is compared to the sphere[172] of the most remote planet Saturn, it is not even as big as a pea. Thus, while the relationships of these bodies to each other and their spheres can indeed be described by numbers, there is no mechanical device which allows them to be displayed on a chart or otherwise pictured.

The sphere of Saturn is tiny compared to the orbit which any near fixed star traces

Moreover, as this terrestrial globe is to the sphere of Saturn, so the sphere of Saturn is to be compared with that of the nearest fixed star. The following facts have been established. Not only are the fixed stars different from Earth and some of them so remote that they manifestly defeat the perception of alert and keen minds, but it is also the case that the nearest of the fixed stars (e.g. Canis Major or Lucida Lyrae) does not allow a parallax with respect to the radius of the earth. If it did allow a parallax — e.g. of two seconds — its distance from the centre of

---

[171] 1 German mile is approximately 7.6 kilometres. This gives a value of 6536 km. In comparison, a modern value for the radius r is 6357 < r < 6378 km., recognising that the Earth is not a perfect sphere.

[172] "Sphere" here is used to mean the orbit of the planet around the sun.

the Earth would be 103 448 times the radius of the Earth.[173] If indeed the parallax was only of one second the distance would be 268 965 times the radius of the Earth which is equivalent to 231 309 900 German miles. (This is in accordance with Scipio Claramons'[174] book on the universe which uses the inerrant sine, tangent and secant tables.) Since none can be perceived — not even the parallax of a nearer star with respect to the radius of the Earth — it is clear that no effort of human ingenuity will succeed in putting a bound to such a great distance.

There is no definite number of stars

As for the actual number of the stars, who can put a figure on it? With astronomical telescopes we can nowadays see many more than in former times and superior instruments allow sharper images of stellar nebulae which would otherwise be invisible to the naked eye.

There are many stars that are at least ten times bigger than even our sun

Even though the magnitude of any given star cannot be accurately measured, it nevertheless cannot be doubted that many of them are ten and more times bigger than our sun.

But bigger than all of these is that immense emptiness, also called Space or Expanse, containing all these spherical bodies, however many in number and however great in multitude. In comparison with Space, all these bodies, even taken together, are only as a tiniest part or atom.

The enormity of space between the bodies of the universe cannot be at all grasped by mortal beings

Long reflection on these matters and frequent puzzling over the construction of the Cosmos has brought me to the following position. On the one hand, the huge masses of these bodies and the distances between them, so immense as to escape real human comprehension, have somewhat intimidated me. On the other, the problem of the vastness of

---

[173] The parallax calculation corresponds to the calculation of the vertical height of an isosceles triangle whose base is equal to the radius of the Earth and whose vertex angle is two seconds of arc

[174] Scipione Chiaramonti (1565–1652) was the author of many works in Italian and Latin including *De Universo*, published in 1644.

the space that exists between bodies and extends endlessly has gripped me and imbued me with an unceasing desire to investigate it. Since everything is in Space, and since it provides a place for things to be and to continue to be, what could Space itself possibly be? Is it perhaps some heavenly material of the nature of fire — solid (according to the Aristotelians) or fluid (as Copernicus and Tycho Brahe think) or is there some fifth transparent essence? Or is Space empty of all material? Is it indeed the perpetually denied vacuum?

Chapter II – On Place and Time

Aristotle's definition of Place[175]

Generally philosophers assert that a vacuum is a place in which there is nothing. This makes it necessary to say something about Place and what it really is. Aristotle defines Place in the following ways.

"It is the surround of something in the way that an immobile vessel surrounds a body it contains."

"Place is the limit of the containing surface corresponding to what is contained."

"Place is the ultimate limit of a containing surface."

Other Definitions

According to other philosophers:

"Place is the external surface of a located body."

Alternatively:

"Place is the unmoving hollow surface containing a body."

However, the Philosopher himself acknowledges (*Physics* Book IV)[176] that many difficulties arise as to the nature of Place and how things are in a place. His conclusion is that not only is it problematic what Place is, but it is even an issue whether it exists at all.

The author's description of the meaning of Place

The truth of the matter is that Place is not something real in itself; but it is rather a certain definite and bounded region in which something manifests its presence with respect so some other neighbouring thing — when it is here, it is not elsewhere.

---

[175] In *Physics* IV, Aristotle provides an extensive discussion of Place (IV.1–IV.5), the Vacuum (IV.6–IV.9), Time (IV.10–IV.13) and the Vacuum. On Place he has this to say (IV.1 [209a/26]): "Again, just as each body is in a place, so, too, every place has a body in it." and (IV.2 [209b]) "Now if place is what primarily contains each body, it would be a limit, so that the place would be the form or shape of each body by which the magnitude or the matter of the magnitude is defined: for this is the limit of each body. .... Hence the place of a thing is neither a part nor a state of it, but is separable from it. For place is supposed to be something like a vessel — the vessel being a transportable place. But the vessel is no part of the thing. .... Hence we conclude that the innermost motionless boundary of what contains is place." (Translation Hardie & Gaye O.U.P)

[176] *Physics* IV.1

And so the common sense of mankind perceives each thing as being *somewhere* — that is, it locates it in some definite proximity or closeness to some other definite thing and calls this proximity Place. So, for example, the place of Peter might be in a certain room, the place of the room in a certain house, the place of the house in a certain street, the place of the street in a certain city, e.g. Rome. But where is Rome? It is in Italy. Where is Italy? In that quarter of the world called Europe. Where is Europe? It is on the surface of the Earth between Asia and America. The question "Where is the Earth?" can again be put and (according to the Copernican system) be answered "In its Sphere or orbit, which is between the Spheres of Venus and of Mars." Where are the Spheres of Venus and Mars? The reply is "Between the Spheres of Mercury and Jupiter." Once again someone can ask "Where are the Spheres of Mercury and Jupiter?" and somebody else can reply "Between the sun and the sphere of Saturn." Where then is the sphere of Saturn? Answer: "In the most remote part of all the planetary spheres around the sun." But where is the sun? Copernicus replies, "In the middle of this universe." But where is the universe? A response to this question will be given in Book VII below.

Place is not something real

Thus, when it comes to Place or asking where something is, one can keep on repeating the question. Nevertheless we can assert that Place is not something real in itself but rather a construction of the intellect, something imaginary and relative. It is a term always used with respect to something and thus having, as it were, a correlative or correspondent. When one is taken away, so is the other. When the thing assigned a place is taken away, so the place itself disappears and vice-versa.

Furthermore, just as Place is not something real, neither, in the same way, is Time.

What Time is[177]

---

[177] On Time Aristotle writes: (*Physics* IV.11) "But we apprehend time only when we have marked motion, marking it by 'before' and 'after'; and it is only when we have perceived 'before' and 'after' in motion that we say that time has elapse. ...... Hence time is not movement, but only movement in so far as it admits of enumeration. A proof of this: we discriminate the more or the less by number, but more or less movement by time. Time then is a kind of number. ....

The Peripatetic Philosophers define Time as:

"the number of motion with respect to the before and after"

and they acknowledge that Time is difficult to think about, but more difficult still to explain. Augustine is reported to have said:[178]

"If nobody asks me, I know what Time is; but if I want to explain it to someone who does ask, then I don't know."

In our opinion, Time is the result of a measurement of duration on bodies based on their motion around the sun. For example, duration on the Earth is measured according to its periodic or annual course around the sun; this measurement is called Time and is divided into years.

In dealing with phenomena on the Earth, measurement can be made using not just using the periodic motion of the Earth around the sun, but also the daily motion of the Earth itself (from which days and hours are defined). Thus Time can be said to be the measurement of duration by years, days and hours where these arise from the daily and annual motions of the Earth.

On Planetary Time

For the other planets and for phenomena occurring on them, duration will need to be measured according to their motion both around the sun and their own diurnal motion. The result of this measurement should be called the planet's Time.

It is clear, then, that time is 'the number of movement in respect of the before and after', and is continuous since it is an attribute of what is continuous."
[178] St.Augustine of Hippo (354–431) Confessions Book 11, Chapter 14.

Chapter III – On the Vacuum

Aristotle's definition of a vacuum[179]

Aristotle defines a vacuum as a Place not occupied by a body but which however is capable of being so occupied. Nevertheless, he does not admit that a vacuum exists as a natural phenomenon and gives the following argument against it.

Objection to the vacuum

A philosopher should not posit the existence in nature of something that cannot be the cause of any natural effect. The vacuum is not the cause of any natural effect and therefore the vacuum is not to be posited.

Resolution

The fact is that, taking a vacuum to be a place not occupied by a body but which is capable of being so occupied, there is a definite something, albeit not real but having, however, a relative existence, which is indeed the cause of very great natural effect. Consider, for instance, a body which is now here but could be elsewhere later and which could occupy with its presence a place (or rather a space) not currently occupied but capable of being occupied, e.g. when Saturn is in Capricorn, its place in Cancer is vacuous but capable of being occupied. This shows that a vacuum is the cause of very great natural effect. If a vacuum, or indeed empty space, could not exist in nature, but all of Space were occupied, one body could not go into the place of another nor possess a motion taking it from one place to another. However the experiments of Book III will clearly demonstrate that this is not the case. We shall show how both air and water rush into evacuated glass vessels and, against the normal order of things, rise up.

One might say that this happens because of the abhorrence of a vacuum. One may reply to this as follows. If the abhorrence of a vacuum is admitted to exist then the existence of a vacuum itself is admitted. For if a vacuum did not exist, neither could the abhorrence of it. How could abhorrence of something exist, without the thing itself being admitted to exist?

---

[179] In *Physics* IV.6–9 Aristotle discusses the vacuum at length.

From the above, someone opposed to Aristotle's position could now argue as follows. A philosopher should posit the existence in nature of whatever is the cause of some natural effect. The vacuum is the cause of the effect associated with the abhorrence of a vacuum, and also of the occupation of empty space by a body (for if there were no vacuum, nothing could be occupied) and of many other experimental phenomena. Therefore, philosophers should posit the vacuum.

Philosophers in agreement with Aristotle

Furthermore, as related by Plutarch[180] (Book I, Chapter 18, *On the Opinions of Philosophers*[181]) the generality of philosophers, from Thales to Plato have shared Aristotle's opinion. But Leucippus, as well as Democritus, Demetrius, Epicurus and Metrodorus[182] and others, admit the vacuum and assert that it is infinite in magnitude. For their part, the Stoics have asserted that inside the universe there is no vacuum, but outside it there is an infinite vacuum.

Other philosophers have concluded that the vacuum is the soul of everything, that it is the spirit of the universe. They think that it is incorporeal and intangible, that it neither possesses a form nor can a form be imposed on it, that it can neither be acted upon or act itself, and that its only property is that it can receive a body.

The opinion of René Descartes

---

[180] Plutarch (46–120) was a Greek historian, biographer and essayist who had an enormous influence on later European literature and drama. The work, *De Placitis Philosophorum*, which von Guericke attributes to him, dates from the 3rd or 4ᵗʰ century AD and, along with other similarly mis-attributed works, is now assigned, in default of knowledge of the true authors, to a "pseudo-Plutarch

[181] The pseudo-Plutarch writes (*The Opinions of Philosophers,* Chapter 18, *Of a Vacuum*): "All the natural philosophers from Thales to Plato rejected a vacuum. Empedocles says that there is nothing of a vacuity in Nature, nor anything superabundant. Leucippus, Democritus, Demetrius, Metrodorus, Epicurus say that the atoms are in number infinite; and that a vacuum is infinite in magnitude. The Stoics say that within the compass of the world there is no vacuum, but beyond it the vacuum is infinite. Aristotle says that the vacuum beyond the world is so great that the heaven has liberty to breathe into it, for the heaven is fiery."

[182] Metrodorus of Chios (4th century BC) was a Greek pre-Socratic philosopher and sceptic. He accepted the Democritean theory of atoms in the void. He is thought to have said "To consider that the Earth is the only populated world in infinite space is as absurd as to believe that in an entire field of millet only one grain will grow."

More recently a certain René Descartes, in his book *The Principles of Philosophy* (Part 2, Article 16 et seq.),[183] aligns himself with Aristotle in denying the existence of a vacuum. He gives as his reason:

"*because the extension of Space or internal Place does not differ from that of a body*".

He goes on to say: (*Principles of Philosophy*, Part 2, Article 18)

"*And accordingly, if it be asked what would happen were God to remove from a vessel all the substance contained in it, without permitting another body to occupy its place, the answer must be that the sides of the vessel would in consequence come into proximity with each other. For two bodies must touch each other when there is nothing between them and it is manifestly contradictory for two bodies to be apart — i.e. that there should be a distance between them — and this distance yet be nothing. For all distance is a mode of extension and cannot therefore exist without an extended substance.*"

The abhorrence of a vacuum is considered by the Peripatetics as one of the affections[184] of the universe

The Peripatetics count the abhorrence of a vacuum as being among the affections of the universe. They think that in the universe there is a perpetual procession of bodies each giving way to the next, and thus that there can be no corner of the universe unoccupied by some substance. It is because of this that the capacity for action of the heavens, being the highest body of all, can make itself felt, via intermediate bodies, on lower ones.[185] A frequently asked question is: "Could God make a vacuum?". Since a vacuum doesn't exist, how may it be said to be the

---

[183] Descartes writes (*Principles of Philosophy* Part 2 Article 16): "That a vacuum or space in which there is absolutely no substance is repugnant to reason. With regard to the vacuum — in the philosophical sense of the term, a space in which there is no substance — it is evident that such does not exist. This is so because the extension of space or internal place is not different from that of body. From the very fact that a body has extension in length, breadth and depth we are right to conclude that it is a substance, because we conceive it impossible that nothing should possess extension. We ought to form a similar inference with regard to the space which is supposed to be void — that since there is extension in it there is necessarily also substance."

[184] The Latin is "affectio" which might translate as a "tendency" or "inclination". In Book Delta of the Metaphysics Aristotle gives as a primary definition "A quality in respect of which something admits of alteration, such as white and black, sweet and sour, heaviness and lightness etc." C.S.Lewis (*The Discarded Image* p. 93) points out, the metaphors used in describing nature changed during the 17th century from the earlier "sympathies" "antipathies" "strivings" and "inclinings" to "laws". Von Guericke does not speak in terms of "laws of nature" as Descartes and later Newton do. Descartes may have been the first person to use the phrase "Law of Nature" in this scientific sense. (*Principles* II.37)

[185] This is an allusion to the mechanism whereby the rotations of the Primum Mobile was transmitted to the inner Spheres.

cause of so many observable effects? To the first of these questions Scaliger[186] replies that God could not have made a vacuum because He cannot make something manifestly dissimilar to Himself. The result of an act of creation is that something should exist. God could not create just nothing. To the second question the philosophers reply that it is not the vacuum but the abhorrence of the vacuum that is the cause of the above mentioned effects. The effects are brought about not because a vacuum does exist but so that it will not exist.

Experiments which are held to argue against the vacuum

Moreover, there are simple experiments which seem to support the idea that a vacuum cannot exist. For example, water, against its normal behaviour, rises when air is sucked out through a straw. Similarly, after the flame has been put out, flesh swells up inside the cupping-glasses[187] which are in frequent use by surgeons. When the air intake of a bellows is blocked so that air cannot enter it from any direction, it cannot be drawn apart. If a vessel with a fairly small inlet is turned upside down, water does not flow out of it. There are other similar experiments. Oviedo[188] rejects the speculation that a vacuum could be created by some angelic power. The above are the objections commonly raised by philosophers to the vacuum. We shall have more to say about them in Book III, Chapters 35 and 36.

We shall show, by many experiments described in Book III, that a vacuum can indeed exist in nature.

The opinion of the author as to what a vacuum is

We do not believe in a vacuum conceived as if it were something real but rather think of it as a privation or an absence. For example, darkness is the absence of light and blindness is the absence of sight but neither of these is something real. Likewise death is the extinction of a life but death itself is not something real. In the same way a vacuum is the privation of fullness. It does not however then follow that the pri-

---

[186] Joseph Justus Scaliger (1540–1609) was a French Huguenot, classical scholar and historical chronologist. His *De emendatione temporum* began the scientific study of chronology.
[187] A cupping-glass is a cup shaped glass in which the air was heated by a flame and which was then applied to the skin. As the air contracts, a partial vacuum is formed inside the glass.
[188] Francisco de Oviedo S.J. (1602–1651) was a Spanish theologian and philosopher and the author of an influential Cursus Philosophicus.

vation or absence (popularly called a vacuum) of this or that substance is something real.

Just as it is for fullness, so it is for the vacuum; there is always a pre-supposition of space or enclosure — a container of some sort that may be empty or full. (For simply to speak of a vacuum without considering or naming an enclosure or container, is to speak of nothing.) Similarly, when discussing bodies whether celestial or terrestrial, an enclosure or space — a container of some sort — is necessarily assumed.

Because this fact is not evident or easily understood, there has arisen a great diversity of opinion on the issue of whether and where there is vacuum or a plenum.

The container of the bodies of the universe is none other than universal Space, or the universal enclosure which contains everything. Of this we say that some region of it is full if a body together with its effluvia[189] occupies the region and we say that it is vacuous when no such body and effluvia occupy it.

The word "vacuum" on its own denotes nothing

Consequently, we do not speak simply of a vacuum without any further qualification (because that would be to speak of a nothingness which the mind is incapable of grasping), but of vacuous space. The recognition of this truth would benefit all philosophy.

---

[189] Von Guericke has in mind the Earth's atmosphere which he regarded as an effluvium of the Earth.

Chapter IV – On Space

Space can be understood in two ways

At this point we do not deal with Space, as ordinarily conceived, in its three-dimensional aspect. Normally one thinks about the size, width, or volume of this or that object or place or building or palace or field or district or distance and so on. Rather, we have in mind the Universal Enclosure or Container of all things. This is not to be thought of in terms of quantity — in terms of length, breadth and depth. Neither is it to be considered with regard to any substance, whether or not that substance consists of points, is capable of being cut into sections, can be divided indefinitely or has direction.[190] Nor should it be considered with regard to either an external or internal bounding surface, nor conceived as something that diffuses or spreads or expands, but as something which is infinite and which contains everything. Everything exists, abides and moves in it while it itself is not subject to variation, alteration or change.

Space should therefore be understood in two ways — either as it is normally conceived, or as the Universal Container of all things.

Description of Space

Space, conceived as the Universal Container of all things, is that in which each body subsists and has its being (here or elsewhere, according to the proximity of other objects) or could have its being. Furthermore, it is not displaced by anything. In particular it is not displaced according to the size of a body occupying a space, but is permanent, immobile, indivisible and everywhere in everything and throughout everything whether corporeal or incorporeal. Nothing gives it being, whether it be here or elsewhere (understood as above), filled or empty.

Space is not to be compared with any object

---

[190] The Latin is obscure. The text is "neque considerandum respectu ullius substantiae, vel punctim, vel sectim, vel divisim vel ex parte." The allusion probably is to Aristotle, Physics Book VI, where the continuum is discussed. Von Guericke's general point is that Space is real and objective but does not exist in the category of substance.

In other words, Space, understood as the container of all things, is all that is conceived by bare understanding[191] as not existing. It is not therefore some or other thing which can be seen, touched, heard or perceived by the senses, but rather something quite apart from every possible state of matter. Every material thing differs infinitely from Space so that no object either exists or could be made which might in any way aspire to be its equivalent.

Another way of looking at it is to say that Space is that through which all things are unified or that in which all things are perceived. (We could not even perceive ourselves except in Space). Accordingly Space is continuous, passes through and permeates everything. From Space all bodies take their magnitude. It subsists around everything, both outside and inside. It accommodates everything without distinction. It is all penetrating without, however, having any capacity for acting or being acted upon. Space itself has no place. (There is no Space of Space.) It is not part of anything nor can it be given a form or possess any quality or accident.[192] In Chapter 6 we shall have much more to say on this.

How is Space to be perceived?

It is definite that each body according to its volume and its three-dimensionality needs also a space for its interior without which it cannot come into being or endure. Suppose for example, there is a certain room in which there is no person or thing present except for the air. (We know that near the Earth's surface all of the space not filled by other visible bodies is filled with air.) But if someone were to enter that air-filled room, he would expel air according to the size of person he was, and would occupy with his own body that space which was previously filled with air. If he were then to retire from the room, either the air would come back again in his place or something else — e.g. a stone statue — could be substituted instead to occupy that internal space.

---

[191] The meaning of the Latin "omne id quod per nudum intellectum concipitur" is not transparent. Schimank translates it as "vom gewöhnlichen Menschenverstand". Von Guericke might be alluding to "natural understanding" as opposed to his "theological understanding", which he develops later.

[192] Von Guericke is using here directly Aristotelian language. If Space were a substance like iron it would be capable of having "form" imposed on it to produce e.g. a sword with certain qualities and accidents.

The space itself nevertheless remains unmodified and without any capacity for acting or being acted upon.

There is a great difference between a space and a body

As our experiments will show, the air, too, could be extracted by a suitable device, leaving everything else unchanged. Nevertheless the space corresponding to the whole room endures. So we have that one and the same space can be filled now by one body and now by another, and that one thing can come into the space left by another thing and also that the entire space corresponding to the room can be emptied of all bodies and also of the air. It thus follows, firstly, that there is a great difference between a space and a body which can fill the space at one point in time and not fill it at another and, secondly, that no body, per se, constitutes a space.

It also follows that the opinion of René Descartes, cited in the previous chapter, is wrong when it was asserted that:

"Space or extension cannot exist without a substance possessing extension."

(See also Book III, Chapter 9, Point 1)

Even though space cannot be seen or touched, it can nevertheless be simultaneously perceived by the eyes and apprehended by the mind. For example, while we are observing the distance or the interval between two towers or mountains it is easy to understand that the intervening body of air does not create the interval but that the interval exists in and of itself, so that if all the air were also removed, the mountains or towers would not become contiguous. Moreover, as we have said, our experiments will provide adequate proof that a space can sometimes be empty and sometimes filled.

In ordinary conversation Space is thought of as something separate rather than as something universal and all penetrating

It should also be noted (as we see here in Magdeburg) that one can often chat about space in ordinary conversation, but can only seriously reflect on it among the learned. People in general understand space according to the width or size of buildings or such like, even though it is actually something that completely transcends this idea.

Chapter V – On the intermediate space, existing between the bodies of the Cosmos, which is commonly called the heavens

Whether the space between the bodies of the Cosmos is materially or immaterially constituted?

The following question arises about the huge space between the bodies of the Cosmos — the Sun, the Earth, the rest of the planets and the fixed stars. Should it be considered materially or immaterially constituted?

We already have said something in Chapter 1 about the sheer scale of the distances, widths, depths and incredible heights associated with the emptiness of the space intermediate between these enormous bodies. In fact, if we wished to compare the volume of this space with the size of the Earth or any other celestial body, it just as astonishing how the size of the former, as acknowledged by experts in these matters, is unbelievably larger in comparison.

The space or expanse between the bodies of the Cosmos is commonly called the heavens. In Book I, Chapter 31[193] I discussed what, in the common opinion of philosophers, the heavens are, from what stuff they are constituted, how diversely this word is understood and the use of the word in at least five or six different senses.

1. It is used as in the phrase "the airy heavens" to denote the region within which the clouds and the meteors are born. Thus one speaks of the clouds of heaven, the birds of heaven or manna from heaven. One says that the heavens are calm, that rain comes down from heaven, that God adorned the heavens with his breath, that God conceals the heavens with thick clouds and so on.
2. It is used for the Sphere or orb of any of the planets.
3. It is used for the Sphere of the (supposedly) fixed stars.
4. It is used for the (fictional) crystalline Spheres.[194]
5. It is used for the (supposed) Primum Mobile.
6. Finally it is used for the Empyrean or the abode of the blessed.[195]

---

[193] See Appendix 1 to Book II
[194] The planets and the fixed stars were, according to the Aristotelian and late medieval model, embedded in transparent rotating spheres. See e.g. C. S. Lewis, *The Discarded Image* Chapter V or A. Koestler, *The Sleepwalkers*, Chapter IV. By von Guericke's time, this opinion had been discredited.

However the ordinary person, because he is unaware of these distinctions, understands the entirety of Space as one heaven and calls it all by this one name.

The opinion of the author as to what, from a philosophical standpoint, ought to be called the heavens

In our view, the truth of the matter is that the word "heavens" denotes an entity that is relative or stands in a relationship to something else. This is similar to what we have already said about Place. It is not of itself something separate and real but something relative, standing in a relationship to some other definite thing. It is because of this relationship that the name can be used. If the latter did not exist, the former could not be spoken of. For example, if the Earth, or some other cosmic body, did not exist, neither would its heavens (i.e. the space surrounding it) although that space would nonetheless exist. Suppose the Earth, or some other cosmic body, were destroyed, then its surrounding Space, which is its heavens, would also disappear. However the space that had been there previously would remain.

Before the creation of the Earth, since there was nothing to be surrounded, there were no heavens of the Earth. Once the Earth was created, so also were its heavens. From the neighbouring space, which was already in existence, the heavens of the Earth were made or arose and when the Earth shall perish, then so also will its heavens. Space however will remain.

What the heavens of the Earth are

From these considerations it follows that the heavens are really just the surrounding expanse or space, in which this Earth or any another cosmic body — both the physical body itself and the extended potencies it exerts[196] – subsists and in which the body executes its orbital motion.

---

[195] The abode of the blessed beyond the Primum Mobile was an elaboration of the Aristotelian model inspired by Christian theology.

[196] The Latin is "extensis virtutibus". Von Guericke understood the phenomena of electrostatics and the Earth's gravitational pull on the atmospheres as the "virtutes" of matter. In Book IV Chapter 1 he writes "Every created thing, especially the cosmic bodies, is constituted from its matter, its life (vita) and its innate powers. These powers are neither substance nor accident, but are effluents of cosmic bodies, which are inherent in them and which flow out of them."

For example, our heavens is that space in which the Earth together with its atmosphere and its moon annually goes around the sun and which is understood to extend as far as the range of their potencies. The heavens of the Earth are bounded by the range of the potencies of Mars and Venus.

The Sphere of the Earth

In other words, our heavens (or the heavens of the Earth) are not just the space surrounding the Earth — the space in which it happens to be at the moment — but comprises all the space traversed in its annual motion and thus it could even be called the Sphere of the Earth. This space is, of course, distinct from that of the Earth's neighbours, Mars and Venus.

Difference between space and the heavens — between external and internal space

Although indeed the heavens of any given body of the Cosmos is one and the same as its space, it nevertheless differs in that the word "heavens" is to be understood only as denoting external space whereas the word "space" applies equally both internally and externally. For internal space, which is within every body of this kind including the Earth, is not seen by us. External space can, as it were, be visually grasped.

How the intrinsic and the aforementioned extrinsic ideas of Space are to be understood

Thus we conclude that the space which a body of the Cosmos occupies, according to its size or 3-dimensionality, is its intrinsic space. Its extrinsic space is, by contrast, its heavens or the expanse from its surface to the remotest boundary.

The opinion of the author as to what the aether is

The heavens, the expanse, the external space of any cosmic body, and the aether, are all one and the same. The only difference is that the term "aether" should strictly be understood as the space outside the atmospheric space of a body, extending to the remotest heights and pervading the remotest regions. It has neither gravity nor levity.[197] It is not

---

[197] "levity" is a word of Aristotelian provenance used to describe the tendency of an element, such as fire, to rise.

forced upwards by the air, but is that pure space in which a cosmic body subsists. Thus in the same way in which for us Saturn exists in the aether, our Earth, as seen from Saturn, is in the aether. Between all cosmic bodies there is necessarily an intermediate space which, from the perspective of any one of them, is called its heavens. Similarly there are as many heavens as there are stars, although Space is a single continuum, and is, in fact, equally outside as inside these bodies. Whether Space is something material or immaterial is a question on which philosophers radically differ, as is to be seen from Chapter XXXI of Book I.

More recent philosophers do not admit the solidity of the heavens

However much philosophers of the past may have imagined solid orbs in the heavens, this opinion has been almost completely discredited among more recent thinkers on the grounds that the planets and comets could not move freely without bodies passing through each other. This is impossible.

Accordingly, Tycho Brahe and all his followers share the opinion of Seneca that there are no real or solid orbs in the heavens of the sort that most astronomers have dreamed about. They believe the heavens consist of a very rarified and transparent substance, such as an air or a liquid, or some invisible and very finely constituted substance having the fluidity of air. This substance, through which the stars journey like birds through the air, is permeable. Indeed, Tycho doubts whether the aether is even material while Kepler[198] says, in the *Epitome of Copernican Astronomy,*[199] (p. 54) that the entire space thought to be occupied by the aether can, without difficulty, be supposed empty. To this opinion we also subscribe for the heavens are indeed pure space and, in and of

---

[198] Johannes Kepler (1571–1630) was a German mathematician and astronomer. He was the first to discover that the orbits of the planets are elliptical rather than circular.

[199] *Epitome astronomia Copernicanae* was a three-volume work published by Kepler in the years 1617, 1620 and 1621. The Epitome contains his elliptical system of orbits and Kepler's Laws for planetary orbits. The facsimile is available on Google books. The text alluded to here, from Book I, p. 54, is:

"Id non posset fieri, si aether vel minimum densitas aut coloris haberet. Nam radii solis, cum per liquorem rubeum translucent, colorem colligant rubeum in transitu. Itaque si per Physicam luceret, astronomus totum aetheris spacium plane Vacuum posset supponere, nec immerito dubitaret Tycho Braheus an aetherem agnosceret materiatum."

itself, void of every material. The words of Ecclesiasticus (Chapter 43) seem also to lead to this conclusion, when they say:[200]

"Who could become sated of gazing at His glory? It is a magnificent height, a clear expanse."

The question as to whether this magnificent height or expanse of space is finite or infinite is one to which we now turn.

---

[200] The *Book of Ecclesiasticus* (or Sirach) 42:26 and 43:1. The Vulgate is "Quis satiabitur videns gloriam ejus? Altitudinis firmamentum pulchritudo eius est." The translation from the Greek text given in the New Jerusalem Bible is "Who could ever grow tired of gazing at his glory? Pride of the heights, a clear vault of the sky."

Chapter VI – Whether Space, the universal container of all things is finite or infinite

We are going to revisit (v. Book I, Chapter 35)[201] the topic of space beyond the Cosmos which is also called[202] Imaginary Space. It will again be evident how diverse are the opinions of philosophers.

Aristotle considered that outside the heavens of the stars there is absolutely nothing[203]

Aristotle explicitly asserted that beyond the heavens of the fixed stars, (which for him was the highest heaven — in other words, the substance underpinning the turning of the Primum Mobile) there was neither place, nor time, nor a vacuum but absolutely nothing.

I understand this in the following sense. There is no doubt that if, outside the Cosmos, there is just infinite nothingness, then there is neither place nor time nor a vacuum, because place presupposes a proximity to some other thing. If there is no such other thing, there is no proximity and, therefore, no place. Time is the distinguishing of duration. Because, however, in infinite nothingness there is truly no duration and therefore much less so is there the distinguishing of duration. A vacuum is an empty space and if we are talking about an infinite nothingness, then there is neither a vacuum nor empty space.

About absolute nothingness, nothing can be said or thought

Can indeed absolute nothingness exist or be spoken about? Can what does not exist be contemplated or imagined? The next chapter will illuminate these questions.

---

[201] See Appendix 5.

[202] Von Guericke is probably alluding to a Peripatetic phrase encapsulating Aristotle's opinion that such space was merely infinite in thought. Of the misguided considerations that lead people to believe in the infinite Aristotle writes: "But above all, the most convincing consideration (because no one finds it easy to cope with) is that number and mathematical magnitudes and the region beyond the heavens seem to be infinite because they do not give out in our thought." *Physics* III.4 [b22]

[203] For Aristotle "nothing" really did mean nothing. He writes (*De Caelo* Book I, Chapters 8, 9 [279a]): "Outside the heavens there is neither place nor void nor time. Hence whatever is there, is of such a kind as not to occupy space nor does time affect it." His idea of the Cosmos, like the mathematical concept of a manifold, does not assume an embedding in a flat ambient space.

Philosophers generally think that outside the heavens there is Imaginary Space

Most philosophers do indeed admit that the space outside the Cosmos is imaginary. This is evident from many passages in the above mentioned last chapter of Book I. Nevertheless many of them say that it is something wholly fictitious — in other words, it is nothing, but understood in a different sense from nothingness itself. Thus they conclude that before the creation of the Cosmos, as there were no minds to imagine anything, there was therefore no Imaginary Space.

Since they maintain that there was nothing, one may ask why, against Aristotle, do they fancy that there was, at the same time, space. For if there is nothing (taken in the sense of Aristotle), nothing to be wide, broad or deep, then there cannot be space. Therefore Imaginary Space is just nothingness, so let it be nothingness.

Other thinkers say that this extra-cosmic space is something devoid of anything real and that it is the same as a spatial vacuum taken in our sense.

The Coimbra School[204] takes the view that this space is as equally inside as outside the heavens and has existed from eternity. The action of God on it is manifest through His immeasurableness,[205] rather than as it is with a real entity. (v. Book I, Chapter 35[206])

From this it necessarily follows that if God is outside the Cosmos in an infinitely extending Imaginary Space, then God is Imaginary Space. It follows because God does not stand in need of any object and consequently not of space. Space is of His very nature and as He is immeasurable so space is also, of its nature, immeasurable.

Lessius has identified Imaginary Space with God

---

[204] The Jesuits at the College of Coimbra in Portugal produced a series of commentaries on Aristotle in the late 16th and early 17th centuries.
[205] The Latin is "Connimbricensibus constat .... Deum actu in illo, non ut aliquo ente reali, sed per suam immensitatem esse."
[206] v. Appendix 4.

According to Lessius[207] (v. Book I Chapter 37)

"Imaginary Space is God Himself, who in accord with His immeasurableness, is everywhere — that is to say, of necessity diffused infinitely."

For if anyone were to transcend all the heavens and search in the space that he fashions by imagining what doesn't exist, he would undoubtedly find God.[208] However if God is Imaginary Space, is He not even more so real space?

The opinion of theologians about Imaginary Space

Those who follow the theology of the Schools hold that, in actuality, there is indeed but one Cosmos. However, there could have been many. Their general view is that God could indeed have created cosmoses or other bodies of arbitrary magnitude in space. They do not admit that there was any primordial abyss, in other words any space before the creation of bodies, but think that space, i.e. the very receptacle of all bodies, was necessarily co-created along with bodies.[209]

The author's response to this type of opinion

But by the very fact that they say "bodies could have been created in space" they admit the existence of place and of the abyss (or space) and that these are all antecedent to the creation of any body. Indeed if space had been created along with matter and had not been antecedently diffused all around it, a body would not have an external realm in which it could move, much less follow its natural motion. Indeed it would be necessary for God to create a new space for the motion of an arbitrary body from place to place. Likewise it would follow that when a body is raised, space would also be simultaneously raised. This, however, goes

---

[207] Leonard Lessius S.J. (1554 –1623) was a Belgian Jesuit and professor of theology at the Louvain 1585–1600. His best known work, *De Iustitia et Iure,* is on commercial ethics. (Catholic Encyclopedia) His *De perfectionibus moribusque divinis libri XIV* was published at Antwerp 1620.

[208] Von Guericke's meaning is obscure. The Latin is "Si enim quis omnes Caelos transcenderet, & in Spatio, quod imaginando format quod non sit, quaereret, Deum certe inveniret." The next sentence develops the argument towards von Guericke's final opinion.

[209] This view was classically expressed by Augustine, Confessions 11:5. "You certainly did not create heaven in heaven or earth in earth, nor in air nor in water because these pertain to heaven and earth; nor did you create the whole universe in the whole universe because there was no "where" that had been made before it was made so that the universe might be."
(neque in universo mundo fecisti universum mundum, quia non erat ubi fieret antequam fieret ut esset).

against the evidence. For when any particular body is destroyed, e.g. when a tower collapses, the space which it used to occupy remains and other edifices can be raised in the same space. Similarly, when a man leaves a room, the space, which he had been occupying, remains and can be occupied by someone else. Likewise air extracted from a glass vessel leaves a space behind it in the vessel, into which other air, water or similar fluid can rush. We conclude that space does not take its existence from corporeal substance but is indeed something autonomous, immobile and omnipresent.

The opinion of René Descartes on Imaginary Space

René Descartes' view is that Imaginary Space is actually something real and that this Cosmos, or the totality of corporeal substance, has no limits on its extension. (This is clear from several passages cited in Book I Chapter 35.[210])

This opinion is false

Throughout the whole of our treatise we shall demonstrate in manifold ways that this opinion is false. Moreover it is idolatrous to hold that any individual thing is infinite and immeasurable. God alone recognises no limits on his extension.

The opinion of the author on Imaginary Space

We shall now come to the question at issue. Is it or is it not the case that there is space outside the Cosmos and, if there is, is it finite or infinite? Since it definitely is the case that the Cosmos has an ultimate boundary, the human mind is led by its spirit of curiosity to investigate this boundary. What is it, in the last analysis, that contains or surrounds all that is? Is it the Primum Mobile (which I think is a fiction) or the Waters that are believed to be above the heavens or the Empyrean Heaven or is it something else?

Assume, in accordance with the opinion most commonly held, that outside the Cosmos there is just nothingness, taken in the sense of Aristotle. Then, if someone were to come to the ultimate boundary of the Cosmos, could he, from the outermost surface of this final heaven,

---

[210] v. Book I Chapter 35 translated in Appendix 5.

stretch out his arm or could he throw a javelin or a stone further into that nothingness? Or could he not?

Suppose the first alternative — that he could. There would be nothing in the way and so, precisely because nothing obstructs his action, there would be space and consequently there would be something. For if there were no space there, the stone could not be thrown further or the arm extended since nothing can be projected into, nor anything abide in, what doesn't exist. What doesn't exist has neither breadth nor width and is absolutely incapable of receiving anything.

Now suppose the second alternative — that he couldn't. There would be some obstacle in the way or something stopping one thing from occupying the place of another. But the cause of the blockage would necessarily be something hard and physical. Therefore there would be something outside the final boundary of the universe, for nothingness cannot be an obstacle; nor can an obstacle be called a non-being. One might argue: "It is not a body or something else that is the obstructing agent but nothing itself. In other words, it is the very absence of space and place that is providing the obstacle. It is its nature to repel, just as it is the nature of a hard body to repel a javelin or a stone."

What the absence of place is

But who can make any sense of something that does not exist but yet could repel and possess some natural capacity for offering resistance? The very evidence of our eyes shows us that a lack of space or place for one body is simply just another body in the way that prevents the first occupying the space of the second. However if one body is removed the other can occupy its space. Furthermore, as it cannot be denied that the Divine Essence is infinite, immeasurable and outside the Cosmos, it stands more to reason that what is immeasurable in breadth, width and depth is to be thought of in terms of space or expanse and not in terms of an infinite nothing. It will be seen in the next chapter that such an infinite nothing doesn't really exist.

It follows that a javelin or a stone, unless it is prevented by another body, can be thrown further and this can be repeated indefinitely. On the one hand, the throwing of a javelin or a stone can be continued beyond the Cosmos and there is nothing preventing this. On the other hand however, any throwing of this kind cannot be accomplished except in space.

Although there is nothing outside the Cosmos, space nevertheless extends infinitely

From this we can draw two conclusions. The first is that the nothingness outside the Cosmos and space are one and the same and that the so called Imaginary Space is actually the real space. For Imaginary Space (in the general opinion of the philosophers) is nothingness. However, nothingness is space and therefore the space which they call imaginary is real. Nor does the objection that whatever is imaginary is not a real or definite entity have force. While it is the case that some imaginary things are indeed not real, we nevertheless have to, at least, imagine the things we have not actually seen or which exceed our ability to take them in. For example, someone who has never actually seen Rome, or a pure spirit, or an exotic animal, or something similar, has to imagine it. In the case of the Infinite, which nobody can truly understand, he must make at least a best effort to imagine it in some way or another. However it does not follow that Rome or a pure spirit or the Infinite is not something real and definite.

Space is immeasurable

If the throwing of a javelin or a stone can be continued indefinitely, then the fact is that no bound can be set on where it is. We come here to our second conclusion. This extra-cosmic space is an extension and an expanse that is homogeneous in direction and without any bound. Consequently it is infinite and immeasurable. However, if it is infinite and immeasurable the question arises as to what it really is. But before we reply to that question, it will first be necessary to look into "the things that are".

Chapter VII – Concerning what IS and what is said NOT to be

There are only two ways of being and there is no third possibility

Everything that exists, is either something that has been created or is something that has not been created. A third category — as if one might say "Everything that is, has either not been created, or has been created, or is nothing" — is not admissible. For nothing is the denial of one of these possibilities and the affirmation of the other. Therefore, there is no third category of being. So what is not a created something is an uncreated something. Vice-versa, what is not an uncreated something is a created something. There is no third category — neither in the mind nor in the intellect nor in speech.

The nature of an uncreated something

In point of fact there is something that has not been created. It is different in essence to all created things and is infinite, immeasurable and eternal. It pre-existed creation, and subsists autonomously, taking its being from its own self. It contains everything and is itself not contained by anything.

The nature of a created something

A created object does not take its being from itself but from something that is uncreated and in which it also subsists and to which it owes its entire being. Such an object is finite and exists in accord with its substance, its way of being and its innate potencies. (This is true even in the case of a spirit, as we shall discuss in the last chapter of this book.)

The nature of what is associated with a created something

While much else is associated with a created object, these associations are not themselves individual created things (for if the original thing did not exist neither would the associations) but are accidents of the object, whether internal or external, intrinsic or relative. Of particular note are[211] quantities, qualities, motions, the capacity for acting on other

---

[211] This list is Aristotelian. Many of these terms are discussed and defined in Book Delta of the Metaphysics. In E.g. on "privation" Aristotle writes: "When something does not have one of the things that it is natural for things to have, even if it would not be natural for the something in question to have it. For example a plant is said to be **deprived** of eyes." On "accidents" he writes "What pertains to something and what it is true to assert of it, but neither necessarily nor for the most part". (Penguin Classics: Hugh Lawson-Tancred Translation)

things, the capacity of being acted upon by other things, potentialities, relations, images in the mind, privations, potencies possessed as accidents, numbers, times, places, names, words and so on.

These are what objectively exist and to these, all that is, can be traced back.

The word "nothing" cannot be intelligibly predicated simultaneously of both these categories of being

There are only two categories of being — but no third. Consequently, where there is nothing of creation or its associates, the uncreated exists. The opposite also holds. Where there is nothing uncreated, the created exists. For nothing, with an intended meaning of a region simultaneously void of both the created and the uncreated, is unintelligible and cannot be the subject of discourse. The word can be used only as the negation of one category of being and consequently the affirmation of the other. In particular, as we have mentioned in the preceding chapter, the word "nothing" is used in an Aristotelian sense to refer to what is outside the Cosmos, as if the intention was to speak intelligibly of something neither created nor uncreated. However as there simply is no third possibility, intelligibility requires that the reference is to one out of the two options. In this context, we also note the common use of the word "nothing". Here no reference to an absolute nothing is intended, for there is always some understood context for the relative use of the word. For example, suppose someone says that a chimera is nothing. He is speaking in the context of animals. He does not mean that chimera is absolute nothing, but just that among animals there is no chimera. What a chimera actually is, is a mental image of the sort that is associated with a created object.

Both possibilities cannot be simultaneously rejected. Consequently, in the present context, it is one and the same thing to say "Outside the Cosmos there is nothing" and to say "Outside the Cosmos there is the uncreated". Apart from this Cosmos, (one supposes) there are no others and what does not exist cannot be said to have been created. Therefore what is outside the Cosmos is uncreated, for what is not a created something is an uncreated something and emphatically not simply nothing.

Thus suppose it were to be asked what should be our conception of what there was before the foundation of the Cosmos. One person might reply "There was something uncreated", and another, "There was nothing". Either response would be right. The latter is using the word in a relative sense — i.e. relative to created objects. He is quite right — there was nothing of creation then. However the uncreated existed then and exists now.

To speak of "nothing of creation" is the same as to speak of the uncreated

Likewise we say that heaven and Earth were created from nothing, i.e. from nothing of creation, which just means from the uncreated. Similarly when we say that everything has been created from nothing and has thus been accommodated by, and established its existence in, this nothing, we just mean by and in the uncreated. For where now created objects exist and continue to be, formerly there was nothing. They have been accommodated in nothing, i.e. in the uncreated. They could not have been accommodated in any created object because none existed. For if a created object had then existed there wouldn't have been nothing. Even if one had existed, one object could not have been accommodated in another. Consequently everything was accommodated in nothing, i.e. in the uncreated.

Therefore it is in nothing that anything you care to mention exists. If God were to reduce to nothing the machinery of the Cosmos that He has created, nothing (as it was before the creation of the Cosmos) would endure — in other words, the uncreated. The uncreated has no precursor. We say the same thing about nothing. Nothing contains everything. It is more precious than gold. It knows nothing of coming to be or ceasing to be. It gives more joy than the sight of a radiant light. It is nobler than the blood of kings. It is comparable to heaven. It is higher than the stars, more powerful than a thunderbolt, perfect and blessed in all its aspects. Nothing always makes itself manifest. The jurisdiction of kings ends where nothing begins. Nothing suffers no injury. According to Job,[212] the Earth is suspended above nothing. Nothing is outside

---

[212] Job 26:7. In the third cycle of Discourses, Bildad of Shuah says "He it was who spread the North above the void, and poised the earth upon nothingness". (New Jerusalem Bible)

the Cosmos. Nothing is everywhere. One says that a vacuum is nothing as one also says that Imaginary Space, and also space itself, is nothing.

Chapter VIII – Whether space, or the universal container of all things, is something created or uncreated

Since the vacuum, Imaginary Space and space itself are all nothing and nothing (as was shown in the preceding chapter) is just the denial of one category of being and the affirmation of the other, it follows that the vacuum, Imaginary Space and space itself all conform to one of the two possibilities. They have either been created or they are uncreated, there being no third option.

The opinion of Jacques du Bois, who, instead of space, thinks there is universal vacuum outside the Cosmos, which he calls the Divine Essence

It is acknowledged by Jacques du Bois,[213] a preacher at Leyden, that the vacuum or Imaginary Space or space itself is not created. On page 39 of his publication, *Theological-Astronomical Dialogue*, (against Galileo Galilei, Phillip Landsbergius[214] and others who put the sun in the middle of the universe and have the Earth revolve around it) he writes:

"He who denies the vacuum above the most remote Heavens, contradicts the infinitude of the Divine Essence. For if the highest of the Heavens cannot, by the testimony of Solomon (Kings 1:8:27)[215] contain God, then outside the heavens some location (Ubi) must exist which is the abode of the Divine Essence and which cannot be contained within any bounds. As this location does not contain any body, we normally call it the vacuum. Accordingly, before the creation of the Cosmos, God abided, in fact was infinitely omnipresent, in this boundless abyss which could not have been filled by any finite body however big, such as the highest Heaven. (Note that this author concurs with Aristotle that the heavens constitute a

---

[213] Jacques du Bois (d. 1661). His *Dialogus Theologico-Astronomico* was published at Leyden in 1653. The full title is "Dialogus theologico-astronomico in quo ventilator quaestiones astronomicae; an Terra in centro universi quiescat & Sol aliaque luminaria coelestia circa eam moveantur: an vero, Sole quiescente, Terra circa eam feratur: et ex Sacris Litteris Terrae quietem, Soli vero motus competere probatur adjuncte refutatione argumentorum astronomicorum, quae in contrariam proferri solent." (Theological-astronomical dialogue in which astronomical questions are reviewed: whether the Earth is at rest in the centre of the universe and the sun and the other radiant heavenly bodies are moved around it or whether, the sun being at rest, the Earth is borne around it. It is shown to follow from Sacred Scripture that the Earth is at rest and that the sun moves. Also adjoined is a refutation of the arguments of astronomers who customarily profess the opposite.) In 1655 he published a work *Veritas et auctoritas sacra* (Truth and sacred authority).

[214] Phillip Landsbergius (1561–1632) Dutch pastor, astronomer and doctor.

[215] "Yet will God really live with human beings on earth? Why, the heavens, the highest of the heavens, cannot contain you. How much less this temple built by me!" (New Jerusalem Bible Kings 1:8:27)

substance.) To agree with René Descartes that the corporeal Cosmos has no limits to its extension is effectively to assert that Creation is infinite — a view that is both impious and against nature.

Jacques du Bois conflates "where" with "space"

From the above it is very clear that Jacques du Bois thinks that God is omnipresent in some place where there is a vacuum. Only he hasn't expressed himself well in saying *"Therefore there is some location which is the abode of the Divine Essence ..."*. What he ought to have said is the following. Therefore there is a region or a space, not 'which is the abode of', but 'which is itself' the Divine Essence. For God cannot be contained in any location, nor in any vacuum, nor in any space, for He himself is, of His nature, location and vacuum, a region void of any created thing, and space, the universal container of all things.

Father Kircher, while admitting that space is filled by God, also allows that He Himself is that space, for God cannot be contained by anything except Himself

On the other hand the famous mathematician based at Rome, Fr. Athanasius Kircher of the Society of Jesus, although a fierce opponent of the Copernican theory of the universe and a man who denies that a vacuum can exist in nature, nevertheless expresses himself about Imaginary Space in the following words. (*Ecstatic Journey*, Dialogue II Chapter 9)[216]

---

[216] Fr. Athanasius Kircher. (1602–1680) *Iter Ecstaticum* (Ecstatic Journey) of 1656 sought to explain what the cosmos looked like in an imaginative dialogue between an angel and a philosopher who discussed its composition while traveling throughout the heavens. In the introduction to the second edition (1671) the author writes:

"Iter extaticum coeleste, quo mundi opificium ... novâ hypothesi exponitur ad veritatem, interlocutoribus Cosmiele et Theodidacto; hac secundâ editione prælusionibus & scholiis illustratum, ac schematismis necessariis, qui deerant, exornatum, nec non à mendis ... expurgatum, ipso auctore annuente, a P. Gaspare Schotto ... Accessit ejusdem auctoris Iter exstaticum terrestre & synopsis Mundi subterranei." (An Amazing Journey in the Heavens, in which the design of the Cosmos is, using a new hypothesis, truthfully explained in dialogues between Theodidactus and Cosmiel. This second edition has been enhanced by introductions and scholia and supplemented with necessary diagrams, which were lacking. Errors have been also corrected by Fr. Kaspar Schott, with the approval of the author. The amazing terrestial journey of the same author has been added along with an account of the subterranean world.) The cited passage appears on p. 437 in Chapter 9 (*De Spatio Imaginario*) of Dialogue II, (*De Providentia Dei in Mundi Opificio elucescente* — On the Providence of God shining forth in the Design of the Cosmos). The words

"Since God is infinite in his actions, it is necessarily the case that He fills the entirety of vacuous and empty space, which one thinks of as immeasurable and infinite, with His own substance and presence. He banishes from it all nothingness, vacuum, emptiness or non-being. Thus outside the Deity there is necessarily no possibility for nothingness, or vacuum or emptiness. If there were nothingness outside God, one would be forced to admit that the Deity is hardly infinite at all as the Divine Substance would be constrained and hemmed in by that nothingness. This is impossible. Thus it again follows, that the Cosmos is accommodated not in nothingness but in the Deity. When one imagines the Space outside the Cosmos as being of the Imagination, one conceives it, not as nothing, but as the fullness of the Divine Substance spreading out infinitely. He who has created and accomplished all things gathers His creation unto Himself and His fullness. He draws it in, supports it, enfolds it, encloses it and preserves it."

Consequences of Fr. Kircher's opinion

From these words the following conclusion is inescapable. Space, the vacuum and the emptiness, which outside the Cosmos we conceive of as being immeasurable, are not nothingness or non-being, taken in the sense of Aristotle, but are simply void of anything created — that is, they are uncreated. Rev. Fr. Kircher is mistaken when he writes that God fills with his substance and presence all of Imaginary Space — i.e. the vacuum or emptiness, whose very existence he himself denies. How could God fill with his substance something which doesn't exist? He ought to have said, concurring with Lessius cited above, that Imaginary Space, i.e. the vacuum and the nothingness outside the Cosmos, is actually God Himself. He does this finally when he says that space outside the Cosmos is not nothingness but the fullness of the Divine Substance.

We are finally brought to the view that the infinite Divine Essence is not contained in space or, in other words, in a vacuum. For God, here and everywhere present, is not <u>contained</u> in space or in a vacuum but is, in and of Himself, space and the vacuum and is so quite separately from all of creation. His Essence is different from that of all created objects. It is not to be circumscribed, nor, if I might put it so, to be corralled in any sort of enclosure, but is infinite and so just as much outside everything as it is inside everything. Accordingly He is present to all our actions; and for these He shall summon us to judgment.

---

are put into the mouth of Cosmiel replying to the query of Theodidactus "Dic igitur, quid sit illud, quod est extra mundum" (Tell me then what is there outside the Cosmos.)

"Does He act only when near at hand and not from far away? No one can hide away so that he does not see Him for He fills the heavens and the Earth." (Jeremiah 23: 23)[217]

The reasons that have led the above authors to think of space outside the Cosmos as being the Divine Essence itself, also apply, as both have the same nature, to the space inside the Cosmos. For when they assert that the space outside the Cosmos is infinite and immeasurable, being, in fact, the fullness of the Divine Essence, it follows that this is also true, for the same reasons, of the space within the Cosmos. For the Cosmos (albeit in comparison with the size of space hardly registering as even a point or an atom) is contained in that infinite space and cannot be separated from it. Otherwise we would have to contemplate the possibility that space would recede to the extent that this Cosmos is accommodated in it. Rather it is the case that space also in-dwells in the Cosmos and permeates it. It is in this sense that all the bodies of this Cosmos are accommodated, drawn in, supported, enfolded, enclosed, contained and preserved by space. Nor, as I shall discuss in the next chapter, does it matter whether the Cosmos is placed here or infinitely many Persian leagues away. As may be seen from Book I Chapter 35,[218] the Coimbra school concurs with all of this.

---

[217] "Am I a God when near, Yahweh demands, and not a God when far away? Can anyone hide somewhere secret without my seeing him? Yahweh demands Do I not fill heaven and earth?" (Jeremiah 23:23) New Jerusalem Bible
[218] v. Appendix 4.

Chapter IX – On the Infinite, the Immeasurable and the Eternal

The philosophers define the Infinite as something inexhaustible. They define the Immeasurable as something that for all distinction of place — above, below, to the right, to the left, in front of and behind — is without end, restriction or limit. By the Eternal they understand duration without limit, equally with respect to both past and future. In other words, the Eternal lacks both a beginning and an end. By an Age they understand an infinity of Time which, however, has a beginning.

But, as the Infinite surpasses the reach of man's understanding, so also does the Immeasurable and the Eternal and all three should be taken as one and the same, to be understood only in terms of the uncreated which we can discuss only according to the human capacity for understanding.

The Infinite utterly exceeds the capacity of the human intellect

Sound reason tells us that the Infinite, the Immeasurable and the Eternal are one and that they are not, and could not be, many. It cannot be grasped in any proper way by arithmetic number,[219] or by a name (except possibly that of "being" which simply tells us that there is an essence without telling us what it actually is) or with words. It is just that which is. Our minds cannot grasp it nor our tongues describe it. Consequently, however great an effort we might make to encompass it in terms of number or quantity or to describe it in words, we always fall short, in fact, infinitely short. For as it permits no limit to be set on its magnitude, it recognises also no division or separation and thus is, in its entirety, said to be one. Nor can any name be adequately ascribed to it. Just as it is immeasurable, so it is incomprehensible and indescribable. Where would we want to begin to limit by a name that which has no bounds to its extension or to assign a beginning, middle, or end to it?

There is no comparability in regard to the Infinite and the Immeasurable

If, in an immeasurable region, (which, of course, has no beginning, middle or end) someone had set out in a long journey into the Infinite and had carried on that journey for countless thousands of miles, then,

---

[219] Von Guericke's understanding of "number" was still the Aristotelian one — v. History of Ideas section.

in respect of the immeasurable, he would still be in the same place. If he were to repeat his action and reach somewhere ten times, or even infinitely many times, further on, the Immeasurable would, be just as much all around him as before and he himself would be in the same place as before. As regards reaching a boundary or meeting his goal of traversing the Immeasurable, he would not have gained a single step. There are no fractions of the Immeasurable. If there were, it would become graspable by our reason or by the reason of some or other created intelligence.

It is the case that such intelligences are also apt to try to understand the Infinite in terms of the created order of being — by thinking of an infinite number[220] or by thinking of multitudes to which the human mind cannot put a limit, such as an elapse of time in years and days, or of collections of objects.

On the so-called infinite number. What is number?

Number really arises by division or separation[221] whereas, as we have said above, the Infinite, being in its entirety One, recognises no division or separation. Also a multitude is formed by gathering together units. And so a number cannot properly and truthfully be called infinite.[222] That which has a beginning and cannot become so big that nothing can be added to it is not the Infinite but finite. Given a number, something can always be added to it. Therefore it is not the Infinite but finite. The addition of one finite quantity to another never makes an infinite quantity. If the Infinite is to be actual, it needs to be realised all at the same

---

[220] By "number" von Guericke understands, not the modern notion of natural number or infinite cardinal, but Euclid's notion that a number is "a multitude composed of units" (Elements, Book VII, Definition 2) i.e. much like the modern notion of a set.

[221] This is probably an allusion to Aristotle's teaching that given a number we can generate a bigger number by dividing one of the units of the original number. (Physics III.6 [207b])

[222] This chapter as a whole and this sentence in particular "ideoque Numerus proprie & vere Infinitus dici non potest" has a remarkable resonance with Cantor's thinking on the absolute infinite. E.g. Cantor writes "(The absolute) surpasses human power of comprehension and, in particular, eludes mathematical determination." (Gesammelte Abhandlungen p. 405) From a post-Cantorian perspective, we can summarise by saying: (a) von Guericke recognised the need to deal with countably infinite numbers (i.e. sets) (b) he also recognised that proper subsets of infinite sets were also infinite (c) he correctly thought that the continuum was a different type of infinity than the countable infinities he discusses (d) he incorrectly thought that the continuum was, like Cantor's absolute infinite, "beyond human comprehension" rather than being of the same cardinality as the power set of a countably infinite set.

time and in a completed form, rather than just in a partially completed form.[223]

An infinite number cannot be expressed

To try and make it accessible to the human mind, one might form a conception of the Infinite in terms of number that can always be added to. However although this is not indeed the actual Infinite and in fact does not bear any comparison with it, it nevertheless still goes beyond the grasp of the human mind. Comparison between these ideas fails because equality, less than, and greater than cannot be applied to the actual Infinite, Immeasurable and Eternal whereas they can be applied to the infinite conceived in terms of number.

If the infinite is conceived in terms of number there can be many infinities

If God were to create infinitely many men, there would be many more infinities of fingers and hairs created than of men. Similarly if He were to create infinitely many suns, round each of which ten stars orbited, there would be more stars than suns. Consider a straight line which I have extended without limit in both directions. Suppose further, that on this straight line God were to create a cosmic body every thousand miles, so that along the straight line there would be an infinity of them where this term is understood, as above, in a numerical sense. If now every second one were removed and placed on one side so that they likewise formed a straight line, say a thousand miles distant from the first, then there would be two infinite parallel lines, both of which were filled with infinitely many bodies. If also this operation were repeated and every second body again removed, and again placed to one side to form another line — this could be repeated again and again — it would always be the case that every such line would be ornamented by infinitely many spheres along it. From this it follows that there can be simultaneously many infinities provided the word "infinity" is understood, as above, in terms of number. Indeed, as there can be many infinities, there can also be infinitely many such infinities of this kind and of these infinities also infinitely many.

---

[223] The issue of the actual, completed infinity versus the potential infinity was much and continuously discussed from classical antiquity to the nineteenth century and even today continues to provoke differences of opinion. The topic is discussed in the History of Ideas section.

Even if for us mortals no adequate understanding of the Infinite, the Immeasurable and the Eternal is attainable, we can nevertheless make more progress in the contemplation of the Infinite by thinking about notations for numbers than in any other way.

Consequently we need to turn our attention to this topic.

Chapter X – On Number[224]

By using arithmetical notation, much that would seem incomprehensible to the uninstructed can be grasped

Although it may be the case that no mortal can picture to himself the Infinite, nevertheless so much can be described using a systematic scheme of arithmetical notation that it can seem that what we can describe is even greater than the Infinite. This is not, of course, so.

There have been, and continue to be, many people unversed in the skill of estimating the size of solid bodies, who think that the number of grains of sand on the shores of the sea is so huge as to be indescribable by words or by arithmetic notations.

Archimedes' number of grains of sand is small.

Contrary to their opinion, Archimedes geometrically demonstrated the existence of, and actually produced, a number which is not only bigger than the number of all the grains of sand on all the seashores, but is even bigger than the number of poppy seeds that the entire Earth, packed to the very centre with them, could hold. We want to follow Archimedes' example but shall introduce our own system of counting which is more extensive than that commonly used, in the hope of being more convincing to the sceptical.

Thirty-eight decimal digits specify a number greater than the grains of sand in the whole Earth

We shall presuppose that the entire Earth is composed of very tiny grains of sand so that 10 000 of them correspond to one poppy seed. This means that each grain is so small as to be invisible. We shall further presuppose that forty poppy seeds laid along a line correspond to the length of a finger. There are ten fingers in one foot. There are five such feet in a geometric pace. There are 10 000 paces in a German mile. We shall take the Earth's diameter, which we would normally estimate at 1,820 German miles, at 10 000 German miles.

---

[224] Throughout this chapter, in the course of which it would have been natural to use logarithms to the base ten, von Guericke does not betray any explicit knowledge of the invention of logarithms by John Napier (1550–1617) and Henry Briggs (1561–1630). Tables of logarithms were published by Briggs in 1624.

With these assumptions, the diameter of the earth comes out as 100 000 000 paces which is the same as 500 000 000 feet, 5 000 000 000 fingers or 200 000 000 000 poppy seeds. Furthermore, as (by Euclid Book XII Proposition 18[225]) the volume of a sphere is proportional to the cube of its diameter, we take the cube of the diameter to obtain a figure of 8 000 000 000 000 000 000 000 000 000 000 000 poppy seeds for the volume of the earth. When this number is multiplied by the 10 000 grains of sand corresponding to each poppy seed, we get a figure of 80 000 000 000 000 000 000 000 000 000 000 000 000 for the number of grains of sand that could be fitted into the Earth.

A number with fifty-three digits represents more than the number of grains of sand that could be fitted into the entire universe

Furthermore there is a number with 53 digits which represents more than the number of the tiniest grains of sand that could be fitted into the entire universe, right to the edge of the firmament, whether this is taken according to the Tychonic or Ptolemaic systems. Quite learned men have often objected to me that so great a number as the grains of sand in the universe could not be denoted with thousands of digits, or even if the digits were laid out to a length of one, three, five or more miles.

But let us tackle the problem by assuming, as Clavius[226] does, that the Ptolemaic system is correct and that the Earth is at the centre of the universe. Let us assume further that the sphere of the fixed stars is not just 45 225 times the radius of the Earth, (Alphraganus,[227] working in the Ptolemaic system, assigned this distance as the maximum to the fixed stars.) but 50 000. Hence the length of the diameter of the sphere of the fixed stars will be 100 000 times the radius of the earth or 50 000 times the diameter of the earth. Next, take the cube of this 50 000 to get 125 000 000 000 000. It follows from the aforementioned proposition of Euclid that volumes are proportional to the cubes of the linear

---

[225] Book XII Proposition 18 is "Spheres are to one another in the triplicate ratio of their respective diameters."

[226] Christoph Clavius S.J. (1538–1612) was a celebrated German mathematician and astronomer, primarily responsible for the Gregorian calendar and for the introduction of the mathematics curriculum in Jesuit schools. He remained a supporter of the geocentric system.

[227] Alphragranus (al Farghani) was a ninth century Islamic astronomer who made computations of astronomical distances.

dimensions, that the volume of the Earth to that of the sphere of the fixed stars is as 1 to 125 000 000 000 000. This is to say that the Earth could be contained in the sphere of the fixed stars 125 000 000 000 000 times. But the Earth contains 80 000 000 000 000 000 000 000 000 000 000 000 grains of sand. This number multiplied by the previous number gives (subject to our assumptions) a bound for the number of grains of sand that the entire Cosmos could hold — that is to say 10 000 000 000 000 000 000 000 000 000 000 000 000 000 000 000 000 000 grains.

From all this it is clear that a given number — limited to the thousands or tens of thousands — is directly comprehensible but when it goes beyond thousands upon thousands upon thousands, it becomes in-comprehensible. Nevertheless, as our earlier examples show, it can be described by digits. Indeed our huge number with 53 digits, though far exceeding the grasp of the human mind, can be written down. At this point someone might wonder what effectively infinite, formidable and completely incomprehensible multitude would be represented by writing down a thousand or more digits.

Only a few people think about what can be grasped using arithmetic digits

By way of enquiry, and also as a sort of wager, I offered one hundred thalers to a certain excellent arithmetician for his trouble, if within a mutually agreed fixed time (three months, as it happened) he could calculate, starting with two, the result of multiplying a number by itself (i.e. squaring it) twenty times. For example, multiplying two by itself once gives four, four multiplied by itself gives sixteen, sixteen by itself 256, and so on.

He promised, betting ten Imperials,[228] that he could work this out and would take just one month to do it, rather than the three months agreed. Furthermore, at the end of the period he would, in the presence of those who witnessed this wager, produce the answer to the proposed problem. He did this, without thinking that the task, because of the

---

[228] The Imperial thaler was an official unit of currency in the Holy Roman Empire. An Imperial thaler was worth 7 kipper thalers in 1785; so from context 100 thalers and 10 Imperials are probably equal.

sheer number of digits that arise, is not humanly possible. This be-comes clear by trying it.

2 on squaring once gives 4.

2 on squaring twice gives 16.

2 on squaring three times gives 256.

2 on squaring four times gives 65 536.

2 on squaring five times gives 4 294 967 296.

2 on squaring 6 times gives 18 446 744 073 709 551 616.

We see from these examples that the number of digits goes up by al-most a factor of two each time. Consequently if we were to do a further squaring, so that two was squared seven times, the answer would have forty digits. If eight times, eighty digits; if nine times 160; if ten times 320; if eleven times 640; if twelve times, 1,280; if thirteen times, 2,560; if fourteen times, 5,120; if fifteen times 10 240; if sixteen times 20 480; if seventeen times 40 960; if eighteen times 81 920; if nineteen times 163 840. And finally, if 2 were squared twenty times, the result would have 327 680 digits.

Who could possibly carry out such an enormous calculation with its equally daunting numbers of multiplication and additions? For even this last calculation alone (squaring a number with 163 840 digits) would entail more than 26 843 000 000[229] digits. This means that there would be as many digits to be written down as the number of letters in at least 1,242 volumes of the *Corpus Juris*.[230] (For if the *Corpus Juris*, including the annotations of Godefroy, contains 1,000 pages and each page four columns and each column 90 lines and each line 60 letters, then the entire book would contain 21 600 000 letters. This figure divides 26 843 000 000 1,242 times.) As if that were not enough, where would one obtain a big enough sheet of paper on which to write down this calcula-tion?

---

[229] Approximately the square of 163 840 — obtained presumably by laying out the calculation as a traditional long multiplication.

[230] *Corpus Juris Civilis cum notis Gothofredi* was a law book written by Denis Godefroy (1549–1622), a French jurist and philologist.

And so we see to what an unbelievable number of digits this computation would lead. But consider, however, the content of an aggregate denoted by so many arithmetic digits. This would be so innumerable, that this multitude of digits, in comparison with the size of what it denotes, would be of no significance whatsoever.

An awe-inspiring and imponderable number which can be described by digits

If these above mentioned 53 digits denote a greater number than the number of very tiny grains of sand that the entire universe could hold, then how awe-inspiring and innumerable would be the number denoted by 327 680 digits. For whenever another digit is added, the number denoted is increased by a factor of ten. For instance, if just six zeroes were added to those 53 the total would correspond to a capacity of a thousand thousand Cosmoses of the same sort.

So we have to accept that we are wretched creatures whose intellects do not measure up to comprehending the infinity of the uncreated. But however that may be and however extraordinarily great a number may be, we still have to admit that every number is finite as it always, in respect of the Before, has a beginning and, in respect of the After, lacks completeness.[231]

---

[231] This is an allusion to Aristotle's discussion of time and his definition of it as "the number of motion with respect to the before and after." (*Physics* IV 10–14 [218a–224a]). Von Guericke is using this language to make the point that any number can be incremented. His way of expressing himself here reminds one of the Kantian doctrine that, as geometry arises from our intuition of space, so the natural numbers arises from our intuition of time.

Chapter XI – On the Heaven which is called the Abode of the Blessed

The Last Judgment

We know for certain that after the destruction of this earth the blessed as well as the damned will still be somewhere. This is so even if the destiny of the Earth is to disappear entirely rather than just be transformed into something better. (v. Book V Chapter 25) For it is our common lot to have to reveal ourselves completely before the judgment seat of God so that each one can render an account of his actions while on Earth to that tribunal which will judge him to be either good or evil. The question thus arises as to where the blessed and the damned are. Is it above the Earth or below it? Or is it somewhere utterly remote from the Earth — perhaps beyond the (supposed) sphere of the fixed stars?

In the Immeasurable there is nothing relative

From the foregoing discussion one notes that space (in other words the universal container of everything) is the Infinite and the Immeasurable and therefore there is no created object which does not subsist in space thus understood. In the case of the Immeasurable, there is no below or above; nothing is far away, nothing is here, nothing is there and there is absolutely no notion of place except relative to another created object. Likewise the abode of the blessed cannot properly be called a place, unless the term is relativised to another created object. Taking all the relevant considerations into account — especially those we shall discuss in Book V, Chapters 5 and 6 concerning the distances of the stars — the natural inference would seem to be that, after the annihilation of this Earth, the place of both the blessed and the damned will perhaps be the very same place which the Earth previously occupied. This is what people commonly call heaven. For otherwise, in immeasurable space no object, whatever it may be, has a place except relative to some other object.[232]

---

[232] Von Guericke's point seems to be that at the Last Day, though the Earth will be annihilated, creation as a whole will survive. Therefore, it will still be possible to speak of the place of created things such as Heaven and Hell, the eternal abode of the saved and the damned, relative to other created things such as the orbits of the other planets. Hence his conjecture is coherent, if

The Earth can only have a place relative to other bodies; otherwise it is nowhere

For example, if a planet did not have a position in the Cosmos relative to other bodies of the Cosmos, then one could not say that such a planet is here or there. This is the case even if it were many, many thousands of miles distant, whether before, behind, above or below, in immeasurable space from the other bodies. However, if there were no other body at all in the universe, and all had perished at the same time as the annihilation of the Earth, then being here, or being countless thousands of miles away, would be indistinguishable. Such huge differences don't make any difference — not as much as one step along a journey to the Indies — to the fact that a planet's being in undifferentiated space is the same as its being nowhere.

The heaven of the Earth

Thus it is without doubt that the heaven of our Earth (as has been said in Chapter 5) is none other than that expanse of space between the heavens of Mars and Venus, which the Earth, together with the Moon, and the regions encompassing the range of the potencies[233] they emanate, occupy as they go around the sun.

And just as space (the universal container of everything) is uncreated and is spoken of in terms of its being greater, so, in the same way, we understand the place of God to be "the highest of the high". The more we can imagine space to be greater, the more we conceive of His nature. Thus the Psalmist says:[234]

"Who is like our God who dwells on high?"

Why a high place or "in the heights" is attributed to God

According to Aristotle,[235] all the barbarians spontaneously attributed the highest place of the heavens to God and they identify the heavens with

---

not, to a modern sensibility, plausible. His general point that it doesn't make sense to speak of the place or position of solitary objects in infinite empty space is completely unexceptionable.

[233] The Latin is "virtutes" The phrase "virtutes mundanae", which, judging by a letter to Leibniz, (Schimank p. 45) is of von Guericke's own coining, is a key concept for von Guericke and is a precursor of the modern "force field" concept.

[234] Possibly Vulgate Ps 88:7 (Jerusalem Ps 89:6) "Quoniam quis in nubibus aequabitur Domino?".

[235] De Caelo I.3 [270b 5–10]

God when they say "I call heaven to witness". We also in the Lord's Prayer call upon God, our Father who is in heaven. This really means that He is heaven. For we know that God is not in heaven in the sense of being in a circumscribed place or some sort of dwelling for even the the heaven of the heavens could not contain him. Indeed, in the same sense that He is in heaven, those who die in His grace are also in heaven. As for those who die beyond the reach of His grace, their destiny is hell where they will suffer in eternal darkness.

After the Last Judgment, there will not be (in our view) any created order — in particular no huge palace built from the finest materials. For if there were still a created order, and God was, as popular opinion would have it, installed in heaven, as if in some circumscribed and bounded region, it would follow that God is now in a better state than previously, as if He had become richer and now has heaven and a Throne of Majesty which He previously didn't have. The true God, who will incorporate the God of mercy, will also incorporate heaven.

What is the heaven of the Cosmos?

As far as the heaven of the entire Cosmos goes, it is just that space that exists between all the bodies of the universe. Before the creation of the Cosmos, this space was, in our view, a vacuum but is now to some degree filled with the bodies of the Cosmos. Thus, there may also be assigned to any such body its heaven or space. Consequently, the heaven of the Earth is the space between Mars and Venus.

The size of the heaven of the Earth

We have no doubt that this heaven can adequately accommodate as many humans as there ever could be. It is clear from Book VI Chapter 13 that the distance between Mars and the sun is 3,739 times the radius of the Earth. Therefore (since according to Euclid, the ratio of volumes of spheres is the cube of the ratio of their respective diameters or radii) the sphere of the orbit of Mars could contain the Earth 52 271 672 419 times. The distance of Venus from the sun is 2,049 times the radius of the Earth. Therefore the sphere of the orbit of Venus could contain the Earth 8 602 523 649 times. Then, subtracting the sphere of Venus from that of Mars, there remains space enough for an intermediate sphere — the heaven of this Earth — which could contain the Earth 43 669 148 770 times. This would seem to be quite large enough to accommodate the human race however numerous it might become, with due respect to the judgment of theologians, who, however, also differ vehemently among themselves on this topic.

Chapter XII – On the greatest and the smallest

Quantity is not absolute but, but like place, is a relative concept

Quantity considered on its own, rather than in comparison, is not something intrinsic to an object but for any created object it arises by reference to something external. For it is in the nature of things that large and small, long and short, high and deep, or wide and narrow cannot be applied to anything except with respect to, or in comparison with, something else. Reason itself tells us that that all created things have some definite limits on how big or how small they can be. Their size must fall between these limits. To be infinitely large or small is not a property that can be possessed by the created but only by the uncreated. Thus whatever is infinite or immeasurable cannot be constrained by a maximum or a minimum. For the Infinite does not admit of comparison. Therefore when it comes to distinct and separate created objects, they can be small or large relative to each other but without a standard of comparison one cannot say that they are absolutely large or small.

What are the upper limits?

However there are in nature objects of maximal size — the heavenly bodies, our own and other suns, the fixed stars, the planets and their associated satellites and so on. For just as creation rejoices in its variety and shows God's omnipotence, so (especially for bodies of the same type) their differences bring illumination to everything. From their differences we can compare one with another. Without such comparison nothing can be said to be big or small. Thus one sun may be compared with other suns, one planet with other planets and so on.

Once the greatest bodies have been identified, one can recognise smaller ones and ones of minimal size and fair comparisons can be made between things of the same type. For instance, on our Earth, animals of different sizes are found — on the one hand, whales, elephants etc. and on the other, mites, lice and midges. There are also grains of sand, dust particles and other very tiny amounts of things which can be cut ever more minutely into fragments of incomprehensible smallness, but not infinitely, so that they disappear into nothing.

What are atoms?

166

The smallest possible parts are called atoms by some. They think of them as indivisibles — i.e. having no further constituents.

What are minimal parts?

Many things, previously invisible, can nowadays be seen with the help of microscopes. Using this optical technique, we now understand that various materials are swarming with tiny living things,[236] which, up to recently, were hidden from our view. Nevertheless it remains the case that the smallest portions of water, air, fire and other fluids are so tiny that there is no way of detecting them.

Although these particles are indeed very small, they nonetheless cannot penetrate glass or metal. In Book IV we discuss how much smaller still are the parts of the effluvia or incorporeal potencies which do penetrate and even pass through all types of metal and glass.

Be all this as it may, the fact of the matter is that every such particle exists in, is contained by, and is penetrated by, this infinite space of ours. This is the case whether we are considering the smallest of all creatures (with its even smaller intestines), or an invisible dust particle, or particles of fire, or of water, or of air or an atom of some other very fine-grained fluid, or some extremely minute little sphere or some rarified, incorporeal effluvium that penetrates all bodies. It is even true of Spirit.

It follows also that there is no created object so huge as not to be infinitely and immeasurably dwarfed by space. At the other end of the spectrum nothing is so small, so constituted of emanation or spirit, but space is infinitely smaller and more rarified.

From these considerations one can readily see that it is not contrary to nature that, when our bodies revert to dust, however little it may be or wherever on the Earth it may be scattered, the particles can be reassembled and our bodies reconstituted. This takes place in and through the space in which they have continued, despite the transformation to

---

[236] When von Guericke was writing this was very recent knowledge. This remark seems to betray either an acquaintance with Hooke's Micrographia (1665) or some awareness of the work of Antonie van Leeuwenhoek, (1632–1723) the first observer of micro-organisms which he called "animaliculae", the same word that von Guericke uses. Though his observations were not published until 1673 by the Royal Society, van Leeuwenhoek was an energetic correspondent of whose work von Guericke might well have heard.

dust, to subsist. Therefore at the Last Judgment, our bodies can be summoned anew and resurrected to give an account of their actions in this life.

Appendix 1 Book I Chapter 31 – On heaven, (or the heavens) and on the aether and the matter of the heavens

The heavens are generally said to be that very extensive, diffuse and completely transparent expanse surrounding our Earth in all directions. They comprise the space, filled with starry spheres of light, which extends from the Earth's land and oceans to the uttermost boundary of what there is. There the heavens cease. This is the commonly held opinion.

The word "heaven" is used in many senses[237]

The word "heaven" is used in many different senses. A first meaning is the atmosphere of the Earth in which meteors are formed. Thus one says "the clouds of heaven", "the birds of heaven", "manna from heaven", "the heavens are clear", "rain falls from heaven", "God adorned the heavens with his breath (the wind)", "God covered the heavens with thick clouds" and so on.

Sometimes the periodic course of a planet is also called its heaven as, for example, the heaven of Mercury, of Mars, of Venus, of Jupiter or of Saturn. But when one speaks of the stars of heaven, one usually means the highest region of the expanse, also referred to as the "starry heavens" or the "eighth sphere". Indeed it is also called "the ethereal heaven". The poet Ovid says:[238]

"I have suffered as many evils as there are stars shining in the aether.".

The crystalline heaven

According to the Peripatetics, there is, as well as these three types of heaven, a fourth — the crystalline heaven, or ninth sphere. This was introduced because of the advances of the equinoxes.

What is the Primum Mobile?

Finally, as the fifth meaning of "heaven" one can understand the Primum Mobile by whose motion, as one assumes, all the spheres of the planets, as well as that of the fixed stars, are dragged from east to west

---

[237] Von Guericke's discussion echoes that of Aristotle who also discusses the different meanings given to the word "heaven". (*De Caelo*. I. 9 [279a])
[238] Ovid. Locus Tristia 1.5.47

in twenty-four hours. Aristotle defines this in Book I Chapter 9 of *De Caelo* as:[239]

"the substance of nature which is located in the furthest turning of the Cosmos".

This is synonymous with saying that the heavens are the remotest substance of the Cosmos which has an innate turning motion.

The radiant heaven

Formerly both Catholic and Evangelical theologians had conceived a further heaven extending the previous ones — the radiant heaven, whose essence was to be seat of God and the refuge of the blessed. The next chapter deals with this in more detail.

What is the aether?

Scholars are divided as to what the aether actually is. Anaxagoras thought it was the element, fire. But, in *De Mundo,*[240] Aristotle writes that the aether is the matter of the heavens and the stars, i.e. of the entire framework of the constellations, the heavens and the fixed stars. This is not because it is on fire and flaming but because it restlessly proceeds along its course and goes around with dizzying speed driven by its ἀεὶ Ιειν[241] to be always moving. It is according to him, an imperishable divine element completely different from the other four. On the basis of this, scholars nowadays distinguish two main constituents of the Cosmos — the elements and the aether, or the elementary and the ethereal Cosmos. Thus, by the aether they mean everything that is above the (supposed) sphere of fire. Some consider that the substance of the aether is the infinite air. Others, for example Virgil, simply think of it as the ordinary air. Virgil writes:[242]

"and the aether reverberates with a great sound".

Following Apuleius,[243] the four elements are called earth, water, air and fire. Lucretius in Book I uses aether as a synonym for Jupiter. So much

---

[239] Aristotole says (De Caelo I [278b]) "In one sense, then, we call 'heaven' the substance of the extreme circumference of the whole, or that natural body whose place is at the extreme circumference." (Translation. J.L.Stocks.)

[240] The *De Mundo* is a work of unknown authorship incorrectly attributed to Aristotle.

[241] Perpetual impulse to move.

[242] *Aeneid* Book V, l. 228 "………resonatque fragoribus Aether".

[243] The Latin is "Apulejo, quattuor elementa, Tellus, Aqua, Aether, Ignis vocantur.".It is unclear why von Guericke should attribute the four elements to Lucius Apuleius (2nd century AD)

then, briefly, as regards the aether. One may consult our opinion in Book II Chapter 5.

Is the substance of the heavens solid?

As the opinions of investigators of nature on this matter widely diverge, so they are similarly divided on the substance of the heavens. The Peripatetics affirm with Aristotle that the eighth sphere, that of the fixed stars, is, along with all the others that carry the planets, composed of a hard impenetrable substance, while the stars themselves are composed of a still denser material. The Church Fathers are also preponderantly of this opinion, perhaps taking their stance from Job:37:18.[244]

"Did you, along with God, then create the heavens, whose solidity has been forged like cast metal?"

Or is it fluid?

Others take a contrary view. They say that the substance of the heavens is fluid, that it is materially constituted and that, like our air, it permeates everything but yields easily to any object it encounters. It offers virtually no resistance, gives way in all directions, and offers a place to anything that penetrates it. Afterwards, just like water, it reunites its separated parts when it flows back together again. The majority of the philosophers of antiquity — including Pythagoras, Plato (in the *Timaeus*) and Seneca — take this view, which has also been adopted by many more recent astronomers, notably Tycho Brahe. This material is so rarefied that it allows the free transit of the comets etc. through it. Even some of the old Church Fathers thought this a reasonable assumption. Fr. Arriaga, in his *Discussions on the Heavens* Part 4.53, writes:[245]

"The seventh heaven is almost infinite in size. In comparison with it, Saturn, which is attached to it, is like a single point. It seems hardly in accord with reason and good sense

---

when Aristotle attributes them to Empedocles, unless he means that Apuleius was the first person to use these four Latin names for the elements.

[244] The Jerusalem translation of Job:37:16–18 is "Do you know how he balances the clouds — a miracle of consummate skill? When your clothes are hot to your body and the Earth lies still under the south wind, can you, like Him, stretch out the sky tempered like a mirror of cast metal?"

[245] Rodriguez Arriaga S.J. (1592-1667) was a Spanish Jesuit. He was a professor of theology at the university of Prague and was a tutor to the future Kaiser Ferdinand III. Von Guericke is probably alluding to Fr. Arriaga's *Cursus Philosophicus* (1632) which contained a section on cosmology.

that to move such a tiny star the entire mass of the seventh sphere needs to move. An explanation much to be preferred is that just the planet itself is moved in a fluid-like material by some Intelligence. All that rigid scaffolding just to set this single star in motion seems simply superfluous."

Aristotle thought the heavens were animate and to the Athenians the sun had a soul

Additionally, in respect of the heavens and its essence, substance, nature, form etc. there are many other opinions, questions and points of discussion. Aristotle thought the heavens were animate and endowed with a rational and comprehending soul. (*De Caelo* Book II and *Meteorology* Book II)[246] Pythagoras, Plato and other ancient writers were of similar mind. This seemed to them so firmly established that, according to Augustine in *City of God*, Book XVIII,[247] Anaxagoras was prosecuted and condemned to death because he held that the sun was not something animate but a shining star. Among others, the Jewish writer Philo expressed the same view as Anaxagoras in *Creation of the World* as did Pliny in *Natural History*, Book II Chapter 8.

Are the heavens perishable?

Furthermore Plato, Anaxagoras, Democritus and others affirmed that the heavens are perishable. In *De Caelo* Book I Chapter III and Book II Chapter II Aristotle taught the opposite. According to him the Heavens

---

[246] This is a strange opinion to attribute to Aristotle and the cited sources do not really bear it out. In *De Caelo* Book II [248a/30] Aristotle writes: "Nor, again is it conceivable that it should persist eternally by the necessitation of a soul. For a soul could not live in such conditions painlessly or happily, since the movement involves constraint, being imposed on the first body, whose natural motion is different and imposed *continuously*." This is taken to be a criticism of the "world soul" idea of Plato's *Timaeus*. He also writes (Book II 12 [292a/20]): "We may object that we have been thinking of the stars as mere bodies and as units with a serial order indeed but entirely inanimate; but should rather conceive them as enjoying life and action. On this view the facts cease to appear surprising." *Meteorology* Book II is a discussion of terrestrial phenomena and does not discuss the heavens.

[247] Augustine: *City of God*, Book XVIIII, Chapter 41: "Did not Athens have two flourishing sects; the Epicureans who contended that human affairs are of no concern to the gods and the Stoics who held the opposite opinion and argued that human affairs are under the guidance and protection of the gods, the helper and defenders of men. Hence I wonder why Anaxagoras was put on trial for saying that the sun is a red hot stone and denying utterly that it was a god, while in the same city Epicurus enjoyed high renown and lived in undisturbed serenity, though he not only refused to believe in the divinity of the sun or of any other heavenly body, but also contended that neither Jupiter nor any of the gods dwells in the universe in any sense, so that men's prayers and supplications may reach him." (Bettenson Translation)

172

did not possess the same essence as the elements, but were possessed of a special fifth essence and were thus imperishable.[248]

Are the heavens capable of being created?

There arises the question whether or not the heavens are capable of being created. The scholars of antiquity had their differences in these matters, even if they all agree, as Aristotle remarks in *De Caelo*, Book I,[249] that the heavens have been created. Xenophon, according to Plutarch Book II Chapter 4, declares them to be not created and not perishable but eternal. Plato changes his point of view. In Laws Book III he asserts that the number of years since the Cosmos was constituted is finite, but in the *Timaeus* he supposes the Cosmos was created by God and in Definition 6 raises the question whether the heavens were created from all eternity or just at an unimaginably long time in the past. Aristotle holds both that the heavens were not capable of creation and that they were not created. He bases this view on a principle that everything that comes into being and passes away has an opposite. But the heavens have no opposite and therefore the heavens cannot come into being or pass away.[250] Elsewhere he frequently defends this view on many other grounds.

Among more recent philosophers one also encounters great differences of opinion. In particular the question as to whether the heavens will necessarily be destroyed on the last day attracts both affirmation and denial. Those who affirm it adduce various passages from Scripture. For example, Psalm 102:26–27:[251]

"The heavens are the work of your hands, they will pass away."

---

[248] In *De Caelo* I.3 Aristotle advances a number of arguments that the heavens are eternal and unchanging: (a) that anything for which circular motion, having no opposite, is the natural motion is unalterable (b) it accords with the religious intuitions of mankind (c) it accords with the historical record of observation (d) from the etymology of the word "aether" as "runs always".

[249] Von Guericke is probably alluding to *De Caelo* I 10 [279b/12] "That the world was generated, all are agreed, but, generation over, some say that it is eternal, others say that it is destructible like any other natural formation. Others again with Empedocles of Acragas and Heraclitus of Ephesus, believe that there is alternation in the destructive process, which takes now this direction, now that, and continues without end." (Translation J. L. Stocks)

[250] These ideas are set out in *De Caelo* I:3 [200a 10–30]

[251] Ps:102:25-27 "Long ago you laid earth's foundations; the heavens are the work of your hands. They pass away but you remain; they all wear out like a garment; like outworn clothes you change them; but you never alter and your years never change." (New Jerusalem Bible)

or Luke 21:33[252]

"Heaven and Earth will pass away."

or Peter 2:3:10[253]

"The heavens will pass with a great explosion."

But Augustine understands, in *City of God*, Book XX Chapters 14, 16, 18 and 24, the term "heavens" to be synonymous with the region of the air — i.e. in the same sense as that mentioned above, whereby one speaks of the "birds of heaven". Suarez[254] follows Augustine and quotes the above letter of Peter just before Verse 5.[255]

"For a long time the heavens had been in existence through the Word of God as was also the Earth, made from water and consisting of water. However the Cosmos, as it then was, perished in the inundation of the Flood. Thus the heavens and the Earth that exist today, established by the same Word of God, are spared to await the fire on the day of judgment and damnation of the godless."

These words allow the following interpretation. The heavens, which perished in the flood at the time of Noah will pass through fire on the Day of Judgment. However the heavenly spheres did not perish at the time of the Flood and therefore will not pass away at the Last Day. (v. St. Thomas[256] Part IV, 47 & 48, Pereira[257] *Commentary on Genesis* Book I,

---

[252] "In truth I tell you, before this generation has passed away, all will have taken place. Sky and Earth will pass away, but my words will never pass away." (New Jerusalem Bible)

[253] Peter 2:3:10 is "The Day of the Lord will come like a thief, and then with a roar the sky will vanish, the elements will catch fire and melt away, the Earth and all that it contains will be burned up." (New Jerusalem Bible)

[254] Francisco Suarez (1548–1617) was a Spanish Jesuit, philosopher and theologian and a leading figure in the School of Salamanca. He had a high reputation as a metaphysician and legal philosopher and is considered the last substantial thinker of the scholastic tradition.

[255] Peter 2:3:3–7. "First of all, do not forget that in the final days there will come sarcastic scoffers whose life is ruled by their passions. 'What has happened to the promise of His coming?' they will say, 'Since our fathers died everything has gone on just as it has since the beginning of creation!' They deliberately ignore the fact that long ago there were the heavens and the Earth, formed out of water and through water by the Word of God and that it was through these same factors that the world of those days was destroyed by the floodwaters. It is the same Word which is reserving the present heavens and Earth for fire, keeping them till the Day of Judgment and of the destruction of sinners." (New Jerusalem Bible)

[256] Von Guericke's reference is unclear. Summa Theologica has only three parts.

[257] Benedict (Bento) Periera (1535–1610) was a Spanish Jesuit philosopher and theologian. He taught literature, philosophy, theology and Scripture in Rome. Von Guericke is referring to his "Commentariorum et disputationum in Genesim tomi quattuor " published in Rome between 1591 and 1599. (Catholic Encyclopaedia)

Queries 1 and 2, the Coimbra School commentary on *De Caelo* Book I, Discussion 3, Question 1 Article 3 and Tanner[258] Part 1 Division 6, Question 4 Objection 5 Point 5). But when it written there that:[259]

"there will be a new heaven and a new Earth"

this is to be understood in the sense that the heavens we experience now will be so renewed that will seem newly created. A comparison can be made with how the Earth appears rejuvenated with the seasonal return of spring when all nature appears in a new dress.

The heavens are thought to be something physical

It is also asserted that the heavens are something substantial. According to some who hold this opinion they are composed of substance only and according to others this is not the case. The first option would imply that the heavens are not composed out of matter and form together and the second would imply that they are.

What is the origin of the motion of the heavens?

The following question is also discussed. Do the heavens move of their own volition in response to an inner urge to motion or are they moved by Intelligences?[260] The opinion of some scholars is that God alone is responsible for their movements, and, according to the general opinion

---

[258] Adam Tanner S.J. (1571–1632) was an Austrian theologian and mathematician. He taught Hebrew, apologetics and moral theology and was a professor of Scholastic Philosophy at Ingolstadt. He was an active participant in the religious and political disputes of the period. His main work *Universa theologia scholastica* was published at Ingolstadt in 1626–1627. The Tannerus crater on the moon is called after him.

[259] Von Guericke is presumably alluding to *Revelations* 21:1 "Then I saw a new heaven and a new earth; the first heaven and the first earth had disappeared now and there was no longer any sea." (New Jerusalem Bible)

[260] C.S.Lewis (*The Discarded Image* p. 115) writes: "The nearest approach to the divine and perfect ubiquity that the spheres can attain is the swiftest and most regular possible movement, in the most perfect form, which is circular. Each sphere attains it in a less degree than the sphere above it, and therefore has a slower pace. This all implies that each sphere, or something resident in each sphere, is a conscious and intellectual being, moved by the 'intellectual love' of God ... These lofty creatures are called Intelligences. The relation between the Intelligence of a sphere and the sphere itself as a physical object was variously conceived. The older view was that the Intelligence is 'in' the sphere as the soul is 'in' the body, so that the planets are, as Plato would have agreed, ζωα — celestial animals, animate bodies or incarnate minds. ... Later, the Scholastics thought differently. 'We confess, with the sacred writers', says Albertus Magnus 'that the heavens have not souls and are not animals if the word soul is taken in its strict sense.'"

of the Scholastics, they are moved by Intelligences. This theory has become so dominant among them that it is almost sinful to deny it.

The shape of the heavens

Generally speaking, astronomers and philosophers have concluded that the heavens are perfectly spherical, as this shape is particularly adapted for circular motion. They justify this from their stance on the vacuum. They argue that if the heavens did not possess a spherical shape there would have to be void outside it. What other opinions are held about this topic will be made clear in the following Book.

Appendix 2 Book I Chapter 32 – On the Firmament and the Waters above it in Sacred Scripture

The Expanse in Sacred Scripture understood as the firmament

In the first Chapter of *Genesis* Moses writes:[261]

"Then God said, be there RAKIAH, (that is the Expanse which in some editions of Scripture is also called the firmament*) between the waters that it might separate the waters, one from another. God therefore made this Expanse, which separates the waters which are below the Expanse from those above the Expanse. And so it was. God called this Expanse SCHAMAIM (*which, according to several authorities, is to say "There, there is water" ; it is also construed as meaning the heavens). *Thus there was evening and there was morning of the second day. Afterwards God said, 'Let the waters which are below this SCHAMAIM flow into one place and let dry regions appear.' And it was so. He called the dry places Earth and the Containers of the water, he called the seas. Later (*Verse 14*) God said 'Let there be lights in the Expanse (*the firmament*) of heaven' "*

The firmament, heaven and the Expanse are all one and the same

From this and its continuation in Genesis it is clear that the Expanse, the firmament, and heaven are all one and the same. For indeed, in this particular chapter of Genesis, as generally in Scripture, heaven is more often understood as the "airy heaven" so that birds are said to be "birds of heaven; the clouds are called "the clouds of heaven" and so on. It follows that the terms Expanse or firmament or heaven refer to that Expanse which begins with surface of the land and the seas and continues to the remotest limit of the Cosmos. According to context, the term is to be understood as referring to this or that region. For instance, in the phrase "the birds of heaven" or "of the firmament" or "of the Expanse", the term cannot be understood as referring to any other region apart from the one where the birds actually fly.

---

[261] The Jerusalem Bible translation of this passage is "God said 'Let there be a vault through the middle of the waters to divide the waters in two.' And so it was. God made the vault and it divided the waters under the vault from the waters above the vault. God called the vault 'heaven'. Evening came and morning came: the second day. God said 'Let the waters under heaven come together into a single mass, and let dry land appear. And so it was. God called the dry land 'earth' and the mass of the waters 'seas'." The New Jerusalem Bible footnotes: "For the ancient Semites, the seeming vault of the sky (the firmament) was a solid dome holding the upper waters in check; the waters of the Flood poured down through apertures in it."

The waters above the heavens or the firmament are understood to be in the clouds of heaven

Thus also in the phrase "waters above the Expanse" or "above the firmament" the term can only be understood as referring to the region where there is water i.e. to where the clouds of heaven actually are. (This is the SCHAMAIM, or "There, there is water."). For God binds the waters together in dense clouds. (Job: Chapter 26)[262] Also when "lights of heaven" are mentioned this is to be understood as referring to that region of the Expanse or of the heavens in which any particular light actually is. It clearly does not follow from the words of Scripture, that the waters which are said to be above the firmament or the Expanse or the heavens, are actually above the fixed stars — they are, in fact, in a more appropriate place — in the heaven of the clouds. It should be noted that the preposition "above" (super) sometimes means the same as "in" (in) or "at" (ad) or "with" (apud).[263] This is illustrated in Psalm 137:

"Super flumina Babylonis sedent filii Israel"

where "super flumina" is the same as "ad flumina".

The word firmament is incorrectly used for the sphere of the fixed stars

Although the relative positions of the fixed stars to each other are fixed and unchanging, that stellar region (assuming that they are in a single region or sphere) cannot, however, correctly be called the firmament, as will be made clear in due course. Much less can the opinion of the Peripatetics be sustained for they attribute various motions to the sphere of the fixed stars. How can they want to call something that they think is moving, fixed?

Two conclusions can be drawn. Firstly the word "firmament" is not an appropriate one in this context and the word "Expanse", which is more in agreement with the Hebrew text, is a preferable term. Secondly there

---

[262] Job 26:7–8. "He it was who spread the North above the void and poised the Earth on nothingness. He fastens up the waters in his clouds without the clouds giving way under their weight." (New Jerusalem Bible)

[263] Von Guericke is here making a point about the meaning of the Latin prepositions "super" "in", "ad" and "apud". The usual translation of the line from the Psalm is "By the waters of Babylon the sons of Israel sit"

are no waters above the expanse of the fixed stars and the term "waters" is, in this context, to be understood as referring to clouds and rain.

The opinion of Origen on the waters above the heavens

By "waters above the heavens" Origen[264] wants to understand angels enjoying the beatific vision and by waters below the heavens, devils expelled for heaven because of sin. This opinion has been rejected by the other Fathers of the Church. Thus Augustine, who had understood "waters above the heavens" as referring to angels, changed his mind, and along with Jerome and many others, came to understand the phrase as referring to clouds. By "heaven" or the "heavens" he understands the lowest region of the air. They also say that this is to be understood as the firmament which divides the waters from the waters. Compton-Carleton[265] expresses this opinion in his *Philosophia Universa* (p. 409).

The Peripatetics put the waters above the Primum Mobile

Others, in particular the Peripatetics, who claim that all the heavens form a continuum, place these waters between the Primum Mobile and the Empyrean heaven. They say that it is not sensible to locate them between the other heavens, as they would stop one sphere from moving another. Hence they say that although the heavens, which are moved, are contiguous with each other they are not however contiguous with, or attached to, the Empyrean heaven and thus these waters are put in between.

Other Opinions

Some think that these waters are dispersed above the outermost surface of the Empyrean heaven and seek to prove this from Sacred Scripture e.g. *Daniel*: 3[266]

---

[264] Origen Adamantius (185–254) was an African Christian scholar, speculative theologian and religious philosopher. He was the author of a number of commentaries on Scripture including one on Genesis. He died in the persecution of the Emperor Decius. Some of his opinions were later anathematised but he remains recognised as a Church Father.

[265] Thomas Compton-Carleton S.J. (1592–1666) was an English Jesuit, educated at Cambridge, who taught at Liege. His *Philosophia Universa* was published in Antwerp 1649 by Jacob Meursius and dedicated to Maximilian of Bavaria. The passage to which von Guericke alludes forms part of a disputation.

[266] Daniel 3:60

"Bless the Lord, all the waters above the heavens."

Likewise Psalm 148:[267]

"Praise Him, O heavens of the heavens, all the waters above the heavens."

Hence they think that the waters of this kind above the Empyrean heaven are to be reckoned in the region of the Space of the Imagination.

Thomas, Bonaventure and Durandus,[268] among others, understand by the Waters above the Heavens, the Crystalline Heaven — in other words the (supposed) ninth Sphere. For they say that just as the highest heaven, on account of its resemblance to fire, is called Empyrean so this one, on account of its resemblance to water, is called Crystalline. Finally others understand the waters above the heavens to be some breathable material in the middle of the Empyrean, thanks to which the saints can speak. But we, as we have said above, understand the waters above the firmament to be the clouds and the rain of the skies.

---

[267] Ps:148:4.

[268] Thomas Aquinas (1225–1274) O.P. (The Angelic Doctor); Bonaventure (1221–1274) (The Seraphic Doctor); Durandus of St. Pourcain OP (c.1275–1334) (The most resolute Doctor). St. Thomas' *Summa Theologica*, Part 1, Q. 68 Articles 2 and 3 consider "Whether there are waters above the firmament" and "Whether the firmament divides waters from waters."

Appendix 3 Book I Chapter 33 – On the Empyrean Heaven

To the particular five heavens described in Chapter 31 of this book the aforementioned theologians commonly add — so to speak superimpose — a sixth and then a final heaven — the Empyrean — which they say is the abode of the blessed, the court of the angels, and the throne of God's Majesty. This is pervaded with a very great light and thus they call it the Empyrean, which means fire. They make the comparison with the light, rather than the heat, of fire. They reckon that it gleams by no starlight, does not move, is not square, nor round, nor has substance, nor has been created but is just some heavenly Where. On p. 39 of his *Dialogue Theologico-Astronomicus,*[269] Jacque du Bois, the preacher from Leyden writes:

"Anyone who denies that the Empyrean heaven is above the visible heavens, either does not believe the inspired word of Scripture, or has not learnt the basics of Christianity."

Various questions on the Empyrean heaven

But as is frequently the case with other topics, so too in this matter various questions can be raised. Is the Empyrean heaven comprised of form and matter? Is it an elementary body, separate from all material substance, and thus a spiritual entity? Is it subject to motion? Does it exert an influence in this sublunary region? Does it feel the flames of the stars? Is God contained in its scope? In what place is the Empyrean heaven located? What shape does it have? What size is it? When did it come into existence?

Some say that the Empyrean heaven was created at the same instant as the Earth and the waters. At any rate, the words of *Genesis* 1

"In the beginning God created the heavens and the Earth."

could be interpreted as being about the Empyrean heaven. Others say that that although God *could* have created the Empyrean heaven at the same instant as the Earth and from a similar substance to the terrestrial, there is no basis for the affirmation that He actually did this.

Is this heaven solid?

---

[269] v. Book II Chapter VIII

Some think that the most remote part of the Empyrean heaven is solid and that it is separated from the lower part as if by some vault made of a coarse and opaque material so that the light and the Empyrean itself is not seen by mortals still living in the world. One is reminded of how, among the Jews, the Holy of Holies was covered by a veil.

The shape of this heaven

The shape of the Empyrean heaven is also problematic, particularly in respect of the outward facing side. As regards the inward facing side the consensus is that it definitely is spherical and, as it were, fits against the (supposed) Primum Mobile. As regards the outward facing side, or the highest part, some think it is spherical in shape, because a sphere is the most perfect of shapes. But because the Empyrean heaven is not ordered for motion but for stability, it seems to some more appropriate that, in accord with Apocalypse 21[270] where the city is said to be square, the outward facing side is a square.

The size of the so called Empyrean Heaven

Some want to measure the size of the Empyrean. They think that the length is more than 10 000 000 miles and the width more than 3 600 000. But these figures are not reconcilable with the enormous distance of the stars. Thus Fr. Antonius Maria Schyrlaeus[271] of the Society of Jesus in the *Oculus Enoch et Eliae*, Book IV Chapter 1 Section 6 p. 195 undertook a different calculation based on his assumption (v. Chapter 27 above) about the distance to the Sphere of the fixed stars. He obtained a value for the height of the Empyrean heaven (neglecting the waters considered to be above the heavens) by reasoning in the following manner. The distance to the fixed stars is the square of the distance to Saturn which is equivalent to 1 000 000 diameters of the sun. Similarly the square of the distance to the fixed stars — 1 000 000 000 000

---

[270] Presumably the reference is to Apocalypse:21:15. "The angel that was speaking to me was carrying a gold measuring rod to measure the city and its gates and wall. The plan of the city is perfectly square."

[271] Fr. Antonius Maria Schyrlaeus of Rheita (1597–1660) was a Czech astronomer and optical instrumentalist. He was a professor of philosophy at Trier. His book *Oculus Enoch et Eliae*, published in 1645, describes the binocular telescope, the forerunner of modern binoculars and also contains a map of the moon. The Rheita crater on the moon is named after him. He was a resolute anti-Copernican. Parts of his life are obscure. Von Guericke appears to be mistaken in supposing him a Jesuit. Up to about 1620 he was a Capuchin and his subsequent religious affiliation is unclear. (Richard Westfall, Galileo Project).

diameters of the sun — gives the distance to the Empyrean heaven. This is 10 000 000 000 000 diameters of the Earth or 20 000 000 000 000 radii or 20 000 000 000 000 000 leagues.[272] As any diameter is to its circumference as 7 to 22, the circumference of the Empyrean Heaven will be 125 714 185 714 285 714 leagues. Thus if one assumes that one of the blessed traverses in one day as much space in the Empyrean Heaven as the circumference of the Earth, then such a blessed could not traverse the circumference of the Empyrean heaven in 10 000 000 years.

Schyrlaeus uses these numbers to emphasise the power, the loftiness and the greatness of God, whom Sacred Scripture asserts to be higher than heaven itself. As regards opinions that may be held about the internal height of the Empyrean heaven, nothing is determined, except that the said author states in the second part (Chapter 1 Page 6) that it is more than 8 000 000 000 times greater than the entire firmament and admonishes the Epicureans to consider from this how great the works of God are. He furthermore instructs them to ponder that the Empyrean heaven is still billions of times higher.

Will the Empyrean heaven pass away?

Will this immense and vast Empyrean heaven pass away, as heaven and Earth will pass away, when the day of the Last Judgment comes? Or will it endure for eternity? On this issue too opinions differ. Some assert that it will be annihilated and some deny it. Some distinguish the airy heaven, the ethereal heaven and the Empyrean heaven and restrict the prospect of annihilation to just the airy heaven, or to the airy heaven and the ethereal heaven. Thus the question arises again, what would remain in the vastness of Space circumscribed by the Empyrean heaven, if the airy heaven or the ethereal heaven or both were to pass away? Would it be a vacuum? Or would it be nothing? What purpose would be served by it? What good it would it be to anybody? Of what substance would the Space be made of, which, according to the opinion of Ricciolus (assuming the distance of the Sphere of the fixed stars from the Earth is 210 000 times the Earth's radius) could comprise 38 808

---

[272] The Latin unit is "milliaribus horariis" which Schimank translates to Wegstunden — the distance a man can walk in an hour. If we take this as four miles, and translate "Wegstunde" as "league", then the radius of the Earth is 1,000 leagues.

000 000 000 000 times the volume of the Earth. See Book II Chapter 11 for our thoughts on all these matters.

Appendix 4 Book I Chapter 34 – Beyond this Cosmos are there others, perhaps many others, and are there a definite number of them, or are they innumerable?

Earlier at the beginning of this book we mentioned some of those who have taken the view that there are many, or even infinitely many, Cosmoses — to wit, Aristarchus, Anaximenes, Xenophanes, Democritus, Epicurus, Metrodorus of Chios,[273] Leucippus, Diogenes and others whom Theodoretus,[274] in Book I of *On healing the ills of the Greeks,* and St.Thomas, in Part 1 p. 9 Question 68 Article 3, enumerate.[275] This is what caused Alexander the Great to burst into tears complaining that, although there were many Cosmoses, he was not even master of one.

Plutarch recounts (*Book on Oracles*) that Plato at one time thought that there were many Cosmoses. The above-mentioned Metrodorus thought that, just as in a big field we don't see just one ear of wheat growing, it is absurd to suppose that there should be just one Cosmos in infinite Space. That the number of Cosmoses is unlimited stems, according to him, from the fact that since there are innumerable reasons why this Cosmos has arisen, there must be infinitely many other cosmoses. Where so many causes are operating there must be a multitude of outcomes. The ultimate causes are either the atoms or the elements. (v. Plutarch, *The Opinions of Philosophers*, Book 1 Chapter 5.)

The nature of the Universe

Empedocles asserted that there was just one Cosmos, but that this Cosmos was not the entire universe but just the small material part of it and that the remaining space is empty. Seleucid took the view that this Cosmos is infinite while Diogenes thought that the universe was infinite but that the Cosmos was finite.

---

[273] v. footnote to Book II Chapter 3

[274] Theodoretus (c.393–457) was a monk who reluctantly became Bishop of Cyrus c. 423. He was an energetic preacher, theologian, philosopher and active participant in the Nestorian controversy against St. Cyril. He attended the Councils of Ephesus and Chalcedon. The *Graecarum affectionum curatio* is an apologetic work in 12 Books. (Catholic Encyclopaedia)

[275] The reference given by von Guericke appears mistaken. The reference should be to *Summa Theologica*, Part I, Question 68 Article 4 which is a consideration of "Whether there is only one heaven". Aquinas gives the opinions of among others St. Basil, St. John Damascene, St. Augustine. Q. 68 Article 3 is a consideration of "Whether the firmament divides waters from waters."

The Stoics drew a distinction between the universe and the totality of being. They taught that the universe and the void are both infinite. According to them, the totality of being is the Cosmos except for the void, so that the totality of being and the Cosmos are not identical. (v. Plutarch Book II Chapter 1, *On the Opinions of Philosophers*)

Authors who consider that there is just a single Cosmos

Thales and his followers take the opposite view and assert that the Cosmos is finite and unique. Plato too shared the view that there was a single Cosmos and universe and supported his opinion with the following three arguments:

(1) It would not be complete if it did not comprise everything.
(2) It would not reflect the model from which it was formed, if it were not unique.
(3) That it would not be incorruptible if there was something outside it.

Aristotle's arguments for there being just one Cosmos

Aristotle seeks to prove, by adducing many considerations, that there is a unique Cosmos. These are as follows.[276]
(1) The Cosmos comprises all the matter which occurs in nature. From this fact it follows that all sensible bodies are located within this Cosmos (this is indeed an assumption he makes) and there are none and can be none beyond it.
(2) He is of the opinion that, if there were other Cosmoses, they would all necessarily be composed of the same matter. Since they are of the same nature, each one of the constituent bodies would have the same potential. If there were many Cosmoses, the Earth of another Cosmos would be carried to the centre of this Cosmos, or vice-versa.
(3) He does not consider that any thing that might be outside the Cosmos could occupy a place, or could be aged by the elapse of Time, nor could be susceptible to change. Thus he concludes that no such thing could exist.
(4) He thinks that the motion of one Cosmos would impede the motion of another at the point of contact of adjoining Cosmoses.

---

[276] The points that von Guericke enumerates here are an offhand summary of Aristotle's arguments in *De Caelo* I.8 [276a.20 –279b.35]

(5) The space between adjoining Cosmoses, which would look like a three sided body, would be a vacuum, a possibility which he denies.

(6) The number of Cosmoses would be indeterminate.

(7) The bulk of matter would be scattered through the several Cosmoses and not concentrated in one, as the economy of nature would seek.

(8) He concludes that it is neither necessary nor desirable that some inhabitants should be separated from others.

(9) There would not be a single First Mover.

The Theological School agree with Aristotle's view that there is just one Cosmos, but disagree with him when he says that it is impossible that there should be many Cosmoses. The theologians emphatically believe that God can and could have created multiple Cosmoses, even if it is the case that, in the exercise of His free will, He created in Time a single Cosmos. These questions are further treated in Book VII.

Appendix 5 Book I Chapter 35 – On the Imaginary Space outside the Universe

Is there anything outside the universe?

According both to Aristotle, effectively the leader of philosophers, and to the widely held views of many other philosophers and theologians, there are not a multitude of Cosmoses beyond this one. Sound reason dictates that the Cosmos will indeed have an ultimate boundary. Since it is against God and Nature that anything (God excepted) should be infinitely extended, the human mind naturally asks what, ultimately, there is outside the Cosmos. In other words what terminates the Cosmos — is it the so called Primum Mobile, or the Caelum Empyreum, or the waters believed to be above the heavens[277] or something else? What contains it all? What surrounds it?

Aristotle held that outside the universe there is nothing

Aristotle (*De Caelo* Book III Chapter 8 & 9) has thought carefully about this. He explicitly states that beyond the last heaven (which for him is the Sphere of the fixed stars, or in other words, the natural body or substance associated with the outermost revolution) there is neither place nor time nor a vacuum but just nothingness. Furthermore he is emphatic that, according to his thinking, no natural body could exist there.

What is Imaginary Space?

Certain thinkers consider that there is some sort of Imaginary Space there which they call "possible localisations". This nomenclature allows different people to form mental pictures or images of this in different ways.

The opinion of the Coimbra School

The Coimbra School (Commentary on Aristotle's Physics Book VII Chapter 10[278] Question 2 Article 4 concerning the Space diffused

---

[277] "Waters above the Heavens" is an allusion to the biblical cosmology (v. Genesis 1:7–9 or Ps:148:4) precariously reconciled with the Aristotelian scheme. Chapter XXXII of Book I, translated in Appendix 2, explores this matter more extensively.

[278] This chapter of the *Physics* is concerned to argue that the First Mover, the agent of all change, has no magnitude or parts and is located at the outer edge of the Cosmos.

equally inside as outside the heavens) has this to say:

"Firstly this space is not a true quantity endowed with threefold dimensionality, for otherwise it could not act as a receptacle for bodies. This is because it is not within the power of nature that many three dimensional bodies should exist in the same place. Likewise it is not some other real thing or definite entity since no objective reality except God has existed from eternity and this space would have always existed and would have to continue always to exist. Secondly it is not a construction of the intellect since by its very nature, without any action of the intellect, bodies within the Cosmos subsist in it and, beyond the Cosmos, could so subsist. Therefore in this Imaginary Space the presence of God is manifest, not as it is with some real entity, but through his immeasurableness, which, as the entire Cosmos cannot encompass it, necessarily extends outside the heavens and exists in infinite space. Thus it is to be noted that God is manifest in different ways — in his own Being, in created things, and beyond the Cosmos. He is manifest in his own Being because His existence is completely autonomous. He is in created things through His essence, His presence and His power. He is beyond the Heavens because no place, whether real or imaginary, can be cut off from Him. Thus we conceive the extra-cosmic Space as something that is truly there, but not in the same way as something real and definite."

The commentary on *De Caelo*, Book I Chapter 5 confirms this. The authors write:

"Note however that there cannot be any body beyond the heavens but there does nevertheless exist space or a Receptacle which could contain bodies."

Various other opinions

Some people say that the space of the imagination is just nothingness itself. Others say that it is a thing void of all reality. Still others proffer the view that it is the negation of all being.

To the first opinion some would make the following response. 'As regards nothing, this, exactly because it is nothing, cannot be imagined as space, for a nothingness (unlike space) cannot possess properties of breadth, width, length or depth.' To the second opinion they argue that if Imaginary Space is space void of all realities and being, then Imaginary Space is a vacuum and accordingly the vacuum and Imaginary Space are one and the same. To the third they would counter that if Imaginary Space is the negation of all being then this space cannot even be spoken of.

Others take the view that Imaginary Space is a purely mental phenomenon, and from this they conclude that, as before the creation of the

Cosmos there was no mind to form images, it follows that there wasn't then an Imaginary Space. Since God cannot be in what doesn't exist (as for instance in a chimera) but only in what does exist and as Imaginary Space, in their view, does not exist, God cannot be in Imaginary Space.

Others understand Imaginary Space as some immeasurable physical substance, representing pure possibility, and spreading out infinitely in all directions. A variant of this view is to understand Imaginary Space as providing a possible location for physical substance of this kind.

Lessius[279] thinks that Imaginary Space is God himself

Some say that Imaginary Space is God himself who in accordance with his immeasurability is everywhere — in other words He is necessarily infinitely diffused. Lessius (Book II, *On Divine Perfection* Chapter 2). For if anyone were to go beyond all the heavens and were to search in the space, which he forms in his imagination but which isn't really there, he would certainly discover God.

Many people give no credence whatever to Imaginary Space. They argue that what is only conceived in the intellect or the imagination isn't something real. For example: anyone could *conceive* that he has a thousand gold pieces when he doesn't even have a single one. Therefore, they argue, there is no reality corresponding to the Imaginary Space.

The opinion of Descartes

A more recent philosopher, René Descartes, thinks that Imaginary Space is something real. In Part 2 Article 21[280] of his *Principles of Philosophy* he writes:

"We further discover that the Cosmos — in other words the entirety of corporeal substance — is extended without limit. For wherever we conceive these limits to be, we can not only imagine space extended indefinitely beyond them, but it is also the case that what we present to ourselves in our imagination we present as reality i.e. that we see this infinitely extended space as objectively real and accordingly containing indefinitely extended corporeal substance. This is so (this is what Descartes claims) because the idea of extension, which we always have for any kind of space, is plainly identical with the idea of corporeal substance. From this it can be easily inferred that the substance of which the heavens are constituted is no different than that of the earth. Even if there were infinitely many Cosmoses, it is incon-

---

[279] v. footnote to Chapter 6.
[280] Von Guericke quotes Articles 21 and 22 from Part 2 of the Principles of Philosophy.

ceivable that they would consist of anything other than this one and the same substance. But then there cannot be many, but just one Cosmos. For we clearly realise that this substance, whose nature is solely determined by the fact that it is extended, already occupies absolutely all imaginable spaces, in which these other worlds are supposed to be. We cannot form any idea of any other sort of matter. Thus one and the same sort of substance exists throughout the totality of being, i.e. that which is recognised as having the sole property of being extended."

The above is Descartes' thinking on this issue.

What is to be finally concluded about Imaginary Space?

Finally, if Imaginary Space is to be admitted, it follows that it is infinite and immeasurable. That is to say, it is an expanse infinite in all directions with infinite length, depth and breadth. It likewise follows that it is incorruptible, eternal, fixed and unchanging so that it cannot be abrogated by any physical or mental exertion. It can accommodate any body whatsoever, whether it be large or small. We discuss this matter further in Book II.

LIBER TERTIUS

DE

PROPRIIS EXPERIMENTIS

Book III
Concerning my own Experiments

Chapter I – On the Air, its origin, nature and properties

To give a better understanding of our experiments we shall, to catch the interest of the reader, present some novel, but definitely established, facts about air. In the following chapters we shall provide the demonstrations.

The nature of air

Air is something physical which emanates from water, from the Earth and from other substances and which then flows into the surrounding space. (v. Book IV Chapter 1) In other words, air is just something that is given off — like an odour or effluvium of water, earth or other physical bodies. This is particularly evident when water or some other humid substance is shaken, tossed or rubbed. (We shall show that wind and the sound of organ notes can be produced through the falling of water.)

Air is not an element[281]

Particularly, when a process of fermentation or putrefaction of a humid body sets in, then, more markedly, an odour or some other vapour is given off. This is just air. Therefore air cannot properly be said to be an element since it is just an effluvium.

Air is not perceived by smell

The most familiar kind of air, emanating both from land and sea, is just the odour of the Earth itself. It is not however detected by our sense of smell because from the very beginning of our lives we accustom ourselves to it by actually living in it. By contrast, we do detect by the sense of smell anything odorous coming from other sources that becomes mixed with ordinary air. This happens in many ways and depends on the properties of the things themselves and our own sensibilities.

Air is something physical

All air or odour is indeed a physical substance. It is however very diffuse and susceptible of expansion or dilation.

What the sphere of the air is

---

[281] This was Guericke's own opinion held against the contemporary consensus that air was an one of the four elements — earth, air, fire and water.

All the air around the Earth is a result of a corporeal potency[282] of the Earth and forms an orb. In other words, air is a substance released from the Earth, which surrounds the entire globe and which sustains all the animals on the earth.

Air is never reduced to water

Once air or odour has arisen from water or from some other source, it never becomes water again but remains as air. This is the case even if moisture is evaporated by the heat of the sun or of a fire into the air and through condensation is reduced again to liquid water. However the air is not reduced to water as can be seen from the experiments described in Chapter 2 and elsewhere. It can also be observed on a really cold winter's day when the air seems to sparkle as if it were made of little scintillating particles. This effect is caused by the diffuse suspension of water particles in the air which freeze and separate from the air. The air itself however never freezes.

Air expands by being heated

Air, according as heat is applied or withdrawn, expands to a greater or lesser degree. Consequently hot air occupies more space and cold air less. This change is commonly, but improperly, called by philosophers a rarefaction of the air. For when the air is expanded, it does not become rarer or more diffuse or better able to penetrate hard substances, but just occupies more space. When the heat leaves it, the air contracts and its volume diminishes. So it is not a question of there being more or less air but of the heat which the air, to a greater or less degree, absorbs and also then releases as it cools.

Air becomes denser through coldness

Just as air is expanded through being heated, so, through being more and more cooled, it becomes denser because of the coldness and consequently occupies less space.

Air can be compressed

---

[282] The Latin is "corporeae virtutis". For von Guericke this is an important general concept to be contrasted with the "virtutes incorporeae". The former means the capacity for giving off a material effluvium; the latter, the capacity to exert an influence that is not mediated by substance — essentially, action at a distance.

Additionally air has the property that it can be made ever denser by strenuous compression but will expand to occupy space that becomes available to it. These properties can be seen from experiments. For example, we see this effect in inflated balls or in little fountains where water is sprayed upwards by the action of compressed air. In the latter case, a syringe or a pipe is used to force in as much air as possible, without risking a breakage of the equipment. When the fountain is opened, the compressed air explosively drives out the water that had previously been poured into it.

There are limits to both the contraction and expansion of air

Just as everything has in the end determinate bounds, so also there are limits, beyond which one cannot go, to the compression and rarefaction of air. Air in a sufficiently strong metal vessel can be compressed by repeated exertion of pressure so that ultimately it behaves as a solid substance similar to water. In the opposite direction, the tiniest little bubble of air, the size of a pinhead, placed in an empty vessel expands a hundred times until it finally disappears into nothingness.

Air has gravity[283] and presses down on itself

Since the air around the Earth is a physical substance and thus has a certain gravity, it presses down upon itself. Of course, the air higher up presses down on the air at a lower altitude. As a consequence, the low altitude air all around us is much more compressed than that higher up. When something is compressed there is more of it, and when there is more of something it is heavier. Therefore here on the surface of the Earth we have more air, with greater gravity, than on the top of towers or mountains and, also of course, the higher the air is the lighter and more diffuse it is.

---

[283] Although von Guericke uses the word "gravitas" one cannot not take this in a clear-cut Newtonian sense. One can either take it as meaning simply "weight" (as Schimank does) or as von Guericke's wishing to make the point that air has "gravitas" rather than the "levitas" attributed to it by Aristotelian physics. In Book II.3 [331a] of the *De Generatione et Corruptione* Aristotle writes "The simple bodies, since they are four, fall into two pairs which belong to the two regions, each to each: For Fire and Air are forms of the body moving towards the 'limit', while Earth and Water are forms of the body which move towards the 'centre'."(transl. H. H. Joachim O.U.P 1930) In *De Caelo*, Book IV.4 [311a/b] a more sophisticated view is presented. "Neither (air nor water) is absolutely either light or heavy. .... All the elements except fire have gravitas and all but earth levitas. ... In its own place each of these bodies has gravitas, even air."

Clouds in the air are associated with their own definite regions

Our view is that the air is divided into separate layers or regions. Each species of cloud, whether heavier or lighter, occupies a definite region of air — a region where the surrounding air has the same density as the cloud. But if the air were everywhere equally compressed, it would be equally heavy at all altitudes. Clouds could not therefore form and be stable in different regions, but, just as in water where a given object either floats or sinks to the bottom, a cloud would either descend to the surface of the Earth or ascend to the most remote part of the air.

Air presses down on everything

On account of its gravity, air presses down not just on itself but on everything below it and almost always with a fixed pressure. This is not felt by us humans because we live in the air itself. This surrounds us, presses equally on us from all directions and at the same time penetrates us. As fish in water do not feel any pressure, so much the more do animals in air not perceive any pressure.

The gravity of the air is like that of a water column twenty cubits[284] high

The gravity of the air upon the earth is as much as the gravity of water about twenty Magdeburg cubits high. If, on the surface of the earth, water stood twenty cubits high, it would press down on everything beneath it. The air presses in the same way.

However it is by no means the case that the air always has one and the same gravity. It becomes lighter when the rain has fallen.

The air around the Earth does not always have the same gravity

If the air did not have some gravity, it would fly off into space and would abandon the Earth on account of its orbital motion.[285] (What

---

[284] The Latin is "ulna" and the German "Ellen". A "cubit" was the length of the forearm from the fingertips to the elbow. The cubit was divided into 7 hands each of 4 digits. The length of the cubit was about 45 cms.

[285] Von Guericke uses the phrase "annuam lationem". He carefully defines "latio", distinguishing it from "motus" (motion) in Book V Chapter 15 and 16. " 'Motus' is an action of a being, which exists autonomously by an intrinsic principle which stimulates unmediated movement i.e. it operates without assistance from anything else, as, for example a living body moves itself and its parts, the eyes, arms, feet etc. 'Latio' is the transport of a being from place to place. It is also called local movement or movement to somewhere."

gravity truly is shall be discussed in Book IV Chapter 3 when we consider the Earth's conserving potency.[286]

Water always seeps into the air of the lower region

Near the Earth some portion of water — sometimes more sometimes less according to the temperature — is always absorbed by the air. Even though the air presses down on water it does not do so to the point where it enters the water because it is lighter.[287]

The effect of air

Air causes change in bodies and can transmit cold and heat to them. It itself is well adapted to absorbing all sorts of things — notably light, sound and smell, but also mists, vapours etc. It has an amazing effect both on the animate and the inanimate. It flows gently over the outsides of animals, protects them, keeps them moist and refreshes them as it changes. In ensuring they maintain an appropriate size,[288] it penetrates them and directly preserves their life by allowing them to breathe.

A flame rises because of the gravity of air

A flame rises in air, as does vapour and smoke, not as an effect of innate levity but because of the gravity of the surrounding air. This causes the flame or vapour or smoke, all of which are just air which has become hotter and consequently more diffuse and less dense, to be lifted up. The effect has the same cause as the rising of a bubble in water. Thus if there were no air, smoke would not rise.

The air surrounding the Earth fills all empty spaces

Near the Earth every part of space relinquished by a body is never left to become a vacuum but is filled with air. The same thing happens to the space in water which a fish occupies with its body. When the fish

---

[286] The Latin is "virtus conservativa". Book IV Chapter 3 is entitled "De Natura et Qualitatibus Virtutis Impulsivae" (On the Nature and Properties of the Impulsive Potency)

[287] Von Guericke appears never to have come to a realisation of the absorption of air by water and its release as bubbles when the pressure is sufficiently low and this phenomenon is distinct from boiling.

[288] The Latin is "ad mediocritatem adducendo". I assume that von Guericke has in mind his experiments with grapes and animals in a vacuum and is alluding to the role of air pressure in the compression or bloating of a body. Equalisation of air pressure is needed to avoid both extremes.

changes place, the space that it used to occupy becomes filled with water.

Chapter II – On my first attempt at creating a vacuum — by the extraction of water

When I was considering such matters as the immeasurability of space (as discussed in Book II Chapter 1) and of its necessary omnipresence, the following experiment came to mind.

Suppose a wine butt or a beer barrel is filled with water and then thoroughly corked so that no external air can get in. Suppose a syringe or a bronze pipe is fixed to the bottom of the butt, through which one may extract water. The water through its own gravity would necessarily sink lower and above it there would be left in the butt a space empty of air and, in fact, of any other physical substance.

See Illustration V Figure 1

To put my idea into practice, I procured a brass syringe $a\ b\ c$, usually used to quench fires, a shaft (c or f) and an accurately constructed piston g so that there was no space for any air to get in or escape around the sides of the piston. Additionally there were two leather valves — the interior one d within the cover a of the syringe to let water in and the exterior one b to let water out. After the attachment of the syringe to the lower part of the butt a, for which I used an iron ring e fitted with four lugs, I tried to extract water. However either the lugs or the metal screws attaching the syringe to the butt broke before water could be extracted from the butt.

The situation was not beyond retrieval. A remedy was sought and with the help of stronger screws we finally found that three strong men pulling the shaft of the syringe could cause water to follow the piston and be ejected through the upper valve b.

Air passes through wood

A noise, like that of violently boiling water, was heard throughout the whole butt. This lasted for quite some time and continued until air had replaced the water which had been extracted from the bottom of the butt.

Some way around this problem had to be found. A smaller butt was procured and placed inside the larger one. A pump with a longer neck going through the wood of both butts was installed. Firstly, I had the smaller butt filled with water and its inlet stopped up. Then the larger butt was similarly filled with water. I repeated the experiment from the beginning. The result was that when water was extracted from the smaller butt, there was left, beyond doubt, a vacuum in its place.

Water passes through wood

But at the end of the day when the experiment was completed and all noise and bustle had been stilled, a varying note was intermittently heard, like the humming of some small bird. This lasted almost three full days.

However when the inlet to the smaller butt was finally opened it was discovered that it was for the most part filled with air and water. There was however a part that was still a vacuum because, in the course of opening it, air rushed in.

Air is generated when water rubs against wood [289]

As a result of this everyone was left wondering how water had found its way into a butt that had been everywhere so carefully strengthened and sealed. I repeated the experiment many times in different forms. Finally I concluded that when under high pressure water penetrates wood and, in rubbing against the wood as it goes through it, some air is always generated in the butt along with the incoming water. (This phenomenon is important in later experiments.) The butt however cannot be completely filled because of the limited permeability of the wood to water. When the pressure is lowered, the penetration of air and water ceases. Consequently what remains is a sort of semi-vacuum.

---

[289] The air observed in the inner butt after three days would now be accounted for by the air dissolved in the water (against which von Guericke does not take any precautions such as boiling the water first) and by the vapour pressure of water at room temperature. The amount of air that can be dissolved in water increases as the pressure rises and decreases as the pressure falls (Henry's Law). At 20⁰C water exerts a vapour pressure of 0.02 Atmospheres i.e. unless this pressure is exerted on its surface the water will begin to boil.

Chapter III – On the second attempt at obtaining a vacuum — by the extraction of air

When I had recognised the porosity of wood, partly by visual inspection and partly by my own experiments, it then seemed to me that a copper sphere of almost any capacity would be more suited to what I was trying to do. (Rev. Fr. Schott in his book "Magdeburg Experiments" calls it a "cooking pot".[290])

See Illustration V Figure II

The one shown as *A* had a volume of 60 – 70 Magdeburg measures.[291] I had this built and equipped with a brass tap at the top. At the bottom a pump with a particularly strong fitting was attached. Then, just as I had previously done with water, I now tried to extract air.

At the start the shaft was easy to move

At the start it was easy to move the handle. However it gradually became more difficult so that pulling it out it was as much as two solidly built men could manage. They continued their pushing and pulling until they were confident that nearly all the air had been extracted.

The copper sphere was crushed by the external air

Suddenly, to general consternation, the copper sphere noisily collapsed on itself like a handkerchief might be crushed in someone's hand. It was as if it had been violently dashed to the ground from a very high tower.

An exact sphere would not have collapsed

I attributed the cause of the collapse to the carelessness of the maker who perhaps had not made it exactly spherical. A flat section, such as it might well have had, would not have been able to resist the weight of the external air. By contrast an exact sphere could easily have done so by virtue of the orientation of its parts so that each reinforces the others.

---

[290] Latin cacabus –i m.
[291] Taking the radius of the copper sphere to be 0.5m a Magdeburg measure comes about to be about four litres.

It was thus vital that the maker should manufacture an exact sphere. This was done and the air sucked out again. As with the previous attempt, sucking out the air was easy at first and became difficult later on. The ceasing of the expulsion of air through the upper valve of the pump was taken as proof that the sphere had been evacuated.

This was the second method of procuring a vacuum.

Air penetrates very easily

When the tap *B* was opened the air rushed into the sphere with such force that it seemed that a man standing in its way would be swept along by the impulse. Anyone letting their face come even to within some distance of the tap found their breathing impaired. One could not safely hold one's hand above the tap for fear that it might be violently drawn towards it.

Even though the sphere seemed to have been completely evacuated, experience showed that, after it had been left for a day or so, it nevertheless ultimately filled up again. This was because air had penetrated around the sides of the piston of the pump and through the valves and the tap. As we shall see below, this problem also had to be addressed.

Chapter IV – On the construction of a special machine to produce a vacuum

Because air, as the most diffuse of substances, has an astonishing way of penetrating little holes and spaces however small they may be, it was always the case that some air found its way past the sides of the piston, or through the air pump or through the valves. It is impossible to obtain a perfect piston and valves that would prevent any air at all from getting past. Accordingly I constructed various machines such that the both the upper and lower valves of the air pump could be immersed in water. Rev. Fr. Kaspar Schott described these, originally in the *Mechanica Hydraulica–pneumatico*,[292] and later in Book I of the *Technica Curiosa*[293] entitled *Mirabilia Magdeburgica*.

Since all this apparatus was difficult to transport and since also His Serene and Potent Excellency, the Lord Elector of Brandenburg, my most clement Master, graciously expressed the wish[294] to see this experiment which had been named "the Magdeburg experiment" by the afore mentioned Rev. Fr. Schott, I accordingly invented the following machine.

See Illustration VI Figures I and II

1. From a blacksmith, one procures an iron tripod *a b c d f* about two cubits high secured at the top with an iron ring *b c* and at the bottom screwed to the floor with iron screws.

See Figures I and III

2. The air pump *g h* is a brass syringe of the type we described in Chapter 2 but at the top it is fitted with a lead flange *y*.

---

[292] *Mechanica Hydraulica–pneumatico*, published in 1657 by Kaspar Schott S.J. was the earliest published account of von Guericke's experiments. The experiment with the valves under water is described and illustrated on p. 445.

[293] *Technica Curiosa* Iconismus II before p. 9.

[294] This request may have been expressed when von Guericke, visiting Berlin in March 1658 on civic business, met the Great Elector personally for the first time. In a letter to Fr. Schott of April 1662 he expressed his appreciation of the Elector's patronage of science and mathematics. On November 21st 1663 he conducted a demonstration for Friedrich Wilhelm at Cölln an der Spree in the Elector's Library. Otto von Schwerin, a tutor to the Elector's sons, recorded the event. (Schneider p. 113)

Figures I and IV

3. For the upper surface of the flange *y* there is a brass covering *m n* fitted with an inlet *n* to which the tap of a vessel to be evacuated can be attached. The covering sits on a circular leather gasket and is fastened with three screws.

4. Let a leather valve (v. Illustration V Fig. I, *d*) be inserted into the middle of this cover from the bottom so that when the shaft *s* of the piston *h* is pulled down it can pull the water or air out of the vessel to be evacuated into the pump *g h* and when it is raised can expel the air or water through the external valve *z*. (v. Illustration VI Fig. IV)

5. Additionally around the lead flange at the top of the pump a vessel such as a copper pail is soldered to collect the water expelled through *z*. (See Fig. I *x x*).

6. The pump *y g h* together with this collecting pail is attached to the tripod by inserting it down through the circular aperture *e* of the above mentioned iron ring and it is then firmly fixed to the ring by three iron screws through the lead flange.

7. To ensure that the lower part of the pump stays fixed, an iron ring *k k* with three arms, which also serve to hold the legs of the tripod together, is secured with iron screws. (v. Fig. I)

8. To one of the legs of the tripod at *w* is similarly attached an iron handle *w u u*, which, pivoting on a dowel at *w*, can be raised or lowered.

9. Finally to this handle is attached an iron rod *u t* which is joined at *t* to the above mentioned wooden shaft *s h*. The piston *h* is fitted to the shaft in the normal manner and in this way the operation of the pump can be got underway.

10. So that no air can get into the pump either from the bottom or around the sides of the piston *h* (Fig. VI) a type of copper cauldron, suspended by three hooks from the three arms *o o o* is used. It is filled with water so that the lower aperture of the pump inside the tube at *k k* and its fittings are always sealed by the water. Thus air cannot get in either above or below.

The extraction of air is brought about by its expansive potency[295]

11. In general, all extraction of air, just as is the case in the operation of this pump, depends on air's own expansive potency, also called its elasticity. (v. Chapter 33) Some air always expands from the vessel to be evacuated into the vacuum inside the pump and from there it is then expelled by the regular movement of the pump. In the end the tiny quantity of air that remains in the vessel does not have sufficient elastic force to push back the leather of the valves which are generally reinforced with brass feathers to ensure that they always close well.

How, using a special tube, even a tiny amount of air can be extracted (Figs. I and IV)

In the upper covering of the pump z m n, between the valve z and the main tube n, a small tube can be fitted together with a little shaft and piston which looks like a nipple. Using this, the leather of the valve within can be artificially controlled. It can be opened and closed so that even the smallest amount of air which might be thought to remain in the vessel is better and more easily able to descend because of its own gravity into the pump. But this is all an aside and really just to satisfy the inquisitive.

When the shaft of the pump is pulled down the internal space necessarily becomes a vacuum

It is clear from the above that this device enables us to produce a spatial vacuum, and that the chain binding matter together, which might otherwise be considered impossible to loosen, can be slackened.[296] If the handle w u u is raised, the piston shaft touches the covering m n and the shaft then fills the entire pump. When however the handle is pulled down, it creates a vacuum in the internal space of the pump into which the air of the attached vessel flows, finally leaving it empty.

---

[295] The Latin is "virtus expansiva"— another example of this comprehensive concept.
[296] Von Guericke is here referring to a Peripatetic doctrine which he also considers in Chapter 19. The Latin is "Spatium Vacuum dari & Vinculum illud, quod alias indissolubile habetur, dissolvi posse."

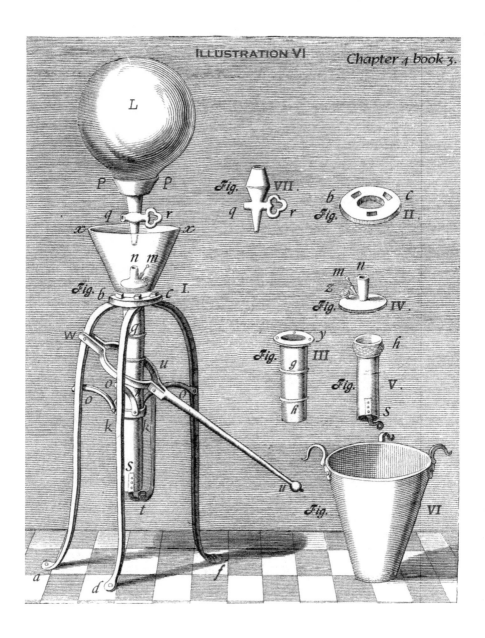

Chapter V – On the third experiment demonstrating a vacuum

For a further demonstration of the vacuum I took the glass flask *L* which is of the type used by apothecaries and commonly called a quarter or half Receiver. Using a pitch-like material, which German goldsmiths call "kitt" rather than solder, I glued a brass bowl *p p* to the neck of the flask. This was in the shape of a lid and was equipped with a tap *q r* designed to fit into the inlet of the pump cover *n*.

Additionally, so that larger objects — birds, fish, mice, clocks, bells candles etc. — could be placed in the flask, I made the tap *q r* removable and so that it could slide in and out of the bowl *p p* making an exact fit, as shown in Fig. VII.

Water burst into the flask with great force and filled it

Having attached this glass flask to the inlet of the pump cover, (one of smaller volume could also have been used) I opened the tap *q r* and sucked the air out of the glass. When no more air could be extracted by moving the piston shaft, I closed the tap, removed the flask and immersed the tap in water. Then when I opened it again, I saw a frenzy of bubbling like a fountain bursting violently from the Earth. This continued, gradually filling up the flask with water to the very top until only a space the size of an Avellan[297] nut was left. I thought, and later confirmed, that this space was filled with air.

My immediate conjecture was that the neck of the tap, from the outlet to the spigot, had filled with air while the flask was being removed and was being taken for immersion in water. This was the air that had formed the spherical air bubble the size of the Avellan nut. Accordingly I thought the evacuation needed to be tried again but this time filling the neck of the tap with water before immersing it. When I did this the flask filled up so that only a space the size of a pea was left unoccupied by water. Even though I repeated the experiment I could never get it to work so that absolutely all the air was excluded.

Air bubbles arise from the turbulent motion of the water

I always observed that the inrush of the water engendered foam and bubbles and naturally conjectured that these bubbles were the reason

---

[297] Avella is a town in Campania near Nola abounding in fruit trees and nuts.

for the unfilled space which remained. However, where they were coming from was by no means evident. Even though I immersed the entire tap together with the cover $p\ p$ which had been glued on, up as far as the glass, the inrushing water nevertheless always produced foam and bubbles. Although while the water was rushing in, the bubbles seemed a hundred times greater than the size of the sphere of air that was left at the end of the process, nonetheless there was always some air left.[298]

---

[298] See footnote to Chapter 2 on dissolved air and vapour pressure.

Chapter VI – On the fourth experiment on making a vacuum — by the extraction of water from a glass vessel

Because it seemed that, using the above technique, some air, albeit less than a thousandth of the volume of the evacuated flask, always remained above the water, I thought about another method. I took a glass vessel, which was spherical at one end and had a long tubular neck at the other (v. Illustration V Fig III) so that water could more easily fall under its own weight from the sphere through the tube. This is commonly called a "phial". I instructed, as previously, that a thin metal vessel welded to a tap, be glued to the tubular neck, as shown in the diagram. I filled the whole vessel with water as far as the mouth of the tap and connected it to the pump inlet *n m* (v. Illustration VI). After pumping was started, I did indeed see water come down into the pump, but at the same time I also saw a fairly large bubble rise up the glass tube. Finally I saw that this was caused by the air trapped in the spigot of the tap. (Generally the spigots of taps are hollowed out and filled with gravel or sand instead of metal.)

The spigots of taps need to be reworked

This made it necessary to obtain a tap whose spigot was entirely cast from brass and then was bored through.

Bubbles arose from the glue

Later when I tried the experiment again, there was no bubble from the spigot, but some small bubbles rose partly from the pitch-based glue, which attached the metal vessel to the glass tube, and partly also in and from the water. Although the experiment was repeated several times over the course of days and no further bubbles rose from the pitch, I nevertheless was unable to find a way of preventing some little bubbles from appearing in the water itself.

The turbulent motion of water caused an emanation of air

Then when I had disconnected the glass tube from the pump and submerged it in water to an adequate depth — so that the spigot was covered — I opened it and saw the same effect of a turbulent inrush of water accompanied by the generation of many small bubbles, as has been described in Chapter 5 in connection with the extraction of air. The tube was again similarly filled with water but almost more so than before. Nevertheless some air remained in it. The remaining air was hardly comparable in size to the upward rush of bubbles. Of a hundred or more bubbles seen when the water was surging up the tube, only about four or five seemed to remain at the end. However some people, who wanted to deny that there ever had been a vacuum in the tube, took this as an excuse to reject the experiment.

In a vacuum bubbles are bigger than they otherwise would be

However these endeavours were not fruitless. A number of things were learnt from the experiment. The first was that the little bubbles had been hidden in the water so that they could not be seen, but when they encountered the vacuum they became a hundred times bigger than they previously had been. The second was that many bubbles were formed in the water in consequence of the forces of compression and friction experienced by the water in the spigot and the neck of the tap.[299] The third was that many little bubbles were generated by the turbulent motion of the water itself. These would not have appeared had the water remained stationary. Even when they had been generated they would have remained invisible but for the encounter with a vacuum which caused them to expand so greatly as to become visible.

---

[299] This echoes von Guericke's earlier statement about water generating bubbles through friction as it passes through wood. The phenomena he notes can be accounted for by the release of dissolved air and temporary boiling in the non-equilibrium state while the water is rushing up the tube. The bubbles due to boiling would re-liquefy when equilibrium is re-established and the released dissolved air would remain.

Chapter VII – On a fifth and more accurate way of demonstrating a vacuum

After the above experiments had been tried and properly understood, I had a glassblower make another glass vessel (Illustration VII, Fig. I *A*), a Magdeburg cubit in length, cylindrical in shape and about the thickness of a man's arm. One end was hermetically sealed and at the other end, where it was open, I glued, as before, a metal covering *B* to which, also as before, a tap *C* had been soldered. Additionally I had this tap fitted with yet another cover *D* and two more taps *E* and *F*. The purpose of *E* was to control the interior tap *C* from one side; the purpose of *F* was to control the connection to the inlet *n* of the pump.

It is necessary that the taps be immersed in water (v. Fig V[300])

Next I filled not just the vessel *A* but also even the covering *D* with water right to the top at *G*, closed the tap and then set it aside for a day or so. Afterwards when I set it up again[301] I saw a small air bubble rise which I thought must have been generated in the water itself from the time when the water was poured in. Over a period the bubble had formed itself into a spherical shape.

In water small bubbles arise because of the motion of the water while it is being poured

I therefore turned the flask upside down, let the bubble out and then refilled the space it had occupied with a drop of water. I repeated this for a number of days.

Then I connected the flask in the usual way to the pump and, by turning the spigots of the taps, pumped out water to about halfway down the flask. This time, in contrast to the earlier experiments, there were no little bubbles and the level of the water sank without any turbulence.

Water in a vacuum makes a noise as it crashes into itself

When the flask was detached and the taps opened, there arose, in consequence of shaking the flask, not just some little bubbles in the water, but the noisy crashing of the water itself against the interior walls of the

---

[300] The reference to Fig. V is ambiguous, but he is clearly dealing with his earlier problem of air entering the system by immersing it in water.
[301] He is inverting the vessel in order to attach it to the pump at *n*.

flask as if it were made of some hard material such as pebbles. The consequence was that the glass itself, for some reason not understood by me, unexpectedly shattered. It was then necessary to obtain another glass tube of the same kind with particularly thick walls and to try the experiment again.

Water in a vacuum separates out and creates small empty spaces

When this was done and the glass vigorously shaken up and down, I saw the water spread itself out and empty space open up within the water itself which then closed back with a bang as if two poles were being beaten against each other. Moreover, by the very collision of the fragments of water a small bubble was always generated in the middle of the water.

Some air is always generated when water collides with itself

From the above, the following was clearly visible. In the hollowed out region formed by the separating water there was absolutely nothing but space emptied of all air. This follows because, as the glass tube was closed from all sides, no external air whatever could get in. As noted, in the very middle of the reflux of the water, a single small bubble was generated. If we assume that this bubble had not been in the evacuated tube to start with, its appearance must be attributed to the turbulent motion and energetic collision of the water. Had the bubble been generated in anything other than a vacuum it would have been so small as to be hardly visible.

A demonstration of an empty pocket of space

Internal air, if there had been any in the upper part of the tube, could not penetrate the water, which is naturally and always below rather than above air. This separation happened either in the bottom of the tube or in the middle of the water. Indeed, the severity and noise of the collision of the separated waters shows that there was no air in that little space of separated water. Such an effect could not be brought about in any other way than in an evacuated tube of this sort.

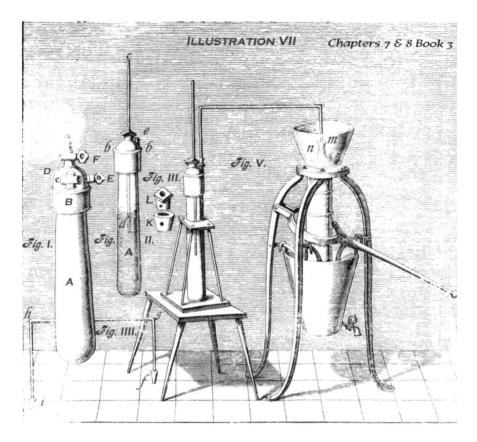

Chapter VIII – The sixth experiment — on the creation of the ulti-mate vacuum

The previous experiment gave grounds for scepticism to those who refuse to admit that a vacuum could exist. The basis of their scepticism was the following observation. Both when the water separated because the spigot of the tap was turned, and when the water vigorously collid-ed with itself when the glass tube was shaken, there was always a bub-ble generated which rose into the evacuated upper part of the tube.[302]

Some people do not admit the elasticity of air but, however, con-tradicting themselves, maintain that the tiniest bubble of air can fill an entire vessel

---

[302] The argument of the sceptics is that bubbles are formed because nature seeks to prevent a vacuum.

In company with some others, Dr. Deusing[303] in his *Disquisition on the Vacuum* does not admit that air, apart from the case where an external force is applied to compress it, has any elasticity or natural impulse to expand. According to this view a small bubble of air of the sort noted above could not fill the tube, as no external force is applied to cause the elasticity necessary to fill the tube. Nevertheless in objecting to the experiment they maintain that an arbitrarily small pocket of air in an evacuated tube expands to fill the whole tube. They say they would only be prepared to admit that the tube is empty if they were to see: (1) all the water sink out of the tube; (2) that absolutely no air could in any way enter the tube in place of the departing water; (3) no bubble, however small it might be, rising in the water.

Another device for creating a perfect vacuum

Accordingly I thought up another little device. This entailed having two tubes, of which one (narrower and longer) would be permanently immune from any inrush of air or generation of bubbles and consequently would preserve a perfect vacuum.

The construction of this device

I took a glass tube of the same kind as described in a previous chapter, of length about one cubit. (Illustration VII Fig. II *A*) To this, at the open end, I affixed a metal cover *b b* just as I had been accustomed to do with other similar vessels. Through the inlet of this cover I inserted a narrower glass tube *c d* of length about one and a half cubits which reached to the middle of the thicker tube *A*, as shown in the figure.[304] To one side of the inlet, at *e*, I soldered the valve *e* (depicted at *K*) which was designed in a special way so that it could replace the tap. Finally I glued the cover *b b* to the tube *A* with the sort of glue that goldsmiths usually use.

I now describe the valve *e*. I had two small brass thimble-like vessels, *K* and *L*, made. The smaller one, *L*, was sealed at the bottom, and so en-

---

[303] Anton Deusing (1612–1666) was a Dutch professor at Groningen and author of works, mostly on medical subjects, but also on physics and mathematics. His *Disquisitio Physico-Mathematico de Vacuo* (Amsterdam 1661) asserts that there neither is, nor could be, a vacuum in nature and claims to survey and refute the experiments adduced up to that time in support of the vacuum.

[304] The tube *c d is* sealed at *c* and open at *d*.

gineered that it fitted very tightly into the bigger one *K*, filling the hollow space in *K* completely. Each of *K* and *L* had a small hole at the side. The holes exactly matched when *L* was placed inside *K*. Thus when *L* was rotated inside *K* the valve opened and closed.

There is no horror of a vacuum

After I had built this apparatus in this way, I filled the tube *A* with water so that the outlet *d* of the narrower tube would always remain immersed in water whether the pump was turned up or down. Then I turned it at an angle so that that the narrower tube *c d* also was filled quite far up with water. When this was done and the tube stood up straight again, the water remained suspended inside the tube *c d*. This was not because of the horror of a vacuum, as people frequently claim but because, as we shall see, of the gravity of the air pressing down on the water in tube *A* which prevents the sinking of the water in the tube *c d*.

After doing this, I positioned this device to one side of the pump described in Chapter 4 and connected it with a special metal tube *f g h i* like a siphon. (v. Illustration VII Fig. IV) This was done so that the end *f* was fitted to the inlet tube *n* of the pump and the other end to the valve *e* of my new piece of apparatus. The fittings were very exact as can be seen from Fig. V.

When all this was duly completed I gave instructions that the air be pumped out. (This made use of the small tube discussed above in Chapter 4, Point 11. With the help of this tube the leather of the inner valve of the pump could be opened and an unimpeded descent of any remaining air enabled.) When this was done I immediately and clearly saw water descend in the glass tube *c d*, with many little bubbles being generated everywhere, equally in the lower, as in the upper, part of the tube.

The bubbles which adhere to the glass are an emanation from glass

At first I thought these arose only from the water. But I presently realised that, as well as from the water, they arose both from the glass and the pitch adhesive. Principally I noted that many of the bubbles formed on the glass and the pitch and then gradually grew until they broke into the water and rose up. When the operation of the pump was continued until the air was completely sucked out of the bigger tube A, the water in tube $c\,d$ sank till it settled at the same level as the water in tube A. This was confirmed by visual inspection.

The so called horror of a vacuum exists as a consequence of the gravity of the external air

This phenomenon can be explained as follows. The insertion of the siphon $f\,g\,h\,i$ into the valve e prevents any exertion of pressure by the external air. At the same time, the air trapped in the tube A loses all its expansive or elastic force through being extracted. (Before the extraction, even though there was no possibility for external air to get into the tube through the sealed vent, the air trapped in A held the water suspended in the tube $c\,d$.) It follows from this that the water sinks in the tube $c\,d$ and seeks a lower place because of its own gravity. There is no "horror of a vacuum" effect because such a thing is not part of nature. For if the water in tube $c\,d$ sank to fill the vacuum in tube A because of the horror of a vacuum why would it leave tube $c\,d$ a vacuum just to fill the other tube A? Is it not also a rule of nature that one should attend first to one's own needs before worrying about anybody else's?

How an empty space can be easily exhibited

When the experiment was completed and all the air extracted so that the water in tube $c\,d$ had sunk to the same level as that in tube A, the valve was closed and the apparatus stored as a demonstration system for exhibiting a vacuum. If one desired to exhibit a vacuum, one simply turns the apparatus towards the horizontal so that the tube $c\,d$ is filled with water. (This is done so that the inlet d always remains under water.) Then the apparatus is turned upright again and one forthwith sees the water in tube $c\,d$ sink leaving behind a vacuum in this tube because the inlet d, remaining permanently submerged, cannot admit any air. Consequently the space left in the tube is necessarily a vacuum.

The water in a vacuum rushes together creating a noise like the collision of stones

Likewise if the apparatus is moved quickly or shaken up and down, one sees, as described in the previous chapter, the water in tube A separate, creating a vacuum in the middle of itself and then coming together again with a bang. If there were not a vacuum, this effect would in no way be possible.

It should moreover be noted that in the first six to eight days, while the water, the glassware and the glue were still new, the above mentioned bubbles always appeared in great abundance. This led me to the firm belief that the air was penetrating the pores of the glass. My view on this matter was strengthened by the fact that (while the tube *c d* was being inclined and being filled again with water) a pocket of air about the size of a pea was always seen in the tube *c d*. Although when the tube was turned so that this air was released into the space of the bigger tube *A,* this effect was nevertheless completely repeatable. This phenomenon motivated me to enclose the tube *c d* in yet another glass tube, to fill the latter with water, and then to seal the upper end of this tube so that the interior tube *c d* was completely surrounded by water. By this means I thought I could prevent the penetration of external air into the tube *c d*, assuming as I did, that the air could not penetrate both tubes and the water as well.

An eye catching experiment that air does not penetrate glassware

Nevertheless it transpired that tiny bubbles were generated in the tube *c d* for up to six or eight days. Through repeated trials I discovered that these bubbles originated with relatively new glass and always gradually decreased over the course of a few days until no more were perceived. Repeated experiments over a period of time confirmed this discovery. For when I left the apparatus unused and open for a few days and then repeated the experiment, then, just as before, little bubbles appeared both within the water and on the glassware.[305]

All bodies have emanations which constitute their odour or air

From these phenomena it was very clear to me that these bubbles had arisen not just as an emanation of the water but also of the glass. Furthermore the corporeal effluvia of bodies (which we shall also mention in Book IV Chapter 1[306]) are nothing but air, and that air is nothing but

---

[305] This effect is clearly owing to the fact that the water had again dissolved atmospheric air. Guericke was still subject to the belief that the air, as the lighter body could not penetrate the water.

[306] Book IV Chapter 1 deals with von Guericke's general views of corporeal and incorporeal potencies. (v. Appendix 1)

the corporeal effluvia of bodies. It is also the case that all bodies have their effluvia or odours. Not only water but also glass, metal and everything else release their effluvia into the nearby surrounding space, as we shall demonstrate in a number of ways in Chapter 10 below.

The effort expended on surrounding the tube *c d* with a second tube filled with water, was thus fruitless, especially as it is definite that no properly made glass allows the passage of air through it.

Water in a totally evacuated tube always releases an air or odour

In the interests of making progress, one should note the following. After the above mentioned six to eight days, no more bubbles appeared and the water sank in the tube *c d* without any turbulence or generation of bubbles. Absolutely no air had any way of getting in. As mentioned earlier, this was exactly what my critics wanted. Nevertheless, after the tube had been evacuated and then tilted by moving the *c* end downwards so that *c d* again filled with water, the above mentioned bubble, about the size of a small pea, appeared. Although this little bubble was expelled again by filling the tube and the water again made to sink by turning the tube upright, I nevertheless always observed that, following the repeated entry of the water into the tube, a bubble, generated from the water itself in the completely evacuated tube, remained.

Although after the apparatus was opened this bubble was so compressed by the weight of the external air vehemently rushing in as to be almost invisible, the following observation could nevertheless be made. Water when it is in a vacuum always releases some air or odour into the surrounding empty space. I also noticed through many repetitions of the experiment, that the bubble that is generated each time in the tube *c d* and then, by tilting the apparatus, released into the space of the tube *A*, finally attains, in this bigger tube, a considerable size. I inferred this from the fact that the water in the tube *c d* did not settle at the same level as previously but at a higher one because of the spontaneous endeavour or expansive force of the air.

The weight of the air prevents even the smallest emanation from the water

And although I frequently extracted this air too from the bigger tube *A*, it remained the case that no matter how many times I did it, a small bubble of this kind always remained in the tube *c d*. The only reasonable inference from this is that the water does not stop emitting its odour, which is just air, into the adjacent space. This is particularly so if the adjacent space is a vacuum, as long as some of the water remains.[307] Thus nature imparts a conservative potency[308] to the Earth (see Book IV Chapter 5) through which the air around it is conserved and a certain force and weight maintained on it. This is what stops all the water from being consumed and flying off, which it would otherwise do by freely emitting its odour into the ambient surrounding space in which, by the influence of the sun, it is perpetually transported in a great orbit, which in Book V Chapter 16 is referred to as annual.[309]

A vacuum cannot be produced beyond the means employed in this experiment

From all the foregoing it is evident that the production of a vacuum has been taken to the point where we can improve on it no further. For our views on the production of a vacuum by the descent of mercury, see Chapter 34 below.

Finally the following observations are worth making.

A remark on beer

1. If a small apparatus is filled with beer up to, say, about half, as was previously done with water, and the air is extracted, them all the beer becomes froth and rises up so that some of it gets through the valve into the siphon.

A remark on the breaking of glass which can happen in three ways

---

[307] Irrespective of any issues of dissolved air, water will exert a vapour pressure of about 0.02 of an atmosphere into a vacuum at room temperature. At pressures below this the water will start to boil.

[308] The Latin is "virtus conservative".

[309] This paragraph sets out von Guericke's ideas on gravity which were a step towards the Newtonian formulation. Book IV Chapter 5 is entitled *De Virtute Conservativa Terrae* (On the Conservative Potency of the Earth) and Book V Chapter 16 is entitled *De Latione Telluris* (On the Motion of the Earth). As well as the phenomena associated with buoyancy (Aristotle's relative gravitas and levitas v.*De Caelo* IV 4) he also postulates a force of attraction exerted by the Earth which maintains its atmosphere, but there is no inkling of gravity as a mutual universal attraction. The geocentric cosmologies did not have the problem of accounting for the maintenance of the atmosphere.

2. One should be aware that, after the evacuation of the apparatus, if the valve is opened very quickly, then the outside air rushes into the bigger tube *A* with such force and exerts such pressure on the water that not only does it vigorously rise up in the tube *c d* but the upper part of *c d* breaks off and goes flying into the ceiling. In fact, the force of the incoming air causes the whole apparatus to rise.

3. This apparatus must always be turned slowly on its side, so that the water will not rush in too quickly into the tube *c d* and cause it to shatter. The reason for this is the following. There is no air in the tube which can resist the inrush of the water. Therefore it flows in with such great force and turbulence that, by the intensity of its inrush, it seems to have the hardness of stones and it is this that breaks the glass tubes. If this were to happen, the external air could rush through the small tube back into the larger tube *A* with such force that it might shatter it, causing a danger to the eyes of the bystanders.

4. One should beware of shaking the apparatus too much. This will break it. This has happened to me.(v. Chapter 7)

Liquids which are well mixed owing to the compatibility of their parts are not separated in the tube without violence

5. At this point it is worthwhile noting that in a certain circumstance water from the smaller pipe *c d* does not sink even, I think, if the pipe were to be made a hundred cubits high. This situation arises when the apparatus is inverted for a period so that the pipe *c d* fills with water and then is later turned upright again. The reason for this effect is the following. The water has become so internally cohesive that there is no stimulus for it to break up and separate unless the apparatus is banged on the table or the floor. Then because of the impact it breaks up somewhere unpredictable with a loud crack and with a high risk to the pipe. Well washed mercury does the same thing. In this case the gravity of the air in the cylinder has no effect, as we shall describe in Chapter 19 and subsequent chapters.[310]

Liquids always give off some air or odour

Although with the passage of time these liquids so thicken, that they will not suffer any disruption except by a sudden shock, the following

---

[310] This phenomenon arises from the adhesion of the liquid to the wall of the tube.

unexpected effect nevertheless occurs. When the pipe *c d* is filled and left upright for a day or so, the water is generally discovered to have descended. For all liquids, especially when they are suspended as the water in the pipe is, give off an air-like emanation which in time gathers in the top of the tube and causes the separation of the particles of the liquid from those of the glass.

Chapter IX – Is there a vacuum in nature or not?

The corporeal effluvia of bodies constitute their odour or air

Since physical bodies give off air as their effluvium and no body exists without some effluvium of this sort, it follows that in these sublunary regions — that is to say near the earth — no space can be discovered, so empty of all effluvia and odours, that absolutely nothing remains in it. This remains the case even for such things as metal or precious stones or glass whose effluvia are so miniscule as not to be observable to man. However in an evacuated glass vessel where the odour has the space freely to expand, small bubbles or little blisters of air can be detected. We shall deal more fully with this in the following chapter.

A vacuum taken in a mathematical or physical sense does not exist in these sublunary regions

It is indeed the case that absolutely all the air can never be excluded with mathematical exactitude. Nevertheless it does not follow that just because on this earth nobody can create a space completely empty of all material, there is not such a thing in nature. (For human scientific experimentation is not in itself a purely mathematical activity but a craft activity based on mathematics. One cannot construct or measure a line or a surface with mathematical accuracy or weigh a body with such accuracy. These operations can only be approximately carried out using some experimental procedure.[311] It is likewise impossible here on the Earth, where all around there are bodies giving off corporeal effluvia — various sort of airs or odours — to procure a mathematically exact spatial vacuum.) Let us rather use our experiments — the preceding ones as well as ones yet to be described — to show that completely empty regions of space do indeed exist in nature.

A mathematically exact vacuum exists beyond the range of the potencies of the Earth

Below we will show the following:

---

[311] v. Preface to first edition of Newton's Principia for a similar thought. "But as artificers do not work with perfect accuracy, it comes to pass that mechanics is so distinguished from geometry that what is perfectly accurate is called geometrical; what is less so is called mechanical. However the errors are not in the art but the artificer."

1. That the air is a corporeal effluvium or odour from the land and oceans of the Earth.

2. That the Earth binds this air to itself as part of preserving itself and indeed keeps it under a certain pressure.

3. Indeed, because of the earth's ability to retain the surrounding air, the air suffers compression and is under greater pressure nearer the earth's surface than when more remote from it.

4. The pressure of the air is subject to frequent variation.

5. The pressure also changes in immediate response to climbing a height or a mountain. The variation depends on how high one climbs.

6. Air, on account of its gravity, rushes into every space not otherwise filled.

7. There is no abhorrence of a vacuum in nature and the appearance of such a phenomenon is an effect of the pressure of the surrounding air.

9. All the air can be excluded from vessels or glass tubes and consequently a vacuum can be procured. A proviso has to be made that the generation of new air from the water or the glass itself cannot be prevented. The amount of such new air is however miniscule and can be ignored.

From the above and other experiments the following conclusions can be drawn.

1. What is given off by the Earth's corporeal potency[312] is nothing other than its odour or air — in other words its effluvium. This effluvium is discharged into the immediately ambient space which is otherwise empty of any substance.

The range of the potency of the Earth is not infinite

Let us compare the small with the great. The odour of a rose permeates the immediately ambient space. It does not extend infinitely but is confined to a certain region within which it constantly attenuates to the point where it vanishes. A similar situation obtains with the air around the Earth. It likewise does not extend infinitely but only up to a limit

---

[312] The Latin is virtus corporea.

beyond which it ceases. This issue is further examined in Book V Chapter 7. Pure empty space, empty of any substance, necessarily begins when the presence of the air falls off to nothing.

There is empty space where the atmosphere ends

There is no good reason for saying that any substance — heavenly fire[313] or anything else whether solid or fluid — is formed in such space. Similarly there is none for supposing that the space between the stars ought to be filled with some vastly extended substance that would serve some useful purpose or bring some advantage. If such a substance did fill space, all the effluvia, influences and effects of the stars would be rendered futile.

Space is infinitely different from substance

There are some misguided people who think that space is the same as substance and that its nature consists solely in extension and that space without substance is a purely intellectual construction or something imaginary, analogous to how an astronomer conceives the equator. What they ought to be thinking is this. The tiny quantity of newly generated air cannot not even fill the space it occupies in an evacuated vessel, much less sustain, constitute or create it. It is hardly credible that if that tiny quantity of newly-generated air were not to be present in such vessels, then they could not sustain a vacuum and their sides would collapse so as to be touching. This is nevertheless the opinion of René Descartes[314] whom we have quoted in Book II Chapter 3. When circular vessels are used this collapse doesn't happen as we shall show in Chapter 26 below.

Where there is no substance there are no effluvia

2. For the demonstration of a vacuum — to show that such a thing does indeed exist in nature — it is sufficient to show water or air or some other substance being evacuated from a vessel in such a way that hardly a hundredth or a thousandths part remains behind and nothing else comes in to replace what has been removed. Even if here on Earth

---

313 Some variants on Aristotelian cosmology supposed that the motion was transmitted from the Sphere of the fixed stars to the inner Spheres by fastenings of fire between the spheres. Anaxagoras thought that the aether was fire.
314 v. Principles of Philosophy Book II Articles 16–18

a vacuum, as mathematically conceived, cannot be realised, we understand why this is the case — because the effluvia given off by substances prevents it's accomplishment. However if there were no substances, as in the heights beyond the Earth, then there would be no effluvia from substances. With the ceasing of a cause comes the ceasing of the effect. Consequently we would then have a spatial vacuum.

As the pressure of the air changes instantly on climbing to a mountain top, it follows that the atmosphere is not going to reach even half way to the moon

3. Since air pressure not only often changes spontaneously, but also immediately reacts to the change in altitude obtained going up a mountain, it is natural to suppose, taking into account the great height of the stars, that the vast space surrounding the Earth is not filled with air as far as the moon, much less to the sun or beyond. It is even more incredible that this air should make, bring about, or constitute, space, so that if the air or elemental fire or some other substance were not present, then the earth, moon, sun and the rest of the stars would become contiguous with each other. Who could seriously imagine that an effluvium from the Earth — the air or the conjectured fire, or anything else whether solid or fluid — could actually constitute the vast space of the interstellar regions? Or who could imagine that if this, or some such diffuse substance did not occupy the space between the stars, then there would be no idea of distance between the heavenly bodies and that they would have to touch each other? It is surely much more plausible to suppose that whether or not there is any substance in the interstellar regions, space is real and continues to exist, neither acting nor being acted upon, and indifferent as to whether any material body is contained in it or not.

If nature allows an almost complete vacuum then it also allows a complete one to exist

4. Those people are deluded who believe that not only the thousandth fraction of the original air that remains in the glass vessel can fill it but even that an arbitrarily tiny quantity of air can. Who, except by excessive deference to the opinions of others, could let themselves be persuaded that a thousandth or arbitrarily small fraction of something could be as big as the whole? (I am not here talking about the type of

person mentioned at the beginning of the last chapter, who does not admit that air has any expansive force.) Common sense itself tells us that the more the air is extracted and rarefied the more vacuum is created in the space previously occupied by the air, so that ultimately as the amount of air is reduced to zero, a vacuum is created.

One portion of air is not more rarefied than another

5. However there are others who deploy a different argument against the vacuum. They claim that a more rarified sort of air enters through the glass once the coarser air has been extracted. Now, the truth of the matter is that such a distinction cannot be maintained. As the preceding experiments and those of Book V Chapter 9[315] clearly show, air cannot pass through glass. Let us suppose, without of course admitting, that there is some aether more diffuse than the air which can penetrate glass. The question then arises — why doesn't it penetrate the glass before the extraction of the supposedly coarser air? There is always some space left in the vessel so that more air could be blown or forced into it. But however it doesn't enter; so there is no type of air that is more finely grained or coarser than any other sort of air. The distinctions to be made with air are between its states when it is rarified and when it is compressed or between its humidity or its dryness. (The former states arise from when it has been allowed to expand or forced to contract.) Humidity and dryness are not essential properties of air and do not make any difference to its ability to penetrate. But assume, as a hypothesis, that there is a type of air which could penetrate glass and other hard materials so that, as water was extracted it would seep its way through the glass into the space vacated by the water, and then when the water came rushing back, it would escape again through the glass. Such a hypothesis hardly accords with common sense because any sort of air that could penetrate glass would also penetrate water and would not retreat from the inrush of the water. It would be present both in the glass and the water before the extraction and would remain so after the extraction. This position really is just a postulation of an incorporeal, all penetrating, air.

Space similarly penetrates everything

---

[315] Book V Chapter 9 is entitled *De Divisione Aeris in Regiones*. (On the Division of the Air into Regions)

In this it is similar to how we speak of space. Space penetrates every-thing. It is immobile and exists in everything. It is the same at all points whether it is filled with a body or not. These latter properties cannot be attributed to any sort of air.

Outside the atmosphere space becomes pure

From the foregoing the following conclusions can be drawn. Above and round the earth, as far as the atmosphere extends, there is indeed no space that is empty, unless procured by means of vessels made out of some solid substance. Beyond and above the region occupied by the atmosphere the presence of air ceases and pure space, void of all physi-cal substance, begins. This matter is discussed further in Book V Chap-ters 7 and 9.

Do the incorporeal potencies also fill space?

The reach of the incorporeal potencies that operate in the Cosmos will be discussed in Book IV. Do they also fill space? A distinction needs to be drawn between the potencies that originate from the sun and those originating from the Earth and the other planets. The latter according to the nature and quality of the potency, are dispersed, at greater or lesser distances, in the ambient empty space around these cosmic bod-ies. However they do not fill the space as they are not corporeal nor do they stay in the one place but move in association with their parent bodies in periodic motion. When they move, they necessarily leave be-hind a vacuum. These potencies really only exist to the extent that some object, susceptible to their influence, presents itself within the range of their action. What doesn't exist cannot fill anything. Consequently the vast space between the bodies of the Cosmos is empty of any sub-stance.

Chapter X – Experiments on odour and fermentation

Each physical object emits a corporeal effluvium by and from itself. This has been shown in Chapter 8 above. The phenomenon becomes even more evident when an object is immersed in water or some other fluid material. This causes the object to begin to be encrusted with many bubbles and (when the immersion takes place in a vacuum) to cause an effect like effervescence or fermentation to occur.

Everything has an odour which is its air

Such an effluvium of an object is its air or odour. For example, immerse a piece of gold, silver, mercury, some other metal, or for that matter, any other substance in a glass vessel which has been filled with water and, even after a short time, you will see the effect on the glass itself. Countless bubbles appear to be attached to the surfaces and then slowly rise to the surface of the water where they disintegrate and merge with the air.

But what is scarcely perceptible in the normal situation is much more observable in a vacuum. As the air in a vacuum expands more and more, so too do bubbles, which are composed purely of air.

Ordinary air does not have a smell

We do not smell ordinary air, which is just the odour given off by the Earth. This is because it is so pervasive that we have accustomed ourselves to it from our earliest years. We do however detect by our sense of smell the odour given off by particular objects. This occurs to a greater or less degree depending on the particular substance — how plentifully it gives off its odour and, also, on our own capacity for smell.

The distinguishing of odours into good ones and bad ones is just a matter of personal preference and does not correspond to any real intrinsic property. An intolerable stink to one creature can be the sweetest of scents to another.

Odours do not penetrate hard substances

Air is something that is physical and has gravity but which doesn't penetrate hard materials such as glass or metal. This is similarly true of every type of odour.

Putrefying substances emit more odour

Mainly however, strong odours or airs are given off from substances that are moist, unstable, or rotting because they are subject to a process of fermentation. Hence all putrefying material, when under water as in a marsh or stagnant pond, always emits lots of little bubbles. This is to be seen when a spear or long pole or some such implement is driven into the bottom, when immediately there is a surge of bubbles.

Why there are bubbles in ice

I have often wondered how from the bottom of ponds, which are underwater, such bubbles can arise, since air, as the lighter body, should rise to the surface of water and not descend into water.[316] This phenomenon also explains why a lot of bubbles are also found in ice of all kinds for when they ascend in water they freeze along with it and are responsible for making ice lighter than water.[317]

Why corpses float to the surface

It also explains why corpses that have drowned rise to the surface. For when after a few days putrefaction begins, the newly generated air distends the corpse, makes it lighter and ultimately forces it to rise.

Experiment on the generation of air

When I had observed this, I carried out the following experiment. I placed a small dead carp in a glass bowl and filled it with water. I then covered the carp with a glass goblet in such a way that all the air was excluded, that the goblet was completely filled with water and that the carp was completely immersed. After some days lots of bubbles were given off, as they are from a dead body, and this ultimately made the corpse rise. Because of the goblet enclosing the carp, the bubbles given off could not become mingled with the ordinary air and they gathered at the top of the goblet forming new air.

This fermentation, or generation of new air, can be most strikingly seen, as we have said, when these experiments are done in an evacuated vessel. For then many more and much bigger bubbles appear, as after a

---

[316] The idea that air could simply be dissolved in water and retained by molecular mechanisms is one that von Guericke could not have conceived.
[317] Irrespective of the presence of frozen bubbles ice is less dense than water.

few days becomes very evident. Ultimately the generation of new bubbles tails off and finally ceases. Fermentation is treated further in the
final chapter of Book IV.[318]

---

[318] Book IV Chapter 16 is entitled *De aliis adhaec Virtutibus corporeis et incorporeis.* (On other additional corporeal and incorporeal potencies)

Chapter XI – An experiment by which the formation of clouds, winds and iridescent colours in glassware can be stimulated

The construction and use of a thermoscope

It has been noted that air expands when heated and contracts when cooled. The thermoscopes or thermometers invented within the last thirty years have particularly shown us this. From the expansion and contraction of the air trapped inside these instruments, the effect of the application of heat and coldness can be studied from day to day and even from hour to hour. However as many other authors have already written on this topic, for the sake of brevity we refer the reader to p. 229 of Rev. Fr. Kaspar Schott's *Mechanica Hydraulico-pneumatica*[319] and to other authors cited there. The reader is also referred to our own discovery described in Chapter 37 below.

Because it is needed for the experiment we are about to describe, it is necessary to have to hand a Receiver *L* as described in Chapter 5. Another transparent glass vessel *M* (see Illustration VIII *M*) is also needed. Pharmacists call this "a cupping glass" but it is also commonly called a flask.[320] In a similar way to the Receiver, a cover and a tap are glued to it so that its tap fits exactly into the inlet to the Receiver.

A wind is created in the lower vessel L

The Receiver is evacuated and both vessels are joined together with the smaller one positioned above the larger one. When both taps are opened the following is observed. The air from the upper vessel rushes into the lower one in violent gusts and the objects that were placed on the bottom of the Receiver — such as little stones or Avellan nuts — are scattered and thrown up in all directions.

Water is evidently absorbed in air; more compressed air can hold more water

---

[319] Fr. Schott describes a Thermoscopium Prognosticum (weather-forecasting thermoscope) of which he writes: "We call this instrument a Thermoscope or, if you prefer, a thermometer. Using it the application of heat and coldness at some arbitrary place can be studied from day to day and from hour to hour from the force of the expansions and contraction. …. Thermoscopes or Thermometers of this sort were constructed in two ways, one for use in winter and the other for summer." He attributes it to Fr. Athanasius Kircher.

[320] Von Guericke uses the Latin "cucurbita –ae f" and then the German "eine Kolbe".

Indeed from this sudden expansion of the air in the upper vessel and its descent into the lower one, it follows that the air remaining in the upper vessel is significantly changed and diminished. A large amount of air can hold more moisture than a little amount and so the air in the upper vessel loses its extra moisture which can actually be seen as tiny droplets steadily falling to the bottom.

This effect becomes more apparent as the humidity inside the glass vessel is increased. Then bubbles arise in greater numbers so that they form a mist which, by allowing some air into it, can be broken up into clouds. (This is especially the case when the tap of the flask that has been evacuated in this way is opened under water. Then it sucks in water and sprays it throughout the whole vessel making the air it contains much more humid.) When the taps are closed, the vessels separated from each other, and the tap of the smaller vessel slowly untightened so that a little air is introduced, then the mist breaks up into clouds.

A lot of air can hold a lot of water

It is evidently the case here that the water, because of the contraction and diminution of the air, separates itself from the air and forms itself into a cloud. Then if the tap is fully opened, the cloud or mist disappears forthwith because it is absorbed by the incoming air.

There is no doubt that mists in air are subject to irregular motion

Furthermore, when the flask containing a mist is stored for a short time, the sinking of the mist and its separation from the clearer air can plainly be seen. Also to-and-fro motions can be produced in the glass, of the kind that perhaps the clouds are subject to in the upper atmosphere. This experiment is thus relevant to obtaining a better understanding of the processes occurring in the air of the atmosphere.

The cause of clouds

Finally from these experiments the cause of clouds and of wind can be learned. For when mists rise from the bases of mountains or from underground caves or even when newly generated air inside them (as one sees in mines which from time to time release air) rises, some alteration

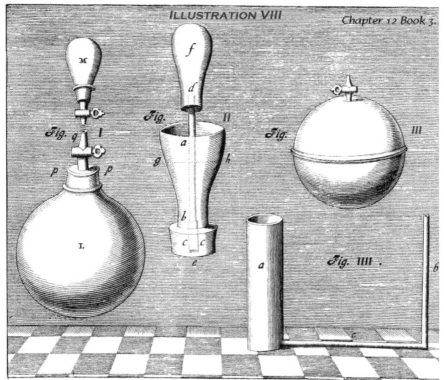

or contraction takes place, according to the characteristic way each of these interacts with the external air. It is because of this that the watery material, which is in the air, separates out and condenses. This explains the formation of clouds.

Why and when the breath of animals is visible

It is for just this reason that the breath of animals in winter appears to be smoke or mist. The warmer air becomes denser as it cools on exposure to the colder air and thus reduces in volume. As a smaller volume cannot hold as much water as a greater one, moisture is released which becomes visible by the coalescence of so many tiny particles.

Why glass vessels appear to sweat

In the summer or in hot places, we see glass and other wine containers appear to sweat when taken from cellars. The reason is that the air surrounding the vessel is cooled by contact with it. This causes it to contract and to give up the water it was holding which then sticks to the side of the vessel.

Creating the colours of the rainbow

Lastly the following observation should not be passed over in silence. When these glass vessels are exposed to the sun in the course of an experiment, the air in the upper vessel first begins to glisten and afterwards exhibits most clearly all the colours of the rainbow.

Chapter XII – On fire in a vacuum

Flame diminishes with the supply of air

I lit a candle made from white wax and placed it in the above mentioned Receiver using the removable tap *q r.* (v. Illustration VIII Fig. I). Then I positioned the Receiver next to the pump (v. Chapter 4) and, operating it vigorously, extracted the air. I saw the flame steadily become lower and contract into itself as the air was sucked out. It turned purple as it sank to the tip of the wick and finally went out. Although for a moment or two after the extinction of the flame the wick remained glowing, issuing a plume of smoke, it too finally went out.

Why the flame of a fire is oblong

From these frequently repeated experiments some points were noted. Fire cannot continue without air and it goes out when the air is exhausted. The oblong shape of a flame is owing to the pressure of the air which lifts it and to some degree propels it upwards in the same way as water, being heavier than air, propels a bubble upward. However the flame remains attached to the tip of the wick because the pressure of the surrounding air is not stronger than the attachment of the flame to the tip of the wick.

Why a flame is extinguished by impure air

Consequently if a lighted candle is placed in a low lying spot where the air is impure and very heavy, we see the flame flare up and then subside and it proves impossible to maintain it for any length of time. If there were no air pressure the flame would not be elongated but round like a ball, as indeed the flame of the sun appears spherical.

Fire cannot last long in a sealed off space

On another occasion, I similarly placed a lighted candle in the Receiver which I sealed in the usual way, so that air could neither enter nor escape. I discovered that the candle remained alight for three or four minutes and then went out. Furthermore I observed that it went out in almost the same way as previously except that there was no blue flame nor did it extinguish itself at the tip of the wick but in the middle of it.

The cause of this phenomenon needs a different kind of explanation

The extinction of the candle can only be understood by assuming that fire takes some sort of nourishment from the air — that it consumes the air and then, because of the lack of nourishment, it can no longer sustain itself. Therefore I set up an experiment which I will describe in Chapter 13.

Concerning the subterranean torches of the Romans

There has been much discussion, based on reports of writers, of the subterranean torches of the Romans. There are no direct witnesses to these torches and in the most credible writings of antiquity complete silence reigns with regard to the inexhaustible oil they burnt. Experiment teaches that fire cannot subsist without air. Nobody will convince us that those torches burnt for centuries.

Chapter XIII – An experiment on the consumption of air by fire

I knew that fire consumes air from the following experiment. I took a glass vessel, called a cupping glass or more commonly a flask, whose base had been removed as shown by *a h b g* of Illustration VIII Fig. II. With the usual glue, I attached the narrower end to the metal covering *c c* and at the same time drew a metal pipe *d e* through the middle of the flask and the covering, so that its opening *e* could be attached to the tap *q* (v. Chapter 11) of the above mentioned Receiver. (v. Illustration VIII Fig I)

Then I had the flask filled with water up to over half way — to the line *g h* — and put another smaller flask *f* over it so that it almost reached to the base *b*. I connected this whole arrangement to the removable tap *q* of the Receiver *L*. At the same time I hung a lighted candle inside the Receiver and ensured that no air could get in or out except through the pipe *e d* into the upper flask.

The air in the Receiver first of all expands

I saw immediately that the flask *f* lifted. This occurred because the heat generated by the flame of the candle quickly expanded the air trapped in the Receiver and drove it through the pipe *e d* into the flask *f*. But since the lower part of the latter remained submerged under water, the air had no way of escaping.

The air is partly consumed

This lasted just one or two minutes and then the flask *f* began to sink again and steadily fell back to the base. It even seemed that all the water in the flask *f* was rising and moreover sucking a host of bubbles into it. This was visible proof that a portion of the air contained in the Receiver had been used up. At least a tenth of the air was consumed[321] by the flame and perhaps all of it would have been consumed had the candle not gone out so quickly.

---

[321] The percentage of oxygen in air is 21%. How far the water will rise depends on considerations which von Guericke could hardly take into account such as Avogadro's hypothesis, the diatomic nature of oxygen and nitrogen molecules, the production of carbon dioxide and carbon monoxide and their solubility in water. This phenomenon is one of the sources of evidence that air, contrary to the deeply ingrained conviction that it must be an element, is a mixture of elements.

What causes the candle to go out

The shortage of air in the sealed Receiver could, of course, be a valid reason for the extinction of the flame. However over and above this, it seems to me that the extinction is also caused by the impurity of the air owing to the dissipation of wax or tallow within the Receiver.

How the impurity of the air can be recognised

When the air that is left behind is extracted from the Receiver, it immediately begins to darken, and leaves behind it a black smoke[322] which was not visible when the air was more abundant.

Whether fire annihilates air

Finally the question arises whether fire consumes air in such a fashion that it annihilates it or it converts it into an earth-like substance. I believe the latter to be the case although so meagre a quantity of this substance is produced that there is no way of actually observing it.

---

[322] The smoke particles, being very much larger than the air molecules, would remain behind as the lighter air molecules escape into the region of lower pressure created by the pump. As their proportion increases they would become more visible.

Chapter XIV – Light in a vacuum

Some people say that our evacuated glass vessels could not be empty of all matter because they can see the objects placed inside them. However the truth of the matter is that if a vacuum did cause an object inside it to become invisible, it would follow that the vacuum was capable of obstructing the illuminating potency.[323] Only a dense substance could impede this potency and consequently the vacuum would be a dense substance. But since empty space is not something substantial it is invisible and as such it cannot appear dark in the daylight. For where would the darkness in the glass vessels come from, since they are surrounded on all sides by brightness and light? Light is in fact present in the air and at the same time in all the surrounding objects, including in the glass vessel itself, which it penetrates.

There is no potency of the sun in a vacuum – the potency of the sun or of light is not exerted on the incorporeal but only on material bodies

It would be quite different, if we did not find ourselves in the air here on Earth, where during the day there is reflected light. This illuminates all points of the empty space in the glass vessel.

Suppose however we were to find ourselves in the remote aether, where the sunlight encounters no resistance and is not reflected off anything but where the potency of the sun (i.e. the light it emits) freely passes through the aether. In this situation we would, as long as our gaze was turned away from the sun, see nothing other than darkness. If we were to look at the space in the evacuated glass, it would appear dark. (v. Book IV Chapter 12[324] and the end of Book III Chapter 9) We have a clear example of this at night. During the night when we have the Earth behind us and our face turned away from the sun, we also see nothing, as there is no illumined body in front of us. (Except in clear conditions we see certain planets or comets that are illuminated by our sun, or by some fixed stars which, like our sun, give out light from their own resources.) Hence the empty space in the Receiver appears invisible or dark, just as during the day it appears bright.

---

[323] The Latin is "virtus lucens".

[324] Book IV Chapter 12 is entitled *De Virtute Lucente et Colorante* (On the luminous and colour causing potency)

Chapter XV – Sound in a vacuum

Bells do not sound in a vacuum

In an evacuated vessel, the sound of bells, stringed instruments and other objects, which normally emit an audible note, is extraordinarily weak. To conduct an experiment on this topic, I attached a clockwork mechanism that made a distinct sound to a string and suspended it from the mouth of the much-mentioned glass Receiver. Previously I had adjusted the mechanism so that, by the striking of the little hammer in the bell, a clear tone sounded at definite intervals during a period of half an hour.

A noise is nevertheless emitted

Then I began to extract the air from the sealed Receiver and noticed that when part of the air had been removed the sound emitted was less audible and that, after a full extraction, no sound at all could be heard. When I brought my ear close to the glass I detected a muffled sound which was caused by the striking of the hammer.[325] It was the same sort of sound one gets when the bell is held firmly and then struck with a hammer. A dull sound is created but no tone generated.

The return of the air makes the bell emit a tone again

When I allowed the air back into the vessel this dull noise immediately again became a proper tone.

The striking emits a noise even in an evacuated glass

I had a cabinet-maker build me, instead of a little bell, a castanet out of four square pieces of wood and of such a size that it would fit through the mouth of the Receiver. I fixed this castanet, which I had previously connected to the hammer of the bell, to the inside of the Receiver and reinserted the stopper. When I moved the Receiver this way and that with my hands, the hammer struck against the sides of the castanet. Before the evacuation the sound the castanet made, when struck by the

---

[325] The only explanation for this is that when the clock strikes some vibration is transmitted to the Receiver through the string on which the clock is suspended.

hammer, was distinctly audible and after the evacuation it was just as audible, so that no difference at all could be detected.[326]

We see from this that sounding bodies, such as bells, cymbals, glasses, strings of musical instruments and so on, emit a note with the assistance of the air — i.e. by means of the impact they make on the air causing it to shake and tremble. In contrast a noise or a sound, created by a rubbing together or collision of objects, does not arise through the agency of the air but by the sonic potency[327] of the objects themselves. This topic will be discussed in Book IV Chapter 10.

A noise is emitted by the power of the sound

Even in the case of a sealed Receiver, when air can neither get in or out, notes as well as noises can penetrate the glass. But when the air is absent, no further notes are emitted, but noises persist whether air is present or whether it has been pumped out. One must note the following difference. A sound which is generated or stimulated by the air itself, will also be propagated with the aid of the air, as we shall see in Chapter 26.

By the collision of air a sound will be emitted, in the same way as by the scraping of hard bodies against each other

In that chapter we discuss how square glass or earthenware vessels are not just broken but that also a loud bang is caused when the surrounding air immediately and violently surges back into a space which had been evacuated.

The noise of firearms is caused by the impact of air colliding with itself

---

[326] The experimental arrangement here is not completely clear and von Guericke did not provide an illustration. For the recorded observations to have been made, it must be the case that the impact of the striking hammer must have been transmitted directly to the glass wall. What I picture is that the four pieces of wood were hinged together with one fixed to the glass wall and the other to the clockwork-operated hammer suspended from a string inside the Receiver.

[327] The Latin is "virtus sonans". Von Guericke believed that the capacity to emit a sound is an "incorporeal potency" of an object, stimulated by the vibration of the object. (Book IV, Chapter 1) In Book IV Chapter 10, entitled "De Virtute Sonante et Resonante" (On the potency that causes sound and echoing), he writes: "Sound, bangs, noise, voice etc. are not propagated through the medium of air as the generality of philosophers believe but just as incorporeal potencies penetrate all objects (other things being equal), so does sound penetrate all objects including those which air cannot penetrate."

A roll of thunder and the crack of a rifle are sounds engendered in the air from a common cause. A sudden outbreak of fire expands the air but when promptly extinguished, it leaves behind it a certain amount of empty space which the air rushes back to fill.

Finally the following should be noted. Suppose a clockwork mechanism were placed inside a glass vessel or a well-sealed copper sphere from which the air cannot escape and then suspended in our familiar Receiver. Suppose further that all the air were pumped out of the Receiver. Then the sound of the bell would be clearly audible.[328] But since such a glass vessel would without doubt be shattered by the air trapped inside it, as is clear from the experiment with the bladder described in Chapter 33, I have refrained from carrying out this experiment.

---

[328] This is incorrect. Von Guericke thinks of light and sound as incorporeal "lucent" and "sonic" potencies. Misled by his experiments he has concluded that both potencies can be exerted through a vacuum. He reasons that notes cannot be heard because notes are created by the string and the sonic potency of the air acting together. Thus when there is no air no notes will be created, but a sound created without any assistance from the air will be transmitted through a vacuum.

Chapter XVI – Behaviour of animals in a vacuum

That much mentioned container, called by the chemists a Receiver, was fitted with the removable tap *q r* (Illustration VI Fig. VII) and set up so that small animals and other objects could be introduced into it. I firstly inserted in it a sparrow which flew back and forth with much flapping of its wings. Then, to drive the air out of the container, I connected it to the machine using the pipes *f g h i* (Illustration VII Fig. IV) as described in Chapter 7. The activity of the bird was immediately inhibited. At first sight there was nothing else remarkable to be seen apart from the fact that, as the air was progressively extracted, it struggled for breath with its beak open. Finally it remained standing with its beak wide open and without any breathing. With his mouth still wide open, it remained motionless for a short time until it fell over and expired. From this it was plain to see that the absence of all physical movement, particularly in the stomach area, was owing to the shortage of air. Its heart had stopped beating in a similar way to the extinction of a flame when the spirit fuelling it runs out.

Behaviour of fish in a vacuum

I had water again poured into the above-mentioned Receiver and introduced fish of various sorts — pike, larger and smaller perch, gouldring, barbells and other frequently encountered types. Different species reacted differently to the extraction of the air.[329] The pike, open mouthed, began to swell up more and more and vomited out small fish which they had swallowed. Their bodies bloated so much that one began to fear that they would explode, until finally they lay at the bottom powerless and seemingly lifeless. I noticed that the bladders of the pike were quite narrow and that they possessed no excretory ducts through which the air could have escaped. It is the expansive power of the air that caused the distension of their bodies. In contrast, gouldring and other common edible fish released air from their bladders. With both sorts of perch a notable difference was observed. In this case they swallowed with astonishingly wide-open jaws and their eyes were forced from their sockets. They died in the same way as the pikes. Even when the air was allowed back in by opening the container, they could not stop swallow-

---

[329] Fish rely on oxygen dissolved in the water. As the air pressure is lowered the fish suffer both a loss of external pressure on their bodies and a loss of oxygen in the water.

ing whereas the rest (provided they were not left too long in the vacuum) stayed alive and revived.

Grapes can be stored for six months in a vacuum

Finally in this context mention may be made of the following phenomenon. When grapes are introduced into a container of this kind, which is then evacuated and stored in a cool place for half a year, the grapes remain, as far as their appearance goes, unchanged but lose all their juice.

This comes from the fact that the juice[330] streams out into the empty space, whereas it would otherwise be forced back by the pressure of the surrounding air and remain inside the grapes.

---

[330] The Latin is "virtus vinaria" —"the wine potency".

Chapter XVII – The construction of a hydraulic-pneumatic apparatus that not only offers the possibilities of making many discoveries, but could be kept in one's study as a diversion

One makes an iron tripod *a b c h i* (v. Illustration IX) whose legs are attached at the top to an iron ring *b c* and fixed with screws. The iron ring is fitted with two moveable iron plates curved so that the glass vessel *e q r* can be suspended between the legs of the tripod container and can also be removed. (The vessel *e q r* is commonly called a quarter-Receiver and is equipped, as described in Chapter 5, with a brass cover so that air can neither get in or out.)

Then a second similar glass vessel *L* fitted with a tap *d* is connected to the lower container *e q r*, as shown in the illustration. The tap is such that its two ends can be inserted, with a good fit, into the covers of the two vessels. Additionally four smaller taps (of which only three, *f x g*, are shown in the illustration) are fitted on the cover of the lower vessel *e q r* surrounding the tap *d*. A pipe, *p p*, serving to suck in or let out water, is carefully connected to the taps *f* and *g*.[331] The tap *g* is attached at its lower end to a brass pipe reaching to the bottom of the vessel.

The remaining two taps (the fourth one could not be represented in the illustration) do not have inlets. Inside the vessel, however, they are attached to pipes, which also reach to the bottom of the vessel, and are so sharpened at their ends that only a small needle could be inserted in the mouth of them.

(Note. All the taps of both types must be engineered to match exactly the opening in the cover so that the fitting is air-tight. To prevent as far as possible any air escaping or entering, they are additionally equipped with a small ring filled with water.)

Furthermore the middle tube *r* should be made out of the same material as the others but of greater width — it should be almost as wide as a finger. It goes from the bigger tap *d* (at the point where it is removable) through the middle of the lower vessel almost to the base, so that water can be channelled through it from the lower vessel to the upper one.

---

[331] The illustration only shows the attachment of *f* to a pipe *p p*.

Finally, the above mentioned pipe, $p\,p$, is made out of iron coated with tin and of such a length that it reaches from the inlets of the taps $f\,g$ almost to the floor of the room. The upper end of the channel should also be fitted with a beak-like brass inlet m which fits exactly the taps $f\,g$. At the lower end it should have a small tap n, as shown in the illustration.

It is left to the interested reader to fill in the rest of the details and to carry this further.

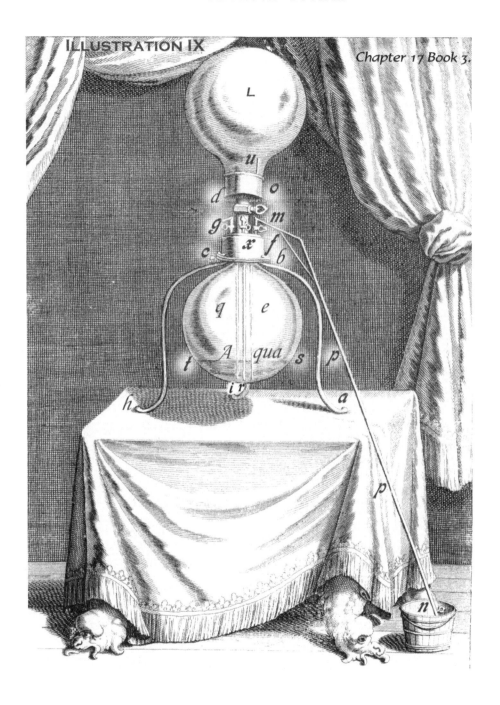

Chapter XVIII – On the use and operation of this apparatus

1. The procedure for evacuating this vessel

The lower glass should be filled with water up to the line *s t*. Then the two vessels are evacuated using the copper sphere, depicted in Illustration VIII Fig. III, which is about the same size as each of the two vessels. The copper sphere is evacuated and connected to the two vessels via the tap *f*, so that the air contained in the vessels moves into the copper sphere. This is to be repeated a number of times until nearly all the air has been extracted. This can be recognised as occurring when no, or hardly any, air from the upper vessel bubbles up in the water from the central pipe *r*.

The first application is to produce an enduring sound

At that point one should close the taps *d* and *f*, but slightly open the remaining two, to which are attached the pipes with the sharpened ends. (If there are three or four such tubes of this sort, so much the better.) Then one sees and hears how the air enters the water, creating a note or a hissing sound whose volume depends on how the keys of the taps are adjusted. This can continue for days on end, even for one, two or three weeks and can consume a lot of time. It is very important to avoid the danger of inadvertently allowing an inrush of air. To produce a sweeter sound it is better if needles are inserted in the mouths of the pipes, so that they become narrower and the air, being more constricted, is forced to become sibilant.

2. Contrary to its usual behaviour the water climbs

Place the tube *p p*, with the tap *n* opened, in a bucket filled with water and, at the same time, attach the end *m* to the inlet of the first tap *f*. Then open the tap *f* and you will see the water in the bucket rush up the pipe into the lower vessel *e q r*. When the vessel is half filled with water, close both the lower tap *n* and the upper one *f*. Detach the tube *p p*, which is now filled with water, and set it to one side.

3. Air rushes violently into the evacuated vessel

If the third tap *g* (the one sitting on the pipe *g q*) is opened, the air breaks in with great vehemence and rushes again through the water in the vessel to the point that one can hardly believe that the glass can withstand the force. This continues until the vessel has been again filled with air.

4. The water of the lower glass rushes, with great force, into the upper glass

When the first tap *f* (now without the pipe *p p*) is opened, so that the air can freely enter the vessel, the tap *d* of the upper vessel *L* can also be opened. When this is done, one sees the water leap into the upper vessel with such noise and force that it seems about to knock holes in it, or to shatter the glass itself into a multitude of fragments. One should be warned that when the water is let in, the air following it should not be admitted in an uncontrolled fashion and that a turbulent inrush should be prevented through the use of the spigot of *d*. If this is not done the whole machine is put at risk by the excessive passage of air through the water.

5. The water in the lower vessel can seemingly be changed into fumes

It was noted at the ends of Chapter 2 and Chapter 4 that owing to the extreme compression and friction occurring in the taps, very many bubbles are generated in the water itself. These escape into the air but cannot be visually detected except in a vacuum. We can use this apparatus to give a visual demonstration of this phenomenon too.

When the upper tap *d* is opened a little, so that the water in the lower vessel is forced to penetrate the narrow opening, then, because of the strong friction effect, the water breaks down into very tiny bubbles. These, being in vacuum conditions where they have free space, appear as a fume at the upper surface of the water. However, in the absence of a vacuum they cannot be seen for the following reason. The pressure of the air on the whole Earth and thus on all the water is so great that the bubbles are compressed to a point where they are no longer visible to the naked eye.

Invisible bubbles become visible in a vacuum

In a vacuum however, where the pressure of the air is prevented by the glass enclosure, the bubbles have space to expand, according to the nature of air.

6. The air is strongly compressed

This apparatus makes it clear that though the air near the Earth is strongly compressed because of its own weight, it tends to expand by its own nature. When the air, by the method explained above, is extracted from these two glass vessels, the air remaining in the upper vessel descends by natural expansion through the tube $x\ r$. It then makes its way through the water and expands into the lower vessel and finally into the copper sphere itself. From this the following is to be noted. If just the lower vessel, (with the tap d closed) were to be evacuated and the tap d then quickly opened, the air of the upper container would rush with such force through the water of the lower vessel that it would cause it to shatter. This, in fact, has happened to me.

7. The so called horror of a vacuum arises from the weight of the air

By means of this apparatus, it can be clearly shown that the so called horror of a vacuum is nothing more than the weight of the air pressing down on itself and everything below it. For when these two vessels have been simultaneously evacuated, water in the lower one shows no tendency to rise or to fill the upper evacuated vessel. However, immediately some air is let in via the tap f to the lower vessel, the water surges with great impetus into the upper one until the tap f is closed again. When this is done, the air which, by the weight of the external air, was forced into the lower vessel holds, by its own expansive force, the water suspended in the position to which it has risen. Again, after the tap f has been opened, the upper vessel becomes filled, initially with water and finally with air. In this situation the water in the upper vessel is maintained in position by the air (pressurised in the lower container) and not by any horror of a vacuum. But even when the tap f is closed, the water is nonetheless unable to descend, for if it were to descend it would compress the air trapped in the lower tube. This cannot happen because the air and the water in the upper vessel are in balance with the air of the lower one. By contrast, when some air is extracted using the copper sphere, all the water descends from the upper vessel following the air until there is none left.

8. The cause of the descent of the water

If it is desired to return this apparatus to its normal state — i.e. to restore the water suspended in the upper vessel back to the lower one — it is necessary to have a little hole somewhere so that air has free passage into the upper vessel. This can be achieved by means of a small tube *u* which goes through the brass cover and the glue into the upper vessel *L*. This tube is fitted with a small stopper. When the stopper is pulled out air is able to replace the water as it is sinks.

9. Through a siphon all the water can finally be extracted

When the water has fallen again into the lower vessel, the end of the tube *p p* is connected to the opening of the third tap *g* and the tap *n* of the tube *p p* is opened. The water previously retained in the tube *p p* descends and all the rest of the water follows as if through a siphon. Thus this machine, which takes in water from one side through the first tap, ejects it from the other side through the third tap *g*. Besides these, there are various other things that can be done with this machine which are best explored by using it in practice rather than by reading lengthy descriptions.

Chapter XIX – On a new discovery, using this apparatus, indicating the pressure of the air on the earth

I kept the apparatus described above standing on a table in my usual room by way of a diversion and showed to friends, and to others interested in such scientific matters, the procedures set out in the previous chapter. Some interested individuals, seeing how eagerly and abundantly the water rose through the pipe $p\,p$ from the floor of my chamber into the evacuated container, posed the following question. (v. Chapter 17, Illustration IX) What is the ultimate height to which water could be raised in this way? This was a question to which, up to then, I did not know the answer, but nor did I assume that a glass tube of infinite length would raise water to an arbitrary height.

Water rises from the ground to the middle storey of my home

I was impatient to do an experiment on this topic. Accordingly I had the pipe $p\,p$ extended so that it could reach through the window from the middle storey of my house to the ground outside. After placing a full bucket of water at the bottom end of the pipe I repeated the procedure described under Point 2 of Chapter 18. I saw the same phenomenon — i.e. that the water, contrary to its normal behaviour, climbed, just as before, into the evacuated vessel.

It climbs still higher

This made it necessary both to transfer the apparatus to a third storey room of my house and to attach a longer pipe to it before trying the experiment again. This time, the phenomenon repeated itself and the water rose to the third storey, but not however as abundantly as before. I betook myself to a room on the fourth floor, made the necessary arrangements and repeated the previous exercise. This time I observed that no water rose up into the vessel but rather that it just reached a certain level in the tube.

Because however the exact level was uncertain, it proved necessary firmly to glue a section of glass tubing at the point where the water level appeared to have risen and to try the experiment for a fourth time. When this was done and the tap opened, I saw the water immediately entering at the bottom and its level oscillate a number of times in the glass tubing until it finally settled down and stabilised.

The water rises to a height of nineteen Magdeburg cubits

I proceeded to make a note of this, dropping a plumb line from this position to the ground and measuring the height in Magdeburg cubits.[332] I found a value of around 19 cubits. Although I did not fail to repeat this experiment many times and in the same manner, I always observed the water level stabilising at the same height.

The height of the water varies

But afterwards when I left the apparatus standing for some days, I noticed some variation from day to day. Sometimes the water level stood one hand, sometimes two or three higher and sometimes it stood lower. I was not easily able to think of the reason for this.

My first thought was that the reason lay in the glass which, with the passage of time, had let in some air, thus allowing the water level to sink somewhat. However I could hardly attribute to the apparatus' not being sufficiently air-tight my observation that on other days the water level would rise to about half a cubit above the previously mentioned height (of 18¾ cubits). In the meantime however, in order to be more certain of the facts, I had the vessel freshly evacuated and carried out the experiment again. On this occasion the water stopped rising at the same level as it had done the first time I had done the experiment and after a few days it again showed variation.

The abhorrence of a vacuum is the gravity of the air

From this experiment, which was unexpectedly suggested to me, I could only draw one conclusion. The abhorrence of a vacuum is the gravity or pressure of the air around the Earth. When it encounters a portion of space free of any other body, it presses down on the water to make it enter and occupy this space and it does so according to its gravity.

There is no unbreakable chain

For if the abhorrence of a vacuum arose, as the Peripatetics would have it, from a chain of being preventing the occurrence of a vacuum in nature, then, necessarily, the water would have pursued the vacuum to any height whatsoever and filled the space. This however is contrary to the

---

[332] A Magdeburg cubit is about 45 cms.

evidence of this experiment, as it was plainly visible that that the water did not pursue the vacuum above 19 or 19½ cubits. The clearest evidence that the rise of the water is caused by the pressure of the external air is provided by the fact that the water does not always maintain the same level. Consider what would be the case if the rise in the water were caused by nature's abhorrence of a vacuum. Either there would be no limit to the height to which the water would follow the vacuum or it would always settle at the same level. The fact that the height of the water does vary is the surest indication that not just the rising of the water but also its variation, arise from an external cause.

The height of the water in the tube is not maintained by nature's abhorrence of a vacuum but because of the balance between a cylinder of water and a cylinder of air.

Chapter XX – On other experiments of this kind demonstrating the gravity of the air on the Earth and the limit of the extent of the abhorrence of a vacuum

The preceding discovery made it plain to see that nature does indeed permit the existence of a vacuum and that what is commonly called the abhorrence of a vacuum arises, at least in regions near the earth's surface, from the weight of air. (For the weight of the external air doesn't just drive the water into a place where there is unoccupied space but also forces it to a height where it is in equilibrium with the air.) Subsequent to this discovery, two other shorter methods of measuring the weight of air and of understanding the phenomenon of the abhorrence of a vacuum presented themselves.

The first procedure

Four brass tubes or pipes *a b, c d, e f, g h* are prepared, making each of them approximately five cubits long and the width of about a little finger. (v. Illustration X, Fig. I) The pipes should be capable of attaching to and disconnecting from each other so that pipes of varying length can be constructed. Furthermore the ends of the pipe are so constructed so that they can fit neatly into one another — *d* into *a, f* into *c, b* into *e* and that they also can be immersed in water by means of small dishes *a c e g* so that the risk of air entering the pipes is avoided.

Next, the first three pipes are connected together and set up beside the wall of my house. The bottom end *b* of the lowest pipe *a b* is fitted with a tap which can open and close. The upper end of third or fourth pipe has an outlet into which another tap, opening to the glass vessel *i k l*, can be carefully inserted so that there is no access for the air. The glass vessel *i k l* is two or more cubits long and is connected as shown in Chapter 2, Illustration V, Fig. III.

Water settles to state of balance with the gravity of a cylinder of air

First, it is checked that when the ends of the pipes are submerged in water not even the tiniest of bubbles can get through.

With the first three pipes *a b, c d* and *e f* connected and set up against the wall of my house and reaching, on, e.g. the first attempt, to a height of 15 or 16 cubits, the lower tap *b* is closed and immersed in the bucket *m n* which was filled to the brim with water. Then these pipes are filled with water. The glass vessel *i k l* is also filled and its tap *l* inserted into the outlet *e* of the tube *e f.* On opening the two taps, *l* and *b*, the water will be seen not to descend from the glass vessel, *i k l.* The reason is that the total height of the pipe plus the vessel is about 17 or 18 cubits and the external air presses more than a column of water of height 17 or 18 cubits has gravity. Therefore the water cannot sink. However if you repeat all this, but first of all attaching another tube of length 2 to 4 cubits so that the total height of the pipe plus the glass vessel is 20 to 21 cubits, or even up to thirty or more, then you see the level of the water in the pipe fall, and even climb again until it finally settles at the above mentioned limiting height of about 18 to 19 cubits.

An important observation – it is not the quantity of water but its height that forces water upwards

It does not matter whether the width of the tubes is large or small because the pressure of the water on a larger surface is no greater than its pressure on a smaller one. For example, let two tubes, *a* and *b*, be erected perpendicularly. Let them be of the same height but of different cross sectional areas and let them be joined together at the bottom by a horizontal tube *c* so that water can go from one to the other. (v. Illustration VIII Fig. IV) Then let one of the two perpendicular tubes, e.g. tube *a*, be filled with water. One sees that the water in both rises simultaneously to the same level and that the greater quantity of water in the bigger tube cannot push the smaller quantity of water, which is in tube *b*, a hair's breadth higher, but that the levels of water in both tubes *a* and *b* remains the same. The reason is this. The air and the water, acting as fluid substances, exert pressure on each other according to their perpendicular heights and thus, in the present case, the decisive factor is not the quantity of water but its perpendicular height.

The second procedure

Tubes or pipes are procured as before and also a glass vessel of the kind that chemists call a cupping-glass but which is commonly called a flask. (Alternatively a ¼-Receiver may be used, but the bigger such a vessel is the better it is for our purposes.) This vessel, fitted with a metal covering and a tap as described in Chapter 5, is completely evacuated

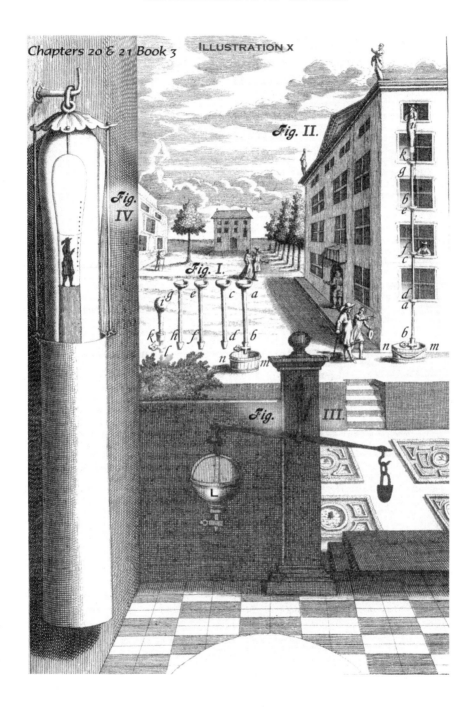

Chapters 20 & 21 Book 3

ILLUSTRATION X

Fig. II.

Fig. IV.

Fig. I.

Fig. III.

and inserted into the opening, *g*, of the pipe which is upright against the wall. (The lower end of the pipe along with the open tap at *b* should be immersed in a bucket of water.) Then, when the tap of the vessel is opened, one observes that the water rises up the tube to the previously mentioned height of about 19 cubits. The reason is that the external air exerts pressure on the water in the bucket, which, finding a passage clear to the evacuated vessel, rises to the height to which the weight of the surrounding air can push it.

It should be noted that water cannot be drawn through a siphon to a height greater than nineteen cubits

These experiments permit the following conclusions.

(1) Using a siphon, water cannot be drawn over a mountain or over anything else more than 18 cubits high.

The height to which water can be raised using a suction pump

(2) Using suction pumps, no water can be raised through borehole pipes if the valve or pump mechanism is more than 18 cubits high. But if the valve and the pump are less than 18 cubits above the water level, then water can not only be raised to that height but then higher still — as high as the length of the shaft used in such borehole pipes permits.

Furthermore because of these experiments, a path is cleared for us to reach an understanding of many other new phenomena. I have written about these in a reply, dated December 30th 1661, to a letter of Rev. Fr. Kaspar Schott. He has printed this letter in Chapter 21 of Book I of his *Technica Curiosa*,[333] entitled *On the Marvels of Magdeburg*. My letter appears, as follows, on p. 52 of this book.

Concerning a little fellow that indicates the presence of a storm

"For detecting the pressure of the air at an arbitrary time, I have devised a rather peculiar invention. It is a small statue fashioned from wood in the shape of a little man. The figure rises and falls inside the upper part of a glass tube, and at certain points indicates with his finger the current pressure of the air. (v. Illustration X Fig. IV) The devices to make this happen are in the lower part of the tube and are concealed from view so that the operation of my invention is kept a secret from onlookers. The glass tube is encased in a metal sheath

---

[333] Von Guericke's letter was in reply to a letter from Fr. Schott's dated December 5th 1661 requesting further information about von Guericke's experiments. Fr. Scott's letter is alluded to on p. 47 of the 1687 edition of *Technica Curiosa*.

which, as well as surrounding it, protects it. It also secures it from being interfered with or broken. I call this machine the 'Semper Vivum' but it might also justly be called 'Perpetuum Mobile.'[334] *However it is not continually in motion but just responds to changes in the air across the length and breadth of the surrounding region. It is not a thermoscope which changes according to heat and cold.*

An evacuated vessel suspended from a balance shows variation in weight

So that your Reverence and all lovers of true philosophy might get the most out of a foretaste of this area of experiment, they should consider the following. Since it is absolutely the case that air does not always have the same gravity, we have the following effect for a globe L from which all the air has been taken out and which has been suspended in air from a precise and sensitive balance. While the external air is at a higher pressure, the globe appears lighter; contrariwise, when the external air is at a lower pressure the globe appears heavier. This is because the denser the surrounding medium, the lighter something in that medium will appear.[335] *For example, as water is heavier than air, the globe would appear lighter in water than in air. The consideration of these facts opens up a new area for discoveries — whether there is rain over a broad region or not and whether it is just starting or about to finish.*

The little fellow gives an indication of stormy weather

Last year (1660), at a time of high winds and stormy weather, I observed, from the experiment I have just related, an unusual and remarkable variation in the gravity of the air. It became so much lighter — far beyond what was usual — that the finger of the little man went off the bottom of the scale marked on the glass tube. When I saw this, I said openly to those who were present that, without doubt, there was a great storm somewhere nearby. Scarcely had two hours gone by before stormy winds blew up in our local area. These were, however, less violent than they had been over the ocean.

---

[334] Perpetual Motion Machine. The possibility of such machines was an open issue until the establishment of the law of conservation of energy and the second law of thermodynamics in the 19th century. Claims to have realised such devices were advanced as far back as the 8th century (Bavarian Magic wheel) and in the 13th century Villard de Honnecourt sketched a design for one.

[335] This is a restatement of Archimedes' Principle that a body in a medium experiences an upward force equal to the weight of the medium displaced.

Chapter XXI – On the weight of air

A twofold understanding of the weight of air

We understand the term "weight of the air" in two senses. Air can be weighed either in a general or in a localised way. By the former we mean its perpendicular or cylindrical weight. For example, imagine a perpendicular cylinder of air (even if the height is not determined) the area and shape of whose base may be arbitrary — for instance in the shape of an obol, a gold coin, an imperial thaler, the head of a man or the rim of hat etc. I claim that the gravity of a cylinder of air, whose cross section is the size and shape of an obol, is the same as the gravity of water standing 19 Magdeburg cubits high in a tube whose cross section is also an obol. This is to say that the gravity of the air exerts as much pressure as the gravity of a column of water 19 Magdeburg cubits high. I shall repeat myself. The gravity of a cylinder of air whose cross section is a Rhenish ducat, is the same as the gravity of the water that stands 19 cubits high in a tube whose cross section is a Rhenish ducat. This proportionality is always maintained as will be seen in the next chapter.

On the weight of localised air

The weighing of a particular region of air (v. Illustration X Fig. III) can proceed from the following basic principle. Since it is the case that air has weight, it follows that when a glass vessel or Receiver, of the kind mentioned in Chapters 4, 8 and 11, is emptied of all the air inside it, it should not then have the same weight as it had before the evacuation. For example, on a set of scales weigh a container of this type with the tap open so that you can be sure that it is full of air. Then remove all the air from it. On weighing it again you will find that it weighs, depending on the volume involved, one or two ounces lighter. When half the air was pumped out of my Receiver and it was then weighed, it was found to be four loht[336] lighter, the equivalent of two imperial thalers. Finally the inlet is gradually opened, so that the air will not rush in so fast as to break the glass. Not only do you hear the sibilant sound of the air as it enters, but you also see the container steadily returning to its previous weight. This is the most perspicuous way of establishing

---

[336] A small German coin.

the weight of air. From these experiments it directly follows that the air presses upon itself — i.e. that the air, on account of its weight, is markedly compressed and dense in the regions near the Earth's surface, whereas the more remote it is from the Earth's surface the less weight it has and, not being compressed to the same degree, is lighter and less dense.

Condensed air is denser

It follows similarly that when air is condensed there is more air in a given volume than when it is expanded, but there is no difference in the nature of the air. The difference lies solely in the greater or lesser quantity of air. This varies according as the air occupies more or less space. At a place of higher altitude where it is not compressed by so great a weight, the air continues to expand, occupying ever more space, until it finally becomes vanishingly diffuse. If a space is so enormous that it cannot fill it, it will necessarily leave a vacuum in the unfilled parts.

This, along with other remarks we have made, should be carefully noted as they are important to the understanding of experiments described below.

A globe on a balance shows a variation in weight

Furthermore, it should be noted that a glass vessel of this kind, even when the tap is left open, shows a variation in weight. For in hot weather, when the air has expanded, the Receiver is also lighter and, on the other hand, in colder weather it is heavier, for the air is denser. (v. the end of Book III Chapter 37)

The true difference in the weight of water and air cannot be found

Finally there have been a number of learned men, who have tried to discover the relative weights of air, water and mercury. All attempts to resolve this are doomed to frustration because it is just a fact that the smaller the altitude of air the greater its compression and thus the heavier it is and, contrariwise, the greater its altitude, the more expanded it is, and thus the lighter it is.

Chapter XXII – On finding the gravity of a cylinder of air for cylinders of arbitrary volume

A cylinder of air exerts the same pressure as a cylinder of water of a height of between 18 and 20 Magdeburg cubits. So the gravity of an arbitrary cylinder of air can be determined by a calculation. First, we will first investigate the gravity of a cylinder of water, e.g. one of height 20 Magdeburg cubits. This can be done as follows.

1. Divide a Magdeburg cubit into 100 equal parts. Measure the dimensions of a large tankard or a Magdeburg measure and you will find that it is 19 hundredths of a cubit in diameter and 38 in height.

2. Using the geometrical fact that the ratio of the diameter of the circumference is as 7:22, the area of the bottom of the tankard comes out to be 285 square hundredths.[337]

The calculation of the circumference goes like this.[338]

$$19 \times 22 = 418 \quad 418 \div 7 = 59\,{}^{5}/_{7}$$

3. Multiply the radius by half the circumference to get the area of the bottom of a cylindrical Magdeburg tankard.

Circumference $59^{5}/_{7}$ → Half Circumference = 30 & Radius = 9½

Half circumference 30 x radius 9½ = 270 + 15 = 285 sq. hundredths
This is the base area.

4. If this is then multiplied by the height of the tankard, 38 hundredths, the result is 10 380 cubic hundredths for the volume of the cylindrical tankard.

The weight of a Magdeburg measure of water

5. When this tankard is filled with water and weighed, the water weighs 4⅛ lbs. (or 4.125 in decimals) where a pound weighs 16 imperial thalers.

The weight of a cylinder whose base is the same as a Magdeburg tankard and whose height is 20 cubits

---

[337] πr^2 (where r = 9.5) = 283.5
[338] The original shows the "carry" digits in the calculation suggesting that the algorithms for multiplication and division were still sufficiently novel as to require detailed setting out.

6. The volume and hence the weight of a cylinder of water 20 Magdeburg cubits high needs to be investigated. For as a Magdeburg tankard, of height 38 hundredths of a cubit weighs 4.125 lbs., so a tankard of height 20 cubits, or 2,000 hundredths, weighs 217 lbs.

To be explicit:

Height of a tankard in hundredths of a Magdeburg Cubit..........38

Weight in lbs. of this tankard …..……………..……………..…4.125

Height of a tankard in hundredths of a Magdeburg Cubit…….2,000

Weight in pounds of this tankard ………....……………….217$^4/_{38}$

This is the weight of a column of water of base area 285 square hundredths of a cubit and height 20 cubits.

Another procedure

The base of a Magdeburg tankard is 285 square hundredths. If this is multiplied by 20 cubits, or 2,000 hundredths, one obtains a volume of 570 000 cubic hundredths. But as 10 380 cubic hundredths corresponds to 4.125 lbs., so 570 000 corresponds to 217 lbs.

To be explicit:

As a volume of 10 830 cubic hundredths corresponds to 4.125 lbs., so one of 570 000 cubic hundredths corresponds to 217 $^{1130}/_{10830}$ lbs.

From this the gravity of any cylinder of air can be found, once the area of the base of the cylinder in question is known. For as the area of the base of a Magdeburg tankard, 285 square hundredths of a cubit, is to the gravity of the corresponding cylinder of air, 217 lbs., so does the area of the base of any cylinder correspond to the gravity of air in such a cylinder.

An example

Suppose the diameter of the base of a cylinder is 67 hundredths of a cubit. Therefore, using the ratio 7:22 of the diameter to the circumference, the circumference will be 210.6 hundredths and the area of the base 3,527½ square hundredths of a cubit.

However a base area of 285 square hundredths corresponds to a weight of 217 pounds. Therefore a cylinder, whose base area is 3,527½ square hundredths will weigh 2,686 pounds. The calculation goes like this.

The area of base of a Magdeburg tankard is 285 square hundredths and the weight of a cylinder 20 cubits high on this base is 217 pounds. Therefore the weight of a cylinder whose base diameter is 67 hundredths is (3,527.5 (the area of the base) ÷ 285) x 217 = (3,527.5 x 217) ÷ 285 = 765 467.5 ÷285 = 2,685.8.

This is the weight of a cylinder of air, whose base has a diameter of 67 hundredths of a Magdeburg cubit.

Another method

As a volume of 10 830 cubic hundredths correspond to a weight of 4.125 lbs., so the volume of the cylinder whose base area is 3527½ square hundredths corresponds to the weight we want to determine. This volume in cubic hundredths is easily found by multiplying the area of the base in square hundredths by a height of 20 cubits or equivalently, 2,000 hundredths, to obtain 2,000 x 3,527.5 = 7 055 000 cubic hundredths. So the weight we want to determine is:

(7 055 000 x 4.125) ÷ 10 830 = 2 910 101 875 000 ÷ 10 830 = 2,687.1

This is the weight in pounds of a cylinder of air whose diameter is 67 hundredths of a Magdeburg cubit.[339]

---

[339] Von Guericke does not comment on the different values he obtains from his two calculations.

Chapter XXIII – An experiment, in which it is shown that, because of the pressure of air, two hemispheres can be so joined together that sixteen horses cannot pull them apart

I commissioned two copper hemispheres *A* and *B* (v. Illustration XI) of diameter about ¾ Magdeburg cubit. (More precisely of diameter 67 hundredths of a cubit but tradesmen do not usually make things exactly as they have been requested.) These hemispheres were made so that they fitted tightly against each other. To one of them a tap, or rather a valve, *H* was soldered so that the internal air could be extracted and external air prevented from getting in, as described in Chapter 8 above and also in Illustration XI Fig. IV. Both hemispheres also have iron rings *N N N N* to which horses can be tied. (v. Illustration XI Fig. V). I also had a circular gasket sewn. This was made of leather well smeared with wax mixed with turpentine, so that air could not penetrate it. I placed one of these hemispheres on top of the other, with the gasket fitted between them and proceeded, using a special tube *f g h i* (v. Chapter 8, Illustration VII Fig. IV) to extract the air. I saw how firmly the two hemispheres, with the gasket in position, were held together. In fact, they were so strongly held together by the pressure of the external air that sixteen horses could not pull them apart, or could do so only with difficulty. When they sometimes, by a great exertion, did manage to pull them apart the hemispheres separated with an explosive noise like a gun shot.

When air is let in the hemispheres can be easily separated

The instant that air is let in by opening the tap *H*, the hemispheres can easily be separated by anyone, merely by manual exertion. So that one may know for certain the magnitude of the weight that was holding the hemispheres together, one should determine, following the investigation of the previous chapter, the weight of a cylinder of air, the diameter of whose cross section is 67 hundredths of a cubit. We chose that particular number as an example with the intention of making it easier to understand this experiment. One finds that the weight of this cylinder of air is 2,686 or 2,687 lbs. This means that the gravity of the air pressing one of the hemispheres against the other is equivalent to a weight of 2,686 lbs. and the second hemisphere is pressed by the same weight against the first. Thus, while striving to pull the hemispheres apart, one team of eight horses are bearing or dragging a load of 2,686 lbs. while the other eight, pulling from the other side, also exert a force corresponding to a load of 2,686 lbs.[340]

How the hemispheres can be pulled apart by a weight

Although eight horses might, without much difficulty, be able to pull a cart loaded with 2,686 lbs, this situation is more difficult because it is being done against the entire column of air and it is, so to speak, more against nature than the pulling of a load on a cart.[341] From this the following is an immediate consequence. Let two hemispheres, which are joined together by a vacuum, be suspended. If from the lower one a weight of 2,686 lbs is hung, then the lower hemisphere will be separated or pulled away from the upper one by such a weight. It should however be noted that the weight necessary to achieve this varies according to the nature of the air which sometimes is heavier and sometimes lighter. This weight represents the entire above mentioned mass of the air around the earth, taking into account, of course, its volume, as determined by the area of the base.

What is the mass of the air in the sky?

Thus if anyone should want to know the total mass of the air in the sky — i.e. the weight of all the air in the Earth's atmosphere — he would first seek to calculate the area of the Earth's surface in square miles and then express this in square cubits and then, following the golden rule[342] set out in the previous chapter, he would discover the desired weight.

The Earth together with its atmosphere constitutes a single distinct heavenly body

Finally we can infer from all this that the Earth (since the air that surrounds it has its own individual and separate weight) is an individual and separate body of the Cosmos, existing autonomously, and neither

---

[340] F. Danneman [p. 112] notes that the assumption that a horse could exert a force of 336 lbs. is much too high. The true average figure is nearer 200 lbs. On the other hand the vacuum within the hemispheres would by no means have been perfect.

[341] Von Guericke seems very confused here. The force required to start a cart moving horizontally depends on the surface over which it is being pulled and the frictions in the bearings and in general will be much less than the force of gravity on the load.

[342] Von Guericke uses this term to refer to the procedure for calculating quantities in direct proportion to known ones.

contained nor surrounded by anything else or any other heavenly substance.

Chapter XXIV – Another similar experiment in which hemispheres, which 24 horses could not pull apart, are separated by letting in air

When these hemispheres were pulled apart they were almost always damaged in some way. This was particularly the case when they were pulled by horses and then fell apart, hitting the ground and being dented out of their perfectly round shapes.

The larger hemispheres cannot be separated by twenty-four or even thirty horses

Accordingly I had two new bigger hemispheres made, each of one whole cubit in diameter. (However, since craftsmen can rarely make vessels of this sort to the specified measurements, I found that the diameters of my new hemispheres were, in fact, only 0.95 of a Magdeburg cubit.) My intention was to show that, while they could not be pulled apart by 24 horses, anyone could separate them by letting in air. We now do the calculations following the pattern of Chapter 22.

Circumference = (95 x 22) ÷ 7 = 2090 ÷ 7 = 298.5 h.

Circumference/2 = 149.3 h. & Radius = 47.5 h.

Base area = Radius x Circumf./2 = 149.3 x 47.5 = 7,091.75 sq. h.

Base area of Magdeburg tankard = 285 sq. h.

Weight of corresponding cylinder of air = 217 lbs.

Weight of given cylinder of air = (7092 x 217) ÷ 285 = 5,399 lbs.

Another Procedure

Volume of a cylinder based on Magdeburg tankard = 570 000 c.h.

Corresponding weight = 217 lbs.

Volume of a column of water with base area 7,092 sq. h. and of height 20 cubits (2,000 h.) = 14 184 000 c.h.

Corresponding weight =

(14 184 000 x 217) ÷ 570 000 = 3 077 928 000 ÷ 570 000 = 5,399lbs

This is the weight of a cylinder of diameter 0.95 cubits.

In the last chapter we saw that it took sixteen horses to pull apart a weight of 2,686 lbs. Now we ask how many horses are needed to pull apart a weight of 5,400 lbs. and we find, using the golden rule, that 34 horses would be necessary. If only 24 horses are harnessed to the task, they will certainly be unable to pull the hemispheres apart and they will remain joined as a single unbroken whole.

How the hemispheres are separated by letting in air

Meanwhile however, just to have some effective technique, the tap of the lower hemisphere (v. Illustration XI Fig. IV) was fitted with a valve, through which, using a syringe, air could flow in but not out. When the tap is opened the air enters and fills the sphere. If more air is pushed in with three or four strokes of the syringe, the hemispheres separate of their own accord.

Larger hemispheres cannot be separated even by 100 horses

From this we can assert that the separation of the hemispheres, although beyond the capacity of 24 or even (if larger hemispheres are chosen) 100 horses, can be accomplished by a single man merely by blowing air in.

ILLUSTRATION XII

Chapter XXV – Another experiment in which the above mentioned hemispheres are shown to be separable by a weight

Experiment to separate the hemispheres with a falling weight and thus to cause a bang

In addition to the experiments which have been done up to now, I have considered the following question. If the two hemispheres *A* and *B* (v. Illustration XII) were separated by a falling weight would they give off a crash like a cannon when a ball is shot from it using gunpowder? I instructed that the hemispheres be set up as before and that the air be extracted. When they were stuck together as a single sphere and the upper hemisphere attached to a fixing, I instructed that a hundredweight, suspended from the lower hemisphere, be released so that it suddenly fell.

How did the smashing apart of the hemispheres go? Since the hemispheres did not separate it was not a success. Because there was also a danger that a suspended weight might unexpectedly come crashing down and either kill or injure one of the onlookers, I abandoned this experiment completely after a third and fruitless attempt at it. Despite the dropping of many weights the hemispheres did not separate.

A method of separating the hemispheres using a weight

So that the construction of the smaller hemispheres, mentioned in Chapter 23, would not appear to have been wasted (for a team of horses cannot be produced just whenever one wants) I employed them for the following purpose. (v. Illustration XII) At the corner of the wooden fence which marks the boundary of my garden, I had a wooden post planted firmly in the ground. To the top end of the post a crosspiece was fitted into which an iron hook, K, was inserted. From this hook, the two hemispheres, already joined together and evacuated, could be suspended from the iron ring L. Next, I procured a solid square platform fitted with chains at the corners. (The platform was of the sort that officials at markets use for weighing goods.) These four chains are attached by the rings $N\,N$ to the second hemisphere, the one to which the valve was fitted. Weights heavy enough to separate the hemispheres are placed on the platform.

To find the weight sufficient to separate the two hemispheres

In Chapter 22 we discussed at some length the weight of the air around the Earth and, in Chapter 23, we described a comprehensive demonstration which showed that the pressure of the air on each of the hemispheres is 2,686 lbs. From this one can infer that the hemispheres, or more precisely the sphere made by combining them, would be pulled apart by a weight of 2,686 lbs. on the platform. When they are pulled apart like this there is a bang, but it is more muffled than if the separation were done by dropping a weight. The reason for this is that, in the latter case the weight has a single impact,[343] while in the former case there is a more gradual building up. Another reason is that the hemispheres are not exposed to the same force in all directions, but are unequally pulled. This causes the effect that that they do not separate equally at all points, but that the air flows in more at some specific point rather than at the same rate all around the circumference.

---

[343] This shows a loose understanding of the force exerted on the lower hemisphere by dropping a weight. The force depends on the mass and how fast it is decelerated when it reaches the bottom of its free fall.

Chapter XXVI – Another experiment which shows that the pressure of the air can cause the compression and even the breakage of vessels

Air fills all the pores of bodies

Since in these terrestrial regions the air around us exerts significant pressure, it follows that it penetrates all bodies that are not completely solid and fills all their internal hollow spaces. We find this to be the case with wood, stones and other similar materials that are not entirely solid. It is much more so the case for all containers which, even if their inlets are narrow, become filled with air. Taking an opposite perspective, a container of that type not filled with air, could not sustain the pressure of the air on it and would be crushed by the surrounding air, unless it happened to be exactly spherical. For example, take the glass Receiver *L* (v. Chapter 21 Illustration X Fig. III) and remove all the air from it. Then fit to it a large square flagon *a* (v. Illustration XIII), constructed so that the connection to the tap of the Receiver is air-tight, so that no external air can get in. The arrangement can be more clearly seen in Illustration XIII.

Then place the bucket *b* under it (to stop fragments of glass being scattered across the room) and open the tap gradually. One will hear the air in the flagon make a hissing sound as it rises into the upper evacuated Receiver. The flagon, not being exactly spherical, is unable to withstand the pressure of the external air and the resulting compression crushes it into a thousand or more shards. At the same time the external air, rushing into the empty space left in the flagon, emits a loud bang.

Objects from which the air has been removed will be squashed by the external air unless they are exactly round

When vessels are spherical they do not break and remain undamaged because a spherical shape inhibits compression. We see this effect in vaults which become stronger the more they are pressed upon. However when they are not exactly spherical one has to fear that they might be damaged or destroyed. I have myself had an unfortunate experience in this regard. It happened when I commissioned a copper sphere (v. Chapter 3) from a metal worker. I have related in Chapter 3 how, as it was not perfectly spherical, it was crushed by the external air.

If someone blew into an evacuated vessel they would die immediately

From this it follows at once that if a man were to blow into such an evacuated Receiver, he would immediately perish. This is because the pressure of the external air would not only suck out all the breath of a man or of any other animal into the evacuated glass but, in doing so, it would also seriously injure the body and all its internal organs.

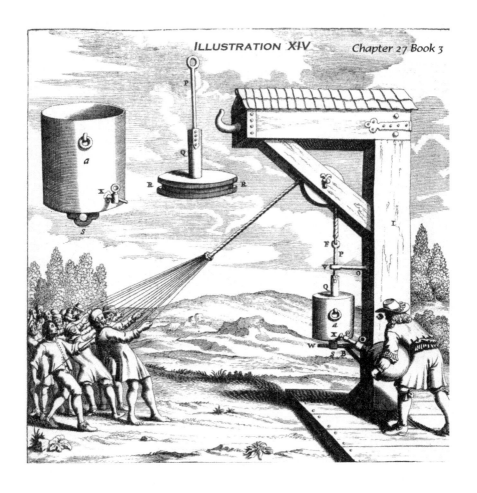

Chapter XXVII – On a glass vessel which is capable of pulling more than twenty, even in fact, fifty or more strong men

Certain experiments which the author showed to His Majesty, the Kaiser at the Reichstag of Regensburg in 1654

When, on municipal business I was attending the Reichstag at Regensburg in 1654, I showed, at their request, some of my experiments including the one, then new, described in the previous chapter to their imperial majesties, Ferdinand III and Ferdinand IV,[344] King of the Romans, both now of glorious memory. In my presentation, I had made a remark that if a man were to blow into a certain vessel (the Receiver), he would be courting immediate death. Fürst von Auersperg[345] could not be persuaded to give any credit to my words and wanted first to see with his own eyes a demonstration using the vessel.

To lay prostrate, just with a glass container, twenty, thirty or even fifty or 100 strong men

Something else also occurred at that time which seemed to cast doubt on the reliability of all my investigations. I therefore set up another experiment, which used a different method and which was designed to show, openly and beyond doubt, the truth of my assertion that this glass vessel could exhaust more than twenty or thirty men. In fact if desired, it could exhaust the strength of fifty or 100 men and if they did not stop pulling could leave them prostrate.

Construction of the apparatus

Firstly, a metal worker was commissioned to make a copper vessel (v. Illustration XIV *a*) in the shape of a kettle except that the sides were parallel and vertical like those of a cylinder. It was over a cubit high and, its volume was the same as the smaller hemispheres described in Chapter 23. A tin handle *S* was attached to the base.

Secondly, a piston *P Q R* which fitted the kettle drum exactly was then procured. The shaft *P* was made out of iron, *Q* out of wood and the piston head itself out of hardwood and grooved around the outside like a pulley wheel. This was done so that an oakum cord could be tightened around it so that an air-tight and water-tight seal was made with the inside wall of the kettle. (The arrangement is the same as is employed in the shaft and piston head of the bellows used in fires.)

---

[344] Ferdinand IV (1633–1654) was King of the Romans, King of Hungary and King of Bohemia. He was the eldest son of Kaiser Ferdinand III (1608–1657). The title "King of the Romans" meant that he was heir to the imperial throne.

[345] Johann Weikhard (1615–1677) Fürst von Auersperg was tutor to Ferdinand IV. In 1653 he was raised to the Reichsfürstenstand by Ferdinand III and subsequently became Herzog of Münsterberg. In 1669, suspected of private dealings with Louis XIV, he was dismissed from court and sentenced to death. The sentence was however never carried out and he was able to retire to his estates.

Thirdly, after I had made sure that *BW* was itself firmly fixed to *l,* the kettle *a* was attached to the large post *I* by fastening it to the arm *BW* using the previously mentioned handle *S*. The piston was positioned above the kettle with its iron shaft *QP* inserted through a hole *V* in another arm *OV* of the post. This had the effect of ensuring that the motion of the piston was completely vertical without any sideways movement as it was raised and lowered and also that *Q* could not be raised any higher than the arm *OV*.

Fourthly, when the kettle had been fixed to the post *I* in this way and the piston head let down almost to the bottom of the kettle, a rope to which a hook was attached was fed through the pulley *T* and attached to the piston at *P*. The tap *X* was then closed. Twenty or more men, pulling on the rope with their hands, did their best to pull the piston out but they managed only to pull it about half way up and not any further.

Fifthly, the much mentioned Receiver was connected to the tap *X* so that the fitting was air-tight. (Although the men were pulling as hard as they could, they remained unable to extract the piston head from the kettle.) Then the two taps were opened, first that of the Receiver and then that of the kettle. The piston head was drawn back down to the base of the kettle overcoming the exertions of all these men. I would venture to say that this glass container could successfully pull against twenty, thirty or even more men (Indeed if the apparatus were bigger as many as 100 could be pulled). If it were to pull just a single man it would rupture all his internal organs.[346]

The reason for this effect

The cause of this effect should be attributed to the pressure of the air. As soon as the internal air is extracted from the kettle, the air pressure immediately presses down on the piston head. Since the kettle is equal in volume to the hemispheres of Chapter 23, the air pressure amounts to 2,686 lbs. Twenty or even thirty or fifty men could not withstand the sudden exertion of such a force.

---

[346] Danneman (Note 18 p. 112) notes that, for this experiment to have worked, the bottom of the kettle must have been curved. Otherwise there would not have been air for the Receiver to suck out and thus to further reduce the pressure inside the kettle to the point where the piston is forced downwards.

Chapter XXVIII – Experiment on raising a large weight

Using the apparatus described previously, a boy of twelve to fifteen years old would be able to lift a weight, however heavy it might be.

One leaves the kettle *A* (v. Illustration XV) fixed to the post *I*. With the piston head *R* extracted to the top of the kettle, one feeds a chain through the pulleys *T* and *H*, the latter of which is suspended from the hook *K*. The piston shaft *QP* is attached to the chain at *P* by the hook *F*. Then the platform, which is loaded with a weight of 2,686 lbs., is suspended from the hook *N*.

Next, one obtains a pump (which should be made fairly narrow so that it can be used by a boy) and, as described in Chapter 2, one attaches it to the tap. The boy is instructed to operate it. As the air is sucked out of the kettle, the piston head is slowly but perceptibly drawn downwards and while the platform holding the weight of 2,686 pounds is raised.

One should note that if one wanted to lift a heavier weight, it would be necessary to use a kettle of larger diameter. In fact the diameter is in proportion to the weight it is desired to raise. The calculation of the necessary diameter may be easily made by the method of Chapter 22.

Because of the variation of air pressure the weight that can be raised also varies

Finally one should note the following. Since the pressure of the air is not always the same and, as we shall show in Chapter 31, can in fact exhibit a variation of up to five percent, it follows that the same weight cannot always be raised. On can read off this variation from the fingers of the little man suspended in the glass tube[347] or one can more accurately determine it and thus be able to establish definitely the pressure of the air at any time or at least to know, more or less, what the variation is.

---

[347] See Illustration X. Von Guericke's barometer, using the "little man" is described in Chapter 31.

Chapter XXIX – Experiment with a new air powered gun of novel design

Some years ago a method was discovered by which, using the compression of air inside a brass or iron tube, a lead bullet could be fired from it just as a bullet is fired from an ordinary gun using gun powder. What others try to bring about in ordinary guns using a plentiful supply of air, we, taking an exactly opposite approach, achieved through the absence of air. Here is how it was done.

The construction of this gun

A tube *a b d* (v. Illustration XVI) is made from a sheet of copper with a diameter suitable for the lead balls that one desires to fire. At the end *a* a type of brass valve is welded (just as in the outlet depicted in Illustration V Fig. I *b*) into which a leather disc *K* can be inserted which covers and blocks the end *a*. At the end *a* the tube should have, on its lower side, at *g*, a slit of about half the length of a finger and whose width should be no bigger than the blade of a table knife. Beneath this slit, a narrow gutter-pipe, running from *g* (below *a*) to *e* (below *b*) and terminating at *e* in a conical shaped nozzle, is welded to the main tube *a b*. This nozzle ought to be of such a width so that it can be fitted exactly to the tap *c* of the (by now familiar) Receiver *L*. If this cannot be done, then the tap may be lined with cord or oakum to ensure that the fit is a perfect seal.

The use of the gun

So far we have described he construction of our gun. Now we turn to its use.

1. The Receiver is completely evacuated and placed on a stool, an open drum or some other similar support.

2. The tube *a b d* is connected, using the conical nozzle at *e*, to the tap *c* of the Receiver.

3. The round leather flap *K* is placed in the brass valve in front of the opening *a*. (The flap is made from leather from Cordoba and round the outside is fitted to an iron ring, in a method often employed by shoemakers.)

4. A lead ball, exactly filling the inside of the tube *a b d,* is positioned at *d* and the gun directed to a target.

5. The key of the tap *c* is completely opened and then closed as quickly as possible. When this is done, the ball is explosively expelled from the tube. Afterwards, if another leather disk *K* is inserted in the valve at *a,* another lead ball placed at *d* and the tap quickly turned again, there will be a second explosive expulsion. This procedure can be repeated until the Receiver fills with air.[348]

So, using a glass Receiver, we can produce by this method explosive expulsions. However this device still falls far short of perfection, but under the instruction of the great teacher, Experience, it can be much

---

[348] Each time a shot is fired the leather flap is crashed into by the onrushing ball and presumably lost. A new ball and a new flap are required each time.

improved. It has, for instance, taught me that the length of the tube *a b d* should be proportional to the size of the lead ball to be fired. I have also noted that when the tube was 4½ cubits long, the ball was ejected with much more impetus, than when the tube was shortened to three cubits.

Chapter XXX – Experiments which show the variation of air pressure with height

The air near the Earth's surface is more compressed and hence is denser

This phenomenon, which some people would otherwise attribute to the horror of a vacuum, arises from air pressure. It follows from the fact that the lower regions of the air, because of the weight of the air lying above them, are more compacted and hence, depending on the height of the air above them, will be more or less dense.

On the tops of mountains the pressure of the air is weaker

It also follows that at the tops of mountains or towers the supposed abhorrence of a vacuum is diminished. This is because in high places the air does not press down as strongly as it does in the lower lying regions of the earth. By way of experiment, let the glass vessel *L*, which we call the Receiver (see Illustration VIII) be brought, with the tap of course open, to a low lying place e.g. to a church or graveyard. Then, with the tap closed, let it be brought to the top of a tower and then let the tap be opened again. An outflow of air will be observed. If the tap is closed again and the Receiver brought down to a lower location, then on re-opening the tap, an inflow of air will occur.

From all this it is clear that in places of higher altitude the air is not as strongly compressed as it is in lower lying ones. This is because the cylinder of air above a place of high altitude is diminished both in height and weight. It should be noted that when this experiment was carried out, the air both inside and outside the church was at the same temperature. For if it had been warmer in the church and colder at the top of the tower, the validity of this experiment would be open to question. It would be better to close the tap of the Receiver in a spot outside the church where the temperature is the same as that at the top of the tower and then, keeping the tap closed, to either carry it or haul it with a rope to the top where one can open the tap again.

Another experiment using mercury

Others have sought to test this phenomenon through the variation of the fall of mercury in a glass tube with the height of the mountain on which the trial was conducted. (See Chapter 34 for more on this topic.)

Also, at Paris M. de Pascal[349] has noted that near the bottom of a certain mountain the mercury in a glass tube had fallen to about 27 thumb widths.[350] About 156 paces[351] higher up the mountain the mercury in the glass tube had dropped to no more than 25 thumb widths. Finally at the top, 206 paces above the bottom, the mercury had dropped to about 24 thumb widths.

Four years ago,[352] I also tried this experiment at Brocksburg. I successfully carried out the experiment at the bottom of the mountain. Then I gave the glass tube, which was in fact enclosed in a metal one, to a servant to carry. In a fall he broke the glass tube, ruining the whole experiment.

Be that as it may, the single cause of this type of phenomenon is that air on the top of towers or mountains is compressed less by the air above it than air at intermediate or lower levels. Consequently it is lighter which results in a shorter column of mercury.[353]

---

[349] Blaise Pascal (1623–1662) was a French mathematician, physicist, philosopher and religious writer. He, aware of Torricelli's work, conducted experiments on the vacuum publishing his work in 1647 under the title *Nouvelles Experiences touchant le vide*. He himself carried out an experiment in a tower in Paris. The experiment alluded to was carried out by his brother-in-law, Florin Perrier, in the Puy de Dome in his native Auvergne. Pascal attributes nature's "horror of a vacuum" to a force of attraction between bodies which had to be overcome to create a vacuum. In the conclusion to *Nouvelles Experiences touchant le vide* Pascal writes: "Apres avoir démontré qu'aucune des matières qui tombent sous nos sens, et dont nous avons connoisance, ne remplissent cet espace vide en apparence, mon sentiment sera, jusqu'à ce qu'on m'ait montré l'existence de quelque matière qui le remplisse, qu'il est vé ritablement vide, et destitué de toute matiere. .... Je tiendrai pour vraies les maximes posées ci-dessus:
1. Que tous les corps ont de la répugnance a se séparer l'un de l'autre, et à admettre du vide dans leur intervalle; c'est à dire que la nature abhorre le vide.
2. Que cette horreur ou répugnance qu'ont tous les corps n'est pas plus grande pour admettre un grand vide qu'un petit, c'est à dire, pour s'éloigner d'un grand intervalle que d'un petit.
3. Que la force de cette horreur est limitée, et pareille à celle avec laquelle de l'eau d'une certaine hauteur, qui est à peu près de trente-un pieds, tend a couler en bas.
4. Que les corps qui borne ce vide ont l'inclination à le remplir.
[350] The Latin for this unit is "pollex" (thumb). From the numbers quoted this must equate to about 2.5 cms.
[351] The Latin is "peda -ae f" which is von Guerickes' translation of the French word "toise", which is a measure of approximately 1.95 m.
[352] i.e. in 1659. It has been dated to approximately June 6th where he made the attempt after the end of a meeting in Quedlinburg which he attended on June 5th.
[353] By post-Newtonian standards von Guericke writes loosely. The atmosphere is a fluid. The pressure at a point is due to weight of the fluid above it and not on the density at the point. Secondly, as he does correctly point out against Dr. Deusing, pressure is exerted equally in all directions. This is the defining characteristic of a fluid. The density at a point is of course also

Doctor Deusing[354] contradicts experiments

It will come as no surprise that Dr. Deusing, in his treatise on the vacuum, wants to rebuke and find fault with M. Pecquet[355] who shares our view. Dr. Deusing writes:

"If the lower regions of the air were so greatly pressed upon by the air above them so that they become more compacted, it would follow that we mortals in this lowest region of the air, supporting on our heads the entire mass of the air above us, would be affected by the weight of the air above us and we would we knocked flat on the ground."

We do not feel the pressure of the air, as it exerted all around the body

Dr. Deusing ought to have borne in mind that the air does not just press on our heads but flows all around us. Just as it presses from above on the head, it likewise presses on the soles of the feet from below and simultaneously on all parts of the body from all directions. Indeed, it so fills the body that it is completely immersed in air and all its crevices and empty spaces are filled with it.[356] As fish do not perceive the pressure of the water around them, we do not perceive the pressure of the air around us.

---

affected by the weight of the air above, but this is a separate issue from the question of pressure.

[354] See footnote to Book III Chapter 8.

[355] Jean Pecquet (1622–1674) was a French anatomist. His *Experimenta nova anatomica* (1651) contains observations on the level of the column of mercury on mountains.

[356] This is an important realisation. Von Guericke is here stating the defining characteristic of a fluid.

Chapter XXXI – Experiments showing the variation in the density of air with changes in the weather

A thoroughly evacuated vessel, suspended from a balance, experiences a change in weight

By means of the experiment related in Chapter 19, I discovered that air does not always have the same density and also observed this phenomenon in the Receiver in which air was weighed. (v. Chapter 21) For when it was completely evacuated and weighed over the course of several days, its weight changed so that we saw both this globe and its counterweight go up and down a number of times, just as we have described in Chapter 20 above. To investigate further, I commissioned a sphere, of about half the volume of the Receiver, made out of sheet copper and with a valve of the kind described in Chapter 8, in place of the tap.

I had this sphere completely evacuated and placed, along with a counterweight of fused lead, on a balance that had been specially adapted to this purpose. The variation in weight could be read from a scale on a semi-circular brass strip positioned at the side. Inspection showed that sometimes a variation in weight was apparent on the same day but sometimes not till the second, third, fourth or fifth day of observation.

When it rains the air becomes lighter

When it rains, a lot of water is released from the air and hence it becomes less dense. In this situation, the evacuated sphere becomes heavier and weighs down the scale. In contrast, it rises (or becomes lighter) when the air becomes denser.[357] The reason is that the denser a substance in which something is contained, then the lighter the contained something will appear to be.

The heavier the ambient material the lighter a body immersed in it will appear to be

For instance, let us take alcohol, which is denser than air. If one immerses this sphere in alcohol we see from the balancing counterweight that it is lighter than it was in air and lighter still if it is immersed in

---

[357] This is a variant of Archimedes principle. The up-thrust on the sphere, being equal to the weight of the air displaced, depends on the density of the air.

water and lightest of all in salt water as this is denser than pure water. Examples of such variations in the weight according to the ambient material could be proliferated. In any case, as far as this sphere is concerned, it becomes heavier or lighter according as the air in which it is suspended becomes more or less dense.

The construction of a completely air-tight sphere is an extremely difficult and laborious business. If it is not completely air-tight then the quantity of air inside the sphere will increase with the passage of time. This in turn impairs the proper working of the experiment and undermines confidence in my ideas. It has also proved difficult to procure a suitable scale and have it modified with just the right parts so that it can detect even small changes in weight. I was therefore concerned to find another better and more accurate way of determining this variation in the weight.

About a wooden statue floating in air

This issue is also discussed at the end of Chapter 20 above where I describe how, by dint of some skill and effort, I placed a wood carving of a little man in a glass tube (v. Illustration X Fig. IV) so that he was supported on air and would rise and fall as the density of the air changed. The little man was arranged so that his finger would show, quite precisely, the variation in the density. The little man could also be used to recognise and, in fact, predict whether there would or wouldn't be, rain and whether it was just beginning or about to finish.

I shall say nothing now about the violent storms and tempests which, although they may be a hundred or more German miles[358] away, can be detected by this apparatus. It would be desirable to know the area where the storms are taking place but this cannot be determined from the apparatus and it is also the case that the apparatus cannot be easily moved from one place to another.

---

[358] A German mile is approximately 7,600 kilometres.

Chapter XXXII – The cause of suction

The air penetrates all bodies unless they are solid like metals

The earth is encircled by a sphere of air that presses heavily upon it. From this it follows that the air penetrates and fills all the holes and cracks in physical bodies, unless they are perfectly solid. This implies that it also fill all the pores in the bodies of animals. It is because of their being filled in this way that the air pressure is not perceptible to them. When something has been once filled to capacity, it does not accept anything more but instead exudes material. When something, which is at least partially empty, is placed on or connected to the external surface of a body and the body is pressed towards it, (just as our own bodies and everything else here on this earth is pressed upon by the ambient air) there will necessarily be a movement of fluid material in the body seeking to fill up the evacuated attachment. For example, when the human body is put under pressure from all sides by the ambient air, it becomes simultaneously filled internally with air which is why the pressure of the air is undetectable. Similarly when an infant is brought to the breast and creates a vacuum by pulling its tongue back — as it does when it suckles — this action, because of the pressure created on the breast, draws the nearest fluid material, which in this case is milk, into its empty mouth.

The same principle applies to cupping glasses. Indeed the bigger the mouth of that type of vessel, the greater the pressure, which we perceive as suction. Consequently, if an evacuated Receiver whose tap has an inlet bigger than the cupping glass were applied to the skin, the flesh would steadily creep into the neck of the tap until it finally ruptured.

Hydraulic machines for drawing water out of wells work in a similar fashion. These are commonly called pumps and they draw up water through pipes by applying suction. When the piston head, which should exactly fill the smooth bore of the shaft, is raised it creates an empty space in the shaft, and consequently, through repeated motions of this kind, the water necessarily rises from the well up the tube to the pump handle. This all happens, not because of any abhorrence of a vacuum, but because of the pressure of the air on the surface of the water of the well. If an abhorrence of the vacuum were the cause then the water would rise to any height whatsoever in the pump shaft. This doesn't occur. When an extraction engine is greater than 19 or 20 cubits tall i.e. when the top of the drawing shaft and the outlet are positioned at more than this distance above the water level, then no water can be raised. This puts paid to any question of a natural "fear of a vacuum". To sum up, the rising of water in a pump shaft is owing to the pressure of the air, which forces the water up, but only to a height of 19 or 20 cubits.

Chapter XXXIII – Experiments on the rarefaction and compression of air

Thermometers clearly show that air, of its nature, enjoys the property of being able to be compressed or made denser and also of being capable of rarefaction or becoming more diffuse. When it is cold, the air coalesces and occupies a smaller space. When it is warm the air expands and occupies a greater space. Human artifacts allow the occurrence of this phenomenon to be seen, sometimes in quite a striking fashion. It is particularly evident in the use of the air fountains[359] which are frequently used in banquets or placed on tables. Into these, we can, by means of a pump attached to an inlet, blow in so much air that they ultimately burst. On the other hand, if no extra air is blown in and the air that normally occupies them left untouched, but a flame placed below, then, provided all outlets are closed off, the fountains also burst.

The air in an air-gun barrel is strongly compressed

Experiment also shows us that the air in an air-gun can be compressed to a fifth of its volume just by the action of a pump operated by hand.

The air nearer the Earth's surface is strongly compressed

The sphere of air surrounding the whole Earth is, through the Earth's conservative potency (v. Book IV Chapter 5), compressed in on itself. As a consequence, the air is held in position, acquires weight and becomes denser in such a way that the lower a region of air is, the denser it becomes. For when bodies are piled up one on top of another, the more bodies there are, the higher the pile becomes and the more pressure there is on the ones at the bottom. It is the same with the air where the lower regions — those nearer the earth — are under greater pressure than the higher up ones. All of this accords with sound common sense. (v. Chapter 30 above)

Air has a natural striving to expand

---

[359] Von Guericke may be here referring to the "pyrobolus fons", described on p. 226 of the *Mechanica Hydraulico-pneumatica*, of which Fr. Schott writes; "I call this device a pyrobolic fountain, for air expanded by the force of fire drives water in an upward jet."

From the preceding and many other experiments, especially that of Chapter 11 where it was described how air flows more vigorously into an evacuated tube, two affirmations can be made:

(a) the entire mass of the air surrounding the Earth becomes compressed through this force of attraction which draws it into itself;

(b) air also enjoys a certain innate tendency to expand.

(Especially in the lower regions, air is compressed with a force that overcomes its natural striving to expand. Only if it has enough power and space, can it express its striving to expand. Philosophers refer to this property as "elasticity".) I had a similar experience of a violent rush of air with the apparatus described in Chapter 18 Point 6 when I accidentally forgot to evacuate the upper glass, but nevertheless opened the tap which connected both vessels. The air rushed into the water of the lower one, which had been evacuated and partially filled with water, with such force that I was genuinely terrified that the whole apparatus would shatter into fragments.

Another experiment using a bladder

Therefore if anybody remains sceptical that air has an expansive force — and indeed there are many who would deny it — let him place a bladder full of air inside a pair of hemispheres, as described in Chapter 23. He should ensure that the hemispheres have been well fitted to each other, and then let him evacuate the air inside them. He will then see that the bladder inside the hemispheres bursts when pumping has hardly begun. Let him also take a bladder of this kind, only half fill it with air and then place it in the Receiver, as we did with the clockwork in Chapter 15. He will discover that the more air is taken out of the Receiver the more the bladder swells until it finally bursts.

Air can be extracted from a vessel even if the evacuating pump is placed at the top of a house

I have also established the following. Let a pneumatic pump be positioned on the top of a building with its pipe going from the pump handle to the ground and let the other end of the pipe be inserted into a Receiver or some other vessel to be evacuated. Then, when the pump handle is operated, the air from the Receiver rises through its own expansive force up the tube of the pump. This experiment makes the expansive force of air absolutely plain to anybody interested in this matter.

From all the foregoing, it becomes clear that there is an atmosphere and that the lower parts of it are more compressed than the upper parts and also that air will expand to fill the space available to it.

How air pressure arises

The underlying reason for air pressure deserves investigation.[360] Some people think that it is caused by the striving towards the centre to which, they believe, everything that has gravity tends. Others assign the cause to the light rays from the stars that come from all directions and exert a pressure on the air.

One really wonders why they want to explain some things by attributing them to a natural and innate striving towards the centre rather than just explaining them as arising from the Earth and its conservative potency. From Book IV Chapter 5[361] one can see that there does exist in nature this sort of innate attractive potency and thus the impulse to fall should not be attributed to the things in themselves but to the operation of a more general potency.[362] Besides, this supposed power of compressing air can hardly originate from the stars above. For if it did come from the stars, then the Earth, as an obstruction in the path of light rays, would also be subject to this pressure from the stars and would offer resistance to it. However when two bodies press against each other, a third body placed between them is pressed equally by them both. Thus it would necessarily follow that the lower regions of the air would experience the same pressure as the higher regions, which is contrary to experiment.

The height of the atmosphere is small compared with the distance of the stars

Finally the lower region of air is under more pressure than the upper region. This is something we can perceive on very high mountains and

---

[360] Nowhere does von Guericke show any inkling of the kinetic theory of gases which explains the phenomenon of pressure.

[361] This chapter is entitled *De Virtute Conservativa Terrae* (On the conservative potency of the Earth)

[362] We see how far away von Guericke is from any idea of the action and reaction principle. The Newtonian concept of gravity attributes the force of attraction equally to both bodies.

even in the steeples of churches. It follows that the air above the surface of the earth does not reach to any very great height. In comparison with the distance to the stars, the height of the atmosphere is insignificant and, in fact, beyond its boundary there is nothing but pure and incorporeal space. This will be discussed further in Book V Chapters 6–9.[363]

---

[363] The titles of these chapters are 6: *De Aere circa Tellurem et Igne Elementari, credito* (On the air around the Earth and the supposed elementary fire) 7: *De Altitudine Aeris circa Tellurem* (On the height of the air around the Earth) 8: *Observatio quaedam, a Davido Fröhlicho in Monte Carpatho Hungariae institute, quae non parum facere videtur, ad judicium de Aeris sensibili altitudine et Regionum eius constitutione, ferendum* (A certain observation made by David Fröhlich of Carpathia in Hungary, which seems to contribute substantially to making an estimate of the height of the atmosphere and the constitution of its regions) 9: *De Divisione Aeris in Regiones* (The division of the air into regions)

Chapter XXXIV – An experiment for demonstrating a vacuum through a fall in the level of mercury in a tube sealed at its upper end

While attending the Reichstag in Regensburg (as mentioned in Chapter 27), though occupied with other matters, I showed certain of my experiments to some of the Prince Electors and Ambassadors. In the course of these demonstrations,[364] I struck up an acquaintance with Most Rev. Father Valerianus Magnus[365] of the Capuchin order. He showed me a particular experiment of his own (or so he said) to show the existence of the much pondered upon vacuum. The experiment was conducted as follows.

1. He took a glass tube sealed at one end and somewhat longer than 1½ Magdeburg cubits.

2. He filled this tube with mercury and, holding his finger to the open end to prevent any mercury escaping, turned the tube upside down and immersed the open end in a vessel filled with mercury.

3. He took away his finger slowly and one saw the mercury slowly falling until it had reached a certain level, about 1¼ cubits above the level in the vessel, where it stabilised and didn't fall any further. This is what happens on the gradual withdrawal of one's finger. If the finger is withdrawn abruptly, then the mercury oscillates up and down a number of times before settling to the same level as before.

---

[364] Based on research by Jerzy Cygan, Schneider (p. 99) gives a different account of their acquaintanceship. Von Guericke met Father Valerian in August 1653 and as a result of scientific conversations with him, was stimulated to bring his apparatus back from Magdeburg, to where he had returned on a visit to his sick wife in October 1653, in order to be able to mount his own demonstrations. Von Guericke returned to Regensburg before the end of 1653, where he showed his experiments, initially to a limited circle, and subsequently, as his reputation grew, to the highest officials of the Empire.

[365] Fr. Valerianus Magnus (1586–1661) was an Italian Capuchin missionary and preacher in Germany, Hungary and Poland. He enjoyed the respect of Ferdinand II and Ferdinand III and was used as a diplomat by King Wladislav IV of Poland. As a scientific publicist he seemed ready to take credit as the originator of experiments which he merely repeated — in this case, those of Torricelli (1608–1647). Pascal was acquainted with him and in a letter to M. de Ribeyre in July 1651, traces how Torricelli's experiment, but without the identification of Torricelli as the discoverer, became known in France in 1644 through a letter to Fr. Mersenne (1588–1648). He (Pascal) alleges that, at some point after 1647, the Capuchin had performed the experiments of Torricelli in Poland claiming to be the originator. This is in accord with von Guericke's experience at Regensburg. His acknowledgment that Fr. Valerian had, in his pamphlet, *Demonstratio ocularis, loci sine locato ... ,* correctly attributed the experiment to Torricelli, acquits the Capuchin of outright fraud.

Rev. Fr. Valerian claims that the space in the upper part of the tube when the mercury falls is really and truly a vacuum. He says that it cannot be the case that any other substance could have replaced the mercury as it fell. He gave me a copy of his pamphlet entitled:

"A visible demonstration of: (a) place which is not the place of anything; (b) of a body in continuous motion in a vacuum; (c) of light that is not associated with a physical body."

I learned then, from this pamphlet as well as from other sources, that this experiment was first discovered by Johannes Torricelli,[366] a most distinguished scholar and mathematician of the Grand Duke of Tuscany.

The opinion of the author of the experiment producing a vacuum using mercury

Here is my opinion of this most ingenious experiment. I don't doubt that in the upper part of the tube the space left behind by the fall of the mercury is almost entirely empty of air. But it is not absolutely empty; for in pouring the mercury into the tube, some tiny bubbles always remain attached to the inner wall where they are visible to the eye. It doesn't seem possible to avoid these when pouring in the mercury. Later when I was back at home, I procured similar glass tubes for myself and tried the experiment many times. I adapted the experiment to produce a true vacuum (Illustration VII Fig. V) in that I was able to connect this tube to the vacuum pump described in Chapter 4 above.

I first filled the tube with mercury until it was about a third full and then connected it to the vacuum pump using the small pipe mentioned in Chapter 8. I could clearly see that little bubbles were escaping into the empty space above the mercury and, at the same time, there was some agitation of the mercury as its level rose somewhat. I also noticed that it did not maintain that level but dropped by about the thickness of a straw. When any more mercury was poured and the air extracted as before, the same thing happened so that, by the third repetition, all the

---

[366] (Johannes) Evangelista Torricelli (1608–1647) was Galileo's successor as grand-ducal mathematician and professor of mathematics at the University of Pisa from 1642. His interest in the vacuum arose from the discovery by the pump makers of the Grand Duke that they could only raise water to a height of about 10 metres. About 1643 he proposed this experiment to his friend Viviani who actually performed it. The experiment was communicated to Fr. Mersenne in 1644. The "other sources" probably include his correspondent Fr. Kaspar Schott who gives the correct attribution in *Hydraulico-pneumatica* (1657) p. 306.

mercury in the tube had sunk by about half a finger width. From this it fairly clear that there is as much air trapped between the mercury and the sides of the tube as accounts for about half a finger's width of mercury. Accordingly, using our vacuum pump technique, vessels can be more completely evacuated than can be achieved by this simpler method of using mercury.

Those air bubbles which insinuate themselves between the mercury and the walls of the tube have to be taken into account. They are not to be compared with the really big ones that come from water in vessels that have been thoroughly evacuated and, because of the vacuum in such containers, expand by a factor of ten or even as much as a hundred-fold.[367] The air bubbles trapped by the mercury are in ordinary air, and thus subject to a weight of twenty cubits of water as well as being further compressed by the mercury itself.

Besides, no one can deny that the use of the vacuum pump to suck out the trapped bubbles creates a more perfect vacuum in the glass tube. The mercury method also has additional disadvantage that the small vacuum created above the mercury cannot be used for other experiments.

An experiment carried out in a longer tubes using water

Finally it should be noted that Rev. Fr. Kaspar Schott, on page 308 of his *Mechanica Hydraulico-pneumatica*, writes:[368]

" …. that others (when they heard that many people wanted to repeat the above mentioned experiment and to try and produce a vacuum) had tried to reproduce this in longer tubes using water, but had not found that the upper end of the tube became an empty space void of water. However when they placed a glass cap on the upper end of the tube, attaching it to the neck of the tube with a good seal so that no air could get in, and then with considerable dexterity they fixed a little bell together with an iron hammer to the walls of the glass cap, so

---

[367] Von Guericke doesn't make a distinction between bubbles arising from the release of air dissolved in the water and bubbles arising from the boiling of the water itself. Both phenomena will occur at low pressure.

[368] This passage is not a direct quotation but a rather loose summary of what Fr. Schott actually wrote. On p.p. 308, 309, on the key issue of the interpretation of the experiment his words (p. 309) are: "Meanwhile it is definite that in the upper part of the tubes void of either mercury or water, there wasn't a vacuum since sound was propagated through that space which could not have happened in a vacuum. Read the most learned discussion of the earlier experiment by Fr. Melchior Cornaeus, professor of Theology at our Society's College in Würzburg, in his philosophy course to be published shortly".

that, by means of an exterior magnet, the hammer could be made to strike the bell, then a clear sound was emitted and heard by all the onlookers. Such a thing cannot happen in a vacuum, for no sound at all can propagate through a vacuum, just as Fr. Melchior Cornae-us[369] has affirmed in his commentary on the previous experiment, which he has included in his philosophy course."

I agree with this up to a point. If they heard a ringing tone, then there was no vacuum, for there is no ringing tone in a vacuum. By contrast a thudding sound or noise can be propagated through a vacuum, as the experiments in Chapter 15 above show.[370]

---

[369] Melchior Cornaeus S.J. (1598–1665) was a German theologian and philosopher. He was a colleague of Fr. Schott and Professor of Theology at the Jesuit College at Würzburg.

[370] Von Guericke did not have the post-Newtonian understanding of the nature of sound and, in seeking to draw a distinction between notes and dull sounds, misinterpreted the experiments of Chapter 15. His view is that notes or ringing tones are associated with the sonic potency of air stimulated by the motion of the hammer of the bell, whereas thudding noises are a consequence of the sonic potency of certain materials.

Chapter XXXV – The common objections to the vacuum and their resolution

On p. 25 of his *Mechanica Hydraulico-pneumatica*[371] Rev. Fr. Kaspar Schott recounts a number of experiments which philosophers are very eager to interpret as proving that a vacuum doesn't exist.

The first objection — the drawing apart of the sides of a bellows

1. If the inlet of a bellows which admits air to the space left between the sides as they are separated, is blocked, then the sides cannot be pulled apart even by an angelic[372] force. Why would this happen, except that a vacuum cannot exist? However if, despite the blocking up of the inlet and the exclusion of air or any other substance, the sides could nevertheless be separated then a vacuum would have to exist.

Response

Even if the sides of a bellows were quite solid and made of thick leather, there would be no obstacle preventing the sides being pulled apart nor would it require the force of an angel to do it. One would just fix the lower side firmly to the ground, and the upper side could be easily raised by hand, or in the case of a larger bellows by using a lever arrangement. In fact from the calculation undertaken in Chapter 22, it can be accurately deduced how great a weight would be required for the separation of the sides of an arbitrary bellows. The weight is in proportion to the size of the bellows. But now since the philosophers admit that a vacuum would exist if the sides could be parted, despite the exclusion of air by stopping up the inlet, the argument is made. A better and clearer experiment with the air pump depicted as *g h* of Illustration VI Fig. I is the following. With the outlet *n* closed, the piston shaft and piston head *s h* is also placed under water. While the piston shaft is moving up and down no air can enter this space because not only is the outlet *n* closed but the operation of the pump is under water. An observer can clearly see that neither air not water enters. Therefore a vacuum exists in the pneumatic pump.

---

[371] The objections to the vacuum are, as von Guericke notes, all taken from Fr. Schott's *Mechanica Hydraulico-pneumatico* Protheoria I. III "Experiments by which it is shown that a vacuum does not exist."(p. 25)

[372] On some medieval views, angels were the Intelligences guiding the Spheres. (v. C. S. Lewis: *The Discarded Image*, p. 116.)

The second objection — the behaviour of a metal sheet

In his discussion of the vacuum Fr. Nicholas Zuchius[373] writes:

"A metal plate was once put in front of a young man who prided himself on the strength of his arms. The plate was to be raised by a handle in the middle of it from a marble tabletop on which it fitted exactly. The young man first laughed at the task as a ridiculous one fit only for a young boy. Then at the urging of his friends he tried it and despite using both hands and struggling for quite some time he could not lift it. He attributed his inability to some strange and strong glue holding the plate to the table top until he saw the plate being lifted easily from the table by somebody else just by sliding it to the edge and then tipping it."

Response

If we knew the surface area of that metal plate, it would, using the method of Chapter 22 above, be easy to calculate how much force would be needed to pull the plate up from the table. In this way we would have refuted the supposed abhorrence of a vacuum.

The third objection — the behavior of a glass immersed in water

Put a glass under the surface of water so that it fills up and then, while it is still in the water, turn it upside down so that the mouth is facing downward. Then, keeping it like this, start to raise it and try to pull it out of the water. What you will see is that the water inside the glass is raised along with the glass itself. If you hold the glass so that it is partly out of the water and partly still submerged, then you see that the water in the glass stays raised above the ambient surface level and the weight, as perceived by the person holding the glass, becomes heavier. Why is this? Because the air cannot succeed in occupying the place between the falling water and the upper parts of the glass which would be left empty as the water falls.

Response

If the glass were more than twenty cubits long, then you would see the water inside dropping. It would in fact drop by the excess of the height of the glass over twenty cubits. Then, because the air cannot get to the

---

[373] Nicholas Zuchius S.J. (1586–1670) Italian philosopher, mathematician and theologian. He was a professor at the Collegio Romano and invented the first reflecting telescope in 1616. He was the author of *Novae de Machinis Philosophiae* and *Opticae Philosophicae*. Fr. Schott wrote to him, among others, at Rome soliciting his opinions on the Magdeburg Experiments. His reply of November 1656 is quoted at length by Fr. Schott in *Experimentum Novum Magdeburgicum*.

space between the falling water and the parts of the glass left empty as the water falls and since the mouth of the glass remains under the water, a vacuum is created in the space above the water.

The fourth objection — the behaviour of vessels used in watering gardens

Suppose that the bottom of the sort of watering can that one sees everywhere is perforated with many little holes and the can is then filled with water and lifted, keeping it level, well away from the ground. The water does not flow out through the holes, as long a finger is held against the open outlet of the neck of the can. This is because the finger stops air from getting in to fill the space at the top of the can that would be left empty by the water, were it to flow out. The water in the can remains in a stable state of suspension where the downward pull of the water is resisted just as it is when the bottom is whole and the neck open. However once the finger is removed so that the air is allowed into the can through the neck, the water immediately flows out through the holes in the bottom. If, while the water is flowing out, the opening of the neck is again stopped up by covering it with a finger, the water once again remains suspended against the pull of its own weight, which is borne by the hand of the person holding the can, and it does not flow out the holes at the bottom.

Response

The weight of the ambient air presses on the watering can from all sides. Thus when the neck is blocked off, water cannot flow through the holes in the bottom because it is held up by the gravity of the air. If the water were twenty cubits high it would press more heavily than the external air. Therefore it is not any abhorrence of a vacuum that keeps the water in the can but the pressure of the surrounding air. In contrast, once the finger is removed so that the air can enter through the neck, the water then can, according to its natural gravity, escape through the holes in the bottom of the can.

The fifth objection — the phenomenon of suction

If you put one end of a straw under water and suck out the air from the other end, the water immediately rises, contending against its own gravity and following the air into the mouth of the person sucking. This occurs to prevent the development of a vacuum in the straw when the air is sucked out.

Response

Because the water does not rise more than 20 cubits, one can infer that the cause of the rise in the water level is the pressure of the external air which presses on the exposed surface of the water and forces it into the space which is empty. If it really did come from the abhorrence of a vacuum, the water would rise indefinitely and fill the tube.

The sixth objection — the behaviour of a sphere moved near a fire and of a cupping glass

Take a solidly built hollow copper sphere that won't break easily, heat it over a fire so that the air inside becomes markedly rarefied and then submerge it in cold water. The air inside, contracting from the forced rarefaction, becomes more dense and occupies less space. Water is sucked into the sphere as no other air can get into the space that has been vacated. This happens so that a vacuum will not be created in the sphere. In the same way, take either a straw with one end closed and the other open or a well-made hollow tube and strongly and continuously suck the air out. When you stop sucking, put your finger or lip to the open end so that no air can get in. The flesh of your finger or lip is drawn inside the straw or tube so that it puckers noticeably and stands proud of the surrounding flesh. The cause is that during the suction the air remaining violently fills the empty space itself, but when the sucking stops, it recoils from this sudden rarefaction and, occupying less space, it summons the nearest other thing to it to fill the vacated space. The same explanation explains why the cupping glasses which are in common use by surgeons pull the flesh upwards. For indeed the air, previously heated over a fire, had become rarified, but when the flame is put out, it gets colder and denser. Contracted to a smaller volume, it would leave some empty space except that the flesh is drawn up to fill it.

Response

The claims that are made for this experiment on straws or cupping glasses, which draw in flesh pressed against them, do not stand in need of any long winded refutation since we have already described these same phenomena in Chapter 32.

Seventh objection — the behaviour of a piston head which is drawn with difficulty from a gun barrel

Insert into a metal rifle, or into the barrel of a cannon, a piston head that fits tightly to the sides so that air cannot get between the sides and the piston head. Seal the opening at the other end from where the gun is fired. Only with difficulty can the piston be withdrawn and when, with considerable effort, it is withdrawn, a turbulence lasting for some time is created behind it.

Response

The same phenomenon always occurs with the piston head of an air pump. It should not be supposed that the reason for it is nature's fearing or fleeing a vacuum, but the pressure of air, which presses on the piston head making it difficult to withdraw. Also when the barrel is of large diameter, the pressure is so great that there is no point in even trying. (v. Chapter 27 above)

Chapter XXXVI – The opinion of Most Rev. Frs. Kircher and Zuchius at Rome as well as that of Fr. Cornaeus, a professor at the College of Würzburg on the Magdeburg experiments

At Regensburg in 1654 the first Magdeburg experiment was exhibited

At the 1654 Reichstag at Regensburg, some enthusiasts for scientific matters pressed me to give a demonstration of my new experiments. I felt I shouldn't, and in any case didn't want to, disappoint them. My demonstrations took place during the final days of the Reichstag when it was already beginning to break up and craftsmen with the necessary skills to build the apparatus I used from scratch were not readily available.

The Lord Elector of Mainz transported the apparatus to Würzburg

Nevertheless that most eminent prince, Johann Philipp, Lord Elector and Lord Archbishop of Mainz, wanted to have the experimental apparatus necessary for my demonstrations at his palace at Würzburg. There, in the presence of the most Eminent Johann Philipp, Rev. Fr. Kaspar Schott (as he himself says in *Experimentum Magdeburgicum*, the appendix to his book *Mechanica Hydraulico-pneumatica*) witnessed the entire demonstration on a number of occasions. He checked it thoroughly, documented it, communicated it to various scholars at Rome and elsewhere and solicited their opinions of it.

The different opinions of various learned men

Particularly notable among these were Fr. Athanasius Kircher and Fr. Nicholas Zuchius at Rome. At Würzburg Fr. Melchior Cornaeus and others gave their opinions as a perusal of the above mentioned *Mechanica Hydraulico-pneumatica* will readily confirm.

At first it was thought was that the piston of the pump could not be moved endlessly

Initially they all took the following view.[374]

---

[374] Though von Guericke presents it as direct quotation, the passage is a summary of views expressed by Fr. Nicolas Zuchius in a letter, written from Rome in November 1656. (*Mechanica*

The shaft of the air pump, after some number of repeated movements, cannot be pulled further into the forward part of the barrel, and one simply has to give up on the task and to stop working the pump as there is no way of moving the piston any further.

Response

This is just mistaken. The shaft can in fact, though towards the end needing a more strenuous exertion, be withdrawn from the barrel. The bigger the piston head the more difficult the task becomes. The difficulty is in proportion to the size of the piston head and can be calculated as described in Chapter 27 above.

Secondly they think that the difficulty can increase infinitely as the air becomes thinner

Secondly they ask "What is the source of so great a difficulty?" Their answer is the following. There isn't a vacuum left after the extraction of the air because the mere absence of the substance that was there previously — i.e. nothingness — has no power of resisting the withdrawal. Therefore some substance remains in the vessel which is not capable of being further rarified either by the motion of the pump or the exertion of the person operating the pump. It has however been thinned out to the point where it cannot permit any more thinning out which might arise from a further withdrawal of the piston in consequence of this sort of exertion. Fr. Cornaeus puts it like this. Because the air is gradually rarified as far as nature will allow rarefaction to take place, it cannot be further expanded or rarified.

Response

The Jesuit fathers, generally the most learned of men, are — I say it with all due respect — mistaken when they ascribe the observed resistance to the air left behind in the barrel, which, as they themselves admit, is either completely empty or just contains a vanishingly small amount of air. The tiny amount of air, which they say remains in the barrel, could not have a bigger effect than if more were to remain behind.

Hydraulico-pneumatica (p. 463). The second passage is also a précis of points made in the same letter. (p. 464).

Thus it is not to the tiny portion of air that remains behind that this effect should be attributed but to the pressure of the external air. It is this that exerts the strong push on the piston.

The third objection is that an evacuated vessel is never completely refilled with water

The third objection is raised by Fr. Cornaeus in points 5 and 6.[375]

The water on entering an evacuated glass vessel carries a lot of foam and bubbles with it and the vessel is never completely filled with water.

Response

An understanding of these effects is to be found in the experiments described in Chapter 6 above.

The fourth objection speaks in favour of the vacuum

Fourthly, Fr. Schott himself admits the vacuum when, in the *Mechanica Hydraulico-pneumatica*, p. 472, point 7, he writes:

"For when the piston fitted with a piston head is pulled from the bottom A of the pipe towards B as far as D, it follows necessarily that the space between A and D would be void of any substance, unless air were to get in from the Receiver. Whence if the tap of the Receiver is held closed, then there is no way that the piston can be pulled from A towards B."

But experiments regularly show that it can be pulled, even if the tap of the Receiver is held closed. Therefore the space between *A* and *D* is void of all substance.

Fifthly, Point 8 of the same series asks:

"When and how is the vacuum in the Receiver formed? Is it formed at one instant throughout the whole Receiver or is it formed gradually and in different parts of the Receiver?"

Response

The Receiver is gradually emptied of air. Because its natural tendency to expand and because of its natural weight the air sinks to the bottom of the Receiver and into the pump, assuming, of course, that the Receiver is arranged to be above the pump.

---

[375] These points are made, with the same numbering, in a somewhat amplified form on p. 471 of the *Mechanica Hydraulico-pneumatica*.

There is a big difference between a vacuum made by a pump and one created by heat

A distinction should be drawn between the rarefaction of air arising from heat or a flame and that which arises by extraction of air by a pump. Through heating, (even if the glass vessel is glowing hot) a fifth of the air in a vessel remains behind, whereas, in contrast, extraction methods leave behind hardly as much as a fiftieth or even a hundredth of the original air.

Sixthly, in point 9,[376] in connection with a very deep well prepared at Paderborn, it is said:

"its pipes, although very thick and made of tree trunks, cracked making a dreadful creaking."

I know that that has happened for a different reason — because the outlet was too high to allow the water to pass through the hollow trunks to it. I have known many examples of this kind. It is certainly not the case that a shaft of a well will break due to sucking or pulling actions, rather that it will be crushed from the outside.

Some objections which are raised against the vacuum are more effectively refuted by experiments than by words

The remaining arguments which, in the same context, they advance against the vacuum are sufficiently refuted by various experiments as to make an extended verbal rebuttal unnecessary. It is also the case that, at Würzburg, experiments have been carried out without all the necessary precautions being taken and this has led to many shortcomings which have been the cause of those misconceptions.

The error of Dr. Hauptmann

---

[376] *Mechanica Hydraulico-pneumatica* (p. 474). The passage alluded to is: "I myself saw at Paderborn 37 yeara ago such a victory of nature. My confrères at the College had made an extremely deep well from which water was very arduously extracted using machines with lots of wheels. In the interests of efficiency, a pump was built from the very bottom by hollowing out tree trunks and connecting them. The depth of the water was greater than is usually the case in Nature and too great to permit air to be extracted from it by a piston and valve arrangement. No effort succeeded in moving the piston. Finally using machines as well as muscle power a host of brawny men managed it with a great exertion, but so that the pipes, although very thick and made of tree trunks, cracked with a great creaking sound and allowed the air to enter."

Finally, there are many others who have written against these experiments before they had even seen or understood them. One such is Augustus Hauptmann,[377] Doctor of Medicine, who says in his *Bergbedenken* (published at Leipzig 1658):

"Nor for an angel or a devil would it be possible to bring about a vacuum. For there is such a binding (these are his own words) in nature that can never break. To which all the waters of the deep, even from the depths of the centre of the Earth, are subject; and if the cord of Nature is stretched to breaking point (as supposedly happens inside the air pump in the Magdeburg Experiments) the heavens themselves would buckle and sink lower as much as necessary to make it good." [378]

I don't think it is necessary to respond to this kind of thing from him or from others. All I would say is that more weight has to be given to experiments than to the ignorance that's always making false assertions about nature without actually having tested its opinions.

---

[377] Augustus Hauptmann (1607–1674) was a German doctor and chemist. He was a speculative theorist on the nature of venereal and other diseases.

[378] Von Guericke is rightly dismissive of Hauptmann's proclivity for sweeping statements. The underlying opinion that "reality" is a substantial, elastic continuum and that it is inconceivable that it could be torn apart to reveal a substrate of "nothing" seems to be at the heart of the anti-vacuist position as expressed by Fr. Kircher and others. This opinion regained currency and respectability in the 19th century following the discovery of the wave nature of light in 1800.

Chapter XXXVII – A new thermometer called after Magdeburg

Thermometers, constructed in many ways, are well known. The water in the glass tube, as it rises or falls in accordance with the changes in the temperature, shows the increases or decreases in heat or cold in the same portion of air. More specifically, the change in the degrees of heat or cold is marked either on the tubes themselves or on an attached scale. We have mentioned such thermometers in Chapter 11 above.

Using the Magdeburg Thermometer one can be determine the coldest and the hottest day of the whole year

I thought, however, of another way of making thermometers which Rev. Fr. Schott has described (*Technica Curiosa* Book XI, Chapter 13, p. 871) in the following words.

"Using another less obvious and much more ingenious technique, the most inventive originator of the Magdeburg experiments, detailed above in Book I Part 1, has devised and shown to others for a whole year a method for finding the degree of heat or cold in a substantial region of surrounding air. At the same time his device displays which day over the course of the whole year was the hottest and which the coldest. Using ordinary thermoscopes or thermometers this is hardly, or not even hardly, possible. Our originator exhibits the device suspended from a wall of his house in such a position that it can never catch the sun's rays."

(v. Illustration XVII Fig. I) *A* is a very large hollow copper sphere of about the size of the glass container which we have been calling the Receiver. *BC* is a copper pipe of the width of a thumb and about seven cubits long coming down from the sphere. Attached to the side of this and joined to it at the bottom *C* is another pipe *DE*, into which a certain quantity of brandy or spirit of wine is poured, according to the width of the pipe. Then a thin tube *KL*, made out of brass and a quarter cubit long, is lowered into the pipe *DE*. The thin tube *KL* is closed at both ends and does not let in any liquid. Before being closed, enough lead shot pellets have been placed inside it to ensure that it has the same density as the liquid. Consequently, when immersed in the liquid, it floats just breaking the surface. A wax thread *EM* is tied to *KL* and, as it emerges from the tube *ED*, it goes over a pulley *F* and has a little figure, in the form of an angel or a cherub, tied to the other end. The figure is cut from a sheet of brass and has a hand, acting as a pointer, extended towards the pipes. The two pipes mentioned, *BC* and *DE*, are encased in a tube in the form of a triangular prism. The tube is made out of metal sheeting so that the encased pipes are not visible and the mechanism thus not betrayed to onlookers. On the outside surface of the triangular prism the little figure moves up and down and its extended hand indicates the degree of heat or cold on the scale engraved on the outside. (v. Fig. II)

The sphere A has at its side an inlet H, which the author has called the navel of the sphere. Using the container described in Illustration VIII Fig. III above, or some other vessel suitable for evacuation purposes (of the kind we suggested earlier), as much air ought to be extracted from the sphere as is necessary to ensure that the figure is poised pointing to an appropriate point on the scale. Let someone who doesn't know the appropriate place, extract air just when the cold and frosty nights are setting in. At such a time the figure ought to be pointing to about the middle of the scale marked on the outer tube. Thus, at this time of moderate coldness, sufficient air ought to be extracted so that the figure advances to an appropriate position. (Everything improves with practice.)

The originator of the Magdeburg Experiments had this sphere hanging in the open for a whole year on a wall of his house which the sun never reached. It was coloured dark blue and speckled with golden stars and had the epigraph "Perpetual Motion" written on it. (See the section of Fr. Schott's book cited above.)

Another method

I also devised another previously unknown type of thermometer. Place a figure, of the sort glassblowers blow from a glass bubble, in a glass tube, two or three cubits long, and then fill the tube with an alcohol spirit. Then, provided the figure is prepared, as described in Book III Chapter 4, so that it can float in the spirit, it will indicate how hot or cold it is — falling when it is hot, rising when it is cold and in temperate weather holding to a position in the middle of the tube.

Yet another method

Suspend the glass vessel, called a Receiver, with its tap open from a balance and you will find that it is lighter in hot weather and heavier in cold weather. The reason is that the air is denser in cold weather and less so in hot weather.

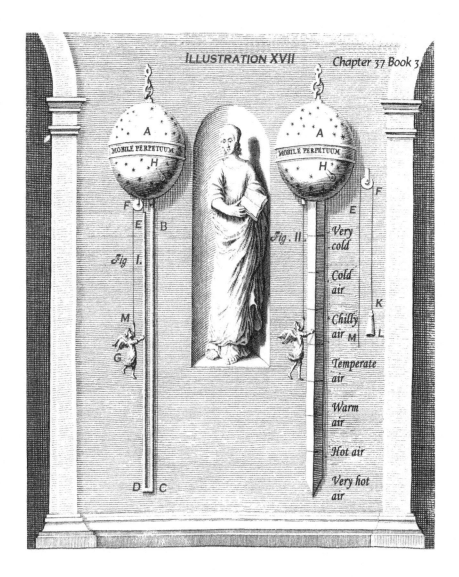

Appendix Book IV Chapter 1 – On universal potencies in general

In Book II Chapter 7 above we wrote that everything in the created order, especially the physical bodies of the world, are composed of their substance, their life and their own innate potencies.

Potencies are neither substance nor accident

These potencies are neither substance nor accident but are effluvia of bodies of the cosmos. Such potencies are innate to them and emanate from them. A distinction should be drawn between the cases where the potencies originate in a body and are emanated from it and those where a body absorbs a potency originating elsewhere. Relative to bodies which absorb them, the absorbed potencies are accidents; relative to the bodies which emit them they are innate capacities which, except in cases of dire destruction or annihilation of the constitution of such bodies, cannot fail.

Why we call them cosmic potencies

We call them cosmic potencies because they mainly manifest themselves through the bodies of the cosmos — that is, through the planets including the Earth, through the sun and also even through parts of the Earth. (See also Book VI Chapter 7)[379]

The potencies are either corporeal or incorporeal

Some of them are corporeal and some incorporeal.

The concept of a corporeal potency

A corporeal potency is an emanation of a rarified material agent from a cosmic body. This emanation does not extend infinitely but only spreads through space as far as the boundaries of a certain sphere of action. It is called corporeal because it does not pass through hard and rigid materials such as glass, metal and such like.

Thus air is a corporeal potency of the Earth — that is, it is a material effluvium of all terrestrial objects, as we discussed in Book III Chapters 1 and 8 above. We become aware of this effluvium through the sense of smell. (cf. Book III Chapter 10) For if we did not possess an organ of smell, situated on the front of our skulls, we could not possibly rec-

---

[379] This chapter is entitled *De Corporibus Mundanis* (On Cosmic bodies).

ognise and distinguish such corporeal effluvia, as we would be unable to smell or recognise smells.

Concept of an incorporeal potency

An incorporeal potency by contrast is something infinitely rarefied that is given off by a body and spreads itself around it to some definite distance. Furthermore an incorporeal potency passes through all rigid and hard materials, in accord, however, with its own and the materials' particular properties. We call the range of action of the potency its "field of action" or "sphere of effectiveness".

What is the field of action or sphere of effectiveness?

Every field of action, whether corporeal or incorporeal, is stronger and denser and more intense at the point where it originates than in more remote locations. As one moves further away from the source of the potency it becomes weaker as it spreads out until its effect becomes vanishingly small.

There are many sorts of potencies

There is no doubt that there are many different incorporeal potencies, which we do not discern because we lack suitable sense organs. However those that do affect our senses and are thus known to us originate in either the sun or the Earth.

Incorporeal potencies originating in the Earth

The following potencies originate in the Earth:

the propellant potencies;

the conservative potency;

the potency of following a straight line;

the potency of turning;

the sonic potency;

the heating potency.

An undeniable incorporeal potency originating in the sun is light

Among the incorporeal potencies that reach us from the sun, the clearest are the luminous potency which gives the light and the colour-giving potency both of which we observe. It is also plausible on various grounds that the moon has a cooling potency.

The potencies of the planets are influences on the Earth

There are arguably many more such potencies originating in the planets, which, corresponding to the various positions of the planets, are beamed down to our Earth. Astrologers refer to these as "influences". Would that we had a better understanding of them!

The potencies operate at a distance

It is of the very nature of these potencies to produce effect at a distance. If they are compatible with bodies that come near, then the potency merges with the body, each possessing the other and together becoming one. But if they encounter an unsuitable body, ill adapted for the uptake of the potency in question, then they will be stopped and reflected. The reflection will be so much more rich and violent, the smoother and more polished the objects are, until it finally abates owing to the diminution in the potency as they become further apart. We will discuss this in more detail later.

The more material a body contains, that is, the denser it is, the more it can absorb a potency

However not every body is adapted to, or capable of, absorbing every potency. The extent to which a potency can occupy or take possession of a body depends on the nature of the potency. This applies whether the potency is being absorbed or emitted. However there are certain incorporeal potencies which can penetrate all bodies.

Potencies can be stimulated through rubbing

Such potencies may be stimulated through rubbing, banging together, touching, or through vibration of bodies capable of originating or absorbing this or that potency. Our Earth has such an effect within its field of action. This may be evoked by touching a suitable body, as the experiments in Chapter 15 show.[380]

---

[380] This chapter is entitled *An in Planetis Animalia?* (Are there animals on the planets?)

Part III

Otto von Guericke's

place in the

History of Ideas

Introduction.

The final part of this book aims to locate von Guericke's scientific thinking on an historical continuum, stretching from antiquity to modern times. This might seem an unrealistically ambitious, not to say foolhardy, undertaking. My plea in mitigation is that the length of this span of time will be offset by the narrowness of the path by which I wish to connect its ends so that the total area covered will be modest. I shall confine myself to a consideration of how the fundamentals of scientific thinking have developed from classical antiquity to the twentieth century. By the fundamentals, I mean the underlying ideas about the shape and content of reality which frame the scientific enterprise — those of number, space, nothingness, the infinite and, most basic of all, that of objective reality. Crises or developments in thinking on these topics are of more profound significance than mere advances in factual knowledge, for it is these background ideas that impart context and significance to facts.[381] Nothing escapes conscious examination as successfully as a prejudice thoroughly inculcated before the age at which some power of critical thinking has awakened. Our universal elementary education systems have made us all unconscious heirs to the fruits of the hard thinking of the seventeenth century on fundamentals. Our unquestioned assumptions were their hard-won judgments and conclusions. Consequently we have become insufficiently aware of the fact that any thinking at all on fundamentals actually took place. For instance, we tend to assume that the notion of natural number is of immemorial antiquity and, give or take a bit of modern logical rigour, that our ideas today are not significantly different from those of antiquity. Similarly we may be inclined to believe that the idea of space as flat three-dimensional, empty, existing independently of matter and stretching infinitely in all directions, has been of similar provenance and only been departed from by the relativistic theories of modern times.

Succumbing to illusions of this sort leads us to credit the great figures of the period with their advances in factual knowledge and experimental or mathematical technique while denying them adequate

---

[381] I still vividly recall how disconcerting it was to realise how apparently objective and factual properties of a moving body, its kinetic and potential energy, dissolve into being meaningless once the framework Newtonian ideas of space and time give way to those of Galilean or Special Relativity.

recognition of their achievement in the century-long struggle to revise the fundamentals. Thus, the credited achievement of Kepler is to have established the elliptical orbit of the planets, of von Guericke to have invented the vacuum pump, of Descartes to have discovered coordinate geometry and the first two laws of motion, of Galileo to have determined the acceleration due to gravity and the moons of Jupiter and so on. We see them perhaps too much as Edisons and not enough as Einsteins.[382] As we tend to be one-sided in our appreciation of the victorious heroes of the time, so we are also too dismissive of their defeated adversaries, ascribing their genuine conceptual bafflement to wanton obscurantism, unscientific attachment to religious views or abject fear of persecution by the Church. This attitude traduces the integrity of men such as Pascal's adversary, Père Noel, or von Guericke's, Athanasius Kircher, whom we should see as men of robust scientific good faith playing an inevitable and necessary role in debating, testing and probing radical new ideas.[383]

---

[382] Writing of von Guericke specifically, Alfons Kauffeldt makes this point strongly. He writes : "Alle diese Verdienste Guerickes sind durchaus bekannt und gebührend gewürdigt worden. Es handelt sich also nicht darum, das diese seine Pionertaten unterschätzt order durch die Leistungen späterer in den Schatten gestellt würden.

Er hat aber noch andere und, wie uns scheint, ebenso bedeutende Leistungen vollbracht. Diese sind es, die kaum bekannt und durch die Leistungen anderer auf gleichem Gebiet in den Hintergründ gedrängt worden sind. Wir meinen seine Leistungen auf philosophischem bzw. Naturphilosophischem Gebiet." (Otto von Guerickes Philosophisches über den Leeren Raum. Akademie Verlag p. 9.)

[383] Kauffeldt (p. 152) provides a good example, saying explicitly what is often conveyed by insinuation. He writes "Einige Jesuiten, z.B. Kircher, Grimaldi, Scheiner, hatten sich durch Entdeckungen und durch ihr Wissen wirkliche Verdienste und eine entsprechende Autorität erworben. Das soll gar nicht bestritten werden. Aber es ging der Societas Jesu und der Kirche nicht um die Förderung der Naturforschung, sondern um die Restaurierung der unumschränkten Vormacht der katholischen Kirche. Deshalb hatte es grosse Bedeutung, wenn die Autorität der an der Front der Naturwissenschaften kämpfden gelehrten Jesuiten erschüttert werden konnte." or (p. 174) "Es konnte also auch hier erleben, dass es gar nicht um die Wahrheit ging sondern um die Aufrechterhandlung eines Machtanspruchs in weltanschaulich-wissenschaftlichen Dingen." This sort of thing is paranoid nonsense that doesn't stand up to the most cursory reading of the contemporary sources. As well to impugn the scientific integrity of American scientists for being loyal citizens of the United States and for hoping to see the world wide triumph of their political values — democracy, trial by jury, equality before the law etc. The fact is that the plenist/vacuist debate has attracted on both sides the greatest scientific minds and has never been decisively resolved. The apparent triumph of the vacuists in the 17th century gave way, in the 19th century, to an apparent triumph of the plenists with their luminiferous aether. The displacement of the luminiferous aether by Special Relativity has still left us with a Space-Time occupied by, among much else, oscillating electromagnetic fields. Is this "incorporeal potency" really nothing? Edward Grant in *Much Ado about Nothing* provides the

The purpose of this section is to show where von Guericke stood in the arch of conceptual developments connecting the thinking of classical antiquity about number and space to the modern concepts. The central points, elaborated in the remainder of this section, can be summarised as follows.

(1) Aristotelian thinking was positivist in outlook and ontologically frugal. Such a philosophy gives rise to a severely realist physics and mathematics.

(2) From the late middle ages, Aristotelian parsimony in respect of objective reality was challenged by two sources of ontological liberalism.

(3) The first of these sources was orthodox Christian theology whose rich ontology challenged, in particular, the Aristotelian denials of the actual Infinite and of the void.

(4) The second was what Jacob Klein[384] has called "symbol generated abstraction". This arose naturally out of the formalistic turn mathematics took with the introduction of the decimal system and the growth of algebraic manipulation. Among much else, this development was responsible for the un-Aristotelian belief in objective natural numbers.

(5) Both these extensions to what constituted objective reality, as well, of course, as the discovery of new natural phenomena, were key building blocks of the scientific advances of the seventeenth century.

(6) Von Guericke developed his own theologically-based idea of absolute space — succinctly described by the Newtonian epithet, Sensorium Dei[385] — as the metaphysical background to his vacuum experiments.

(7) The same concept was either appropriated, or independently arrived at, by Newton and became a foundation stone of his development of mechanics.

---

following example of the technique of insinuation. On Gassendi he writes: (p. 207) "Atomist though he was, Gassendi was only too well aware that full blown Greek atomism, with its infinity of eternal atoms generating an infinity of worlds, was utterly unacceptable to the Church and its theologians. Not even the God-created version devised by Campanella would do."

[384] Jacob Klein. *Greek Mathematical Thought and the Origin of Modern Algebra*. Dover.1992

[385] In the response to Query 31 in Book III of the *Opticks*, in the course of discussing the similarities in the physical structure of animals, Newton writes of "the Wisdom and Skill of a powerful ever-living Agent who, being in all Places, is more able by his Will to move the Bodies within his boundless uniform Sensorium and thereby to form and reform the Parts of the Universe, than we are by our Will to move the Parts of our own Bodies."

(8) During the eighteenth and nineteenth centuries mathematics continued to depend on syntax-generated concepts which conferred objective reality on entities such as differentials, functions, imaginary numbers and much else. These developments caused neo-Platonism to be considered the natural philosophy of mathematics.

(9) By the late nineteenth and twentieth centuries it had become clear that the theological assumptions of figures such as von Guericke and Newton could, for scientific purposes, be attenuated to a simple acceptance of the objective existence of an infinite set. This realisation also freed scientific understanding from any dependence on Kantian doctrines of Space and Time as forms of human intuition.

(10) This period also brought the insight that "symbol generated abstraction" was an unnecessary departure from the standards of rigour prevailing in antiquity. Moreover it brought the realisation that mathematical concepts, previously justified in this way, could be formulated much more satisfactorily in terms of Euclid's number concept suitably excised of the restriction that the whole be greater than the part.

(11) These developments have led to the modern dispensation whereby mathematics is neo-Euclidean arithmetic[386] and theoretical physics is a neo-Copernican[387] enterprise dedicated to "saving the phenomena" via mathematical model-making.

Let us, however, begin at the beginning, with classical antiquity and, in particular, with the titanic figure of Aristotle. Before embarking on saying anything about Aristotle, I make a disclaimer. Aristotle, at least in English translation, is a difficult and convoluted read. Furthermore, from his own writings, or from the millennia of scholarship lavished upon them, there emerges no clear, coherent, comprehensive,

---

[386] In the sense that set theory, which is really the study of arithmoi (Euclid Book VII) extended to include arithmoi for which the "whole is greater than the part" fails, has been shown capable of both giving formulations of (arguably) all useful mathematical concepts e.g. natural numbers, functions and differentials, and of proving, on the basis of evident properties of sets, all theorems whose proofs had earlier rested on other less secure foundations.

[387] The preface to Copernicus' *De Revolutionibus* contains the following passage which is modern in spirit. "For it is the duty of an astrologer to compose the history of celestial motion through careful and skilled observation. Then, turning to the causes of these motions or hypotheses about them he must conceive and devise, since he cannot attain to the true causes, such hypotheses as, being assumed, enable the motions to be calculated correctly from the principles of geometry, for the future as well as the past. ..... For these hypotheses need not be true or even probable; if they provide a calculus consistent with the observations, this alone is sufficient." (A. Koestler. *The Sleepwalkers Part 3: The Timid Canon.* Note 59)

consistent-in-detail, unified system of thinking. The fame and reputation of Aristotle has never rested on the insights afforded by the specific details of what he wrote — in the way that the fame of Newton or Maxwell rests on sharply defined impressive intellectual achievement — but rather on the more nebulous appeal of something one might call the "spirit of Aristotle".

Aristotle is an attractive figure in many ways. He is always completely rational, ready to consider and debate points of view he disagrees with, respectful of the expertise of others and committed to a scientific outlook which holds that the truth is to be discovered by observing and reflecting upon nature. Somewhere near the heart of his appeal lies the approach he takes to the vexed question of knowing what is truly objective. He steers an intermediate course between two poles. On the one hand he avoids the Scylla of extreme solipsism that would claim that what I think of as objective reality is, in fact, conjured up by my brain either just to keep itself stimulated or to ensure its survival in an unknowable world. On the other hand he eschews the Charybdis of an extreme Platonism that would hold that to virtually every noun-phrase utterance or thought, provided only that it fall short of being a logical impossibility, there is something objective to which it corresponds.

Whether or not Aristotle's middle course is correct still divides people according to their intellectual temperament and experience of life. An adherent of any of the great world religions or a mathematician of a certain type — e.g. a set theorist studying sets of large cardinality — will probably be inclined to think that there are more objective realities in heaven and earth than are dreamt of in Aristotle's philosophy. On the other hand, an evolutionary biologist,[388] inclined to believe that there are fewer things in heaven and earth than many believe, will find the spirit of Aristotle attractive and sensible.

As I have said above, the "facts" are not our primary interest. Nevertheless, Aristotle looms so large in the background to von Guericke's thinking that a brief account of the former's teaching on physics and cosmology, before considering his "framework" teaching on number, space and the infinite, will be useful.

---

[388] For instance, the eminent evolutionary thinker and philosopher of religion, Professor Richard Dawkins, has summed up his ontologically sparing Weltanschauung with the pithy aphorism "There are no fairies at the bottom of the garden".

Aristotle's Cosmology & Physics

In the later chapters of Book I and in Book II, von Guericke provides a lucid and dispassionate overview of the Aristotelian system from the point of view of someone for whom making the case against the system was still work in progress. In the version of it presented by von Guericke, the Cosmos comprises eleven concentric spheres around a fixed Earth. These spheres are real material spheres to which the corresponding bodies are attached like lights to a ceiling.

The first sphere is that of the moon or Luna. This sphere marks the boundary of the sublunary Cosmos. Beyond this the Cosmos was constituted of different material and operated according to different physics. The superlunary Cosmos comprised the spheres of the planets Mercury, Venus, the sun, Mars, Jupiter and Saturn. Beyond Saturn there is the sphere of the fixed stars — the Coelum Stellatum which von Guericke also calls the firmament. The Coelum Stellatum was the outermost material boundary of Aristotle's Cosmos and beyond it there is nothing.. In a way that is reminiscent of a modern geometer pointing out that a manifold does not need to be embedded in a flat ambient space, Aristotle rejects any idea of "outside the Cosmos". His view is that "beyond" the Coelum Stellatum, as a matter of proper understanding of the meanings of the words "cosmos" and "nothing", spatiotemporal thinking breaks down. In particular, there are no bodies, no motions to underpin time, and no disembodied places, where there might be bodies but which just happen to be unoccupied. Von Guericke notes:[389]

"In the days of Aristotle, the entire substance of the Cosmos consisted of these eight spheres. In the course of time, other observed motions created a clear necessity to add new ones."

The ninth sphere, also called the Secundum Mobile, was added to account for the advance of the equinoxes. Beyond this there was the sphere of the Primum Mobile, the idea of which goes back to Aristotle. Von Guericke quotes a letter to a sophisticated cardinal, outlining what was commonly held in the sixteenth century.[390]

"Above the stars, there is thought to be another heaven, which the wise men of old called the Primum Mobile as, moved by the power of the most high God (for nothing else is believable)

---

[389] *Experimenta Nova* Book I Chapter 4
[390] Book I Chapter 4. Letter from Johannes Pierius Valerianus to Alexander Cardinal Farnese

it whirls incessantly with breakneck speed rushing from east to west and then back from west to east. It drags with it the sphere of the fixed stars and the spheres of all the planets. Although some are dragged along more slowly, others are dragged more quickly as they are more or less remote from the first rapidly moving sphere."

This picture is relatively crude. C. S. Lewis gives us a better insight into the attraction of Aristotle's idea of the First Mover, as it was reconciled with Christian orthodoxy by medieval theologians.[391]

"All power, movement and efficacy descend from God to the Primum Mobile and cause it to rotate. …. The rotation of the Primum Mobile causes that of the Stellatum which causes that of the sphere of Saturn and so on down to the last moving Sphere that of the moon, ……God, we have said, causes the Primum Mobile to rotate…. How? It was obvious to Aristotle that most things that move do so because some other moving object impels them. … But it was also fundamental to his thought that no infinite series can be actual. We cannot therefore go on explaining one movement by another ad infinitum. There must in the last resort be something which, motionless itself, initiates the motion of all other things…..But we must not imagine Him moving things by any positive action……. (for) we should then not have reached an utterly unmoving Mover. How then does He move things? Aristotle answers 'He moves as beloved[392]'. … The Primum Mobile is moved by its love for God and, being moved, communicates motion to the rest of the universe."

Speculative theologians richly elaborated Aristotle's austerely conceived First Mover — a being existing beyond the Primum Mobile outside of which there is neither place nor void nor time and thus a being of such a nature as not to occupy space or be aged by time.[393]   In Book I, Chapter 31 von Guericke notes:

"To these heavens both Catholic and Reformed theologians add another one, the Empyrean heaven, instituted by God that it might receive and be the abode of the blessed."

He devotes all of Chapter 33 to a detailed discussion of the Empyrean heaven including estimates of its size and speculations about its shape. He is frankly sceptical of the Empyrean heaven but his scepticism is of Aristotelian cosmology, rather than of Christian orthodoxy about heaven. In Book II, having set out his own view of space, he returns to the topic in Chapter 11, *On the Heaven which is called the Abode of the Blessed.* Here he now proposes his own theory, again furnished with detailed estimates of size, that the location of heaven is the space

---

[391] C.S.Lewis. *The Discarded Image* p. 102 and p. 113.
[392] Aristotle *Metaphysics* Lambda 7 [1072b]
[393] Aristotle *De Caelo* Book I.9 [279a]

that will be vacated by the orbit of the Earth after its destruction at Judgment Day.

The physics of the superlunary heavens was based on a single incorruptible element, aether, and a single perfect form of motion, circular motion. As the heavens were organised into concentric spheres, the central problem of celestial physics was to give an account of how the motion imparted to the Primum Mobile by the First Mover was transmitted to the inner spheres in such a way as to produce the observed astronomical phenomena. Aristotle, in order to account for the observed motions of the heavenly bodies supposedly attached to the spheres, actually postulated some fifty-five spheres, grouped into two groups of thirty-three and twenty-two rotating in opposite directions.[394] The outermost sphere of the fixed stars, the Coelum Stellatum, owes its motion to the First Mover. It would seem that originally Aristotle would have preferred a scheme by which the motion imparted by the First Mover to the outermost sphere induced motions in the inner spheres and that, within this framework, reasonable hypotheses could be made to account for the observed phenomena. However the scheme had difficulties accounting for what actually was observed and it proved necessary to postulate some spheres in counter rotation to the others. In the Metaphysics, Aristotle rather lamely appears to allow the possibility that each of fifty-five spheres had its own "unmoved mover".

In the sublunary part of the cosmos, matter consists of four elements — earth, water, air, fire. These are not elements in the modern sense of the word for, as well as blending together to form other substances, they are also acknowledged as being capable of transmuting one into another.[395] It is not clear that a completely coherent picture emerges from Aristotle's discussion of them[396] and how they relate to the properties "hot" "cold" "moist" and "dry".

His account of motion, seemingly extrapolated from human and animal experience, is that the motions of ordinary experience are purposeful, occurring to restore a proper natural order to things which have become displaced. Once the striving of things to attain their proper place has been gratified then there will be neither need nor motive for further motion. The heaviest of the elements, earth, has gathered

---

[394] v. Arthur Koestler. *The Sleepwalkers Part 1, The Heroic Age, Chapter 5, The Divorce from Reality.*
[395] E.g. Physics IV.9 [26a] where he discusses air turning into water.
[396] v. Book II of the *De Generatione et Corruptione*

itself together at the centre of the Earth. On the Earth the next heaviest element, water, lies above the earth and above the water there is the air. Fire, the lightest of all, rises through the air forming a spherical shell just within that of the moon. When we observe bubbles rising in water, or stones falling to the ground, or rain falling to the sea, or flames rising through the air, we are to understand these motions as the striving of elements to attain their natural place. However, one should be aware that Aristotle's views on "motion, "heaviness" and "lightness" are more elaborate[397] than a brief sketch can convey.

The sublunary cosmos forms a plenum of substance and he argues[398] that a vacuum, i.e. a place devoid of all substance, cannot exist. Elevated into the scientific axiom "nature abhors a vacuum", this view acquired the status of a physical principle which could be invoked to explain the phenomena both of suction and projectile motion. The elevation dated back to Aristotle, but, more tellingly, the most acclaimed thinker of von Guericke's own generation, Descartes (1596–1650), had, in the midst of revolutionising much else in physics and mathematics, preserved this principle. There is some analogy with how the principles of conservation of energy and momentum, whose roots lie in atomist, Newtonian physics, were preserved through the conceptual revolutions of relativity and quantum mechanics.

Aristotle's system, somewhat like the theory of evolution, is strong on offering a general qualitative account of virtually every natural phenomenon, but much weaker on precision of detail and prediction. A mark of a successful modern system like the theory of electromagnetism is that it compensates for its ontological extravagance by offering both detailed quantitative accounts of known phenomena and a capacity to predict new ones. The price of success has been a blurring of the clear lines that Aristotle sought to establish between the subjective and the objective. No one doubts the objectivity of a scientific statement such as "Jupiter has four moons". But the objective reality corresponding to concepts such as "the electromagnetic tensor field" or "matter as curved space-time" is much less clear. These can seem like a sophisticated version of Ptolemy's epicycles, justified solely as conceptual schemes that save the phenomena and enable predictions to be

---

[397] Book IV of the *De Caelo* is dedicated to a consideration of "lightness" and "heaviness"
[398] *Physics* IV.6–9

made, rather than as descriptions of objective reality. They are neo-Copernican in spirit. C. S. Lewis puts it well: [399]

"But I do not think it was doubted that there was a concrete reality about which the mathematics held good, distinguishable from the mathematics as a heap of apples is from the process of counting them. We knew indeed that it was in some respects not adequately imaginable; quantities and distances if either very small or very great could not be visualised. But, apart from that, we hoped that ordinary imagination and conception could grasp it. We should then have through mathematics knowledge not merely mathematical. We should be like the man coming to know about a foreign country without visiting it. He learns about the mountains from carefully studying the contour lines on a map. But his knowledge is not a knowledge of contour lines. The real knowledge is achieved when these enable him to say 'That would be an easy ascent', 'This is a dangerous precipice', 'A would not be visible from B', 'These woods and waters must make a pleasant valley'. In going beyond the contour lines to such conclusions he is (if he knows how to read a map) getting nearer to the reality.

It would be very different if someone said to him (and was believed) 'But it is the contour lines themselves that are the fullest reality you can get. In turning away from them to these other statements you are getting further from the reality not nearer.' All these ideas about 'real' rocks and slopes and views are merely a metaphor or a parable; a pis aller permissible to the weakness of those who can't understand contour lines, but misleading if they are taken literally."

I shall now briefly describe Aristotle's thinking on topics — what objectively exists, number, space and the infinite — which were of particular relevance to von Guericke and, more generally, to the development of science in the seventeenth century.

---

[399] C.S.Lewis. *The Discarded Image*. C.U.P. Canto edition. 2009 p. 217.

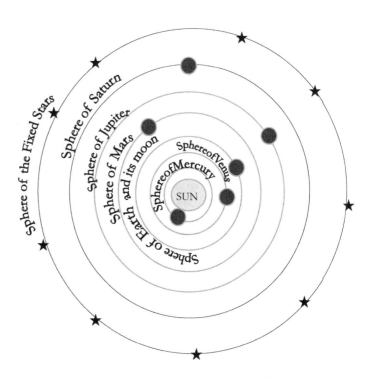

Diagram of the Copernican System with the sun in the centre of the Cosmos but the Earth being placed among the planets.[400]

---

[400] This diagram is based on Book I, Chapter 5, Iconismus 2 of the *Experimenta Nova*.

Aristotelian Ontology

Aristotle spent some twenty years of his life — from 368 BC when he was about seventeen to 348 BC — in Plato's Academy. The most salient characteristic of Plato's philosophy is its dualism.

Dualism is ultimately a belief in a chasm at the heart of things. The chasm divides good and evil, matter and spirit, body and soul, the intellect and the senses, the eternal and the fleeting, the here and the hereafter. Dualism and the reactions it has provoked have been important both in scientific thinking and in the wider arena of moral and religious thought.

Russell[401] attributes to Pythagoras the first clear articulation of the dualism which opposes the intellect to the senses and postulates a transcendental realm of Ideals accessible only to the light of reason and to the eye of the intellect. The doctrine as elaborated by Plato maintains that the things of the senses are imperfect copies of these Ideals and not as worthy of contemplation as the Ideals themselves. Physics, being grounded in the things of the material world, is thus, to Plato, an inherently inexact and provisional science.

To a question such as "Is Pythagoras' Theorem true in nature?", Plato's answer would emphatically be "no". He believed that a proven geometrical proposition is categorically and exactly true only of transcendental entities in a realm of Ideals. The theorem is only approximately and imperfectly true of actual sensible right angled triangles in so far as they resemble the ideal right angled triangle. The practical applicability of, say, Pythagoras' theorem arises from the fact that sensible objects are approximations to the ideal objects which are the true subject matter of geometry. Once truth and insight about the ideal objects have been obtained, the real-world approximations by which we may have been led to contemplate the Ideals are of incidental importance. Copleston notes the thoroughness of Plato's dualism.[402]

"Thus in the Phaedo, he teaches that the soul existed before its union with the body in a transcendental realm, where it beheld the subsistent intelligible entities or Ideas, which would seem to constitute a plurality of detached essences. The process of knowledge, or getting to know, consists essentially in recollection, in remembering the Ideas which the soul once beheld clearly in its state of pre-existence."

---

[401] Bertrand Russell: *History of Western Philosophy*, Chapter 3. Allen and Unwin. (1969)
[402] Frederick Copleston S.J. *History of Philosophy*. Volume 1 p. 192 (Doubleday Image)

The espousal of dualism tends to lead, as much in modern times as in ancient, to a certain disparagement of practical and concrete activity in favour of a more theoretical high-mindedness. The outlook of the fifth century Manichean dualist, Secundinus, writing to St. Augustine is recognisably similar to that of the 20th century mathematician G. H. Hardy. Secundinus writes to St. Augustine:[403]

"I knew you were one who loved lofty things, things that shunned the Earth, that mortified the body, that set the soul alive."

A similar sentiment (apart from the allusion to mortification) is expressed by Hardy in his Apology.[404]

"But is not the position of the ordinary applied mathematician in some ways a little pathetic? If he wants to be useful, he must work in a humdrum way and he cannot give full play to his fancy even when he wishes to rise to the heights. 'Imaginary' universes are so much more beautiful than this stupidly constructed 'real' one."

Aristotle, probably in reaction to the spirit of the Academy, proclaimed a philosophy whose most salient characteristic is its ontological frugality. Just as Plato does, Aristotle exerts a perennial appeal as a paradigm of a certain type of mind — in his case one that is inclined to the concrete and tangible, which seeks understanding of the world through experience in the world and which is disinclined to populate reality with entities beyond those warranted by the senses. Without any offence to historical truthfulness, any of the Humanist societies of the western world today could fairly enlist Aristotle as a deceased distinguished supporter. While Aristotle may have resiled from the gratuitous sneer it is hard to imagine him fundamentally disagreeing with A. J. Ayer.[405]

"For we shall maintain that no statement that refers to a reality transcending the limits of all possible sense experiences can possibly have any literal significance; from which it must follow that the labours of those who have striven to describe such a reality have all been devoted to the production of nonsense."

In the three areas of number, space and the infinite, which I will now look at separately, the common theme of Aristotle's thinking is an ontological parsimony that resists any idea that there are objective entities beyond those accessible to the senses.

---

[403] Peter Brown: *St. Augustine of Hippo* p. 50. Faber&Faber 1967
[404] G.H. Hardy: *A Mathematician's Apology* p. 135. C.U.P. (1967)
[405] A. J. Ayer: *Language Truth and Logic* p. 34. Victor Gollancz Ltd. 1970.

Aristotle and Number

As noted in the Introduction, we need to disabuse ourselves of the idea that ever since men began to think quantitatively the notion of natural number — one, two, three .... — forced itself upon human consciousness and that this idea has been essentially stable throughout history and is of immemorial antiquity.[406] The actual situation is that the Greeks had a clear notion of number and we, today, have also a clear but different notion of number. The process of transition began in the 16th century and not till the 19th century, amid much mathematical soul searching, was the older notion definitively supplanted. Von Guericke and his contemporaries such as Isaac Barrow at Cambridge were transitional figures, inheriting the opinions of antiquity while being carried on a slow historical tide towards the modern view.

The notion of "arithmos", invariably translated as number, which was transmitted from classical antiquity to medieval Europe, is Aristotle's notion. In the generation following Aristotle this was set out by Euclid in Book VII of his Elements written c. 300 BC. There is nothing obscure about what Euclid means by "arithmos". An arithmos is "a multitude of units"[407] and a "unit" is "that by virtue of which each of the things that exist is called one." In modern language this seems to just say, essentially, that an arithmos is a set or collection of well individuated things, or, as we say nowadays, elements.

The identification of "arithmos" with "set" can only be made with qualifications. The first qualification is that the Greeks would not have admitted the empty set or one element sets as arithmoi. This is consistent with the view Aristotle expresses that an arithmos derives its ontological legitimacy only from its units. Aristotle writes:[408]

"The sciences of mathematics are not going to take perceptible entities as their domain just because the things being considered have the accidental feature of being perceptible. (Though, of course, they are not studied qua perceptible.) But on the other hand neither will they take as their domain some other entities separable from the perceptible ones. ....In fact the

---

[406] The contrary opinion is still the prevailing one. E.g. "The natural numbers were there before there were human beings, or indeed any other creature here on earth, and they will remain after all life has perished. It has always been true that each natural number is the sum of four squares and it did not have to wait for Lagrange to conjure this fact into existence." Roger Penrose: *Shadows of the Mind*. p. 413.

[407] T. L. Heath: *Euclid – The Elements*. Book VII Vol. 2 Dover (1956)

[408] *Metaphysics* Mu.3 [1078a] (Lawson-Tancred translation p. 399)

best way to conduct the study into each thing is as follows. Do what the arithmetician and the geometer in fact do. Suppose what is not separable to be separable. A man, for instance, qua man, is an indivisible unity and so the arithmetician supposes a man to be an indivisible unity and then investigates whatever accidental features a man has qua indivisible."

The empty set cannot derive ontological legitimacy from nothing. Similarly the Greek concept does not concede legitimacy to the formation of one element sets. Arithmoi — doublets, triplets etc. — exist because there exist pairs (e.g. the two coffee cups on my desk), triples (e.g. New York, San Francisco, London) etc. of units in the world and not by virtue of the linguistic sleight of hand of putting curly brackets on each side of the name of a unit.[409] Aristotle writes explicitly:[410]

"The smallest number in the strict sense of the word 'number' is two"

This issue was still a vexed one for von Guericke's younger contemporary John Wallis (1616–1673) whose *Mathesis Universalis* (1657) discusses at length whether a unit should count as a number[411] before concluding, with some anxiety that important distinctions were being ignored, that such a procedure was legitimate.

A second qualification needs to be made in the light of Euclid's Common Notion 5, where "common" is to be understood as common to the parallel studies of arithmetic and geometry. Common Notion 5 affirms:[412]

"The whole is greater than the part".

To understand the relevance of this we also need to be acquainted with Common Notion 4, which affirms:

"Things which coincide with each other are equal to one another"

Heath notes that the original Greek, here translated as "coincide", might be more clearly rendered by a phrase like "can be applied with an exact fit". For geometrical figures this common notion affirms

---

[409] Aristotle would have found statements which are routine in textbooks today e.g. "let φ be the empty set and let {φ} be the set whose single element is the empty set" objectionable on the grounds of postulating entities over and above what really exist.
[410] *Physics* IV.12. [220a]. *Metaphysics* Iota 6 [1056b]- [1057a] provides an extended discussion of this issue. There Aristotle writes: "Thus the opposition between one and the many in numbers is like that between the measure and the thing measured." (Lawson-Tancred Translation p. 304)
[411] v. Jacob Klein: *Greek Mathematical Thought and the Origin of Algebra.* p. 211 Dover
[412] T. L. Heath: *Euclid: The Thirteen Books of the Elements.* Vol. 1 p. 155. Dover (1956)

congruence as the principle of equality between figures. For arithmoi, the natural understanding of it is as an assertion of the principle that if a one-to-one correspondence can be established between two arithmoi, then they are equal.

When Common Notion 5 is applied to geometrical figures it asserts that a part of a figure cannot be superimposed on the whole of the figure. Applied to arithmoi, it asserts that a part of an arithmos — in modern language a proper subset — cannot be put into one-to-one correspondence with the whole arithmos. Euclid requires arithmoi to conform to Common Notion 5 and his notion is thus, subject to the above qualifications, equivalent to the modern notion of finite set.

The Euclidean concept constitutes the meaning of the word "number" from antiquity to at least the end of the 16th century. When St. Augustine writes about "the defined number of the elect" or St. Matthew writes[413] "even the very hairs on your head are numbered", these phrases are to be understood in the context of the Greek notion. Towards the end of the seventeenth century we still find no less a figure than Newton feeling the need explicitly to articulate dissent from a received idea. In his *Universal Arithmetic* he writes:[414]

"By a Number we understand not so much a Multitude of Unities, as the abstracted Ratio of any Quantity to another Quantity of the same kind, which we take for Unity."

That is to say that number words e.g. "five" should not be thought as denoting a quintet of units but, at first sight more obscurely, the fraction "5/1". The motivation for the change is, of course, to permit the manipulation of integers and ratios of integers — fractions — on the same footing. This important conceptual innovation, worthy of explicit mention by Newton, is, of course, now finessed past the unresisting minds of children as part of the teaching of fractions.

In his thinking about numbers von Guericke is representative rather than original. In the preface he looks forward to the harmony and mutual enrichment of mathematics and experiments. He applauds mathematics for its power to give a certainty denied all the other sciences. After such an encomium, it is almost embarrassing to see how

---

[413] Matthew 10:30

[414] Isaac Newton: *Universal Arithmetic*. This contained the substance of Newton's lectures on Algebra and was first published in 1707 by William Whiston, his successor as Lucasian professor.

elementary his use of mathematics then actually is. In Chapters 22 and 24 of Book III he embarks upon elementary multiplication of up to seven digit numbers with an elaborate explicitness that would now be found excessive in a primary school homework. The probable reason for his not taking such algorithms for granted is simply that he wasn't taught them in childhood.

Decimal algorithms for multiplication and division, though previously used by Chinese and Arabic writers, did not become routine in Europe until the beginning of the seventeenth century. The major stimulant of the popularisation of the decimal system was the publication by Simon Stevin[415] in 1585 of a pamphlet, *The Tenth*. This work, originally written in Dutch but quickly translated into French, introduced decimal fractions and was directed towards meeting the need for efficient, practical and routine calculation. Stevin's notation was improved by the introduction of the decimal point (or comma) by Napier[416] in 1616 and the algorithms set out by Stevin were integrated into mathematics curricula. During the seventeenth century the material was considered an appropriate topic for undergraduates[417] and subsequently, with the development of universal education provision, for much younger students, as it is today.

Von Guericke's Chapter 10 of Book 2 is entitled *On Number*. The chapter is not however a discussion of the concept of number but consists of some exploratory calculation of the decimal notations for describing very large sets far exceeding those described by Archimedes in antiquity. It is clear that the power and scope of decimal notation was still, at that period, something new and fresh whose merits deserved and needed advertising. The most interesting part of his reflection on number is in Chapter 9 of Book 2 — *The Infinite, the Immeasurable and the Eternal* — where he asks "What is number?" His first blush reply is to recapitulate the Aristotelian notion. He writes:

---

[415] Simon Stevin (1548–1620) was a Flemish mathematician and engineer. He was a religiously tolerant Protestant, a supporter of William of Orange against Spain and an advocate of double entry book keeping.
[416] John Napier (1550–1617) was a Scottish mathematician and physicist who is best known as the inventor of logarithms.
[417] Newton's *Universal Algebra*, based on his lectures at Cambridge, contains an exposition of the decimal algorithms.

"Number really arises by division or separation ..... Also a multitude is formed by gathering together units. And so a number cannot properly and truthfully be called infinite."

All of this is Aristotelian orthodoxy. The unlimited divisibility of matter was part of the doctrine of his *Physics* and Aristotle himself had argued that there could be no largest number because any unit of a number could be divided.[418] In the passage that follows this quotation, in which the possibility of an infinite number is discussed, von Guericke appears as a typical figure of his time in feeling himself free to advance beyond Aristotle and to question the latter's rejection of the existence of an actual infinite. Von Guericke puts the issue squarely.

"If the Infinite is to be actual, it needs to be realised all at the same time and in a completed form, rather than just in a partially completed form."

If such and actual infinity exists then there are infinite numbers and if not, not. He is particularly explicit because he wants to maintain the distinction with the potential infinity, which was admitted by Aristotle. This term was used for operations, such as dividing a line, which could be continued indefinitely, at least in thought. It was also used of pluralities such as the revolutions of the sun around the Earth which, in Aristotle's view, had no beginning. Given this, we would nowadays be inclined to allow "all the revolutions of the sun" as an infinite totality. But Aristotle's position was that the units of such a supposed totality did not objectively, separately and simultaneously exist in such a way as to underwrite the existence of an objectively existing arithmos of all of them.

With three centuries of hindsight, it is clear that von Guericke was asking the right questions at the wrong time. He shows, along with many earlier thinkers,[419] an awareness that arithmetic on infinite numbers would be radically different from that with finite numbers and a correct intuition that the sense in which space is infinite is different from that in which points marked at intervals along an infinite line are infinite. Not until Cantor's diagonal arguments of two centuries later were decisive answers given to a range of questions about the infinite

---

[418] In *Physics* III 6 [207b] Aristotle sets out his view that numbers are potentially infinite because units composing a number can be divided arbitrarily many times.

[419] P. Duhem *Medieval Cosmology* (Translation Roger Ariew) Chapter 3, The Infinitely Large, singles out Gregory of Rimini (c.1300–1358) as particularly prefiguring 19th century developments.

with consequences that transformed mathematics. More precisely, the 19th century developments allowed mathematics to return to its arithmetic Euclidean roots, to resurrect the ancient ideals of rigour, and to complete the unification of the sister disciplines of arithmetic and geometry.

Aristotle and Space

Aristotle extensively discusses place and the void in *Physics* IV. There is an analogy between his opinions on numbers and on space. In both cases there is a sceptical turning away from the seeming conceit that would confer objective existence on anything beyond the realities perceivable by the senses. He views the Platonic tendency to believe that numbers have an objective existence beyond and transcending the concrete units which comprise them as a temptation firmly to be resisted. In the *Metaphysics* he writes:[420]

"Universal assertions in mathematics are not about separable entities which are beyond and apart from magnitude and numbers. They are about these very things, only not qua such things as have magnitude and are divisible."

Similarly, in the *Physics* he views the natural tendency to think of "place" as having an existence independent of matter as ontologically profligate. He writes:[421]

"The extension between the extremities is thought to be <u>something</u> because what is contained and separate may often be changed while the container remains the same (as water may be poured from a vessel) — the assumption being that the extension is something over and above the body displaced. But there is no such extension."

and more explicitly:[422]

"Let us explain again that there is no void existing separately, as some maintain."

It is certainly not the case that Aristotle was simply unaware of the possibility of thinking of space in an absolutist way. He knew his views were in diametrical opposition to those of some of his predecessors notably Leucippus,[423] who argued that there could be no motion without a vacuum, and his more famous pupil Democritus.[424] Charac-

---

[420] *Metaphysics* Mu 3. (Lawson-Tancred Translation. p. 398)The meaning is that, although units may have magnitude or be numbers — discrete collections of things —, one can, for mathematical purposes, ignore their internal constitution. A universal statement, say, $3 + 4 = 7$, is not about separable entities 3,4, and 7 but about triplets, quartets and septuplets of things which we can, ignoring their other properties, reckon as units.

[421] *Physics* IV.4 [211b] (Hardie & Gaye Translation)

[422] *Physics* IV.7 [214b] (Hardie & Gaye Translation)

[423] Leucippus c. 430 BC was one of the earliest pioneers of the idea of atomism

[424] Democritus (c.460–c.370BC) articulated a fuller theory of atomism and conceived the important scientific foundational programme of reducing all phenomena to motion of atoms in the void.

teristically, he gives a fair hearing to views he disagrees with and writes of Hesiod:[425]

"At least he says: 'First of all things, came chaos to being, then broad-breasted earth' implying that things need to have space first, because he thought with most people, that everything is somewhere and in place. If this is its nature, the potency of place must be a marvellous thing, and take precedence of all other things. For that without which nothing else can exist, while it can exist without the others, must needs be first; for place does not pass out of existence when the things in it are annihilated."

He was also aware of experiments with air and remained as unconvinced of their bearing on the question of the existence of a vacuum or void as many of von Guericke's contemporaries. Reiterating his characteristic scepticism of any objective reality over and above sensible objects, he writes in criticism of attempts to disprove the void and gives expression to his plenist convictions:[426]

"What they do is demonstrate that air is something by torturing wineskins and showing that air offers resistance. .... However what people mean by 'void' is an extension in which there is no perceptible body. .... What needs demonstrating is not that air is something but that the only kind of extension there is, is the extension of bodies, and that this cannot be separated from bodies or exist without them in actuality, and cannot break up the material universe so that it is not continuous (which is what Democritus, Leucippus and plenty of other natural scientists claim)".

His resistance to the kind of thinking represented by Hesiod stems at heart from a resolute philosophical conviction that things of the mind and the imagination — even when they form part of an aesthetically pleasing or practically successful system of thought— are just not in the same category as things "out there".

In his own, not entirely happy, attempt to frame a definition Aristotle wants to meet two requirements. Firstly he wants to tie "place" firmly to "body". In keeping with his ontological parsimony, he is not going to cede any objective reality to place disconnected from actual lodged bodies. Secondly, in tension with the first aim, he wants to accommodate motion (except when something is just spinning) as "change of place", so that the "place of a body" remains immobile while the body itself moves and its motion can be considered as a change of place. His definition, advanced after much discussion of the

---

[425] *Physics* IV.1 [209a]
[426] *Physics* IV.6 [213a] (Waterfield Translation. O.U.P.)

issues, is given in the following paragraph which, I imagine, I am not the only one to find unclear. He writes:[427]

"Place is thought to be something important and hard to grasp, both because the matter and the shape present themselves along with it, and because the displacement of the body that is moved takes place in a stationary container, for it seems possible that there should be an interval which is other than the bodies which are moved. The air too, which is thought to be incorporeal, contributes something to this belief. It is not only the boundaries of the vessel which seem to be place, but also what is between them, regarded as empty. Just, in fact, as the vessel is transportable place, so place is a non-portable vessel. So, when what is within a thing, which is moved, is moved and changes its place as a boat on a river, what contains plays the part of a vessel rather than that of a place. Place on the other hand is rather what is motionless; so it is rather the whole river that is place, because as a whole it is motionless. Hence we conclude that the innermost motionless boundary of what contains is place."

This is difficult and there is no doubt that the general position becomes easier to hold if one accepts his physics rather than his metaphysics. Von Guericke attributes to Aristotle a position that allows the possibility of a void but denies that the possibility is ever realised. He writes:[428]

"Aristotle defines a vacuum as a place not occupied by a body but which, however, is capable of being so occupied."

He then goes on to note that Aristotle does not admit the existence of a vacuum as a natural phenomenon. Within the sublunary part of the Cosmos, the idea of a vacuum — a place unoccupied by body — is intelligible but, as it so happens, the possibility is not realised. Apart from an Occam's razor philosophical argument,[429]

"What is not the cause of any effect in nature should not be supposed by a philosopher to exist in nature. The vacuum is not the cause of any effect in nature. Therefore the vacuum should not be proposed in nature."

Aristotle also had other arguments for denying the vacuum of which I shall mention two.

The first is the modern sounding one that there is no preferred direction[430] in the void and consequently the fact that actual motions do

---

[427] *Physics* IV.4 [212a]
[428] Book II Chapter 3.
[429] *Experimenta Nova*, Book II Chapter 3.
[430] The loose idea of there being no preferred direction can nowadays be made completely precise by using Mac Lane and Eilenburg's analysis of naturality. For instance there is a perfect-

have preferred directions — down for earth and upward for fire — is incompatible with the void. He writes:[431]

"Further, things are now thought to move in the void because it yields; but in a void this quality is present equally everywhere, so that things should move in all directions."

Elsewhere, touching on this same idea that where there is no reason to choose one rather than another, the only natural choices are all or none. He writes:

"Grant only that mass is anywhere and it follows that it must be everywhere."

The first point is well made. In the Newtonian system, all motion arises because of interactions between bodies along the preferred direction — the direction of the line joining the bodies — that comes into being when we have two bodies. When there is no preferred direction, as in the case of a single isolated body, there is no influence to which it can be subject.

A second argument comes from his view on how the motion of a projectile, once it has left the hand of the thrower, proceeds. It is quite characteristic of Aristotle that he doesn't think the projectile has acquired something objective but intangible — later called its impetus by Philoponus,[432] later still its vis viva — from the thrower, but wants to give an explanation in terms of the projectile's "natural locomotion" downwards and its direct interaction with the medium through which it is projected. He writes:[433]

"Further, in point of fact, things that are thrown move, though that which gave them their impulse is not touching them, either by reason of mutual replacement, as some maintain, or because the air that has been pushed pushes them with a movement quicker than the natural locomotion of the projectile wherewith it moves to its proper place. But in a void none of these things can take place, nor can anything be moved save as that which is carried is moved.

---

ly precise and satisfying way of turning an imprecise statement such as "the only natural subsets of set S are S itself and the empty set" into a precise consequence of a precise definition of "natural". Similarly, ideas expressed in terms such as "there is no preferred direction in empty space" can be precisely formulated in terms of naturality.

[431] *Physics* IV.8 [215a/20] (Hardie and Gaye Translation)
[432] John Philoponus [490–570] was a commentator on Aristotle, who ridiculed Aristotle's "explanation" of projectile motion and advanced a theory of transferred impetus which prefigured the Newtonian dynamics — v. e.g. Sorabji, *Matter Space and Motion*, Chapter 9. Duckworth.
[433] *Physics* IV.8 [215a/12]

Further, no one could say why a thing, once set in motion should stop anywhere; for why should it stop here rather than there? So that a thing will either be at rest or moved ad infinitum unless something more powerful gets in its way."

The possibility that these last few lines consider and reject became, when recast as Newton's First Law of Motion, a foundation stone of the edifice that displaced Aristotle's physics.

The general principle of the non-existence of vacuum came to be formulated in the aphorism "nature abhors a vacuum" or simply alluded to as "the horror of vacuum". It acquired a status, somewhat like that of conservation of energy today, or the limiting nature of the speed of light,[434] not so much that of an observed truth, but of a fundamental principle with which the observed facts are to be reconciled.

---

[434] Fr. Schott was probably representative of many when he argues in *Mechanica Hydraulico-pneumatico* (p. 444) that while these experimental phenomena are interesting and admirable, one should seek to explain them in accordance with well-established principles among which was the abhorrence of a vacuum. He writes: "Thus far the vacuum has been a chimera as the indestructible plenitude of nature stand in the way of trying or even hoping to produce one." (Sunt qui huiusmodi Machinamentum vacuum (quod hactenus phantasma fuit, sive tentasse, sive sperasse, obstitente invulnerabili, vel ab Angelo, plenitudine Naturae) modis omnibus evincere tentant.)

Aristotle and the Infinite

Aristotle discusses the Infinite in Physics Book III 4 – 8. He gives a masterly summary of the considerations which might lead one to suppose the infinite to exist. He writes:[435]

"Belief in the existence of the infinite comes mainly from five considerations:
(1) From the nature of time — for it is infinite.
(2) From the division of magnitude — for the mathematicians also use the notion of the infinite.
(3) If coming to be and passing away do not give out, it is only because that from which things come to be is infinite.
(4) Because the limited always finds its limit in something, so that there must be <u>no</u> limit if everything is always limited by something different from itself.
(5) Most of all, a reason which is peculiarly appropriate and presents the difficulty that is felt by everybody — not only number but also mathematical magnitudes and what is outside the heaven are supposed to be infinite because they never give out in our <u>thought</u>."

The last point reiterates the Aristotelian leitmotiv— one cannot populate objective reality on the basis of intellect and imagination alone. In deciding the true nature of reality the evidence of the senses is decisive. He expresses himself strongly on the risks of a too facile inference from what we can think to what there is. He writes:[436]

"To rely on mere thinking is absurd, for then the excess or defect is not in the thing but in the thought. Someone might think that one of us is bigger than he is and magnify him ad infinitum. But it does not follow that he is bigger than the rest of us, just because someone thinks he is, but only because he <u>is</u> the size he is. The thought is an accident."

Crediting processes "that never give out in our thought" lead to the sorites[437] fallacy which is an even more beguiling temptation than that of supposing there are entities of which nouns such as triangle or five are the names. Of course, we can *imagine* indefinitely continuing to divide a material object, or to augment an arithmos, or extend a line. However, this does not confer a right simply to suppose that our imaginative capacities prove the existence of an objective reality corresponding to a process carried on infinitely. Succumbing to the sorites fallacy leads one to suppose that there is a natural number sequence and that

---

[435] *Physics* III.4 [203b/10] (Hardie & Gaye Translation)
[436] *Physics* III.8 [208a/15] (Hardie and Gaye Translation)
[437] There is an extended discussion of the sorites fallacy in J. P. Mayberry, *The Foundation of Mathematics in the Theory of Sets.* C.U.P. Chapter 8.

an axiomatically evident principle of induction can be based on a recollection of a line of dominoes falling and imagining that such lines can be extended without limit.

Aristotle would simply and emphatically disagree with Roger Penrose when the latter writes:[438]

"What right do we have to say that the Platonic world is actually a 'world' that can exist in the same kind of sense in which the other two worlds exist? It may well seem to the reader to be just a ragbag of abstract concepts that mathematicians have come up with from time to time. Yet its existence rests on the profound, timeless and universal nature of these concepts and on the fact that their laws are independent of those who discover them. The rag-bag — if indeed that is what it is — was not of our creation. The natural numbers were there before there were human beings, or indeed any other creature here on earth, and they will remain after all life has perished."

Aristotle acknowledges that the difficulties associated with the concept of the infinite and, characteristically, proceeds to draw distinctions. He writes:[439]

"If the infinite exists we still have to ask how it exists; as a substance or as the essential attribute of some entity. Or in neither way, yet nonetheless is there something which is infinite or some things which are infinitely many?

The problem which especially belongs to the physicist is to investigate whether there is a sensible magnitude which is infinite.

We must begin by distinguishing the various senses in which the term 'infinite' is used.

(1) What is incapable of being gone through because it is not in its nature to be gone through (the sense in which the voice is 'invisible').

(2) What admits of being gone through, the process however having no termination or what scarcely admits of being gone through.

(3) What naturally admits of being gone through but is not actually gone through or does not actually reach an end.

(4) Further, everything that is infinite may be so in respect of addition or division or both."

As far as the proper preoccupations of the physicists are concerned Aristotle concludes:[440]

"It is plain from these arguments that there is no body which is __actually__ infinite."

Nevertheless he goes on to point out that there are senses in which the term "infinite" can be used. He writes:[441]

---

[438] Roger Penrose: *Shadows of the Mind* p. 413. O.U.P.
[439] *Physics* III.4 [203b–204a]
[440] *Physics* III.5 [206a] (Hardie and Gaye Translation)

"But on the other hand to suppose that the infinite does not exist in any way leads obviously to many impossible consequences; there will be a beginning and an end of time, a magnitude will not be divisible into magnitudes and number will not be infinite. ...... Clearly there is a sense in which the infinite exists and another in which it doesn't."

The sense in which he allows it to exist is that the infinite "potentially" exists. He is at pains to circumscribe this word with a caveat to pre-empt possible confusion. He writes:[442]

"But the phrase 'potential existence' is ambiguous. When we speak of the potential existence of a statue we mean that there will be an actual statue. It is not so with the infinite. There will not be an actual infinite."

In the concluding part of his discussion he clarifies his meaning by considering examples, the most important of which are the infinite in time, the infinite arising from the unlimited divisibility of a continuous magnitude and the infinite arising from the unlimited increase of an arithmos.

As regards the sense in which the "generations of man" (Aristotle assumed that the human race had no beginning.) is infinite he has this to say:[443]

"... the infinite has this mode of existence; one thing is always being taken after another and each thing that is being taken is always finite but always different ...... we must not regard the infinite as a "this" such as a man or a horse but must suppose it to exist in the sense in which we speak of the day or the games existing — things whose being has not come to them like that of substance, but consists in the process of coming to be or passing away; definite if you like at each stage, yet always different."

As regards the infinite arising from indefinitely increasing numbers he writes:[444]

"Number, on the other hand, is a plurality of 'ones' and a determined quantity of them. Hence number must stop at the indivisible; for "two" or "three" are merely derivative terms and likewise with each of the other numbers. But in the direction of largeness it is always possible to think of a larger number; for the number of times a magnitude can be bisected is infinite. Hence this infinite is potential, never actual; the number of parts that can be taken always surpasses any assigned number. But this number is not separable from the process of

---

[441] *Physics* III.5 [206a/10] By "number will not be infinite" he means the species of all arithmoi, not individual arithmoi. (Hardie and Gaye Translation.)

[442] *Physics* III.5 [206a/20] (Hardie and Gaye Translation)

[443] *Physics* III.6 [206a/30] (Hardie and Gaye Translation.)

[444] *Physics* III.6 [207b/10] (Hardie and Gaye Translation).

bisection, and its infinity is not a permanent actuality but consists in a process of coming to be, like time and the number of time."

Towards the end of his reflections on the infinite Aristotle gives the following hostage to fortune. He writes:[445]

"I have argued that there is no such thing as the actual infinite which is untraversable, but this position does not rob mathematicians of their study. Even as things are, they do not need the infinite because they make no use of it. All they need is a finite line of any desired length. But any magnitude whatever can be divided in the same ratio as you would divide an enormous magnitude and so, for the purposes of their proofs, it makes no difference whether the magnitude proposed is one of those that actually exist."

Were he to return to Earth, among the questions one would like to ask him is whether, in the light of the successful mathematical experience of just assuming the actual infinite over the last century and a half, he would withdraw this statement. Or would he maintain it, claiming that mathematics, having surrendered to Platonism, has lost its realist character and its subject matter is now a blurred composite of the objective and the subjective?

---

[445] *Physics* III.8 [207b/30] (Waterfield Translation O.U.P.)

THINKING ABOUT NOTHING – PERSPECTIVE

The Retreat from Aristotelianism

There were two distinct lines of retreat from the positivist outlook of Aristotle. The first was theologically inspired and manifested
itself through intense efforts to forge an integrated world view based on
Christian orthodoxy. The second line of retreat was inspired by the
mathematical developments of the sixteenth and seventeenth centuries
associated with the triumph of algebraic and formal methods. I shall
discuss these two developments separately.

The Theological Inspiration

The early Christian centuries were Platonic in spirit. Plato maintained an otherworldly doctrine of a realm of ideals of which objects of
this world were at best imperfect realisations. This doctrine gave a ra-
tionale to the natural conviction of mathematicians that a geometric
proposition — e.g. Pythagoras' theorem — is, in some sense and of
some objects, true *exactly* despite its being only approximately true of
actual sensible right angled triangles. This kind of thinking, akin to the
teaching of Christian orthodoxy that this world is but a prefiguration of
a perfect life to come, made Platonism naturally congenial to Christians.

It is therefore somewhat surprising that the society that most
took Aristotle to its bosom was Europe between the twelfth and the
sixteenth centuries. The temperamental and philosophical discord between Aristotle and Christian orthodoxy is so dire as to render his appeal to a Christian society explicable only in terms of the attraction of
opposites. The attempted unification of their ways of thought was a
marriage whose difficult character and final divorce one might have
predicted. Christendom did not achieve the position it occupied in medieval and Renaissance Europe as the fruit of a policy of judicious
moderation and statesmanlike compromise but by the daring and exhil-
arating embrace of extreme ethical and philosophical positions.[446] At
every juncture where an opportunity for pursuing a middle course
arose, orthodoxy steered resolutely towards the Scylla or the Charybdis
of the extreme view. Would it not be more reasonable and prudent to
believe, with Arius, that Jesus was a great teacher and prophet worthy

---

[446] Lytton Strachey (*Eminent Victorians, Essay on Cardinal Manning*) vividly describes this aversion
to doctrinal moderation as "that unyielding intensity of fervour, that passion for the extreme
and absolute, which is the very life-blood of the Church of Rome".

of being followed for his own sake? This would have been easier to accept and would have mitigated tensions between the followers of the Abrahamic faiths. However, Christian orthodoxy insists that Jesus is God incarnate. Would not a doctrine of the resurrection be less problematic in its details and less defiant of common sense if it allowed for an understanding in some less challenging spiritual and immaterial sense? It would. But orthodoxy insists on a resurrection of the body. Not without reason did Tertullian[447] express himself with a mixture of exasperation and breath-taking amazement at its liberating and paradoxical inversions of the normal modes of thought.

"The son of God was born – there is no embarrassment just because it is so shameful. The son of God died – this is believable precisely because it's absurd. Having been buried He rose again – this is certain because it's impossible."

The definitive attempt at a synthesis of Aristotle and Christianity was made by St. Thomas Aquinas (1225–1274) in his master work, Summa Theologica. Shortly after his death the tension reached breaking point. On March 12th 1277 the Bishop of Paris, Etienne Tempier,[448] accompanied by the Doctors of Theology of the University, issued, as it were, the decree nisi for the ill-assorted bed fellows of Aristotelianism and Christian orthodoxy, adducing reasons why a divorce on grounds of incompatibility was inevitable. In the Articles of Condemnation, Tempier enumerated 219 grounds of disagreement with Aristotelian teaching.

Of particular relevance to us are the articles condemning the following Aristotelian opinions:

Article 34:[449] The First Cause cannot create many universes.
Article 49: The First Cause could not move the heavens in a straight line and the reason is that a vacuum would remain.
Article 79:[450] If heaven stood still, fire would not burn flax, because time would not exist.
Article 86:[451] Time and eternity have no existence in reality but only in the mind,

---

[447] De Carne Christi V 4

[448] Etienne Tempier (also known as Stéphane d'Orléans) was Bishop of Paris from 1268 till his death in 1279.

[449] Quod Prima Causa non posset plures mundos facere. It is something of an irony that Tempier wishes to allow the possibility of many universes to defend the omnipotence of God, while a modern thinker, Richard Dawkins, espouses the same proposition to argue the non-existence of God and to attribute the universe we inhabit, apparently fine-tuned to support human existence, to a process of evolution from multiple universes.

[450] Si caelum staret, ignis in stupam non ageret, quia tempus non esset.

The fact that Tempier and his colleagues felt the need to condemn these propositions shows, of course, that these views commanded some support in the University of Paris. Tempier's position rested solely on dogmatic Christian orthodoxy. The condemnation shows how men were led by religion beyond what one might imagine to be the Christian religion's natural concerns — the leading of a virtuous life, the existence of souls, the nature of an after-life, and so on — to take positions on wider questions of perennial scientific interest. The first two condemnations bear on Aristotle's opinions on the question of what is outside our Cosmos. As we have seen, he held the view that absolutely nothing exists — neither body, nor space nor time nor a void. The fact that, apparently hard-wired in our imaginations, we have a picture of a never ending space is not a telling argument against his position. In fact, as we have seen earlier in the section on his views on the Infinite, he warns against assuming that anything objective corresponds to what we can imaginatively envisage. Christian Aristotelians had sought to reconcile Aristotle's position with Christian convictions about the omnipotence of God by arguing that the concept of the plurality of universes entailed a logical contradiction, the only acceptable limitation on God's power.

Arguments about the possibility of multiple universes were closely connected to arguments about the void and one can convincingly sustain the Aristotelian position on this issue only by holding to Aristotle's position on the void. Tempier's Articles 34 and 49 are thus, implicitly, an attack on Aristotle's doctrine on the void. Duhem writes:[452]

'For thirteenth-century scholasticism, the proposition, 'the void is impossible' appeared as a kind of axiom whose negation would constitute a real absurdity. .... The axiom seemed able to serve as the major premise for some deductions. That is how the impossibility of the void served to justify — by a method Aristotle had not used — the Peripatetic proposition, "several worlds cannot exist".

We first find this argument in the commentary on the Sphere of Joannes Sacrobosco that Michael Scotus[453] had composed for the emperor Frederick II. ....The noted astronomer summarily reproduces Aristotle's reasoning but he precedes it with the following argument.

---

[451] Quod aevum et tempus nihil sunt in re, sed solum apprehensione.

[452] Duhem p. 387.

[453] Michael Scotus (1175–c.1232) was born in Scotland and studied at Durham and Oxford. His main interests were in philosophy, mathematics and astrology. As a translator at the court of Frederick II, he translated works of Aristotle and the Commentaries of Avicenna from Arabic to Latin.

'Between the convex surfaces delimiting the different worlds, there necessarily exists a certain amount of space. Therefore either a body exists occupying this space or not. But there cannot be a body filling this space; this body, in reality, would be estranged from all worlds since it would be outside the spheres delimiting the worlds. If there is no body filling this space, it is then a void; and there can be no void in nature, as Aristotle has demonstrated in the fourth book of the Physics; therefore there cannot be a plurality of worlds."

With regard to Time the Peripatetics pushed the logic of Aristotle's positivism — the conviction that there is nothing over and above the tangible and concrete and that the concept of Time cannot be divorced from the procedures to measure it — to an extravagant and apparently absurd conclusion. Their logic is radically positivist. The argument is that, as there is no objective Time over and above individual motions, a definition of Time simply involves choosing a particular motion, typically a celestial motion. Once that motion is chosen as the defining motion it becomes impossible to say that this motion is fast or slow or even if it has stopped altogether. It is only in modern times, with the abandonment of the definition of a second in terms of the Earth's rotation,[454] that it became conceivable to "correct" for a slowing down of the Earth on its axis by adding in leap seconds. Of the Peripatetic view of Time, Duhem writes:[455]

"For Peripatetic physics, time was inherent in the diurnal movement; if the diurnal movement did not exist, there would be no time. From this the Averroists derived the following conclusion: if the diurnal movement stopped, all other movements, all other changes would have to stop, for there would be no time to measure their duration."[456]

Tempier's Articles 79 and 86 insist on the objective reality of Time over and above any motions by which its elapse might be measured. Tempier did not specify the nature of this objective reality. However, drawing on the enriched ontology of religious orthodoxy, a proposal could be formulated. In the generation after Tempier, a pupil of Duns Scotus,[457] Francis of Mayronne,[458] advanced a theological, abso-

---

[454] The modern definition of a second was adopted in 1967 and is based on the frequency of rsdiation emitted by the caesium atom.

[455] Duhem p. 297.

[456] The interaction of this kind of thinking with Christian religious belief caused enormous philosophical significance to be attached to Joshua 10: 12–13. "And the sun stood still, and the moon halted, until the people had taken vengeance on their enemies." (New Jerusalem Bible)

[457] Duns Scotus (c.1265–1308) was born in Scotland and ordained a Franciscan in 1291. He studied at Oxford and Paris and taught at Oxford. He is also known by the soubriquet, "the subtle doctor". His philosophy was a particular inspiration to Gerard Manley Hopkins.

lutist understanding of Time and Space that seem to foreshadow that of von Guericke and Newton. Francis writes:[459]

"Time is a relation, but it cannot be a relation with respect to any creature, for even if there existed only a single creature, there would be a before and an after. I therefore hold that time is the fluxion of presentness with respect to God, in the same way that I have asserted of place that it is a certain presentness with respect to God."

In this intellectual climate the question of the actual infinite could be considered in ways that Aristotle would not have permitted himself. He was subject to reproaches which, given his own ontological economy, seem hardly fair. Duhem writes:[460]

"When Aristotle was writing had not the world already travelled through and infinite multitude of cycles? Had not the starry sphere and the sun accomplished an infinity of revolutions? These infinite multitudes which had unfolded in time, these multitudes whose previous units had ceased to exist at the moment their present units came into being, did not seem worthy to Aristotle of the name "actual infinity"; the name "potential infinity" for these multitudes was more to his liking. He was careful to state that if he allowed the notion of potential infinity it was precisely to safeguard these three truths:
(1) Number can be indefinitely augmented by means of addition
(2) Continuous magnitude can be indefinitely subdivided
(3) Time had no beginning and will have no end.
Belief in the individual survival of the human soul gives the objection to Aristotle's views a more pressing formulation. At each instant of time it is true that an infinity of men had in the past been born, lived and died; but according to the belief in the individual survival of the human soul, the souls of each of these men actually subsist and remain distinct from each other. Hence at each instant of time, the souls of the dead form an actual infinite multitude of distinct objects."

Thinkers such as Duns Scotus and Gregory of Rimini (1300–1360) became with practice more accustomed to the apparently paradoxical properties of the infinite and dispelled apprehensions that a contradiction lurked in the very notion of the infinite. Duns Scotus tackled the frequently made objection that if the infinite existed, a part would be equal to the whole, contradicting Euclid's Common Notion 5. He writes:[461]

---

[458] Francis of Mayronne (c.1280–1327) was a Franciscan monk and a teacher at the Sorbonne. He and William of Ockham were both pupils of Duns Scotus.
[459] Duhem p. 323.
[460] Duhem p. 5.
[461] Duhem p. 89.

*"The words equal, greater and smaller are not suitable for large quantities unless finite.
…... The reason by which a quantity is greater than another lies in the fact that it exceeds,
the reason of equality, in the fact that it has the same measure. Everything indicates that
these concern finite magnitudes. One must therefore deny that an infinity can be equal to
another infinity; more and less also designate differences between finite quantities and not
between infinite quantities."*

Rather than simply acceding to a ban on their use, Gregory of
Rimini thought hard about how terms such as equal, greater, smaller,
whole and part could be applied to the infinite. He tried to legitimise
the use of the application of these terms to the infinite by drawing, not
altogether successfully, certain distinctions. However, the key idea
which underpinned the successful attack on the problem of the infinite
in the 19th century — that of one-to-one correspondence between sets
— is missing. He wishes to preserve Euclid's principle by using the
terms whole and part in a restricted sense. He writes:[462]

*"These terms can be taken in two ways, according to their common meaning or according to
their proper meaning.
According to the first way, anything containing another (or a third thing distinct from the
second and from what the second comprises) is said to be a whole with respect to the second
and anything contained in a whole is said to be a part of the whole in which it is contained.
According to the second way, for a thing to be called a whole with respect to another it is not
sufficient that it contain the other, as is assumed in the first way, but it has to contain a
determined number of things of determined magnitude (tot tanta) not contained within that
which is included. …….. In this (first) way an infinite multitude can be part of another
infinite multitude. ……. In the second way an infinite multitude cannot be either whole or
part of another infinite multitude; there is no determined number of groups of such units (tot
tanta) contained in one of the multitudes and not in the other."*

By the middle of the fourteenth century we find the Franciscan
Nicholas Bonet[463] mildly observing:

*"The possibility of actual infinity does not seem to hold any contradiction for modern philos-
ophers."*

It is the nature of theological thinking to insist on possibilities
and realities beyond anything directly accessible to the senses. Thinking

---

[462] Duhem p. 110.
[463] Duhem p. 105. Nicholas Bonet (d. 1360) was a teacher of theology in Paris and subsequently
a missionary in Mongolia where he was the Pope's emissary to Kubla Khan. The Latin of the
quotation is "Modernis philosophis non apparet aliqua impossibilitas quin sit possibilis infinitas
actualis."

of this type can interact, in certain circumstances, fruitfully with the natural positivism of scientific thinking. Duhem attaches enormous significance to Tempier's condemnation and, through the thought of many scholars between the fourteenth and sixteenth centuries, traces the growth of daring and radical speculation inspired by theological ideas. He argues that theology played a role somewhat similar to that of mathematics in post-Newtonian physics in prompting men to entertain ideas that transcended and often seemed to defy the more grounded ways of thinking arising from experiment and respect for traditional patterns of thought. The culmination of this tendency was the scientific revolution of the seventeenth century which established a new canon of scientific orthodoxy.

Duhem portrays the centuries to whose thinking von Guericke was heir as a period of preschool child-like freshness and energy. Life abounds in new ideas, new observations and new phenomena and no institution has yet arisen where an established orthodoxy is taught that codifies, disciplines, and organises the multifaceted enrichments of experience. It was a time of glimpses and fragmentary insights into foundations of possible new physical theories. Until Newton, no attempt at a synthesis of the fragments into a system was so clearly superior as to definitively eclipse its rivals. Only in the light of the completed jigsaw of the Newtonian system could one have, with the wisdom of hindsight, a perspective on the merit and significance of the individual pieces.

Von Guericke and his contemporaries were heirs to the expanded possibilities that theological notions offered to the study of the natural world. In his time scientific greatness lay as much in the capacity to create a synthesis to account for known phenomena as in the accumulation of new facts about nature. On this criterion, Newton is of course the nonpareil but von Guericke is not a nugatory figure. In the generation before Newton, he carried through a thorough, comprehensive and original program of experimental investigations and interpreted his discoveries in accordance with, firstly, a theory of the Earth's atmosphere which remains essentially correct to this day and, secondly, a doctrine of absolute space and time which proved an adequate underpinning of scientific thinking for the next two hundred years. This is what great scientists do.

The Mathematical Inspiration

Theology provided one line of ontological liberalisation; mathematics provided the other. The character of Greek mathematics was strongly realist. Mathematical statements were either about arithmoi or about lines and geometrical figures. Mathematical arguments convinced through their possession of a quality which is well expressed by the German word anschaulichkeit. This roughly means that one follows an argument about, let us say all triangles, by holding in the imagination a particular instance, shorn of any particular features that might compromise its ability to go proxy for all, and seeing the validity of the argument as it is applied step-by-step to this imagined individual instance. An example whose historical importance we shall mention below is the proof that the sum of the first r odd numbers — *1+ 3 + 5+* .... *+ 2r–1* — is a perfect square. The anschaulich proof of this proposition invites us to consider a typical square arithmos — i.e. a square array of units — and to see that such a square can be partitioned, beginning with the bottom left unit, then the three units touching the bottom left one and then the five units touching these three on the outside and so on until all the units of the square are exhausted. Any reader who has either studied Euclidean geometry or ever explained to children why $ab = ba$ by using rectangles knows the force and appeal of anschauliche arguments as the most fundamental sort of mathematical argument.

What supplanted anschaulichkeit was a process, which Jacob Klein, the historian who first drew attention to this development, called "symbol generated abstraction". This process happened again and again between the sixteenth and twentieth centuries, bequeathing us among much else, zero and one as numbers, the natural numbers, the complex numbers, differentials and functions. These are the things with which Platonist mathematicians, to this day, populate objective reality.

The process of symbol generated abstraction generally starts with an innocuous notational innovation typically offering just a convenient shorthand description of something already clearly understood but described in a somewhat more verbose way. For instance we might introduce the notation a x b is introduced to describe the rectangular arithmos formed from the arithmoi a and b and the notation $a + b$ to describe the arithmos formed by combining the units, assumed to be distinct, of a and b into a single arithmos. Although initially in using the notations we might keep very much in mind what they were originally

intended to denote, one soon realises that one can fruitfully and effi-
ciently proceed simply by manipulating the symbols according to syn-
tactic rules without having to advert at every step to the underlying
meaning. So, of course, if one were pressed as to the meaning of, say,
ab(cd + ef) = abcd + abef one could track back to a statement about
arithmoi but this style of explication quickly begins to seem unconvinc-
ing as well as tedious and soon one begins to freewheel guided only by
the rules, originally based on their intended meaning, of manipulating
our symbols. Two further developments soon turn our detachment
from the original meaning into a more resolute determination to ignore
it altogether.

The first of these occurs when we discover that our notation allows, in fact encourages, us to form terms and make statements of
which the explication according to the underlying meaning is not just
tedious but impossible. If, following Aristotle's views that the smallest
arithmoi are doublets, we began with the notation *"2"* for doublets, *"3"*
for triplets, *"4"* for quartets etc., we will at, at some point, find ourselves having to choose whether to follow the prompting of the notation and treat *7 – 6* on the same footing as *7 – 5, 7 – 4, 7 – 3, 7 – 2*, or
to consult the meaning according to Aristotle and decide that while *7 –
5* refers to the arithmos obtained by removing a five (i.e an arithmos of
5 units) from a *7*, there is no arithmos corresponding to *7 – 6* and such
a term is consequently meaningless. Jacob Klein points out that the last
attempt to subordinate notation to the underlying meaning was made
by Wallis as late as 1670 when he discussed whether it is legitimate to
consider a unit as an arithmos.[464] Once the first step is taken and we
elect to let ourselves be guided by the notation rather than the meaning,
the rest follows inevitably. There is no reason to stop at *7 – 6*, so we
allow ourselves *7 – 7, 7 – 8, 7 – 9* and so on.

The second development was the discovery that, despite the
problem of giving a meaning to what our notation has led us to do, the

---

[464] Klein (*Greek Mathematical Thought and the origin of Algebra* p. 211) writes: "The final act in the
introduction of the new "number" concept is due to Wallis (1616–1703). .... Since he is in the
habit of combining his mathematical presentations with thorough historical and philological
discussions and is therefore much better able than his predecessors to do justice to the ancient
conceptions, he presents to us, for the last time and with the greatest distinctness, a clear picture of the reinterpretation which these conceptions undergo within the framework of symbolic
intentionality." Chapter 4 of the *Mathesis Universalis* (1657) contains a discussion of whether one
is a number. (An Unitas sit Numerus?).

extended formalism had practical usefulness. For instance the negative numbers, which certainly were not names for arithmoi, were useful in dealing with debtors to banks or when considering how cold it was. However, having an application is not the same as assigning a meaning and no one was tempted, for example, to identify a negative number with, say, a debit balance at a bank, or with degrees of frost. The natural numbers, and subsequently the integers, came into being as a way of giving meaning to the terms arising in a successful formalism. One, two, three etc. became names for supposedly objective natural numbers rather than descriptive words for concrete arithmoi. Thus the injunction of Aristotle against supposing that mathematics dealt with an objective reality "over and above" concrete lines, arithmoi etc. was set aside. Natural numbers, instead of being the arithmoi occurring in nature, came to be thought of as a sequence beginning at *1* and being generated by repeating finitely often an operation of forming a successor. The notion of finite was already compromised in Euclid, where on the one hand, a sharply ontological criterion for finiteness — the whole is greater than the part, i.e. there exists no proper subset of a set that is in one-to-one correspondence with the whole — is given and on the other, finiteness is also thought of in an operational way — if an arithmos can eventually be exhausted by some (necessarily idealised) process of removing one element at a time it is finite.[465]

Mayberry[466] refers to the latter concept of finiteness as the "sorites fallacy". The recourse to the sorites fallacy as a method of proof in Euclid is, as shown in great detail by Mayberry, a removable defect rather than a fatal flaw. However for the notion of natural number that emerged in the sixteenth century, the dependence on the sorites fallacy is fundamental. By referring to it as a fallacy one does not intend to imply that it has not been fruitful in essentially the same way that many other intuitions, which one would not wish to admit into a mathematical proof, have proved fruitful. The particular fruit of the sorites fallacy was that it made the principles of proof by induction and definition by

---

[465] For instance, Euclid (Book VII Definition 15) defines multiplication according to the iterative idea of finiteness. He writes: (T. L. Heath translation) "A number is said to multiply a number when that which is multiplied is added to itself as many times as there are units in the other and thus some number is produced."

[466] J. P. Mayberry. The Foundations of Mathematics in the Theory of Sets. C.U.P.

recursion seem axiomatically evident. The free use of these methods[467] allowed mathematicians to subsume all the previously established arithmetic propositions into the new methodology and, in addition, greatly extended the scope of what could be proved.[468] The first proof by induction was accomplished in 1521 by Francisco Maurilico who used it to show that the sum of the first n odd numbers is a perfect square. His completely formalistic proof requires no visualisation of actual squares and illustrates the characteristic features of the new methods. On the one hand there has been a great gain in power and uniformity buy on the other there has been a loss of anschaulichkeit.

From the seventeenth to the nineteenth centuries the natural outlook of mathematicians was a neo-platonism that conferred the status of objective reality onto the abstractions that had arisen from the manipulations of successful and useful formalisms. Mathematics, like any other scientific subject, needs a subject matter and in its case the subject matter was deemed to be objectively and eternally existing entities such as the natural numbers, the real numbers etc. As the citations from Hardy and Penrose show, this outlook remains attractive to many, if not most, mathematicians.

Von Guericke shows no awareness of the accomplishments of the great French mathematicians of the period — Fermat (c.1601–1665), Vieta (1540–1603) and Descartes (1596–1650). Although he does use decimal notation, the decimal algorithms for multiplication and division which had been popularised by Stevin in 1585 and the decimal comma introduced by Napier about 1612, his conceptual thinking about numbers is Aristotelian. In Book II Chapter 10 he give us his thoughts on the topic. He thinks of numbers as multitudes of units and speculates, two centuries prematurely as it transpired, in the tradition of advocates of the actual infinite, about the possibility of infinite numbers.

---

[467] Mayberry (The Foundations of Mathematics in the Theory of Sets) gives a careful analysis of the extent to which proof by induction and definition by recursion are valid principles in a context where "the whole is greater than the part" is accepted as an axiom.

[468] The solution of the cubic and quartic equations obtained by Cardan and Ferrari in the 16th century were among the early triumphs of the new method, decisively going beyond Greek mathematics.

The Modern Dispensation

Scientists of the eighteenth and nineteenth centuries retained the robustly realistic outlook of their seventeenth century predecessors. Their ideal was to give an exact and true account of nature using the language of mathematics. If the precision with which the account was experimentally confirmed was inevitably limited, this was because, as Newton famously put it, the error was not in the art but in the artificer.[469] In the Preface to Copernicus' De Revolutionibus, Oisiander had written that scientific theory need aim no higher than to be an efficient and compact scheme for describing the observed phenomena. To later generations this dissident voice seemed insufficiently ambitious and even pusillanimous. The religious temperament of these later centuries was increasingly sceptical and uncomfortable with an ontology drawn from theological conviction. The religious inspiration of much seventeenth century scientific thinking came to be seen as a rather embarrassing eccentricity of otherwise great men.[470] To most Christians today, von Guericke's religious beliefs are disconcertingly literal and, in the modern sense of the word, fundamentalist, as Book II Chapter XI on the Abode of the Blessed strikingly illustrates. Feeling uncomfortable with theologically underpinned ideas of space and time is not however the same as being able satisfactorily to replace them.

Alternative foundations for space and time are associated with the names of Descartes, Leibniz and Kant. Rather like Aristotle, Descartes avoided the problem of empty space by positing a plenum of substance. Leibniz held that space was an illusion arising from the mind's awareness of the relationships subsisting among co-existing bodies. His position, with its denial of any objective reality over and above what is accessible to the senses, is also Aristotelian in inspira-

---

[469] "But as artificers do not work with perfect accuracy, it comes to pass that mechanics is so distinguished from geometry that what is perfectly accurate is called geometrical; what is less so, is called mechanical. However the errors are not in the art but in the artificers. He that works with less accuracy is an imperfect mechanic; and if any could work with perfect accuracy, he would be the most perfect mechanic of all." (Newton's Preface to the 1st Edition of Principia) (Cotes translation).

[470] J. M. Keynes famously remarked that Newton far from being "the first and greatest of the modern age of scientists, a rationalist, one who taught us to think on the lines of cold and untinctured reason" was "the last of the magicians, the last of the Babylonians and Sumerians, the last great mind who looked out on the visible and intellectual world with the same eyes as those who began to build our intellectual inheritance rather less than 10 000 years ago".

tion.[471] Kant, essentially, modified Newton's view to the effect that space and time, instead of being the sensorium of God, became the sensorium of humanity. We see things in space and time as a consequence of the structure of our faculties of perception. The comparison often made is with a man who sees everything as blue because he wears blue glasses. These theories were more philosophically congenial to the growing humanism of the time than the theological absolutism of von Guericke and Newton.[472] Nevertheless, they did not gain the traction or prestige that scientific fruitfulness would have garnered for them. None of them enabled people to think more clearly and effectively about experimental phenomena and none of them underpinned solid advances in physics in the way that Newton's ideas had.

The remainder of this final section of this book is an outline of the new dispensation created by a remarkable development of the late 19th and early 20th centuries. This permitted a clear separation of the formulation of the different understandings of space and time from the philosophical or religious systems that provided the soil in which the ideas originally grew. The development did not assert that any particular such system was false, but just that none of them were necessary for the formulation of the basic concepts of physics. The most obvious beneficiary was the already triumphant Newtonian system, in that the new development permitted the complete separation of the ideas of absolute space and time from the theological notions with which von Guericke and Newton had underpinned these concepts. However, the true major beneficiaries were the relativistic ideas inherent in the systems of Descartes and Leibniz which, for the first time, became susceptible of a clear formulation that allowed them to serve on an at least equal footing with the Newtonian system as a foundation for classical physics.

---

[471] Max Jammer. *Concepts of Space* (Dover) p.p. 117–122 discusses the relativist views of Leibniz and Huyghens as they emerge from their correspondence with each other and with Samuel Clarke. Jammer writes: "Leibniz goes on to explain that the relation of situation is a wholly sufficient condition for the idea of space. *No absolute reality need be invoked."* (my italics)

[472] A comparison can be made with Hoyle's Steady State Theory of the universe which seemed philosophically more congenial than its competitor, the Big Bang Theory. In the 1920s and 1930s almost every major cosmologist preferred an eternal steady state Universe, and several complained that the beginning of time implied by the Big Bang imported religious concepts into physics; this objection was later repeated by supporters of the steady state theory. This perception was enhanced by the fact that the originator of the Big Bang theory, Monsignor Georges Lemaître was a Roman Catholic priest.

These ideas, adumbrated by Descartes and Leibniz and explicitly advocated by Mach[473] in the middle of the nineteenth century, were only clearly formulated in the early twentieth century under the name Galilean Relativity. Assertions from which von Guericke, Newton and their successors would have resiled — "absolute position is meaningless", "only relative velocity makes sense", "particles have no three dimensional velocity vectors", "the kinetic energy of the universe (as it depends on the absolute velocity of the bodies) is, prima facie, a meaningless concept as is the potential energy (as it depends on the absolute positions of the bodies)" — became matters of mathematical deduction rather than of philosophical speculation. Despite these apparently radical assertions, to which Leibniz's eager assent can be easily imagined, all the consequences of Newtonian physics can be reconstructed in a way that, although mathematically more difficult, adheres more closely to Ockham's razor that ontological frugality is to be preferred to liberality.

When experimental and theoretical developments in electromagnetism prompted Einstein's revision of fundamental thinking about space and time, Minkowski showed how his ideas could he formulated in accord with the new development. Einstein's later discovery of the interaction between matter and space, General Relativity, could hardly have been formulated at all except within the new dispensation. As a vehicle for putting forth different conceptualisations of space and time in a clear, objective, precise and dispassionate manner the new dispensation realised, as closely as is ever likely to be achieved, Leibniz's dream of a universal language.[474]

---

[473] Ernst Mach, in *The Science of Mechanics*,(Open Court Classics 1989) first published in 1883, writes (p. 293): "The view that "absolute motion" is a conception which is devoid of content and cannot be used in science struck almost everybody as strange thirty years ago, but at the present time it is supported by many and worthy investigators. Some relativists are Stallo, J. Thomson, Ludwig Lange, Love, Kleinpeter, J.G. McGregor, Mansion, Petzoldt and Paearson. The number of relativists has grown very quickly and the above list is certainly already incomplete. Probably there will soon be no important supporter of the opposite view."

[474] In "La crise de la conscience européenne" Paul Hazard writes vividly of Leibniz's character and encyclopaedic range of interests. Of his dream of a universal language he writes: "Ne serait-il possible de supprimer (quelques-uns au moins) des obstacles dont la seule vue choque la raison, et pour commencer de s'entendre sur le sens des mots? On créerait une langue qui vaudrait pour tous et qui non seulement faciliterait des relations internationals, mais porterait dans son être de tels caractères de netteté, de précision, de souplesse, de richesse qu'elle serait evidence rationelle et sensible. On s'en servirait pour toutes operations de l'esprit, comme les mathematiciens se servent de l'algèbre; seulement ce serait un algèbre concrète, chaque terme offrant la vision de ses rapports possible avec les termes voisins au premier coup d'oeil. On

The new dispensation was even more revolutionary in mathematics than in physics. The neo-platonic philosophical tradition of hypostatizing mathematical systems, such as the natural numbers and the complex numbers, to provide a worthy semantics for successful formalisms was, like the philosophical systems underpinning physics, reduced to a matter of personal inclination. One could of course continue to believe, with Hardy, Penrose and many others, that the natural numbers exist eternally and objectively in some incorporeal, imperishable realm of being, but such beliefs are fortunately not necessary for the actual practice of mathematicians.

I shall now describe what this development was and how it replaced the ad hoc neo-Platonism, which had become the dominant philosophy of mathematics, with a principled and fruitful neo-Aristotelianism.

It is somehow fitting that the mathematician at the heart of this new dispensation was himself given to speculative theology in the medieval and seventeenth century style. Cantor returned to a question which to many in the nineteenth century must have seemed a barren and typically scholastic preoccupation — that of the existence of the actual infinite.

The achievement of Cantor and the movement he launched began by cutting the Gordian knot which centuries of discussion had failed to unravel, and simply assuming that the proposition that there exists an infinite set is true. His assumption was equivalent to asserting that Euclid's Common Notion 5, "the whole is greater than the part" is, at least as applied to arithmoi, false.

For two separate reasons, neither of which would have commended itself to Aristotle, many thinkers thought this proposition obviously true. The first stemmed from religion. Von Guericke, Newton and many of their contemporaries and predecessors were among those convinced by theological considerations. In Book II, Chapter 9 von Guericke points out how points marked along an infinite line in space would constitute an infinite arithmos and that following the removal of every second point along such a line an infinity of points would still remain. Von Guericke believed all this to be objectively true because of

posséderait ainsi une caracatéristique universelle, l'instrument la plus fin dont l'esprit humain se soit jamais servi."

his theological understanding of space. The second reason stemmed from the neo-platonism that arose in response to the success of algebraic and formal methods in mathematics. According to the neo-platonic convictions of many mathematicians, the natural numbers objectively, if incorporeally, exist and are infinite in multitude. They thus constitute an infinite arithmos proving Cantor's assumption true. This question-begging justification of the Axiom of Infinity continues to be offered in textbooks introducing set theory. Aristotle would not have been persuaded by either the Christian dogma of von Guericke or the neo-platonism of moderns such as Hardy and Penrose. For him the key question would have been the following: does the Cosmos contain an infinite collection of simultaneously existing, distinguishable, material things? If the answer to this question is in the negative, as it appears to be, then Aristotle would consider himself justified in holding to his denial of the infinite.

A second major advance lay in distinguishing between different types of infinities. A key realisation was that the criterion of equality — that two arithmoi could be put into one-to-one correspondence — was not, at heart, a question about possible or idealised procedures for bringing one set into coincidence with another. Rather it was a question about the existence of sets satisfying certain properties. Just as in the seventeenth century the apparently important distinctions between arithmoi and the ratios of arithmoi had been "flattened" into the concept of rational number, so the apparently important distinctions between arithmoi and operations on their units — i.e. functions[475] — was "flattened" into the general concept of "set" and functions just became sets of a certain type. Von Guericke and no doubt many others had suspected that the sense in which space was infinite differed from that

---

[475] Textbooks from the late 19th century contain (by modern standards) the most appallingly muddled definitions of a function. See, for instance, Sylvanus P. Thomson's *Calculus Made Simple* in which the constant function is defined as "the function which doesn't function at all". Another such textbook, Forsyth's *Theory of Functions of a Complex Variable* (1893), devotes some 500 words, quoted in J.E. Littlewood's *Miscellany*, to the concept of function. Forsyth writes: "The earliest occurrence of the idea of functionality is in connection with functions of a real variable; and then it is co-extensive with the idea of dependence. Thus if the value of X depends on that of x and on no other variable magnitude, it is customary to regard X as a function of x; and there is usually an implication that X is derived from x by some series of operations." Contrasting the modern definition with attempted definitions by abstraction, Littlewood remarks "This clear daylight is now a matter of course but it replaces an obscurity as of midnight." (*Littlewood's Miscellany* p. 77, edited by Bollobas C.U.P 1986).

in which the set of points marked at discrete intervals along an infinite line was infinite. In an argument of stunning simplicity and originality,[476] Cantor showed that the sense in which the continuum was infinite was indeed different from the sense in which equidistant marks along an infinite line were infinite. He also proved that the former did not correspond to the absolute infinite as von Guericke, relying on his theologically based intuition, thought would be the case. Cantor famously showed that while there are infinitely many infinite arithmoi, no two of which are in one-to-one correspondence with each other, there are nevertheless multitudes which cannot be apprehended as a single arithmos. Von Guericke's term for such multitudes is "the infinite not graspable by number".[477] The modern term is "proper class".

Cantor's discoveries of the different types of infinite arithmoi established a branch of mathematics dedicated to infinite sets. Of much more importance however, was the realisation, which emerged over the half century between 1875 and 1925, that all of mathematics could be formulated in an essentially Aristotelian way — as arithmetic, i.e. the study of arithmoi, freed of the restriction that the whole is greater than the part. This new outlook was summarised in such aphorisms as "Set theory is a foundation for mathematics" or "Mathematics is the study of structure". What is meant by the former is that all mathematical concepts, many of which had hitherto seemed to be floating on philosophically muddied waters,[478] could be recast, simply and unambiguously, in terms of sets. The understanding of mathematics, given the acceptance of infinite sets, was restored to a pristine Aristotelianism. No mathematician, qua mathematician, need be a Christian, as Newton and von Guericke were, or a neo-platonist, believing with Hardy and Penrose in a transcendental realm of mathematical entities, or a Kantian, believing

---

[476] Cantor showed that the real numbers are in 1–1 correspondence with the subsets of the rationals. He then showed that a set A and its set of subsets of A, P(A), cannot be in 1–1 correspondence by supposing that there was such a correspondence F: A →P(A) and considering the subset of A, S ≡ {x: x ∈ A and x ∉ F(x)}, letting s be such that F(s) = S and asking "Is s ∈ S?".

[477] v. Book II, Chapter 9 where von Guericke appears to distinguish infinities that can be comprehended as number i.e. understood as sets, and those that cannot.

[478] E.g. continuity, smoothness, constructiblity with ruler and compass and computability were all originally defined in operationalist terms which only make sense in terms of some idealised conception of human capacities exercised through an interval of time.

with Hamilton that algebra is the science of pure time,[479] or a constructivist, believing with Brouwer in an idealised notion of human capacity for iterating a procedure. Of course, qua human being, a mathematician can subscribe to any of these beliefs, but mathematics itself is a neutral bystander to the disputes that arise between the advocates of such different philosophies. As von Guericke prophetically remarks in his *Preface to the Reader*:

"Mathematics isn't aggressive but its unhurried pursuit of the most inoffensive truths triumphs. The conclusions of other philosophical disciplines can be argued about because they lack the evident certainty which mathematics has the power to give. Thus it is that the human spirit, after long wanderings through the whole range of studies, finds at last rest in the solitary certainty of mathematics."

The second aphorism "Mathematics is the study of structure" refers to the relatively modest technical refinement of the Greek idea of equality — two figures or arithmoi are equal if they can brought into coincidence with each other[480] — to the modern idea of isomorphism. Whereas the term "arithmos" or "set" refers to some particular multitude grasped, as one, the term "structure" is used for a number of arithmoi standing in a specified relationship to each other and having certain properties.[481] Just as words like "five", "dozen", "score" and so on describe arithmoi, so words such as "partial ordering", "group", "ring", "field" etc. describe structures. The realisation that Cantor's ideas could be applied to supplant the formalistic conceptions of mathematics that had arisen over the previous three centuries, seems to have first taken firm root in the minds of mathematicians of the early 20th century, in particular of Emmy Noether at Göttingen which was then a major centre of world mathematics.

The modern idea of isomorphism between structures is the natural extension of the Greek idea of equality between figures and arithmoi. The corresponding natural extension of the teaching of Aristotle is that, just as there is no abstractly existing number *5*, hovering over the individual instances of quintets and somehow extracting their several quintuplicities into a single essence, so there is no abstract entity

---

[479] This obscure assertion of Hamilton is best understood as arising from a view that algebra deals with numbers in an abstract way and that the natural numbers i.e. the possibility of unlimited finite counting from 1, arise from our intuition, understood in a Kantian sense, of time.

[480] v. T. L. Heath: *Euclid The Thirteen Books of the Elements.* Volume 1 p. 155. Dover (1956)

[481] E.g. a partial-ordering is a set S and a subset "<" of S x S satisfying the conditions "

"group", or "ring" or "field" existing apart from individual groups, rings and fields. There are, of course, structures for which all instances are isomorphic, just as all triplets are isomorphic to each other. This is the case for all instances of such structures as the natural numbers, Newtonian Space and cyclic groups of order *6* and indeed many others. This fact makes it understandable that one should speak of "*the* natural numbers", "Newtonian Space", or "*the* cyclic group of order *6*" instead of "*a* natural number structure", "*a* Newtonian Space structure" and "*a* cyclic group of order *6*". The use of the word "the" is however merely a linguistic courtesy title. It does not conjure into existence a unique objective "natural number system", "Newtonian Space, or "cyclic group of order *6*" over and above the individual instances of natural number structures, Newtonian Spaces or cyclic groups of order *6* any more than the fact that all the individual actors who play Hamlet speak the same lines conjures into existence an objective Hamlet over and above the individual actors. If one is asked "What is the natural number *2*?", the only sensible answer is "It depends on what units constitute the instance of the natural number structure you have in mind."

I conclude this book by briefly describing the natural numbers and Newtonian Space as structures, so that the reader, with some knowledge of mathematics, can see for himself how complete the triumph of the modern version of Aristotelianism has been and how drained these concepts have become of the sort of philosophical and religious reflection which was so marked a feature of von Guericke's thinking.

The Natural Numbers

A structure (N S <) is a natural number structure if :

(i) N is a set, S:N→N is a function and < is a linear ordering of N.
(ii) For each n in N, S(n) is the immediate successor of n in the ordering <.
(iii) Every non-empty subset of N has a first element in the linear ordering N.

It follows from the assumption of the existence of an infinite set that there are infinitely many isomorphic structures, satisfying conditions (i), (ii) and (iii). All of these structures have equally valid claims to be called "the natural numbers", and, say, the third elements of any instance has as good a claim to be called "3" as the third element of any other instance. Mathematicians pursue the study of natural number structures because they find it useful, interesting and challenging rather than because structures of this particular type are in some privileged relationship with human consciousness.

For the definition of Newtonian Space I will assume the reader is familiar with (or can easily look up) the definition of a real n-dimensional vector space and a positive definite scalar product on such a space.

<u>Definition 1.</u>

An n-dimensional affine space is a triple $(S\ V\ -)$ where S is a set, V is an n-dimensional real vector space and $-: S \times S \to V$ is a function satisfying $(p - q) + (q - r) = (p - r)$.
Intuitively S is the set of points forming space and $p - q$ is the displacement vector of q from p. Immediate consequences are that $p - p$ is the zero vector, that $(p - q) = -(q - p)$ and that $(p - q_1) = (p - q_2) \Rightarrow q_1 = q_2$. By making an arbitrary choice of origin S becomes a vector space isomorphic to V.

I can now give the modern definition of Newtonian Space.

<u>Definition 2.</u>[482]

Newtonian Space is a 4-tuple $(S\ V\ -\ *)$ where $(S\ V\ -)$ is a 3-dimensional affine space and $*$ is a positive definite scalar product on V.

Once again, all structures conforming to the conditions of this definition are isomorphic, so the study of one instance is the study of all on an equal footing. Under the influence of the triumph of Newtonianism, the majority of scientists believed, up to the late nineteenth century, that there was an objectively realised instance of a Newtonian space structure — absolute space as conceived by von Guericke and Newton. This is no longer a tenable view and today this absolute space seems merely to correspond to the "space of the imagination" and to

---

[482] Strictly speaking, this over-defines space in that it specifies distances between points as well as angles between lines. Only the latter is intrinsic while the former is supplied by a choice of units.

serve as a cautionary tale to buttress Aristotle's warning against too readily assuming a close correspondence between, on the one hand, thought, imagination and their expression in language and, on the other, truly objective reality.

Index

Secundinus, Roman Manichee, 330
Seleucid, 185
Selle, Dr. Bertram, 51–60, 64
Sorabji, Prof. Richard, 340
Sparr, Otto Christoph, Freiherr von, 80
Spee, Fr. Friedrich von S.J., 114
Stajus, Jacob, 41
Stanfel, Fr. Valentine S.J., 68
Stayger, Heinrich, 49–52
Stevin, Simon, 334, 356
Stiehler, Dr. Ernst, 95–96
Struve, Berthold, 35
Suarez, Fr. Francisco, S.J., 174
Sudenburg, Suburb of, 19, 21, 33, 37
Tanner, Fr. Adam S.J., 175
Tempier, Etienne, Bishop of Paris, 347, 348, 352
Thales, 127, 186
Theodoretus, Bishop of Cyrus, 185
Tilly, Johann Tserclaes, Graf von, 16–22
Torricelli, (Johannes) Evangelista, 44, 66, 287, 297, 298
Torstenson, Fieldmarshal Lennart, 24, 27, 30, 31, 32, 38, 41
Transdorff, August Adolph Freiherr von, 26–31
Trautmannsdorf, Maximilian, Graf von, 36, 37, 40, 42, 47, 48

Ulchen, Hedwig von, daughter-in-law of Otto, 10
Vegelin, Philip Ernest, 74
Vienna, 4, 5, 10, 30, 38–46, 50, 73, 79, 90
Virgil, Publius Maro, 170
Viviani, Vincenzo, 44, 66, 298
Volmar, Isaac Reichsgeheimrat, 36, 42
Waesberge, Johann Jansson van, 75, 90, 104
Wallenstein, Albrecht von, 15–17, 26, 36
Wallis, John,Savilian Profesor, 332, 354
Wanzleben, 80, 81
Weikhard, Johann, Fürst von Auersperg, 279
Wellington, Arthur Wellesley, Duke of, 33
Westphalia, Peace of, 9, 15, 32, 36–45, 47, 48, 55–57, 74, 80, 82, 113
Whiston, William, Lucasian Professor, 333
Wrangel, Fieldmarshal Carl Gustav, 30, 41
Würzburg, 26, 63, 66–70, 82, 87, 104, 114, 299, 300, 306, 309
Xenophon, 173
Zuchius, Fr. Nicholas S.J., 66, 302, 306
Zweidorff, Anna von, mother of Otto, 8